THE LAST OF THE
TSARS

THE LAST OF THE
TSARS

NICHOLAS II AND THE RUSSIAN REVOLUTION

ROBERT SERVICE

PEGASUS BOOKS
NEW YORK LONDON

THE LAST OF THE TSARS

Pegasus Books Ltd
148 West 37th Street, 13th Floor
New York, NY 10018

ISBN: 978-1-68177-501-2

10 9 8 7 6 5 4 3 2 1

Printed in the United States of America
Distributed by W. W. Norton & Company, Inc.

TO LARA, DYLAN, JOELY AND KEIRA

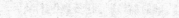

CONTENTS

★ ★ ★ ★ ★

LIST OF ILLUSTRATIONS

1. Nicholas II and son Alexei (Bridgeman Images)
2. Nicholas in Muscovite garb (Hoover Institution Archives)
3. Grigori Rasputin, the one man who could settle young Alexei in his bouts of haemophilia (Hoover Institution Archives)
4. The imperial train in which Nicholas II signed his act of abdication (Hoover Institution Archives)
5. General Mikhail Alexeev (Hoover Institution Archives)
6. Grand Duke Mikhail (Hoover Institution Archives)
7. Abdication draft (Hoover Institution Archives)
8. Nicholas, Alexandra, their four daughters and son (Bridgeman Images)
9. Alexandra nursing her son Alexei (Hoover Institution Archives)
10. Alexandra in her wheelchair at Tsarskoe Selo (Hoover Institution Archives)
11. Letter from 'Niki' to his mother Maria Fëdorovna from Tsarskoe Selo (Hoover Institution Archives)
12. Olga Romanova and Anna Vyrubova (General Collection, Beinecke Rare Book and Manuscript Library, Yale University, Romanov Family Album 3, page 53, image no. 7)
13. Nicholas II and George V (Hoover Institution Archives)
14. Alexander Guchkov (Hoover Institution Archives)
15. Alexander Kerensky (Hoover Institution Archives)
16. Pavel Milyukov (Hoover Institution Archives)
17. Sir George Buchanan (Hoover Institution Archives)
18. General Lavr Kornilov (Hoover Institution Archives)
19. Alexander Kerensky among army officers and troops (Hoover Institution Archives)
20. Freedom House, Tobolsk (Hoover Institution Archives)
21. Guard detachment section at Freedom House (Hoover Institution Archives)
22. Nicholas and Alexandra on their Tobolsk balcony (Hoover Institution Archives)
23. Letter to his mother two days after October Revolution (Hoover Institution Archives)
24. Nicholas and Alexei tending the hens at Freedom House (Bridgeman Images)

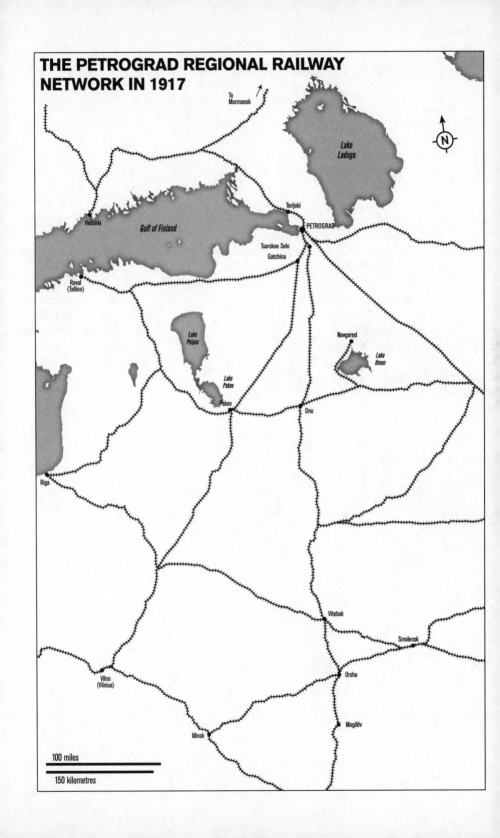

THE FORMER RUSSIAN EMPIRE, 1917–1918

① Eastern front, March 1917

② Limit of occupation after Treaty of Brest-Litovsk, March 1918

ARCTIC

GREAT BRITAIN

Norwegian Sea

North Sea

NORWAY

•Kristiania

SWEDEN

Barents Sea

Kara Sea

NETHERLANDS

DENMARK

•Copenhagen

Stockholm•

Finland

Murmansk•

GERMAN EMPIRE

Berlin•

Baltic Sea

Helsinki

Lake Lagoda

Reval (Tallinn)

Riga

Petrograd

Lake Onega

Archangel•

AUSTRIA-HUNGARY

Warsaw•

Vilno (Vilnius)

Brest-Litovsk•

Minsk•

Mogilёv•

Vologda•

R U S S I A N

Ob

①

②

Moscow•

Vyatka•

ROMANIA

Kiev•

Dnieper

•Bucharest

Danube

Odessa•

Kharkov•

Kazan•

Perm•

Ekaterinburg

Tobolsk•

Ob

Irtysh

•Istanbul

Sevastopol•

Yalta•

Black Sea

Don

Volga

Samara•

Ufa•

Tomsk•

Angora•

Rostov-on-Don•

•Tsaritsyn

Trans-Siberian Railway

OTTOMAN EMPIRE

Tbilisi•

Erevan•

Baku•

Caspian Sea

Aral Sea

Syr Darya

Lake Balkash

Euphrates

Tigris

Amu Darya

ARABIA

•Baghdad

•Tehran

•Tashkent

PERSIA

AFGHANISTAN

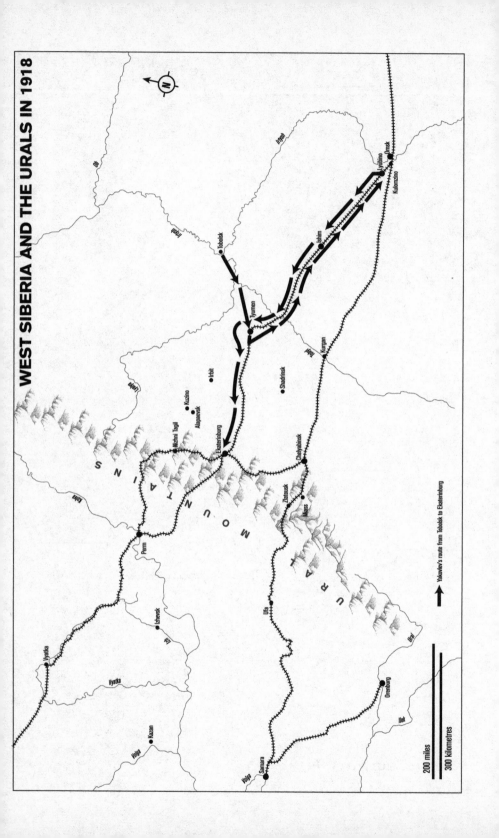

WEST SIBERIA AND THE URALS IN 1918

N

Ob

Irtysh

Irtysh

Tura

Tobolsk

Omsk

Lyublino

Kolomzino

Ishim

Yumen

Kurgan

Tobol

Irbit

Shadrinsk

Kuzino

Alapaevsk

Nizhni Tagil

Ekaterinburg

Chelyabinsk

Zlatoust

Miass

M O U N T A I N S

U R A L

Kolva

Perm

Izhevsk

Volga

Ufa

Vyatka

Vyatka

Kazan

Volga

Samara

Orenburg

Ilek

Ural

→ Yakovlev's route from Tobolsk to Ekaterinburg

200 miles

300 kilometres

ACKNOWLEDGEMENTS

My thanks and love go to my wife, Adele Biagi, who read the complete draft of the book. The last of the Russian tsars is a new interest for me, and Adele's comments were, as always, of inestimable value. I could not have written these chapters without her help. Others who examined the draft were Semion Lyandres, Simon Sebag Montefiore and Ian Thatcher. Semion shared his expertise about the February 1917 Revolution; Sebag advised on the whole Romanov dynasty as well as on the national question in Russia; Ian provided helpful counsel on general questions about interpretation of evidence. I am indebted to them them for their willingness to take time away from their own projects.

I am also grateful to Katya Andreyev for help with Russian Orthodox Church nomenclature; to Richard Clogg for advice about the origins of Russian studies of Byzantine history; to Paul Gregory for tips on books to read on Siberian history; to Lena Katz for explaining the linguistic history of Jews in Russia; to Norman Naimark for clarifying aspects of Jewish history in the revolutionary period; to Robert Sells for his help at an early stage of the research with Romanov medical questions; to Nick Walshaw for sharing his family newspaper clippings on British naval action in the Black Sea; and to Andrei Zorin for our discussions of Russian imperial law and traditions about abdication and succession. Linda Bernard, Lyalya Kharitonova, Carol Leadenham, Anatole Shmelev and Lora Soroka at the Hoover Institution Archives assisted unstintingly whenever I had queries; I should also like to thank the Hoover Institution Library's Maria Quinonez and Terry Gammon for their efficient delivery of rare books and microfilms, and at the Russian Library at St Antony's College, Richard Ramage has cheerfully ferreted out missing data for me. My literary agent, David Godwin, has been an inexhaustible source of encouragement throughout the project; Macmillan editor Georgina Morley actively enhanced the final draft.

The Hoover Institution under directors John Raisian and Tom Gilligan, and its head of archives, Eric Wakin, have consistently supported the research, and I deeply appreciate the sponsorship of the Sarah Scaife Foundation. My thanks are also due to Andrew Romanoff, grandson of Grand Duchess Xenia Alexandrovna, for permitting access to his family's papers in the Hoover Institution Archives.

In the interests of readability I have referred to Nikolai II as Nicholas and used the conventional way of rendering names for other well-known individuals such as Kerensky (rather than Kerenski). Otherwise an amended version of the Union of Congress transliteration pattern is applied. Until January 1918, Russians used the Julian calendar, which was thirteen days behind the Gregorian one. In order to avoid misunderstanding I have changed all dates, where necessary, to the Gregorian calendar. The exceptions to this are in the endnotes where if someone continued to use the Julian system in his or her diary even after the change, I have left the reference intact and added the abbreviation OS (for Old Style) – Nicholas in particular was a traditionalist who disliked any change to the way that time was recorded. All translations from the Russian are my own. I have also included maps of rail networks which, as we shall discover, are useful tools to understand events in the February 1917 Revolution as well to explain why Commissar Yakovlev took Nicholas and his family on such a strange itinerary in April 1918 before reaching Ekaterinburg.

The final draft of this book was written at a time when our family experienced an energetic burst of expansion; it is dedicated to grandchildren Lara, Dylan, Joely and Keira.

INTRODUCTION

Tsar Nicholas II is a controversial figure in twentieth-century history. Admirers defend him as a loving husband and father who did his best for Russia against the tide of malignant revolutionaries who dethroned him in the February 1917 Revolution and murdered him and his family in the following year. Detractors provide a very different account; for them, he was a stubborn, reactionary tyrant whose actions destabilized the country and destroyed opportunities to avoid the catastrophe of later decades. In my opinion, it is wrong to prefer one image to the other. The truth is that he was both things at the same time, a complex, contradictory man and ruler.

I have set out in this book to look at Nicholas in the sixteen months after his fall from power. Throughout that period, he was under detention in Tsarskoe Selo, Tobolsk and finally Ekaterinburg, with little hope of release. He had seldom spoken his mind to ministers and had been notorious for saying one thing and doing another. After his enforced abdication, however, he lost the incentive to give a misleading impression except in so far as he tried to alleviate the worries of his wife and children while they were all under arrest. Parts of this story have been told many times, usually with a justified emphasis on the family's gruesome execution in a Urals cellar in July 1918 and often with less than justified claims that one or more members escaped the scene of butchery. I have come to think that parts of the English-speaking literary world have an almost sociopathic readiness to believe that a well-armed and disciplined communist firing squad in a closed cellar was capable of such staggering incompetence. Nevertheless, the evidence, much of which has long been available, ought to be subjected to conscientious examination, and I shall endeavour to do so here.

In 1917 there was much discussion about sending Nicholas to safe exile in the United Kingdom. But even if his cousin George V had not overruled the idea, how realistic would it have been in the light of contemporary political obstacles in Russia? And what of the persisting mysteries of Nicholas's troubled last journey, from Tobolsk to Ekaterinburg, in April 1918?

Although the deaths of Nicholas and his family on 17 July 1918 certainly require a fresh look in the light of old and new documentation, the previous months also call for attention. In confinement, Nicholas had the time to reflect on his period of rule since 1894. Even so, it is surprising how seldom his diary and recorded conversations have been employed to shine a light on his thinking. In addition to what he wrote for himself and said to others there is a source that has habitually been overlooked, namely the long list of literary and historical works that Nicholas read as he whiled away the period of enforced inactivity. Throughout his lifetime there was dispute about his political purposes, and his choice of books provides us with a mirror of his private meditations. Taken together, his diary, oral comments and reading material in the sixteen months before his death offer a unique chance to examine whether he had any regrets about his decisions in power. They tell us exactly what kind of ruler he had wanted to be, and they allow us to discover whether, as some have alleged, he was truly a convinced autocrat and rabid anti-Semite who made political concessions only under duress.

They can also illuminate Nicholas's thoughts on the revolutionary situation in 1917–1918 and on his vision of the prospects for Russia. He was trying to make sense of circumstances that were out of his control and subject to unpredictable change. Outside his entourage, there were three individuals with whom he exchanged ideas. One was Alexander Kerensky, who was responsible for his care on behalf of the Provisional Government that ruled between the February and October Revolutions of 1917. But two other persons had more intimate discussions with the former tsar that have yet to be chronicled. These were Vasili Pankratov and Vasili Yakovlev. Pankratov was a Socialist-Revolutionary, Yakovlev a Bolshevik, and they were successive officials in charge of the detention of the Romanov family in Tobolsk. Did their conversations with the former emperor of all Russia make any dent in the barrel of his assumptions?

The book will also highlight the political, economic and social environment around the Romanovs' places of detention. This, too, is a topic that has been only lightly treated in the historical literature. The Bolsheviks in Tobolsk and Ekaterinburg had their own opinions about how to handle the Romanov question, and relations between them and the Soviet government were subject to strains. Tobolsk was a town that was overrun by Red Guards from other areas who sought to correct what they regarded as Lenin's failure to hold the family securely; Ekaterinburg had a Bolshevik leadership including several who were willing to kill Nicholas with or without approval by Lenin.

The ultimate decision was to execute not only the former tsar but also all the members of his family in Soviet custody. Russian investigators since the 1990s have immensely expanded the documentary base for an inquiry into who gave the orders and why. I hope to bring these sources together with those I have found in Moscow and California to pinpoint exactly why the murders took place when, where and how they did. The cable traffic between Moscow and Ekaterinburg has often been examined, but it is not enough in itself to explain what happened, and I aim to look at the whole military and security situation in both Ekaterinburg and – just as important – Moscow in the weeks immediately preceding the executions. Moscow's relations with Berlin are also a factor that needs to be taken into account. Only then, I believe, can the degree of Lenin's likely involvement be ascertained – the part that he played has been a matter of intense controversy and speculation in Russia in the past three decades. Such are the questions underpinning this book.

The research for it began when I stumbled upon some exceptional documentation concerning the last months of Nicholas II. In summer 2013 I was burrowing in the Hoover Institution Archives, as has been my habit for several years now, when deputy archivist Linda Bernard asked whether I might be interested in the Romanov items in the archives safe. These included the Nicholas II abdication papers. Next year Lora Soroka, who administers the Russian Archives Project, mentioned some recently catalogued papers – the Agnes M. Diterikhs collection – from the anti-Bolshevik inquiry of 1918–1920 into the killing of the Romanovs. At that point I discovered that Hoover also had a box of documents that once were dubbed 'the file on the Tsar' – the basis for the long-unchallenged suggestion that one or more of Nicholas's family escaped from Ekaterinburg, which is the exact opposite of what the documents reveal. While these sources constitute the spine of my researches, I have also uncovered copious fresh material about other Romanov family members.

Nicholas's thoughts and experiences after the February 1917 Revolution have much to tell us about what happened to Russia in the first two decades of the twentieth century. In the last sixteen months of his life, this modest, inadequate, rigid ex-ruler suffered personal tragedy in a country he had played no small part in bringing to catastrophe. He was spared knowledge of the worst stages of the mass terror that followed only because he was executed in the first year of the October Revolution. But for him, what he did know of, even from behind the closed doors of his places of imprisonment, was already quite enough.

1. TSAR OF ALL RUSSIA

In 1916 a grand ceremony took place in wartime Irkutsk, the great Siberian city south of Lake Baikal, at a time when the Great War was exacting its dreadful toll in lives on the Eastern and Western Fronts in Europe. The purpose was to raise morale in that out-flung region of the Russian Empire. It had been twenty-five years since Nicholas II had visited Siberia when he was still only heir to the throne of the Romanovs and was finishing a global tour that had taken in Vienna, Trieste, Greece, Egypt, India, China and Japan.[1] To commemorate that visit, Governor-General Alexander Pilts gave a keynote speech to the Siberian dignitaries in which he commended the bravery of the imperial forces: 'At a recent audience with our Sovereign Emperor, he kindly told me: "As soon as the war is over, I'll gather my family and come as your guest to Irkutsk."' The audience greeted the announcement with a loud hurrah. It was a remarkable fact that no ruling emperor had come to Siberia since its conquest by Russian traders and troops around the end of the sixteenth century. Siberians high and low felt unloved and neglected, and loyal inhabitants looked forward to a visit by Tsar Nicholas and his family.[2]

No one could know that, in less than a year, he would be returning to Siberia not as the ruling Tsar of All Russia but under arrest as Citizen Romanov. He who had dispatched thousands of political prisoners to Siberian forced labour, imprisonment or exile would himself be transported to detention in Tobolsk. Thrown down from power in the February 1917 Revolution, he and his family would be held under strict surveillance in the little west Siberian town that, by a twist of fate, possessed one of the empire's largest prisons, although the Romanovs were spared the unpleasantness of being locked up inside its walls and were instead confined to the provincial governor's residence. The Bolsheviks overturned the Provisional Government in the October 1917 Revolution and after a few months transferred the imperial family to Ekaterinburg, their power base in the Urals, while they considered what to do with them. In July 1918 the decision was made to kill them all. Taken down into a cellar, they were summarily shot along with their doctor, their servants and one of their pet dogs.

A short, slight man, Nicholas had succeeded his huge bear of a father, Alexander III, in 1894. Nicholas had inherited a pale complexion from his Danish mother Maria Fëdorovna (née Dagmar) and lost his summer ruddiness as autumn drew on.[3] He engaged in few recreations except hunting in the winter and shooting pheasants in the autumn, but felt it right to drop these pursuits in wartime.[4]

There was an ascetic aspect in Nicholas's character, and even on winter nights he left the window open. He loved the fresh air in any season and spent at least two hours in daily exercise out of doors – four if he had the chance.[5] He thought nothing of striding from his palaces without an overcoat on the coldest December day. The emperor, mild of manner, was tough as old boots.[6] He was indifferent to luxury. When in civilian dress, he wore the same suit he had used since his bachelor days. His trousers were on the scruffy side and his boots were dilapidated. For food, he favoured simple Russian dishes like beetroot soup, cabbage soup or porridge – European-style refined cuisine was not to his liking. He was no drinker, and when champagne was put before him at banquets he just took a few sips as a token of conviviality; he handed bottles from the Alexander Palace wine cellar to his guard commander with the comment: 'You know, I don't drink it.' One witness claimed that at dinner with the family, he usually took a glass of aged slivovitz followed by one of madeira. Although others mentioned different beverages, all agreed that he was unusually restrained in the amount that he quaffed.[7]

Tradition was important for him. Among his ancestors, he disapproved of Peter the Great as having broken the natural course of Russian historical development. He disliked Russia's capital, St Petersburg, because he believed it out of joint with the customs of old Muscovy. To Nicholas's way of thinking, the city had been founded on 'dreams alone'.[8] The Russian heritage from the centuries before the reign of Tsar Peter appealed to him. With this in mind, he frequently wore a long red shirt. He ordered his entourage to refrain from using words of foreign origin and scored them out of reports that came to him from ministers and generals. He even considered a project to change official court dress to something more like what people had worn in the reign of Emperor Alexei, the founder of the Romanov dynasty in the early seventeenth century.[9] He thought of himself as a quintessential Russian. He adored the music of Tchaikovsky.[10] After a concert in Livadia by the singer Nadezhda Plevitskaya, he effused: 'I always had the thought that nobody could be more Russian than I. Your singing has shown me to be wrong. I'm grateful to you from the bottom of my heart for this feeling.'[11]

Though Nicholas was a devout Christian, he abhorred long church services and having to get down on his knees.[12] His faith was grounded in ideas that even some in his entourage regarded as being no better than superstitions – his favour for the self-styled 'holy man' Grigori Rasputin, whose drunken binges and serial promiscuity became a public scandal, was taken as proof of his eccentricity. Nikolai Bazili, the Ministry of Foreign Affairs official at the high command HQ, was to recount: 'He was born on the saint's day of Job and believed that fate condemned him for this. He thought that he had to pay for his ancestors whose task had been so much easier.'[13]

Although few people feared him, Nicholas inspired respect and had a 'presence' that discouraged anyone from contradicting him.[14] Sydney Gibbes, who tutored his children, gave this description: 'He was usually rather dignified and reserved, though he unbent in a charming way with those whom he liked and trusted. Though not more than middle height, he looked every inch an Emperor. His tastes were simple, just those of a country gentleman. He abhorred intrigues and all kinds of pretence and insincerity.'[15] Certainly, the tsar listened attentively to each of his leading ministers and had an aversion to open disagreement. But Gibbes was a doe-eyed admirer. In fact, Nicholas was downright duplicitous in the way that he left people with the impression that he concurred with their advice. He thus disappointed many of them when he went on to do the exact opposite of what he had appeared to promise. He had been tsar for over two decades and had outlasted all his ministers. Longevity in power had given him an unwarranted confidence in his own judgement. He aimed to appoint obedient public figures to head the Council of Ministers, and when one of them, Pëtr Stolypin, showed signs of independent conservative opinions, he ceased to trust him – Stolypin had known that his political star was on the wane for years before he was assassinated in 1911. Tension between emperor and prime minister was recurrent, and Nicholas got rid of those who refused to toe the line.

At his coronation in 1896 he swore an oath to maintain his autocratic powers and urged critics to abandon any 'senseless dreams' of democratization. As a boy he had been tutored by the arch-conservative Konstantin Pobedonostsev, under whose guidance he imbibed the principles of absolutism, dynasty, military greatness and the official religious tradition. From this he had never seriously diverged.

Revolutionary tumult had nearly overwhelmed the Russian Empire in 1905 when almost all classes of society, from top to bottom, clamoured for change. Workers went on strike and, guided by revolutionary militants, elected their own councils ('soviets') in defence of their interests. Many peasants took to violent action against gentry landlords. Poles, Georgians and others in the imperial borderlands rose up in revolt. There were mutinies in the Black Sea fleet and among soldiers returning from defeat in the continuing war with Japan in the Far East. In October 1905, Nicholas issued a manifesto promising fundamental reforms. Next year, a State Duma was elected with his consent and under terms that involved the legalization of political parties and the relaxation of censorship restrictions. But when the Duma refused to support his policies, he and Stolypin redrafted the electoral rules so as to produce a less recalcitrant body of representatives. When even this coup against the movement for democracy in Russia failed to quell dissenting voices in the Duma, Nicholas got used to ruling in the teeth of continuing criticism.

His actions were those of a ruler who always thought he was right. He dealt with public disparagement by cocooning himself in the warmth of his family. His wife, Alexandra, born Princess Alix of Hesse and brought up in England at the court of her grandmother Queen Victoria, sustained his inclination to rule without consulting the popular will. Theirs was a close partnership based on shared values and a strong sexual attraction.[16] Alexandra strengthened his determination to manage without advice whenever the advice appeared to damage his personal authority and status. She counselled severity towards those who withheld support from him: 'Be Peter the Great, John [i.e. Ivan] the Terrible, Emperor Paul – crush them all under you.'[17] Several members of the extended Romanov family were horrified by his reluctance to compromise, and his own mother thought that Alexandra exerted an undue and malign influence in this direction. Rasputin was just one of the individuals whom polite, educated society felt that he ought to reject from his court. But Nicholas went his own way, and it was noticed that vehement critics of the boisterous 'holy man' were likely to be removed from the imperial entourage.[18] Count Vladimir Frederikhs, the elderly court minister who had served both Alexander II and Alexander III, was one of the few who got away with it, albeit also with a curt instruction not to interfere in politics: 'This,' said Nicholas, 'is my business.'[19] The fact that the Russian Orthodox Church hierarchy took against Rasputin did not bother the emperor, who was drawn towards folk traditions of religiosity. Rasputin in his eyes epitomized the nation's essential wisdom and goodness.

Nicholas was a devout Christian as well as a military patriot who revered the Russian Army and wanted to leave Russia mightier and more prosperous than when he came to the throne. His nationalism had been with him since childhood. He had a lifelong contempt for Germans, even though he had married one.[20] He also shared his father's hatred of Jews, whom he accused of seeking to dissolve the bonds that bound ordinary Russians together. Nicholas believed that dark Jewish forces had been behind the revolutionary tumult of 1905–1906, and when reactionary nationalist organizations were formed he gave them his endorsement. The chairman of the Council of Ministers, Stolypin, was aghast at how the Union of the Russian People and the similarly named Union of Russian People fomented disorder with their pogroms in the western borderlands.[21]

Despite assuring Stolypin of his support, Nicholas refused to accept the judicial verdicts against those charged with violent excesses. The Unions were forerunners of mid-century fascism. Nicholas was happy to accept a membership card from the Union of Russian People, declaring: 'The burden of power placed on Me in the Moscow Kremlin I will bear Myself, and I am certain that the Russian people will help Me. I will be accountable for My authority before God.'[22] Alexandra sustained his inclination, thinking that such organizations contained her husband's 'healthy, right-thinking, devoted subjects'. 'Their voice,' she assured him, 'is Russia's and not society or the Duma's.'[23] Nicholas was not the sole monarch of his day to have crude political inclinations and an ignorant, opinionated wife. Nor was he unusual in having a poor acquaintance with his nation's high culture. Nicholas shunned intellectuals and drew confidence from the belief that he had a sound understanding of the Russian people. When meeting peasants on his frequent pilgrimages to religious sites, he felt sure that if only they could be kept insulated from pernicious alien propaganda, all would be well for Russia. It did not occur to him that the Russian peasantry might hold genuine grievances against the system of power that his ancestors had imposed. He lived and breathed complacent extreme conservatism.

Nonetheless, he was more complicated than he seemed. Despite his contempt for elections and for most of the Duma's politicians, he had no personal obsession with absolute power – in this matter he was more liberal in his ideas than the wife he adored. He explained this to his offspring's tutor, Pierre Gilliard: 'I swore at my accession to guard intact the form of government that I received from my father and to hand it on as such to my successor. Nothing can relieve me of my oath; my successor alone will be able to modify it at his accession.'[24] This was not a passing idea. Before the Great War he had told Sophia Buxhoeveden: 'Alexei won't be bound. He'll repeal what's unnecessary. I'm preparing the way for him.'[25]

But while he was emperor, he fulfilled his coronation oath as best he could. Beneath his soft exterior there lay a stubborn, hard kernel. Whether they were loyal subjects or active revolutionaries, people saw only inflexibility in him. Loyalists admired him as a strong tsar who confronted those who were working against the empire's finest traditions, and they had celebrated the tercentenary of the Romanov dynasty with gusto. Revolutionaries saw him as Nicholas the Bloody or Hangman Nicholas. Between these two poles of opinion there were millions of subjects who wanted change but feared the turmoil that revolution was likely to unleash. The experience of disturbance and revolt in 1905–1906 had intimidated many into political passivity. At the same time there was a widespread feeling that things could simply not continue as they were. The educated strata of the empire felt embarrassment about Russia in comparison with the world's other great powers – and Nicholas was held to blame for his insistence on conserving the maximum of personal power and responsibility. It was a toxic situation long before the outbreak of the Great War in 1914.

2. AT GHQ

From 1915, when the Eastern Front was stabilized, the Russian armed forces established their general headquarters, known as Stavka, in nearby Mogilëv. Standing on the left bank of the Dnieper, the town had for decades been linked with Kiev by river steamers, and there was a railway station lying a mile to the south-east. But commercial traffic remained at a low pitch even in peacetime conditions. Mogilëv was a place where little happened in daytime, far less in the evenings. Despite being a provincial capital, it was irrefutably dingy. Although most of the 50,000 inhabitants were Russians, there had long been a substantial Jewish minority.[1] Life went on just as it had done for centuries. The nearest thing in Mogilëv to a modern transport system was its four horse-drawn trams. The Hotel Bristol served wine but no vodka after the inception of a 'dry law' in 1914 that was scheduled to last until the war came to an end. Still, though, the town had a problem with hooligans. The tsar's presence did little to enhance the capacity of police and army to maintain law and order. Russia in peacetime was always ructious. In time of war it was becoming less and less governable.[2]

At ten o'clock every morning Nicholas walked from Governor's House, a two-storeyed, nineteenth-century building, to the military quartermaster's offices and received the day's oral report from Chief of the General Staff Mikhail Alexeev. Once Alexeev had explained the latest plans, Nicholas returned to Governor's House and busied himself with his correspondence from ministers in Petrograd (as St Petersburg had been renamed to make it sound less Germanic) or with visits from foreign attachés.[3]

At midday Nicholas would enter the dining hall to greet the two dozen selected officers who had received a card stating: 'You are invited to His Majesty's breakfast tomorrow.' Nicholas with a smile shook hands with each of his guests and, with Alexeev at his right hand, listened to their thoughts about news from the front. Two simple courses were served, and Nicholas hung around afterwards to talk to individuals he had picked out. There followed a break of one or two hours. This was a time when Nicholas usually took a stroll with a member of his retinue while the general staff's personnel returned to work. Supper began at six o'clock and Nicholas again presided. When the courses were finished, he would announce: 'Gentlemen, permission to smoke.' He himself had set a fashion for using a cigarette-holder. More often than not he stubbed out his first cigarette – a sign of nervousness because he immediately lit up and smoked a second. Every evening there was a film or musical show, which Nicholas attended together with his son. A military band struck up the Preobrazhenski march as the emperor took his place in the governor's box and made courteous conversation with the wives of Stavka personnel.[4]

Although Nicholas enjoyed his time with the men of his armed forces, he had to stay abreast of state affairs in the rest of the country. Apart from military matters, he had always been preoccupied with foreign policy and exerted personal control over decisions of prime importance. The Ministry of Foreign Affairs in the capital kept him regularly informed about Russia's changing situation in international relations. Nicholas also expected his Council of Ministers chairman and his Minister of Internal Affairs to apprise him of news affecting political security.

On other matters, he followed rather than led policy. Pëtr Stolypin had persuaded him that if revolutionary disturbances were not going to be repeated, there had to be a new agrarian policy to foster the emergence of a class of yeoman farmers. Stolypin argued that the communal traditions of Russian peasants subsumed individual responsibility. He also emphasized Russian national pride at the expense of the other peoples of the empire – and the two men were at one about this even though Nicholas himself took no initiative. On other items of governmental business he was even less active. The pre-war years were a period when industry was recovering from the near-revolution of 1905–1906. Nicholas left the process of oversight to ministers, dutifully reading reports but contributing little to the discussions. After the Great War's outbreak it soon became obvious that Russia badly needed to improve the coordination of manufacturing output. This led to the creation of so-called war-industry committees involving both industrialists and their workforces. The result was a public debate noisier than the autocrat in Nicholas would have wished, but he went along with it. In truth, he had no other option if he wanted victory on the Eastern Front.

He did, though, sense that he was losing his grip on politics in Petrograd. The empress kept him informed as best she could, drawing his attention to what she saw as nefarious speeches and activities in the Duma. He reserved the most powerful ministries for individuals of dependable loyalty. At the outbreak of hostilities he had saddled himself with the aged, incompetent Ivan Goremykin, who was all too aware that he failed to understand the requirements of modern governance. In 1916 Goremykin successfully pleaded to be released into retirement and Nicholas replaced him with the uninspiring younger bureaucrat Boris Shturmer, only to get rid of him in favour of the no more dynamic Alexander Trepov. This carousel of appointments and sackings from top to bottom in the Council of Ministers brought disruption to civil administration, and Nicholas was made aware of the growing difficulties it produced in securing food supplies to the towns and the armed forces. There was also increasing disarray in industrial output. Nicholas overruled those who said that his next council chairman should be a man whom the Duma leaders could trust. Instead he appointed Prince Nikolai Golitsyn, who was no more eager to take the post than Goremykin had been.

It never occurred to Nicholas that something must be awfully wrong if there was no longer anyone who wanted to head the government for him. Debates in the Duma teetered on the verge of overt criticism of him. Liberal leader Pavel Milyukov was determined to secure the creation of a cabinet that he and his political allies could choose, and when attacking the chaos and corruption at the apex of power in November 1916, asked repeatedly: 'Is this stupidity or is it treason?'[5] Nicholas took scant notice. His interest remained with the armed forces, and he spoke sadly to the commanders at GHQ at the moments of failure in military operations. He wanted them to know that he was as committed to crushing the Germans as they were. When he heard of the growing difficulty in getting supplies to the front, he said: 'I can't get to sleep at all at night when I think that the army could be starving.' People noticed 'his sad eyes and gloomy, agitated face'.[6]

The war years weighed him down so much that he became almost emaciated in appearance. His wife's confidante Baroness Sophie Buxhoeveden wondered whether he had problems with his kidneys. When she put the question to Dr Evgeni Botkin, he confided: 'His heart isn't in order. I'm giving His Majesty iodine, but that's between you and me.'[7]

Defeats at the front in 1915 had depressed him as German armies rampaged over Russia's Polish territory, but in summer 1916 the Russians at last registered a substantial victory in the Austro-Hungarian sector of the front when General Alexei Brusilov experimented with the use of formations of shock troops. Brusilov's success compelled the Germans to redeploy forces from the Western Front and Russia no longer appeared one of the weakest of the Allies. Nicholas felt encouraged. He always wanted to do whatever he could to assist the war effort, and his pleasure in the company of soldiers who were putting their lives at risk was unmistakable. Nobody at Stavka was in any doubt about his fundamental sincerity. Whereas he was at his happiest when alone with his family, he was eager to fulfil what he regarded as his dynastic duty near to the front. The obvious drawback was the fact that his military training equipped him with qualifications no higher than those of an average guards officer. He was out of his depth on strategic and operational questions, and he knew it – leaving such business strictly to Alexeev.[8] His principal contribution, as he saw it, was to act as a figurehead for the imperial war effort while providing fatherly encouragement to commanders, including those like Alexeev who were a lot older than him. His simple dignity and earnest care for all 'his' officers and soldiers impressed everyone at GHQ.

He got on well with Alexeev, who had headed the general staff since 1915 when Nicholas moved to GHQ and parted with the services of Grand Duke Nikolai Nikolaevich, his first cousin once removed, whom he appointed as Viceroy of the Caucasus.[9] For Alexeev, this was a chance to overhaul the high command in his own image. He cleared out the aristocrats and filled the general staff with competent technicians like himself. By early 1917 he had concentrated seven generals and eighty-seven officers as the core personnel to run the machinery of war from Mogilëv. All were expected to sleep, eat and think about the Russian war effort. Such supplies as Alexeev brought to Stavka did not include a library. The general staff, except when it broke for meals, were allowed no moment of distraction during the working day.[10] Alexeev inspired awe among his subordinates by working at his desk for hours at a time.[11] Like the emperor, he disliked luxury and favoured simple clothing and diet, but he was driving himself to the point of exhaustion after medical crises with bladder stones and migraine. He shrugged off advice to let up. Brusilov's advance on the Eastern Front convinced him that Germany and Austria-Hungary could be beaten. Alexeev was setting an example of belief and dedication. The war was there to be won.[12]

Alexeev's personal loyalty to his sovereign, however, had quietly crumbled and he had even begun to talk secretly to individual
politicians who aimed to transfer the throne to a less reactionary
Romanov.[13] It was in this spirit that he tried to persuade Nicholas
that it was in his and the country's interest to compromise with the
Duma leadership. While reporting on operational questions, he took
his chance to mention the worsening political situation. Nicholas listened but would not budge.[14] He had a tender spot when speaking to
generals who had served with his revered father Alexander III, and
one of them – Kaufman-Turkestanski, who was a member of the State
Council – approached him with the same thoughts as those expressed
by Alexeev. The result was the same: Nicholas was stubbornly against
letting Duma leaders set his agenda even though he was not averse
to appointing ministers with a view to improving relations between
Duma and government.[15] Romanov family members were equally
unsuccessful. Grand Duke Dmitri Pavlovich, young and passionate,
found himself rebuffed when he implored Nicholas to change his line.
Even Nicholas's mother, Maria Fëdorovna, failed to dent his determination. Mild-mannered Nicholas acted as if he had already made
one too many concessions by allowing the creation of the Duma in
1906. His mind was closed and no one else at Stavka dared to raise the
matter, even though nearly everyone agreed with Alexeev.[16]

If the emperor had ever toyed with the idea of appointing a government 'responsible to the Duma', he certainly had no such intention
after December 1916 when a cabal of aristocrats, high-society figures
and politicians assassinated Rasputin. Nicholas and Alexandra were
horrified. Rasputin had endeared himself to them as the one person
who could bring calm to their son and heir Alexei, a haemophiliac,
when he fell ill – the doctors had proved inadequate at frequent times
of crisis. Rasputin told them that the family's prayers alone would
help.[17] But during the war his notoriety had continued to grow.
Rumours spread that he took advantage of Nicholas's departure for
Mogilëv to conduct an affair with Alexandra herself. He was known to
take bribes to intercede in the matter of ministerial appointments. He
had his own ideas on foreign affairs and had warned against entering
the alliance against Germany and Austria-Hungary. Opinion formed in
the Duma and other public circles that he might well be promoting the
German cause at court and hoping to convince the emperor of the
desirability of a separate peace with Germany. The imperial couple
knew of the stories about him but stubbornly ignored them, and were

distraught when his corpse was pulled from the ice in the River Malaya Nevka in central Petrograd.

Two of the conspirators, Prince Felix Yusupov and the arch-reactionary Duma deputy Vladimir Purishkevich, were hoping to confound the rumoured moves being made at court towards withdrawal from the war. In broader political circles the news of Rasputin's death gave rise to the hope that Nicholas would be brought to his senses and agree to compromise with conservatives and liberals in the Duma. In fact the murder, by robbing Nicholas of the only person with the capacity to settle young Alexei, served to harden his resolve to stick to the path he had always chosen. Reform was intolerable to him.

3. THE FEBRUARY REVOLUTION

At the beginning of 1917, there was a strong possibility of renewed trouble in Petrograd. Workers had for years been discontented about conditions that had worsened in wartime. Although wages rose with the expansion of armaments production, they failed to keep pace with rampant financial inflation. Housing, sewerage facilities and healthcare deteriorated. In December 1915 and again in December 1916 there was a wave of strikes which were broken with difficulty by the political police. Although revolutionary activists were regularly arrested, working-class grievances remained strong.

The grumbling persisted in the Duma, where disappointment mounted about Nicholas's refusal to compromise after the Rasputin murder. At court, it was understood that the imperial couple wanted no mention of the monk by name: they found the whole matter acutely painful.[1] However, liberal and conservative politicians wanted action. Talks grew about the desirability of a coup d'état in the light of the emperor's intransigence. On 27 February the Duma sessions reopened and, as Minister of Internal Affairs Alexander Protopopov discovered, seditious plans were soon under consideration. What made the situation doubly volatile was the fact that the strike movement had begun to escalate again in the armaments factories which were crucial to the army's chances on the Eastern Front at a time when the Germans were setting up a fresh offensive. Moreover, the female workers in the textile enterprises that produced greatcoats for the soldiers were angry at the deterioration in food supplies. Nicholas was with Alexandra at Tsarskoe Selo and received warnings from the Department of Police about the rapidly worsening situation. The imperial couple took these with a pinch of salt, believing that the security agencies had an interest in trying to scare them.[2] This was not entirely fanciful. Secret services everywhere try to justify the powers and resources bestowed upon them, and it is not uncommon for them to play up threats to the status quo.

Nicholas II consequently saw no reason to put off returning to Mogilëv on 5 March.[3] He told Sophie Buxhoeveden that a pressing message from Alexeev was the reason for his departure:

> He is insisting that I go immediately. I cannot imagine what's the matter since it mustn't be anything important in my opinion, but he's telegrammed a second time and perhaps he really does need to discuss something personally with me that he can't write down for an army courier to deliver. In any case I'll go for three or four days and then come back. A lot of stupid things have been going on here while I was away.

This had stirred Alexandra into making a protest against his trip to general headquarters, but she made no fuss after learning that Nicholas had already informed Alexeev that he would soon join him in Mogilëv, and nothing was going to change his mind.[4] Alexandra was unhappy about his decision, but she did not try to stop him. Nicholas was a stubborn character and once he had resolved to do something, it was seldom easy to deflect him.

Both Nicholas and Alexandra drastically underestimated the growing political dangers. Alexandra herself was preoccupied with the care of her children, who had gone down with measles. Protopopov phoned the palace and reported on the street disturbances to the tsar's valet, Andrei Volkov. Alexandra refused to accept that there was an emergency, telling Volkov: 'No, it's not like that. There cannot be a revolution in Russia. The Cossacks won't mutiny.'[5] She deluded herself. Shots were fired near the Alexander Palace three days after Nicholas's departure, and the building's water supply was cut off.[6] Even if the Cossacks were to stay loyal, other troops were already showing defiance of the monarchy.

Strikes and demonstrations spread next day to every district of the capital and the army garrisons had difficulty in controlling the crowds. Clandestine organizations of revolutionaries – Socialist-Revolutionaries, Mensheviks and Bolsheviks – saw a renewed opportunity to destabilize the political order and began to call for the monarchy's overthrow. On 7 March, the Putilov arms factory workers joined in a general strike and it became evident that some of the troops were going over to the demonstrators. Nicholas ordered the immediate arrest of the rebel leaders, which was his usual reaction to challenges from the labour movement, but the garrison commanders and the police were unable to quell the surge in both industrial conflict and army mutiny. The ban on demonstrations proved impossible to enforce. Petrograd had become ungovernable, and the troops sent out to suppress the workers were instead joining in the protests and lending it their armed support. Duma politicians met privately to discuss how to deal with the crisis. Regiment after regiment turned against the monarchy. Commanders who strove to maintain order were ignored; some were even lynched. All the grievances that had festered since the 1905–1906 revolutionary emergency rose back to the surface.

When talking to officers of the Alexander Palace bodyguard, the empress described the insurgents as fools who would soon have second thoughts and calm down. When reports grew ever more depressing, she exclaimed: 'For God's sake, let there be no bloodshed on our account!'[7] Even more dramatically, she said to the guards: 'Don't repeat the nightmare of the French Revolution by defending the marble staircase of the palace!'[8] She feared the worst when shots were heard in the park outside: in fact, the gunfire was from garrison troops shooting at black swans on the pond. They also killed some goats and gazelles as they grazed. No violence was threatened against the imperial family, but Alexandra saw it as a sign of things to come, declaring: 'It's starting!'[9] Although she bore everything stoically, her servants noticed that she had been crying when alone. Her toughness was nonetheless exceptional and was reinforced by her Christian faith. When chambermaid Maria Tutelberg tried to console her, she replied: 'Our sufferings are nothing. Look at our Saviour's sufferings and how he suffered on our behalf. If this is necessary for Russia, we're ready to sacrifice our life and everything.'[10]

Grand Duke Mikhail, the emperor's younger brother, phoned Duma Chairman Mikhail Rodzyanko from his residence in Gatchina on 10 March in despair about the Petrograd situation. Rodzyanko could offer him no comfort. The two of them agreed to meet in the capital for a discussion in front of witnesses, and Rodzyanko laid bare what he thought was the minimum that urgently had to be done and advised Mikhail to cable his brother and tell him that he was standing on the edge of an abyss. Nicholas had to accept the need to transfer Alexandra to his palace at Livadia by the Black Sea so that people could see that she no longer influenced public policy. At the same time he should permit the State Duma to announce the intention to form a 'responsible government'.[11]

Rodzyanko wrote to plead with Nicholas to get rid of his government and appoint a new one, warning that, if Protopopov remained in office, there would be trouble on the streets. Golitsyn, chairman of the Council of Ministers, gave eager support to Rodzyanko, and they both urged the emperor to recognize the urgency of the situation. A cabinet had to be formed that might command broader political backing, and the idea was proposed that either Prince Lvov or Rodzyanko himself should head it. Grand Duke Mikhail called Alexeev on the direct line, begging him to contact Golitsyn and put the same case to Nicholas. Although Alexeev was suffering from a fever at the time, he found the strength to leave his bed and seek an audience, and he pleaded with Nicholas along the lines that Rodzyanko and Golitsyn had asked.[12] Nicholas heard him out but refused to change his position: he had made up his mind that people were out to deceive him or were themselves deceived. He left Rodzyanko's telegram without an answer. He did, though, write to Golitsyn stating briskly that a change of government was inappropriate in the current situation.[13]

He was reacting to public political challenge as he had always done. In time of war, moreover, he was even less patient about the revolutionary threat than usual. He always assumed that swift repression was the best option. Although he was in regular contact with Petrograd by telegram, his ministers did not give him a timely warning about the sheer scale of the revolt. He took it for granted that loyal troops would quell the insurgents while he focused on Alexeev's plans for the Eastern Front. He was hopelessly out of touch. On 12 March he prorogued the Duma session in an attempt to quieten the political situation in Petrograd. But the leaders in the Duma refused to remain passive observers. In the afternoon of 12 March they formed a Provisional Committee under Rodzyanko's chairmanship with a view to intervening in events regardless of Nicholas's orders. Socialist militants were active on the same day. Responding to the mood on the streets, they made arrangements to elect a Petrograd Soviet of Workers' and Soldiers' Deputies, and an Executive Committee was established that evening. With workers and soldiers flouting the will of government with impunity, it was a revolutionary situation.[14]

While the Provisional Committee already regarded itself as the embryo of a future government, it saw that it needed to obtain approval from the soviet. A framework of 'dual power' was in the making, and the soviet's socialist leaders were determined to maintain their influence over the course of events.

4. ABDICATION

In the night of 13–14 March 1917, Alexeev at GHQ telegrammed General Ivanov, who would be arriving in Tsarskoe Selo that morning; he wanted him to press for a deal between Nicholas and the Duma before it was too late.[1]

In the course of the day Alexeev went further after coming to the conclusion that time was up for Nicholas and that he should step down from power. Although he felt bad about appearing disloyal, he could not see how the army could fight a successful war while the capital was in turmoil. At a time when Nicholas was on his train in Pskov, Alexeev took the unprecedented step of cabling commanders at the front to ask them whether they agreed with him. He expressed his fear that revolutionary militants were about to disrupt the entire rail network; he predicted civil war if drastic action were not taken. He promised fellow commanders to put his ideas to the emperor if they approved. Their swift replies were overwhelmingly in favour. Alexeev communicated this consensus to Nicholas in Pskov and added his own appeal to Nicholas's sense of patriotic duty at a time when the high command had lost confidence in him.[2] If Nicholas had been aiming to cling to power, Alexeev's telegram shattered his will to resist and he wired back that he would make whatever sacrifice was required for the good of Russia.[3]

Even so, he had not yet reached the point of surrender, and nobody knew what he would do next. Recognizing this, Alexeev told the legal adviser Nikolai Bazili to draft a manifesto for Nicholas to sign which would empower Rodzyanko to select a new government.[4] But the news showed that the authorities in the capital had lost all control. Alexeev, who had not properly recovered from a severe attack of influenza, concluded that any such manifesto would be too weak. Nicholas, he reasoned, would have to step down altogether. If he held on to the throne, there would be chaos. Nicholas had to go.

On 15 March 1917 a barrage of advice reached Nicholas in Pskov via a cable from Alexeev. The emperor's cousin, Nikolai, told him bluntly that he should hand over his inheritance, presumably to Alexei. The word 'abdication' was not used. General Brusilov was somewhat less direct, saying that Russia would collapse unless he agreed to renounce the throne in favour of Alexei with Mikhail as the regent. Speed, Brusilov added, was essential. Alexeev passed on both messages while sending one of his own. He could not bring himself to tell his sovereign what to do, but his meaning was clear enough: 'I beg you without delay to take the decision that the Lord God inspires in You.'[5] He emphasized that he and his fellow commanders agreed on the need for him to abdicate.[6] Whereas previously he had gently pressed the emperor to work in tandem with the Duma, now he could see no alternative to his agreement to relinquish the throne – and for the very first time Alexeev spelled out his opinions to Nicholas without the usual display of deference. Russia was being overwhelmed by political insurgency. At the very least there had to be a change of ruler if military effectiveness was to be maintained at the Eastern Front.

Nicholas put up no struggle. Whereas he had no high opinion of ministers and despised most politicians, he loved the armed forces and their high command. He also loved Alexandra, but she was in Tsarskoe Selo, not with him. There has been speculation that Rodzyanko and others in the capital exaggerated the intensity of the Petrograd disturbances when they wrote to him. Undoubtedly Rodzyanko was exasperated by Nicholas's persistent refusal to work in cooperation with the Duma, and he was secretly plotting how to remove him from power. Even so, his messages to Stavka accurately reflected how workers and soldiers were acting in the capital, and now Alexeev was telling Nicholas that if the war was to be won, he himself had to step down. For a ruler who cherished his country's military achievements, this was an almost unbearable shock. The Union of the Russian People was no use to him, and anyway he had no regular acquaintance with its leaders. With the general staff he was in daily contact. When Alexeev revealed his considerations about the revolutionary situation, Nicholas had no reserves of political or emotional resistance left.

Before doing anything else, however, that afternoon he summoned Professor Sergei Fëdorov to his carriage. Fëdorov, a surgeon, had been involved in Alexei's medical care since before the war – in discussion with Dr Botkin and a paediatrician called Dr Raukhfus, he had proposed trials of some more drastic procedures than the others thought prudent. This disagreement reflected the helplessness of the medical profession in the face of haemophilia: doctors were experimenting with treatments that often seemed to do more harm than good. But Fëdorov was a knowledgeable doctor who kept abreast of the latest theories in world medicine; he could also explain what he was doing in a reassuring manner and in language that lay people could understand.[7] In 1915 he had moved as Nicholas's personal physician to GHQ, where he received his own coupé in one of the trains and was in regular contact with commanders and court officials. He had become one of the emperor's most trusted retainers.[8] Fëdorov received no alert about what the emperor wanted to discuss. The doctor could hardly believe his ears. The emperor was turning not to a minister or a general but to him, his mere physician, to consider the most momentous question of succession in the dynasty's history.

It became clear that Nicholas took it for granted that twelve-year-old Alexei would continue to live with him. Fëdorov thought he was being naive: 'Do you suppose, Your Majesty, that Alexei Nikolaevich will be left with you after the abdication?' Nicholas asked: 'Why ever not? He's still a child and naturally ought to remain inside his family until he's an adult. Until that time, Mikhail Alexandrovich will be regent.' Fëdorov replied: 'No, Your Majesty, that will hardly be possible, and it's obvious from everything that you completely cannot count on this.' Nicholas, obviously troubled, changed the subject to medicine and enquired: 'Tell me frankly, Sergei Petrovich, your opinion about whether Alexei's illness is really so incurable.' Fëdorov was blunt: 'Your Majesty, science tells us that this illness is incurable but many people live with it to a significant age, though Alexei Nikolaevich's health will also always depend on every contingency.' Nicholas, almost as if talking to himself, said quietly: 'If that's the case, I can't part with Alexei. That would be beyond my powers ... and, furthermore, if his health doesn't permit it, then I'll have the right to keep him next to me.'[9]

After Fëdorov left, Nicholas pondered his options and quickly made a decision of equally historic importance: he would transfer his powers not to Alexei but to his brother, Mikhail.[10] This way, at least, the Romanov dynasty would be preserved. Mikhail was his closest male relative after Alexei; he was also known for having reservations about the way that Nicholas had ruled the empire. This could help to ensure a peaceful transition as Nicholas disappeared into retirement. Nicholas was soon to justify his decision by pointing out that he had been training Mikhail for the throne until Alexei was born. Mikhail was therefore a suitable candidate for the throne.[11]

While this made some medical and genealogical sense, it flouted the law on the succession introduced by Emperor Paul in 1796. Paul had hated his mother, Catherine the Great, and his legislation was one of his retributions for her maltreatment of him. He knew that she had connived in the murder of his father – her husband – Peter III. Paul aimed to make it impossible ever again for an ambitious woman to accede to power in such a fashion. Until then it had been open to the incumbent tsar to designate his heir, who might be of either sex. Paul changed all that with a stroke of the pen, laying down that the first son of the monarch should automatically succeed. If the monarch had no male offspring, succession would pass down the line of male relatives, starting with the oldest brother. The dynasty could be continued by an empress only in the unlikely event that it ran out of male candidates. Inadvertently, Paul deprived his successors of the right to influence what happened if any of them chose to abdicate. An emperor could lose power by dying or by abdicating, but he could not name his successor: the law alone prescribed who could occupy the throne.

But Nicholas was autocratic by upbringing, and desperate. He was tsar. He still believed that whatever he wanted, he could get. The draft abdication manifesto that Bazili prepared for Alexeev was transmitted from Mogilëv to Pskov a little before 7.30 p.m. on 15 March.[12] At that time neither Alexeev nor Bazili was aware of Nicholas's decision to exclude his son from the succession; their draft mentioned Alexei as emperor and Mikhail as regent. Tension mounted in Mogilëv as they waited for the response from Pskov. A small group including Grand Duke Sergei and Bazili congregated in the duty officer's room next to the Hughes telegraph apparatus in the general staff building. General Lukomski looked in from time to time. After being notified about the imminent transmission of a message towards half past one on 16 March, the group sped to the apparatus and watched as it produced the final variant of the manifesto. In nearly every respect it was the same as that which Bazili had composed for Alexeev. The main difference, however, was of huge consequence. Nicholas passed the throne not to his son but to his brother, Mikhail. Grand Duke Sergei collapsed on the sofa; everyone was stupefied.[13]

Bazili in particular knew from his undergraduate lectures by constitutional expert Professor Nikolai Korkunov at St Petersburg University that abdication was not mentioned in the entire corpus of Russian law, and whereas a potential emperor could forswear the throne, nothing was laid down about how an emperor could rescind it. What was clearly specified, however, was the automatic succession of the emperor's first-born son. Nicholas had no right to cut Alexei out of the dynastic inheritance. His plan was utterly illegal.[14]

Events had meanwhile prodded the Duma's Provisional Committee into action, and in the night of 14–15 March it had chosen two of its members, Alexander Guchkov and Vasili Shulgin, to travel by rail to Pskov and call upon Nicholas to abdicate.[15] The journey took them seven hours, being frequently disrupted by troops who crowded every station on the way. Guchkov and Shulgin reached their destination at 10 p.m. on 15 March 1917.[16] By that time the entire political environment had changed in Petrograd because the Provisional Committee, meeting early in the afternoon, threw its lot in with the revolution and established a Provisional Government with Georgi Lvov as minister-chairman.[17] The new cabinet decreed freedom of the press, organization and assembly while committing itself to holding elections to a Constituent Assembly on the basis of universal adult suffrage. Ministers felt that Russia's performance in the Great War would benefit from the revolution that they headed. They were convinced that Nicholas's removal would allow them to rally patriotic support. Obviously it would ease the situation if he could be persuaded to step down without a struggle – and this sharpened the importance of the mission that Guchkov and Shulgin were carrying out.[18]

They alerted General Nikolai Ruzski, who commanded the northern sector of the Eastern Front, about their intended arrival; but they gave no hint about what they intended to say to the emperor.[19] The trip had been a tiring one, and Shulgin felt embarrassed about having failed to bring court dress with him. Nicholas was ready to receive them despite the lateness of the hour. Count Frederikhs ushered them into the imperial carriage along with Ruzski. The visitors from Petrograd were surprised by his calm, friendly demeanour as he sat at his small table and welcomed them to take a seat. Kirill Naryshkin stayed to take notes on the emperor's behalf. Shulgin privily felt some concern that Guchkov might ruin the atmosphere by raking over the coals of past disputes. He need not have worried; Guchkov was at his most courteous, even though he scarcely looked at Nicholas – not out of diffidence but rather because of his habit of looking downwards when having to concentrate.[20]

Guchkov talked frankly about the implications of mutiny in the garrisons. Nicholas, he told him, should accept how catastrophic it would be to hang on to the throne; he had to recognize that all was lost for him in Petrograd and that Moscow was already in a state of agitation.

There was no organized plot but rather a great anarchic movement of the people. Guchkov reported that Duma leaders had established a Provisional Committee to stabilize the situation and control the troops. The Social-Democrats already dominated events and were calling for a 'social republic'. Promises were being voiced to transfer the land to the peasantry, and this could soon have an impact at the Eastern Front. If Nicholas wanted to prevent this, he had to abdicate in favour of his son Alexei with Grand Duke Mikhail as regent. Guchkov stressed that he was speaking on behalf of a group containing a majority in favour of a constitutional monarchy. He asked Nicholas to face up to reality: 'You see, you can't count on anything whatever. There's only one thing left for you, which is to carry out the advice that we are giving you, and the advice is that you must abdicate from the throne.'[21]

When he suggested that the tsar would require time to consider this, Nicholas courteously cut him short and said: 'There's no need to think anything over. I've made my decision to abdicate from the throne. Until three o'clock I was willing to move to an abdication in favour of my son, but then I understood that I cannot part with my son.' A short silence followed, then he calmly added: 'You will, I hope, understand this . . . That was why I've decided to abdicate in favour of my brother.'[22]

Nicholas's statement of intent threw Guchkov and Shulgin back on their heels. They had arrived expecting they would have a tussle over the question of abdication, although they hoped to proceed by persuasion – they were monarchists who thought they knew what was best for the monarchy. Guchkov later recalled that he had known that, if his enterprise came to naught, he would be arrested and might even be hanged, but he had resolved to persist, for he thought that a regency was Russia's only salvation.[23] He knew that it was going to be difficult to achieve his objective in the currently heated atmosphere of the capital. As he read the situation, the best thing would be to get the formal documentation completed at dead of night and announce the results to Russia in the morning. He refused to accept that this would amount to a coup d'état, but he and his sympathizers were clearly intent on clearing out the worst of Nicholas's governing team: he had 'the Shturmers, the Golitsyns, the Protopopovs' in his sights.[24] He did not want Mikhail to be a strong regent. On the contrary, he opted for him precisely because he thought him 'lacking in will'. Mikhail in his eyes was a 'pure and good person'.[25]

Guchkov explained his thinking as follows: 'We considered that the image of little Alexei Nikolaevich would be a mollifying factor in the transfer of power.'[26] As he later explained, the idea was to persuade Nicholas that this was the best way to wipe the political slate clean. Alexei was 'a boy whom it was impossible to say anything bad about', and the feelings of popular fury that were flooding on to Petrograd's streets would soon subside.[27] Guchkov was trying to ensure that the next emperor would exercise no genuine power, and Alexei was meant to be the lightning conductor that saved Russia from the political storm.[28] But Nicholas's unexpected remarks cast aside this whole scenario. There was a moment of mutual empathy as the two emissaries from the capital said that they appreciated the importance of a father's feelings and would not put any pressure on him. They expressed agreement to the unexpected proposal for Mikhail to ascend the throne.[29]

This consoled Nicholas, who asked whether they could guarantee that his decision would restore calm to the country. They answered that they foresaw no complications, and Shulgin handed over a draft act of abdication. They were leaving for Petrograd in an hour's time and had to carry back a signed document with them. Nicholas took the draft away, returning to the carriage twenty minutes later. Guchkov and Shulgin read through the text that the emperor had received from Bazili at GHQ. They endorsed all of it, except that Shulgin wanted to insert a requirement for Mikhail to rule 'in complete and unbreakable unity with representatives of the people in legislative institutions'. Guchkov added that Nicholas should include in his act of abdication an order appointing Georgi Lvov as chairman of the Council of Ministers.[30] Nicholas consented, and went to his compartment to amend the wording. Guchkov took the opportunity to leave the imperial carriage and announce to those gathered in the open air: 'Our Father Tsar [*tsar batyushka*] is in total agreement with us and will do everything that needs to be done.' Bystanders raised a hurrah. Guchkov then went back into the carriage to wait with Shulgin for the emperor.[31]

A legend was to arise that Guchkov and Shulgin had no idea what they were agreeing to. Shulgin would remonstrate against all this: 'As regards the idea that we did not know the basic laws, I personally had a poor knowledge of them. But, of course, not to the point that I didn't know that the abdication in favour of Mikhail did not correspond to the law on succession.'[32]

At 11.40 p.m. Nicholas reappeared with the signed abdication manifesto in his hand. Without undue formality, he handed over a copy to Guchkov. So that it might not be said that he had acted under pressure, he pre-timed the manifesto at 3 p.m. the same day.[33] Guchkov and Shulgin received what they wanted.[34] According to Alexander Kerensky, the leading lawyer and Socialist-Revolutionary activist, the news was immediately communicated that night by a direct line to Petrograd. Nicholas also wrote a letter to Prince Georgi Lvov putting his security into their hands.[35] It was over. The emperor of all Russia had stepped down from the throne without a fight. The man who had been clawing backing his autocratic powers since the 1905–1906 revolution was now reduced to the status of mere citizen. The strain on him was beginning to dissolve and although he was exhausted, he was also strangely relieved. At 1.45 a.m. on 16 March 1917, he sent the following telegram to his brother Mikhail: 'Petrograd. To His Highness – I hope to see you soon, Nicky.'[36] This was the first time that anyone had addressed the Grand Duke in this way.

No Romanov had abdicated in the three centuries of the ruling dynasty. Assassinations were another matter. Peter III had perished in the palace coup of 1762, Paul in 1801. A terrorist group killed Alexander II in 1881. This last incident was burned into the Russian public memory; it occurred on 1 March in the Gregorian calendar – or 14 March in the Julian one. Shulgin noted with relief that Nicholas had signed his abdication on 15 March and not on the anniversary of that last assassination.[37]

Nicholas's calmness was not replicated at Stavka when the news reached Mogilëv. General Alexeev, Grand Duke Sergei Mikhailovich and Bazili all felt crushed. Nicholas had rejected their proposal for the succession.[38] Grand Duke Sergei sprawled in distress and said: 'This is the end!' Modest, gentle and unassuming, Mikhail seemed to everyone at Stavka inadequate to occupy the throne. Nobody could imagine him as emperor. Alexeev repeated that Alexei and a regency would have been the better option.[39] But it was Nicholas, not Alexeev, who signed the abdication papers. Alexeev could only advise and persuade and make the best of whatever the emperor decided. To regularize the process, he ordered Bazili to go and meet Nicholas on the railway before he reached Mogilëv from Pskov. Bazili travelled out to the imperial train on the rail line at Orsha, where he and the emperor held a discussion. Nicholas astonished him with his tranquil, impassive manner, giving no hint of the momentousness of recent events. His long reign was coming to an abrupt end and yet he appeared to have not a care in the world.[40] From Orsha, Nicholas proceeded to Mogilëv where the train arrived at 8.20 p.m. Ranks of troops awaited him on the platform.

Before leaving the carriage, Nicholas called Alexeev inside. At last giving play to some emotion, he embraced his general.[41]

Meanwhile events in Petrograd remained in unpredictable flux. In the middle of the day on 16 March a group of Provisional Government ministers and Duma leaders met at Mikhail's small salon in Petrograd to discuss the idea of his becoming emperor. Guchkov and Shulgin had just arrived back from Pskov, and Rodzyanko invited them to join the gathering. Rodzyanko also asked them not to publicize the news of Nicholas's act of abdication. Politicians had to prepare for whatever might be the next stage in the emergency in Petrograd.[42]

Rodzyanko, Guchkov, Milyukov, Kerensky and the liberal industrialist Alexander Konovalov were among those present, and there was a forceful exchange of opinions. It was a painful occasion for everyone. Guchkov insisted that the country needed a tsar; he pleaded with Mikhail to accept the throne from his brother with a commitment to convoking a Constituent Assembly. Milyukov too wanted the throne to pass to Mikhail, but got into a short though fiery dispute with Guchkov about the Basic Law. This boded ill for the Provisional Government's prospects of settling the political situation in the capital. Guchkov argued that each and every action taken by ministers could be justified in the light of the wartime emergency. But whereas Guchkov and Milyukov agreed that Mikhail should become tsar, Kerensky strongly opposed the whole idea and urged Mikhail to reject the throne in recognition of the fact that the streets were full of thousands of angry workers and soldiers demonstrating against the monarchy. He warned of civil war if Mikhail tried to succeed his brother. For Kerensky this was the main practical point rather than any republican principle. He added that Mikhail would be putting his own life in danger if he complied with what Nicholas wanted.[43]

Mikhail took Rodzyanko and Lvov aside while everyone else waited in trepidation. Guchkov feared that Mikhail might also be about to consult his ambitious wife, who was widely suspected of wanting to become empress and was at home in Gatchina. The tension affected everyone in the salon. When Guchkov walked out to use the telephone, Kerensky demanded to know who he wanted to speak to. Guchkov replied that he was simply contacting his wife. Kerensky was as agitated as everyone else, but he was enough in control of himself to tell Mikhail not to speak on the phone to anyone. Mikhail remonstrated that he would talk exclusively to his wife but would appreciate time to consult his own conscience: it was his only act of self-assertion. When he rejoined the gathering, it was to say in a firm but anxious voice that he intended to renounce the throne. The disagreement between Kerensky and the advocates of a monarchical solution was rendered redundant. Guchkov said that he could no longer consent to serve in the Provisional Government – he did not relent until Kerensky appealed to him.[44]

Mikhail signed his own act of 'abdication', which really should have been one of renunciation, early in the afternoon of 16 March. It was published a short while later at the same time as the one that his brother Nicholas had already signed. Mikhail urged citizens to obey the new Provisional Government; he expressed the hope that elections would be held for a Constituent Assembly.[45] Alexandra heard in a patchy fashion about events. Around 4 p.m. on 16 March 1917 Count Pavel Benkendorf, the grand marshal of the court, told her about the rumour that her husband had abdicated. She could hardly believe that he could have taken so momentous a decision in such a hurry. Nicholas knew how ill their son was. He surely could not have stepped down from the throne with Alexei as his successor. News sheets arrived from Petrograd an hour later that clarified what had happened, and Alexandra discovered that Nicholas had passed on his powers – or tried to do so – to his brother Mikhail.[46] Meanwhile, the same information shattered Nicholas's composure. He had been counting on Mikhail's agreement to succeed him. For Nicholas, the dynasty was a sacred trust. But he refused to blame Mikhail: 'I cannot judge his actions without knowing the circumstances.'[47] But he regarded Mikhail's manifesto with intense distaste, writing in his diary: 'God knows who was responsible for getting him to sign such garbage!'[48]

When Major General John Hanbury-Williams, the head of the British military mission, was called to see the emperor in Mogilëv on 19 March 1917, he noticed a difference in the surroundings of General HQ. Outside the gates there were just 'loafers'. But barring the way stood 'a sentry with the red band of revolution round his arm'. Already the soldiers were signalling that they were the real power in the land. The sentry stopped Hanbury-Williams from walking up the muddy path to his appointment until one of the emperor's retinue emerged to resolve the matter.[49] The emperor's quarters gave a grim sign of changed times. The grand piano remained, but the vases of flowers had been removed and the photos that once adorned his table had been packed. Nicholas sat in his khaki uniform. Tired and white, he had dark lines beneath his eyes even though he still managed to offer a smile of greeting. He had received a letter from his wife through an officer who had felt the need to hide it in his tunic.[50]

Mogilëv, where just days earlier there had been people shouting their hurrahs for their sovereign, was undergoing the same political transformation as Petrograd and the rest of Russia. Two huge red flags now hung from the windows of the town duma.[51] Residents walked about with red ribbons pinned to their clothing. The police were nowhere to be seen. The revolution was triumphant.[52]

5. TSARSKOE SELO

In the long hours when Nicholas and his brother Mikhail were coming to their momentous decisions, Empress Alexandra was stranded in the Alexander Palace at Tsarskoe Selo. She was waiting frantically to hear what was going on. As the news worsened for the Romanovs, Rodzyanko phoned Major-General Alexei Resin, the Composite Infantry Regiment commander, advising the empress to leave the Alexander Palace and to take her family with her. When Resin replied that the children were ill, Rodzyanko remained unmoved, saying: 'When a house is in flames, one carries out the children.' According to her maid, Anna Demidova, when this message was conveyed to Alexandra she at first consented but then dug in her heels because the palace at Tsarskoe Selo was her home, which she refused to abandon.[1] Alexandra was later to blame Rodzyanko for Nicholas's decision to abdicate. By implication, Nicholas had not really needed to step down.[2] For a woman who was used to offering political advice to her husband, it was a time of acute frustration. Russia was entering a revolutionary emergency and the imperial couple for the first moment in their marriage were unable to confide in each other. Nicholas had relinquished the throne and his sole thought was to get back to her with all speed.

Tsarskoe Selo, as its name ('Tsar's Village') implies, had started as a rural retreat for the ruling family. At its heart was the Alexander Palace, which Nicholas and Alexandra had made their home. After 1905 it was their permanent place of refuge from the hurly-burly of the capital. The building was more like the country house of a British aristocrat than the other great Romanov residences and it was where the imperial family felt most comfortable. In peacetime they could stay there and reach the capital within an hour if the situation demanded, and its parks and lakes provided them with the restful landscape they appreciated. Nicholas, a keen hunter, had mounted his sporting trophies in the entrance hall. In her rooms, Alexandra surrounded herself with signed photographs of current and deceased monarchs, including the late Queen Victoria and King Edward VII. Nicholas's study was always strewn with the maps that he used when scrutinizing military plans. The palace also contained a life-sized painting of Queen Victoria as well as portraits of Nicholas's forebears as tsar: Nicholas I, Alexander II and Alexander III.[3]

Over the centuries the surroundings acquired many mansions and barracks. Indeed, it became a great military centre. A railway station was constructed to enable the Romanovs to travel out easily from the Winter Palace in the capital. Beyond the inhabited area there were swamps and bogs where the mosquitoes made life a misery in the summer months, but the Romanovs stayed safely inside the palace curtilage.[4] The barracks held over 40,000 troops.[5]

Most of Tsarskoe Selo's population were thus not permanent residents but conscripts who served to guarantee the family's security, and their behaviour in regard to the Romanov family changed when revolution came to nearby Petrograd. Immediately there were reports of political celebration fuelled by copious draughts of vodka. In some regiments the 'Marseillaise', marching song of the French Revolution, was played. For a while there was talk of a plot to fire cannonades at the Alexander Palace. The guard unit received orders to take precautions against such aggression.[6] Outbursts of rifle fire, however, continued, and everyone knew that the situation was volatile.[7] Alexandra bore all this with fortitude. While she waited for her husband's return, she wrote sympathetically to him – emotion getting the better of grammar: 'You, my love, my Angel dear, cannot think of what you have gone and are going through – makes me mad. Oh God: of course we will recompense 100-fold for all your suffering.'[8] As she listened to the noise outside, she drew on her reserves of courage. The family's fate was no longer in Romanov hands.

The Provisional Government's measures regarding the Romanovs were kept under scrutiny by the Petrograd Soviet, whose pressure was heavy and continuous. Meeting on 16 March, the soviet's Executive Committee had demanded the arrest of 'the Romanov dynasty' and contemplated its own independent action if the Provisional Government refused. At the same time the Executive Committee recognized that Mikhail Romanov was no genuine danger and could be spared imprisonment but held under supervision by 'the revolutionary army'. As to Grand Duke Nikolai, he should be recalled from the Caucasus and kept under strict surveillance en route to Petrograd. There was a reluctance to arrest Alexandra and the other female Romanovs, and it was resolved to implement a gradual process in accordance with how each individual woman had behaved under the old order.[9] The Soviet leadership remained determined to prevent Nicholas from going into foreign exile, and Nikolai Chkheidze, one of the Menshevik leaders in the Soviet, reported with satisfaction to its Executive Committee that a minister had warned the cabinet that the soviet might arrest Nicholas if such a concession were made.[10]

Ministers aimed to settle the matter on 20 March by decreeing that Nicholas and Alexandra should remain confined to Tsarskoe Selo for the foreseeable future, and the hope was that the question of monarchy would fade from the public agenda.[11] But when Kerensky appeared at the Moscow Soviet on the same day, he still had to listen to calls for Nicholas's execution. Kerensky replied that the Provisional Government would not endorse any such thing and he himself was not going to become the Marat of the Russian Revolution.[12]

The cabinet meanwhile ordered General Alexeev to assemble a unit to guard the emperor on his journey from Mogilëv. A group of Duma deputies would be sent to Mogilëv to oversee the process.[13] Alexeev distributed a message to the railway stations on the route repeating the governmental guarantee of Nicholas's safety in travelling to the Alexander Palace.[14] Four Duma deputies – Alexander Bublikov, Vasili Vershinin, Semën Gribunin and Saveli Kalinin – left Tsarskoe Selo for Mogilëv on the government's behalf at 11 p.m. on 20 March, arriving at Vitebsk before going on to Orsha. Bublikov and Vershinin dealt with questions from the public at the stations that they passed through. They reached Mogilëv in the middle of the afternoon of 21 March, being cheered as they made their way by car to GHQ, where Bublikov spelled out the terms of his mission to Alexeev. After a brief discussion of practicalities, Alexeev accompanied the emissaries to the imperial train to convey the requirements to Nicholas himself. At that moment Nicholas was talking to his mother in the adjacent train.[15] He came out after making the final arrangements for departure. His most difficult task came in bidding farewell to the staff at GHQ. After his speech, there were tears.[16] It was as if none of the officers could believe what was happening.[17] He had also signed a leaving statement to the armed forces wishing them well in the struggle with the external foe, but the Provisional Government refused permission for its publication.[18]

Only one officer in his personal bodyguard was allowed to accompany him to Tsarskoe Selo because anxiety remained about a possible violent attempt to reverse the act of abdication.[19] Nicholas had become a private citizen, and his security was now a matter for the Provisional Government. The engine built up steam and left Mogilëv at 4.50 p.m.[20] The train consisted of ten carriages. The Duma people travelled in the one at the rear. A whole carriage was reserved for the retinue, where sat the aristocrats Vasili Dolgorukov, Kirill Naryshkin and others along with Professor Fëdorov. Once men of influence, they huddled together and discussed an uncertain political and personal future. Authority was exclusively in the hands of Bublikov and his Duma colleagues, who alone could change the route or send and receive telegrams. They stopped first in Orsha, then in Vitebsk. The Duma members took turns to be on duty. As they started on the last leg of the journey, they telegrammed instructions for a reception party to stand ready at Tsarskoe Selo station.[21]

General Lavr Kornilov had already visited Tsarskoe Selo on 21 March accompanied by Colonel Evgeni Kobylinski.[22] With a red bow pinned to his chest, he left no room for doubt that he approved of the revolution. As he entered the Alexander Palace, the servants told him that the empress was still in bed, to which Kornilov replied: 'Pass on to her that now is not the time to be sleeping!' Only then did he disclose who he was.[23] She kept them waiting another ten minutes before receiving them in the nursery. Kornilov addressed her as 'Your Highness' and talked of his 'heavy task' in announcing the government's decision to put her and the imperial family under arrest. From then onwards, she was to contact Kobylinski with any requests. The Romanovs could keep their retinue but those who chose to stay with them would have to accept the same conditions of confinement in the palace. Kornilov removed the entire current guard, replacing it with a riflemen's regiment that he felt he could trust.[24]

He appointed Kobylinski to take charge of the Tsarskoe Selo garrison with Pavel Kotsebu as his subordinate and the Alexander Palace commandant.[25] Kobylinski had been wounded early in the war and was still suffering from an inflamed kidney.[26] He had recuperated briefly in one of the Tsarskoe Selo convalescent homes, where he was transferred to a reserve battalion (and recovered enough to begin an affair with the nurse and teacher Klavdia Bitner).[27] Fellow officers respected him as 'tranquil, calm and balanced'.[28] But whereas Kobylinski could act with political discretion, Kotsebu behaved as if the revolution had not happened. Guards noticed his intense conversations with Anna Vyrubova, whom everyone knew to be Alexandra's confidante. Kornilov soon replaced him with Col. Pavel Korovichenko, a specialist in military law who was one of Kerenski's associates; and as for Vyrubova, she was removed soon afterwards in the course of a visit by Kerensky himself. After a tearful farewell with the empress, witnessed by Kobylinski and Korovichenko, she was taken to prison in Petrograd.[29]

The Romanovs were allowed total privacy inside the Alexander Palace and no soldier would patrol their rooms.[30] But there were rules about how the family were to behave outside its walls, and they could go out into the park only by prior arrangement.[31] Everyone staying at Tsarskoe Selo was automatically agreeing to house arrest for the foreseeable future. Those who were unwilling to submit to this were required to leave immediately. Few, in fact, departed, for loyalty to the emperor and his family was strong. Soon the implications were made manifest. Residents of the palace could walk around the park but only at specified times and always under constant surveillance. Correspondence with the outside world would occur only with permission from the new palace commandant, Korovichenko.[32]

The train reached Tsarskoe Selo station at 11.30 a.m. on 22 March 1917. Nicholas and Dolgorukov still thought they could count on the public respect that had been part of their earlier life. They were in for a surprise.[33] The usual military contingent had been completely replaced four hours earlier – some of the officers had been planning to raise a hurrah for the emperor in the traditional fashion, something that the new revolutionary authorities were determined to prevent.[34] As far as Nicholas could judge, no general but only NCOs were in charge of the troops waiting on the platform.[35] Somehow he overlooked the part played by Kobylinski.[36] When the limousine drew up to the gate at the Alexander Palace, the guard unit was strangely slow to open it to them. This was no accident. Both the troops and their officers wanted to indicate the change of times. The pattern was maintained inside the palace. Nicholas involuntarily tipped the peak of his hat to the guards. For the first time in his life, no one responded with any kind of salute.[37]

Citizen Romanov was having to learn rules that others were setting for him. Russia had become a republic through his abdication, and he had lost the high status that had been his since birth. His wider family underwent the same transformation. It was also on 22 March 1917 that the Provisional Government revoked Nicholas's appointment of his cousin Nikolai Nikolaevich as military commander on the Caucasus front. This was done in a decorous fashion. A message was dispatched to him before he arrived in Mogilëv that asked him to resign the post.

Lvov did not like to fire him. Instead, he applied moral pressure by stating that the Provisional Government could not be indifferent to the voice of the people, which was wholly against employing anyone from the house of Romanov in an official position.[38] Grand Duke Nikolai reached GHQ on 23 March before receiving the message. On 24 March 1917 he complied with Lvov's request and devolved his responsibilities to Chief of the General Staff Alexeev.[39] As a result no relative of the former emperor had an official post of any importance. The February Revolution had spread its effects to Romanov kith and kin.

Everything seemed topsy-turvy; the world had changed and was still changing. The guard detachment around the Alexander Palace for the first time had failed to welcome his arrival. Instead, Nicholas had to wait for the duty officer to appear. The embarrassment was deliberate. The authorities in Tsarskoe Selo were giving a signal about the transformed situation: tsarism had fallen and a new era in Russian history had begun. Not that Nicholas was going to be prevented from joining his wife and children. On the contrary, ministers aimed to have him confined within the palace curtilage, and as soon as the duty officer appeared, he shouted in a full, clear voice: 'Open the gates to the former sovereign!'[40] (The verbal formality served to confirm that things had been turned upside down.) Nicholas maintained his dignity and none of the troops said or did anything untoward as he made his way into the residence. Alexandra was the first to greet him in the first room of their children's quarters. They smiled, kissed and embraced. Then they left the room to be with their son and daughters.[41]

The palace was closed to outsiders and the Romanov family were subjected to house arrest. Nicholas, his wife and their offspring were the sole Romanovs in residence, and none of his other relatives gained permission to visit them. His mother, Dowager Empress Maria, left Mogilëv at the same time as he did but made straight for Kiev. On arrival there, she announced her desire to proceed southwards to Crimea. She left with a reduced military escort on 5 April 1917. She gave signed photographs to the bodyguard unit before it dispersed.[42]

Nicholas and his immediate family adjusted themselves to their new circumstances, but one small episode disturbed them. They had had Rasputin buried quietly in the church inside the palace grounds. When the new troops found out about this, they dug up the coffin and tore off the lid to examine the corpse. They found, next to his right cheek, an icon signed by 'Alexandra, Olga, Tatyana, Maria, Anastasia and Anya [sic] [Vyrubova]'. The order was given to move the coffin to Srednyaya Rogatka railway station for secret reburial nearby.[43] Minister-Chairman Lvov himself countermanded this plan and instructed Kobylinski to give up the coffin and its contents to Commissar Kupchinski, who went out to meet him. Despite Kupchinski's attempt to disguise what he was doing, word quickly got round and Kupchinski was stopped by a crowd before he reached Petrograd. After a tussle broke out over the corpse, Kupchinski thought it prudent to have it cremated rather than risk its theft.[44]

A nearby group of college students and troops carried out the task by transporting the corpse to a wood and arranging to incinerate it in a pyre. Old women who venerated Rasputin's memory were shooed away. But insufficient accelerant was used. Almost as soon as the fire was lit, the petrol was exhausted and the flames failed to do the job. By then there were bystanders, some of whom convinced themselves that this was proof the dead man had been a saint. The students rebuilt the pyre and this time it burned successfully, leaving only his skeleton behind. The little group decided to scatter the bones in the clearing, but this only encouraged the old women to pick them up with a view to setting them in icon frames. As a commotion grew, the tired students gathered the remaining bones, returned to the college and threw them into a large furnace.[45] Rasputin had proved almost as indestructible in death as he had been in life. Even so, the news was withheld from the imperial family. Since they were no longer active players on the political scene, they were being told nothing except what was strictly their family business. They were prisoners in all but name.

6. FAMILY LIFE

Nicholas and Alexandra adored each other. Her letters to him exhibited an undimmed passion after decades of marriage, and he was no less affectionate in return. But their mutual dependence blinded him to her weaknesses in her role as his consort. Alexandra had an hauteur that empresses and queens elsewhere balanced with a degree of 'theatricality'. She simply could not display false emotion or pretend to enjoy herself when she felt apathetic or miserable. Her failure to put on a show of warmth to people in high society did her harm in Russian public opinion.[1] Imperious and opinionated, she alienated most of his relatives including his mother Maria Fëdorovna. Alexandra was content to remain aloof. She always behaved as if she could be sure of having God and common sense on her side.

This would not have mattered so much if the Russian Empire had not been bedevilled by deep crisis, a crisis widely blamed on an emperor too weak to resist the political counsel of an imperious wife. As internal and external difficulties mounted, so hatred of her grew. She had always seen it as her duty to bolster his confidence about sticking to autocratic traditions. Days before the February events she wrote: 'I so passionately would like to help you carry this load! You are courageous and enduring – I feel with all my soul and suffer with you, *much more* than I can express in words.' She added the consoling thought that the late Rasputin – 'our dear Friend' – was praying for him in another world.[2] Nicholas and Alexandra could not have been more different in temperament: she was fiery while her husband was even-tempered. She was quick to make up her mind; he was slow to take decisions. Every evening they had a tête-à-tête when they would discuss the matters that were bothering them, but they never talked about politics in the presence of others.[3] About most things, they agreed, and although she influenced his choice of ministers there is no evidence that she diverted him from a course of policy that he favoured.[4]

But she incurred more blame than he ever did. Kobylinski, who was typical of his time in thinking that a man should dominate his wife, claimed that 'she ruled over the family and subjugated the sovereign'. Nicholas was loath to decide any practical matter of importance without consulting her, at least after the abdication. When asked about something, his typical response was: 'What does my wife think? I'll go and ask her.'[5] Alexandra was opinionated and disliked pusillanimity. One of her catch-phrases was: 'Better to make mistakes than not to take decisions.'[6] She had an aversion to ostentation and luxury and wore just two strings of pearls. This was the extent of her self-indulgence.[7] She was by preference a vegetarian – this much she shared with the 'heretic' Lev Tolstoy.[8] When annoyed, she turned red in the face.[9] She wore a pained expression for much of the time but she also found it easy to empathize with people in distress.[10] Usually she behaved with restraint, and many thought her haughty. But when something tickled her fancy, she had a smile that conquered hearts. Her daughters knew this better than people outside the family; they called her Little Sun.[11]

The imperial couple usually conversed in English. Born a princess of Hesse in imperial Germany and baptized as Alix, she lost her mother at the age of six and spent much of her long holidays with her grandmother Queen Victoria in the United Kingdom. After the Japanese war of 1904–1905 she resolved to speak Russian on formal occasions so as to demonstrate commitment to her adopted country, the only problem being that she talked rather slowly as she carefully enunciated every word.[12] Hating meetings with high society, she surrounded herself with a set of confidantes who were as highly strung as she was. Their chief qualification for being at court was that they always deferred to her and shared her prejudices. She herself practised her sewing and in wartime she spent many hours nursing the wounded at the Tsarskoe Selo hospital. She avidly studied devotional literature. For recreation, she sometimes played piano duets with Sophie Buxhoeveden, who modestly said that she herself must have had Wagner, Grieg and Tchaikovsky turning in their graves.[13]

Alexandra knew – this was her torment – that it was her own biological inheritance that passed the dreadful disease of haemophilia to their only male heir Alexei. She told intimates that she was a bird of ill omen.[14] Her uncle, brother and two nephews had perished prematurely from the disease. She knew that the same fate could await her son. This was one of the reasons she turned to God.[15] She could never forget or probably even forgive herself for Alexei's condition. Evgeni Botkin, one of the family's doctors, made his own quiet study of the Romanovs. Medical science of that era had reached an awareness that the syndrome of fatal bleeding affected only boys who were haemophiliac. But, it was thought, women too could experience symptoms that were anything but pleasant. Female members of families that inherited the illness from one generation to another were said to have a predisposition towards hysteria after going through the menopause – and Botkin concluded that this explained Alexandra's episodes of religious ecstasy.[16] But he would never voice such thoughts to her or her husband. He was devoted to the imperial family and was proud to serve them to the end, whatever that end might be.

She had a penchant for mysticism and found an outlet in Russia's old religious traditions. After adopting Orthodox Christianity, she threw her heart and soul into her new faith.[17] She never regretted her transition, declaring: 'Protestantism is so dry!'[18]

She continued to see the late Rasputin as the embodiment of Orthodoxy's primordial truth and virtue. When her maid Maria Tutelberg raised suspicions about him, she cut her short. The empress commented: 'The Saviour chose his disciples not from scholars and theologians but from simple fishermen and carpenters. In the gospel it's said that faith can move mountains.' She pointed to a picture of one of Christ's miracles and claimed: 'This God is alive today. I believe that my son will rise again. I know that I'm considered mad because of my faith. But surely all who believed were martyrs.'[19] Devout and prayerful, she could not fail to notice that her prayers brought no improvement in her son's condition. The medical emergencies recurred, and he could easily die at any time. This was why Rasputin became so important to her, as Pierre Gilliard was to recall:

> Then when she gained acquaintance with Rasputin she was convinced that if she were to turn to him during Alexei Nikolaevich's illness, he would live. Her son would live. Alexei Nikolaevich would somehow be better. Call it coincidence if you like but the facts of togetherness [obshchenie] with Rasputin and alleviation of Alexei Nikolaevich's illness did coincide.

Alexandra believed. She had nothing else to cling to and found peace for herself in this. She was convinced that Rasputin had been a semi-saint and an intermediary between her and God.[20]

Without Rasputin, she dedicated herself to saving her son as best she could.

Alexei and his mother were closely bonded. Gilliard would recall:

If he went to her twenty times a day, there wasn't a time when she didn't kiss him. I could understand that every time she said good-bye, she was afraid that she wouldn't see him again. What is more, it seems to me that her religion failed to give her what she expected of it: the crises with him continued to occur with their threat to his life. The miracle that she had been waiting for never happened.[21]

Alexei remained in poor health throughout much of the year. But although 'our friend' was dead, fortunately there arose no crisis involving a wound or haemorrhage.[22]

He always tried to be brave. He had frequent excruciating pain in his legs, but when people asked whether he was in pain he would often deny it.[23] Occasionally he himself would enquire: 'What do you think, will this ever go away?'[24] When he was fit enough, his tutor Gibbes played 'Robbers' with him.[25] Alexei also loved to play with his set of toy soldiers and amused himself on the balalaika.[26] Kobylinski remembered him as a bright and spirited lad who could speak English and French. (He was never taught German.)[27] His parents and sisters nicknamed him Baby – a sign that they were not hurrying his passage to adulthood – and he had become used to thinking of himself as but a child. Although he was not unintelligent, he was not a precocious pupil, and his tutors Pierre Gilliard and Sydney Gibbes were expected to join in whatever games he had in mind outside the palace. Both men, like Botkin, were too enamoured of their association with the Romanovs to feel they were demeaning themselves, and anyway they had a jolly time. The same was true of lads such as Kolya Derevenko, son of one of the family's doctors, who was asked to play with him in the daytime. All the Romanovs and their retinue appreciated Alexei's sweet nature.

Nicholas abdicated at a time of family illness when all four of his daughters Olga, Tatyana, Maria and Anastasia lay stricken with measles, probably catching it from Alexei. Olga and Tatyana in addition suffered from pleurisy.[28]

Olga was a modest young woman who spoke French, English and German. She liked singing and had a good soprano voice. She drew well. She avoided glamorous clothes.[29] People noticed that Olga loved her father more than she did her mother.[30] Tatyana was more like Alexandra and was always close to her.[31] Decisive and somewhat bossy, she helped to keep order in the household, and one of her teachers was to say that if the empress had been removed from the scene, Tatyana would have easily filled her family role.[32] Maria was the family beauty. Known to the others as Mashka, she had a talent for drawing and was the most sociable of the sisters. She talked regularly with the guards, discovering the names of their wives and asking how many children they had and how much land. Robust and ever willing, she reminded some people of her grandfather, Alexander III. Alexei would call out: 'Mashka, come and carry me!' and Mashka would always happily comply.[33] Anastasia was short and well built. She loved to discover people's weak spots and was never averse to teasing them; on the positive side, she was 'a natural comic'.[34] Her pet name in the family was Shvibzik.[35]

The happy family found itself in circumstances that it had never imagined possible. The Romanovs, however, were resilient. Only Alexandra found it difficult to smile. Aggrieved by what she saw as a plot by leading politicians to force her husband from the throne, she was often in a sombre mood. She badly missed her active work in the Tsarskoe Selo sanatoriums. But even she could see that she had to put on a brave face. And she and her daughters fell back on the simple pleasures that united them: reading, indoor games and sewing. Alexei played with his toy soldiers and military equipment. Nicholas spent hours sawing wood for the fire. Without their old public responsibilities, they all seized their opportunities for distraction. The whole family wanted to keep up morale while they waited on events.

7. THE PROVISIONAL GOVERNMENT

The Provisional Government felt no impulse to treat the Romanovs harshly, and Nicholas was careful to do nothing to embarrass the cabinet. The two sides cooperated to make the Tsarskoe Selo confinement as bearable as they could. Even so, there remained a desire among ministers to ascertain the truth about stories that Nicholas or Alexandra had engaged in illicit wartime negotiations with the Germans, and the cabinet appointed a Supreme Extraordinary Investigative Commission, its members experienced in legal and official inquiries, whose brief was to discover whether any Romanov had tried to pull Russia out of the war and sign a separate peace accord with Germany. If incriminating evidence was found, it was likely that the imperial couple would be charged with high treason.[1]

The Petrograd Soviet sent soldiers out to Tsarskoe Selo under the leadership of Socialist-Revolutionary Colonel Sergei Mstislavski. They travelled in armoured cars. Mstislavski was on his party's left wing, and it looked for a while that there would be violence. Dressed in his military uniform, he waved a letter from Chkheidze asking Kobylinski to render him every assistance. Mstislavski demanded to see Nicholas in person.[2] According to Kobylinski, he also demanded Nicholas's transfer to custody in the Peter-Paul Fortress in Petrograd.[3] When Kobylinski point-blank refused, Mstislavski exclaimed: 'Well, Colonel, you know the blood that will now flow, and it will be on your head that it falls.' Kobylinski replied: 'Well, so be it. If it falls, it falls; but I still can't fulfil your request.' As Mstislavski trudged away, Kobylinski assumed that it was the end of the matter. In fact Mstislavski inveigled his way into the Alexander Palace, convincing the captain on duty to let him into the building on condition that he would only observe the emperor without speaking to him. Mstislavski returned to Petrograd, reporting that the Romanovs were being kept under proper control.[4]

Of all the cabinet ministers it was Kerensky who had most direct contact with Nicholas after all Romanov questions were placed under the care of the Ministry of Justice.[5] He had too many other things on his desk until 3 April, when at last he found time to go out to Tsarskoe Selo and talk to the former emperor. At his first meeting with Nicholas he addressed him as 'Nikolai Alexandrovich', as if he were just another ordinary Russian. But Kerensky slipped back to 'Your Majesty' [*Velichestvo*] whenever he forgot himself. The emperor mentioned this to his retinue; it was one of the few amusing things he found in the course of his conversation with the justice minister.[6] The court retainers were less indulgent and took poorly to him. Kerensky wore a Russian shirt and rather tattered double-breasted jacket whereas they were accustomed to presentations at court in which ministers always wore tailcoats, and they did not see why a mere revolution should make a difference.[7] They also glumly observed that he travelled to Tsarskoe Selo in the emperor's limousine driven by his old chauffeur. This did not go down well in the palace.[8]

Kerensky carried out his duty with assiduity, talking not only with Nicholas but also with Alexandra and Alexei. Despite being famous throughout Russia as a lawyer who had attacked the bulwarks of tsarism, Kerensky now felt it was important for him to get to know the imperial family and asked what they thought about the idea of asylum in England; he also checked personally on matters of security in and around the Alexander Palace.[9] It was in this way that he heard from a palace servant that the former empress and Anna Vyrubova had set about burning a pile of documents in the stoves. Enquiries made of other servants confirmed the story. Armed with this proof of Alexandra's capacity for deviousness, Kerensky requisitioned all official and personal documentation so that she could not obstruct the work of the Extraordinary Investigative Commission.[10] He also acted to remove Vyrubova from the palace. She was ill and in bed on the day of his visit and her déshabillé appearance disgusted him: he thought she lacked any sense of shame or self-respect. Without further ado he ordered her arrest along with another of Alexandra's confidantes, Lili Dehn, and they were both sent to the Peter-Paul Fortress.[11]

Kerensky returned to Tsarskoe Selo a few days later with Colonel Korovichenko, whom he appointed as commandant of the cantonment. He wanted to quarantine the Romanovs. Retainers would be subject to the same conditions and were to be told to make their choice whether to stay or leave. The palace was to be cut off from the world. Kerensky's permission was going to be required before anybody could step on to the curtilage. He laid down that all correspondence would undergo censorship.[12] Kerensky carefully followed the work of the Extraordinary Investigative Commission and demanded the right to have the chest containing Nicholas's past letters inspected. Nicholas complied but held back a letter that he insisted was private. When Korovichenko snatched the letter from him, Nicholas lost his temper but was helpless to resist, exclaiming: 'Well, in that case I'm not needed. I'm going out for a walk.'[13]

Alexander Guchkov was another politician who made his way to Tsarskoe Selo. Having become the army and navy minister, he wanted to establish that everything was satisfactory with the garrison. He turned up unannounced and his interview with Nicholas was very different from the ones of an earlier period, including the occasion on the train in Pskov a few weeks previously. This time Guchkov was neither supplicant nor petitioner and, as Nicholas was all too aware, could make things difficult for the family if he so decided. But Nicholas could handle the situation and the conversation was businesslike and courteous. The sole unpleasantness occurred as Guchkov made his way out, when it became clear that the officers who were escorting him included a fiery fellow who spoke curtly to the Romanov retinue: 'You're our enemies. We're your enemies. All of you here are mercenaries.' There was a suspicion that drink was getting the better of him. The valet Volkov gave him a dusty riposte: 'You, good sir, are mistaken about our gentility.' This was short of a challenge or a threat, but it was a sign that the imperial entourage retained a feeling that there were certain acceptable ways to address them. Guchkov affected not to have heard the outburst, and did not even turn his head.[14]

In June 1917 Kerensky, who had replaced Guchkov at the Ministry of War, took the step of physically isolating emperor and empress from each other. This would facilitate the job of the Extraordinary Investigative Commission if it was thought necessary to interview them. Kerensky informed Nicholas in person while Korovichenko received the unenviable task of telling Alexandra. The order was also explained to Count Pavel Benkendorf and Elizaveta Naryshkina, who had overseen daily business at court. This was enforced in as decent a way as possible and the couple were allowed to share their evening meals, the only stipulation being that Korovichenko should always be their dining companion. In fact the Extraordinary Investigative Commission could find no evidence whatever that Nicholas had worked for a separate peace with Germany. Kaiser Wilhelm had indeed written to him with such a proposal, and Nicholas had ordered an official to reply that he had no intention of making any response. Kerensky was not equally confident about Alexandra's behaviour, and Rasputin's known leanings towards finding a way to end the conflict added to his continuing suspicions. But in the end Alexandra's name was also cleared, and Kerensky revoked the order to keep husband and wife separated.[15]

Alexandra had never expected to get on with him since he was one of the Provisional Government's most revolutionary ministers. She regarded Kerensky with intense suspicion, and he shared the widespread public hostility to her over the role she had played in politics before the February Revolution. It could have remained a fractious relationship, but after his first dishevelled appearance at the Alexander Palace, Kerensky began to arrive dressed smartly in a tailcoat and garters.[16] This amused her. Gaining a sense of his embarrassment, she was tickled about his general air of confusion and uncertainty.[17] When he asked to talk to her in Nicholas's office, she sent back word that Kerensky should instead come to her room. Kerensky saw no point in arguing and complied with her request. To their joint surprise, they got on well. From behind the closed doors, the valet Volkov could hear plenty of laughter. Volkov asked Alexandra about this afterwards. Alexandra divulged that Kerensky had promised that the family was not about to be consigned to the Peter-Paul Fortress. Indeed, he had cracked some jokes. Alexandra was warming to him and on one occasion said: 'He's no problem. He's a fine fellow. One can talk to him.'[18]

Nicholas nevertheless failed to understand the government's inability to rule with greater firmness. 'Surely,' he asked, 'Kerensky can stop this licentiousness? How is this possible? Alexander Fëdorovich was placed there by the people. The people must obey and not run amok. Kerensky's the soldiers' favourite.'[19] But he also applauded Kerensky for endorsing a resumption of active operations at the front, which was music to Nicholas's ears. At last there was attestation that the Provisional Government had not given up the fight. Nicholas applied for permission to hold a service of intercession on behalf of Russia's forces at church in Tsarskoe Selo.[20] It was all he could do after losing power. He yearned to identify himself with the country's military purposes.[21] Alexandra was less restrained whenever they discussed who was most responsible for their misfortune. Her angry outbursts agitated Nicholas, who took to telling her to shut up. This had not been his usual way with her, either in front of their retainers or alone. In past years if they disagreed, he had dealt with it by proceeding to ignore her advice. The new abruptness was a sign of the depth of his own distress – he liked to talk calmly and with decorum.[22]

But usually Nicholas exempted Kerensky from blame. One day, conversing with Sophie Buxhoeveden, he said: 'That's a person who could have been useful to me; it's a pity that I didn't know him earlier.'[23] But he was less generous about those politicians who in his view had engineered his downfall:

> I forgive Rodzyanko because he loved his country. He deceived himself and was himself tricked, for he wasn't intelligent and submitted too easily to the influence of his entourage. But he was an honest man and a patriot, after his own fashion. As regards Milyukov, I again believe that he loved his country, after his own fashion, but that he was a man of party, a sectarian – and the party for him took the place of his fatherland. In working for his party, he worked against his country. Guchkov, well, he's a man I deeply distrust, for he is filled with ambition; he would be capable of anything to gain power. He never understood that his self-interest never had a side that was dictated by love of his country. Everything that he did, he did for the glory of Guchkov.[24]

There was little rancour in his tirade, only a bitterness about the ensuing Russian turmoil. The only architect of Nicholas's downfall whom he truly detested was Guchkov, and he liked to remember how he had denied him his hand at one of their meetings.[25]

It continued to pain Nicholas that the authorities refused to publish his final summons to the army to show obedience to the Provisional Government. But he rebuked Sophie Buxhoeveden when she failed to cross herself as prayers were being said for the cabinet: 'The Provisional Government is Russia's government. You may well not like Prince Lvov and his colleagues but you have to pray that Our Lord should give guidance in the matter of rule.'[26] Ever the man of duty. Ever the patriot.

8. THE BRITISH OFFER

His abdication had led both Nicholas and the Provisional Government to consider resolving the Romanov question by putting the family into some kind of exile. The Russian exilic tradition had two basic variants. Most people who fled the empire in the reigns of Nicholas and his father moved to escape either the grinding conditions of poverty or the attentions of the security police, the Okhrana. Their favoured destinations were Switzerland, France, Germany, the United States and England. Émigré 'colonies' were vigorous in all these countries and only started to shrink in size after the February 1917 Revolution. The Provisional Government might have chosen this option – and for a while England was under intense consideration – but it also had an alternative possibility. If ministers wanted, the authorities could send people to distant parts of the empire. This system of 'administrative exile' had existed for centuries as a way of stopping miscreants from interfering in public affairs and was frequently used to sideline individuals whose offences did not merit outright imprisonment.

On 15 March 1917 the Provisional Government at its first meeting was already looking at the possibility of exiling the Romanovs. Foreign affairs minister Pavel Milyukov led the discussion. He advocated residence abroad on the grounds that the family's safety would be difficult to guarantee in Russia. It did not take long for ministers to decide there was no necessity to dispatch absolutely every member of the large Romanov clan. Instead, they focused on Nicholas and Mikhail and their families, who could become a source of trouble if they stayed in or near Petrograd. Without coming to a hard and fast conclusion, the cabinet endorsed the idea of evicting them from Tsarskoe Selo. Milyukov's proposal that the Romanovs be definitely sent abroad was rejected, although it was left open as a possibility alongside internal exile. Ministers planned to ascertain whether Nicholas would agree to move to somewhere in Russia designated by the Provisional Government; they also expected to impose conditions on his freedom of movement.[1]

Nicholas was having thoughts along the same lines as Milyukov. He had lost the throne and wanted to depart from the Russian political scene. No sooner had he arrived back in Mogilëv after abdicating in Pskov than he pencilled out a note stating his wish to settle in a foreign country. He asked that the family be allowed to stay at Tsarskoe Selo until such time as his children recovered from the measles, after which he and his party were to travel unhindered to the Murman peninsula and take a ship from Russian shores. At the same time he sought an assurance that he could return to Russia at the end of the Great War to live at his Livadia palace in Crimea.[2]

On 17 March General Alexeev forwarded Nicholas's ideas – except for the Livadia stipulation – to Minister-Chairman Lvov and Minister Milyukov. Two days later he received a telegram of approval from Petrograd. The Provisional Government agreed to let him stay at Tsarskoe Selo until such time as he could travel to the White Sea coast and take a ship abroad. Using the Hughes apparatus (which allowed users to have live written exchanges by means of the telegraph), Lvov and Guchkov contacted GHQ to ascertain the emperor's intentions in greater detail. They wanted to know where he wanted to go. Alexeev could not give them an answer since Nicholas was still consulting his mother and his first cousins once removed Sergei Mikhailovich and Alexander Mikhailovich about the same question. His thinking was made clear later that evening when he asked to discuss the possible journey with Hanbury-Williams. Nicholas entertained the idea only on condition that the British government gave its consent and was willing to offer the Royal Navy's assistance. Hanbury-Williams immediately wired London endorsing the emperor's request.[3]

Milyukov was pleased to learn that the deposed monarch agreed with him. The perils still facing the Romanovs in Russia had not faded, and the Provisional Government did not yet have satisfactory control over the situation in the capital. On the same day he talked to the British, French and Italian ambassadors and indicated the likelihood of a decision to expel the Romanovs. French Ambassador Maurice Paléologue spoke again with Milyukov next day, emphasizing the need for this to become one of the Provisional Government's priorities. Both Paléologue and Milyukov had the bloody precedent of Louis XVI in mind. Later that afternoon Paléologue went over the options with Sir George Buchanan at the British embassy. While taking tea with them, Lady Buchanan expressed her own worries about the danger for the Romanovs if they were forced to stay at Tsarskoe Selo, a mere fifteen miles from Petrograd. The two ambassadors concurred that the best option was to arrange for a Royal Navy cruiser to pick them up in Murmansk.[4]

Milyukov took the initiative with Buchanan on 21 March 1917 and asked him to hasten the process of decision in London. He asked for the British to promise that Nicholas would abstain from interfering in Russian politics from exile, although he did not make this a requirement of the deal: his urgent wish was to secure the departure as soon as possible.[5] Buchanan returned with the British reply on 23 March. Both the king and the cabinet were glad to provide asylum until the end of the war. Their main query was about where the financial support for the Romanovs would come from. Milyukov gave an undertaking that the Provisional Government would make a liberal allowance but asked for this to be kept confidential.[6] Money would be a sensitive matter in both countries. In Russia, few of his former subjects were likely to approve of subsidizing Nicholas; in Britain, millions of people regarded him as a tyrant whose downfall had been long overdue.

Nothing in any case could occur at the apex of Russian politics without the Petrograd Soviet's approval. When its Executive Committee held a debate on 22 March, there was fury at the possibility that Nicholas might be permitted to leave the country. The Soviet leadership had already given instructions for army units to seize control at all railway stations through which the train might pass, and when Colonel Mstislavski had paid his visit to Tsarskoe Selo two days earlier, he had been carrying orders to arrest Nicholas if there were signs of any attempt to move him. The Executive Committee continued to make clear its willingness to break with the Provisional Government. The pressure achieved its desired effect when Minister of Justice Kerensky promised Chkheidze that the cabinet had agreed to drop the idea of sending Nicholas into English exile.[7] The Petrograd Soviet passed a resolution arguing that if Nicholas went to England, he would gain access to funds enabling him to conspire against the revolution. A committee was created to maintain the pressure on Lvov and his cabinet. On no account were the Romanovs to leave Russia. The Soviet's military section cabled to army units at all border points and on all the railways to this effect. Nicholas, having returned to Tsarskoe Selo, was to be kept there for the foreseeable future – and the military section sent commissars of its own to ensure compliance.[8]

Milyukov was depressed by the turn of events, and at his next meeting with Paléologue, after expressing satisfaction about the British official attitude, he informed him: 'Alas, I fear it is too late.'[9] Kerensky had convinced the Provisional Government that the Petrograd Soviet would take every step to prevent the Romanovs' departure.[10] On 24 March 1917, Milyukov repeated this verdict at the formal ceremony at the Marinski Palace which ratified international recognition of the Provisional Government.[11]

London politicians and the British royal family were in the dark about the latest political events in Petrograd. On 25 March 1917 Buchanan handed over a personal telegram from King George to Nicholas. Next day Milyukov told the ambassador that such communications were no longer acceptable. Russia had gone through a revolution and Nicholas had been forced from the throne. Direct contact between the royal cousins was undesirable at a moment when the Provisional Government had difficulty in keeping the Petrograd Soviet on its side, and anyway, the imperial family could not move until the daughters recovered from the measles.[12] Milyukov had already explained that the Soviet leaders would never grant its consent to the plan. Minister of Justice Kerensky acted as the Petrograd Soviet's watchman inside the cabinet so that Milyukov as foreign affairs minister had to steer a delicate course if he hoped to advance his cause of foreign exile.[13] Milyukov explained his frustrations to Nikolai Bazili, who was liaising with the Provisional Government on General Alexeev's behalf. Guchkov felt less inhibited and made the proposal to pause for a while and then organize a rail journey for the Romanovs without consultation.[14]

But the fact remained that the Petrograd Soviet was implacably opposed to the family's departure abroad and had the necessary support in the garrisons and among railway workers to enforce its wishes. George V's readiness to offer asylum was a side issue. The Provisional Government did not dare to antagonize the Soviet leadership as it strove to impose its authority over the country. Until ministers had adequate control, it mattered little what King George or Prime Minister David Lloyd George proposed.

Kerensky came to the Petrograd Soviet soldiers' section on 26 March 1917 to take the heat out of the question. He asked his listeners to believe in him as someone who had fought long and hard against the monarchy. He declared that no one in custody at Tsarskoe Selo could gain freedom without his consent. With a rhetorical flourish he asked the soldiers either to exclude him from their midst or else to give him their trust. Rumours about his indulgent attitude to Nicholas II caused him some annoyance. He admitted that Grand Duke Dmitri Pavlovich remained at liberty, but he defended this situation by citing Dmitri Pavlovich's active role in the assassination of Rasputin. For Kerensky, indeed, there was no doubt that this particular member of the extended Romanov family deserved recognition as an enemy of tsarism – and he saw no reason why he should not continue to serve in the Russian Army in distant Persia. Kerensky was equally firm about permitting General Ivanov to live merely under house arrest. Ivanov was a sick man whom the doctors diagnosed as being at death's door.[15]

But the Provisional Government continued to support the idea of foreign exile. Consequently, it is unsurprising that Nicholas and Alexandra were confused about their future. Cut off from the previous channels of information, they relied on what Kerensky told them in the Alexander Palace and on what they read in the daily newspapers. As the shock of what had happened to them diminished, they were beginning to have mixed thoughts of their own which they shared with people near to them. The idea of living in London as deposed monarchs was unappealing to them, and Alexandra told Pierre Gilliard that if indeed they moved into exile, they would prefer to live in one of the British colonies or in Norway.[16] Sydney Gibbes wrote to his Aunt Hattie: 'Our fortunes are completely broken and it is more than possible that I shall leave Russia & return to England with my "pupil".'[17] Evidently Nicholas and Alexandra had not entirely abandoned the idea of finding asylum in the United Kingdom. Permission to travel, however, was not in their hands. Not even the Provisional Government could guarantee their safety on the way north from Tsarskoe Selo.

9. RULES AND ROUTINES

The Provisional Government drew up detailed regulations for the Romanovs at the Alexander Palace. They were compelled to stay indoors most of the time and were allowed on to the balcony and into a section of the park only between the hours of eight in the morning and six at night. Two entrances alone were to be kept in use and the pre-revolutionary police were removed. (In fact they had already vanished from every station in Petrograd and elsewhere.) All telephones were cut off except for the one used by the palace commandant; the telegraph facility was put out of action. The family's correspondence was subjected to regular inspection. Those members of the imperial retinue who wished to continue in service could stay on the sole condition that they never left the palace. When a doctor was called, a military officer was required to be in attendance.[1]

Sydney Gibbes happened to be on a trip to the capital on the day the regime was introduced. Troops barred his way when he returned to Tsarskoe Selo. Gibbes appealed to the British ambassador, Sir George Buchanan, to intercede with the Provisional Government. After much delay, a letter of refusal arrived which was signed by five ministers – and Gibbes remained barred from the palace.[2] Probably the cabinet feared that Gibbes might operate as an intermediary between Nicholas and the British authorities at a time when the Provisional Government aimed at total control of communications with London. Not everyone in the retinue of Nicholas behaved as loyally as Gibbes had done. Several imperial officials trickled out of court after the abdication. Within days, Nicholas found himself abandoned by Count Pëtr Apraxin, Kirill Naryshkin, Count Alexander Grabbe, aide-de-camp Alexander Mordvinov and aide-de-camp Duke Nikolai Lichtenberg.[3] The Romanovs grew accustomed to the routines of isolation and inspection. When people wrote to them, they had to append their names so that the authorities could trace them if the need arose.[4] The regulations were copied to the Petrograd Soviet with a view to assuring the revolutionary parties that the former dynasty remained under proper control.[5]

Although the palace was cordoned off from the rest of Tsarskoe Selo, the noise in the barracks was often audible. Throughout March and April there were political processions accompanied by military bands. The family disliked the commotion, and Nicholas deplored the endless rendition of the 'Marseillaise' and Chopin's Funeral March. His nerves were strained to the utmost on the day the new authorities dug a mass grave inside the palace park in which to bury and commemorate the people who had perished in the struggle to overthrow the monarchy in the February Revolution. The Chopin melody embedded itself so deeply in the Romanovs' heads that they could not stop whistling it.[6] To that extent, and to that extent alone, the Romanovs absorbed the spirit of revolution. In every other respect they shunned and abhorred it as they always had done.

For their information about politics and the war, they followed the press. Kobylinski witnessed the daily delivery of a package of newspapers which included *Russkoe slovo*, *Russkaya volya*, *Rech*, *Novoe vremya*, *Petrogradskii listok* and *Petrogradskaya gazeta*. There was also a delivery of British and French newspapers. *Rech* was the official organ of the main liberal party, the Constitutional Democrats (or Kadets) and was the most left-wing of them – and, of course, it was a publication that had been anathema to the imperial couple before 1917. The Kadets themselves had moved somewhat to the political right after the revolution and perhaps Nicholas found them less displeasing than he once had done. He felt no need, however, to ask for the Menshevik and Socialist-Revolutionary dailies, far less the Bolshevik ones. Evidently he thought that he already knew enough about them. He sealed himself inside a wrapping of ideas that had served him since his accession, reserving his curiosity for things that he regarded as seemly and appropriate. His intellectual rigidity was total.

Nevertheless, he and the family recognized that they had to get used to the fact that they no longer occupied the summit of power and prestige, and a regular daily routine was one of their comforts. All except for Alexandra rose early from their beds, and Nicholas took a morning constitutional walk with Dolgorukov to discuss the latest situation. He liked to do some physical work before going back indoors – sawing or chopping firewood was a favourite chore. Alexandra, herself ailing and no longer allowed to nurse troops in the Tsarskoe Selo sanatoriums, concentrated on needlework. Seated in her chair all day long, she found relief by working with her hands – some of the gifts that she handed to people had lines of prayers sewn on to them.[7]

The whole family took a meal together at one o'clock. Afterwards the younger Romanovs went outside for some exercise in the garden before returning to their studies. Tea followed at four, after which they sometimes went outside again for a breath of air. Dinner was served at seven.[8] There was no material hardship and culinary standards were maintained; the family also retained a substantial retinue of courtiers and servants. Although they complied with the imposed regime, they seldom lost an opportunity to complain about anything they found objectionable – Alexandra was predictably vociferous. The Romanov detainees were left to themselves inside their palace chambers. Self-isolated from high society before the February Revolution, they were now deprived of contact with the hospital wards where Alexandra and her daughters had nursed wounded soldiers. Nicholas and Alexandra had guarded their children from what they regarded as undesirable influences, and no discussions had taken place with other European royal families before 1914 to find suitors for any of the girls. Now the war had made it impossible to arrange a match. The youngsters were contained within an emotional enclosure. Olga, the eldest, was already twenty-one but she, like her sisters, was less mature than other young women of her age. They and their brother knew of no other conditions of existence and were also predictably immature.

The whole family reciprocated the respect that they received from Colonel Kobylinski, who got on well with Nicholas but desisted from calling him 'Your Majesty', addressing him simply as Nikolai Alexandrovich.[9] The troops under his command were not so polite, and there was often an edgy atmosphere out in the park. The garrison's diet suffered from the general deterioration in food supplies to northern Russia. The troops were irritated at having to eat lentils rather than bread. This had been a cause of discontent in the February Revolution and still annoyed them under the Provisional Government, their ire taking expression in the form of anger shown towards the imperial family.[10]

One day a soldier shot one of the two small goats that were kept in the palace park. Anna Vyrubova reckoned that he had been aiming at her and made a complaint. Neither the troops nor their officers took any notice: the days were gone when the imperial retinue could click its fingers and secure obedience. Next day another soldier shot the second goat.[11] Sometimes, moreover, the troops hurled abuse at the

Romanovs. One soldier, catching a glimpse of Nicholas, shouted to his comrades: 'Here's where our money's gone! Look at how they live!' Nicholas himself never ceased to try to get on good terms with people whom he continued to regard as 'his' troops. He greeted them individually with a friendly 'hello' (*zdravstvuyte*). Volkov was witness to an encounter when the soldier failed to return the salutation. Nicholas assumed that he was merely somewhat hard of hearing and repeated the greeting in a louder voice. But the soldier still declined to respond. From that moment, Volkov believed that everyone in the garrison was in favour of the revolution that had overthrown the monarchy.[12]

General Kornilov periodically changed the guard to maintain distance between the family and their captors. At the departure of one regiment, Nicholas bade them farewell and stretched out his hand to their commander. A pitiful scene ensued. The officer took a pace back rather than be touched by Nicholas, who left his hand dangling in the air. Nicholas was so distraught that he stepped forward and with tears in his eyes held the officer by the shoulders as he asked him: 'My dear fellow, what's all this about?' The answer was blunt: 'I come from the people. When the people stretched out its hand to you, you wouldn't accept it. Now I'm not going to give you my hand.'[13]

Even so, the valet Alexei Volkov detected a softening of comportment as the soldiers got used to seeing Nicholas at work with axe and saw. Some of their officers asked for signed photographs of the Romanovs. Volkov passed on such requests, which the family was only too pleased to satisfy. Other officers were more hostile and declined to shake hands with Nicholas when they came on duty.[14] The old Russia was being turned on its head. For instance, there was an army tradition at Easter of presenting half a bottle of table wine to each regimental commander. Troops in the 2nd Regiment objected to being left out of any such largesse; they created a noisy fuss until Kobylinski relented and gave out fifty bottles of wine. Discipline, already undermined, fell ever further apart – and the same regiment rebuked one of its own ensigns for kissing the emperor's hand. It was bewildering and painful for Nicholas.[15]

He was not the only Romanov who suffered from the behaviour of the garrison soldiers. On 10 June 1917 his son Alexei was playing outdoors with his toy rifle – his proudest possession – when the troops on guard took fright. Alexei was not wielding an instrument of war but a miniature object made for him by a Russian factory, and although it could be fired if loaded, Alexei no longer had any bullets. He had been brought up to feel part of the country's military tradition and just liked to wave his gun around like a soldier. The troops thought otherwise; they claimed that he was brandishing a dangerous weapon. When told to put it down, Alexei burst into tears. The incident was reported to Kobylinski, who discussed it with Gilliard and the children's nanny Alexandra Teglëva. Kobylinski sympathized with the tsarevich but saw the prudence of impounding the little rifle.[16]

Incidents of this kind fanned the flame of Nicholas's horror about the revolutionary situation. All his worst fears were being realized. Usually he avoided political comment even inside his own entourage. He was even more cautious in his correspondence, knowing that everything he wrote could be read by the authorities. But in one of his letters to his mother, Maria Fëdorovna, he could contain himself no longer and told her: 'Words cannot express what a terrible crime is being committed by those who are corrupting the army!'[17] Alexandra refused to bridle herself. On 10 June she wrote to her former patient and war hero General Alexander Syroboyarski about 'the Sodom and Gomorrah in the capital'.[18] With all the confidence of an ex-empress she added:

> The psychology of the mass[es] is a terrible thing. Our people is lacking in culture – this is why, like a flock of sheep, they go with the flow. But if only they can be helped to understand that they've been deceived, everything can move in a different direction. They are an able people but very grey and don't understand anything. While the bad are everywhere bent on destruction, please let the good try and save the country.[19]

10. ON THE LIVES OF RULERS

Nicholas guarded his inner thoughts from those outside his family – he had always been known for his reticence and even his personal diary is a parsimonious source of self-revelation. But there was one area of his life where he left a trail of informative clues behind him. In Tsarskoe Selo, the former emperor became an avid reader. Summer in the Russian north is famous for its 'white nights', when the darkness is of short duration. In the long hours of daylight, when not sawing or chopping timber for the fire, Nicholas caught up with the literature that he had failed to examine in earlier years, and his choice of books illuminates the former emperor's attempt to make sense of the recent extraordinary events.

The themes with which his mind was throbbing were the same as they always had been: duty, fate, religion, nationhood, military greatness and rulership. It had never been his habit to talk to his ministers about them. Now, of course, he anyway had no ministers to talk to, and when he touched on these subjects in conversation with courtiers such as Dolgorukov or Gilliard, he still acted the emperor: he was not seeking a genuine exchange of views with them and they themselves felt no temptation to breach his privacy. It would seem that Nicholas did not unburden himself even to Alexandra, who in turn buried herself in the Bible and Christian devotional tracts. Nicholas was adamant about the need to look strong and keep his dignity. It would seem that the only way he found to commune with the thoughts of others was to sit down with the works of favoured authors. His 'interlocutors' could not answer back, which was how he liked things to be. He had been brought up to assume that to be a Russian tsar was to be answerable to no one. Nicholas was a human fortress.

But he was a fortress with a heart. In the evenings, he cheered up his family by reading to them. He started with stories by Anton Chekhov.[1] Then he chose Arthur Conan Doyle's *The Valley of Fear* and *The Hound of the Baskervilles* – Sherlock Holmes had long been a

Romanov favourite.[2] Detective stories by other writers were popular, too, including those of Gaston Leroux, starting with *Le mystère de la chambre jaune*.[3]

In his own reading, he indulged his lifelong passion for the imperial army's history by looking at two works that had appeared not long before the outbreak of the Great War: L. A. Kasso's *Russia on the Danube* and General A. N. Kuropatkin's *Russia for the Russians*.[4] Kasso focused on the treaty of Bucharest of 1812 that had given 'the best bit of Moldavia' to the Russian Empire – in Kasso's opinion, to the inestimable benefit of St Petersburg.[5] Kuropatkin's sprawling trilogy recorded Russian military campaigns from the distant Muscovite past to the twentieth century, and argued that in recent decades there had been a lamentable failure to pursue the objective of 'Russia for the Russians'. Kuropatkin railed against the scale of foreign ownership in Russian industry, and he also contended that the empire's own Jews exercised a malign influence upon the national interest. In a sharp burst of anti-Semitism, he repeated a story about a pamphlet found on the corpse of a Jewish soldier killed in the Russo-Japanese war of 1904–1905. Kuropatkin cited the alleged secret instructions of a rabbi who urged Jews to infiltrate ruling circles throughout Europe. Supposedly there was a Jewish plot to secure authority by financial control, to treat Christianity as their enemy and to undermine whole countries by fomenting working-class discontent.[6]

Kasso was an imperial patriot and conservative, Kuropatkin a rabid racist and extreme nationalist. He loved 'his' army and never stopped thinking about it. For him, as always, the honour and greatness of the country lay in the hands of its armed forces. He continued to endorse the idea that triumphant alien forces were at work against the well-being of his beloved Russia. The very fact that Nicholas turned to books by Kasso, and especially by Kuropatkin, showed the direction his thoughts were taking.

Nicholas also read *The History of the Byzantine Empire* by F. I. Uspenski, who shone a light on the different historical paths taken by the lands of Eastern and Western Europe under the influence of the Orthodox and Catholic Churches, respectively. Uspenski's best chapters recounted the ill-fated attempt by Roman emperor Julian in the fourth century to abolish Christianity as the established state religion.[7] The work contained lengthy quotations from Julian's pamphlet titled *The Beard-Hater*.[8] Uspenski did not confine himself to events in Byzantium but surveyed the early stirrings of nationhood and religious specificity throughout Europe and the Middle East until the era of the Muslim invasions.[9] It was essentially a sequel to Edward Gibbons's *Decline and Fall of the Roman Empire*, and there was nothing like it in contemporary historical writing around the world. Nicholas, admittedly not someone given to effusive self-expression, found it 'a very interesting book'.[10]

But if he had a favourite author at Tsarskoe Selo, it was not Conan Doyle or Kuropatkin or Uspenski but the poet and novelist Dmitri Merezhkovski. Day after day he read the series of novels grouped under the title of *Christ and Antichrist*. Merezhkovski himself was a leading member of the Symbolist literary group that included the poets Alexander Blok and Merezhkovski's wife Zinaida Gippius; these were novels that offered a vivid reimagining of historical episodes from fourth-century Rome through to nineteenth-century Russia. Merezhkovski had a zeal for the social and religious traditions of old Russia. His quirky theology had got him into trouble with the Orthodox Church to the point that there were moves to excommunicate him. The experience of revolutionary ferment in 1905–1906 had deeply disturbed him, and although his series ranged from one country to another, it was current Russian problems that lay at the core of his concerns. Nicholas read each of the novels in the space of a few days.

The first, *Death of the Gods*, had the Roman emperor Julian as its central character calling himself the Antichrist. Julian ruled from AD 361 to 363 and overturned the decree of his half-uncle Constantine that had designated Christianity as the empire's sole official religion. Merezhkovski depicted Christians as being in constant internal strife, a widely found phenomenon in twentieth-century Russia. The novel described a Julian who was willing to discuss theology with the Christian members of his family and entourage. Julian appears in a light that is far from unsympathetic, but he is also seen as bull-headed and resistant to well-intended advice. As his life and reign come to a bloody end in battle with the Sassanid Empire of the Persians, the last line of the novel runs: 'Night and Tempest, hand in hand, were striding on apace.' Merezhkovski failed to make clear whether he regarded Julian as the genuine Antichrist of centuries of Christian theological thinking. His main implicit purpose was to point to the imperfection of life on earth even among Christians. Truth, for him, lay with God alone.

Nicholas recorded: 'I finished reading *Julian*, which I liked.'[11] The hero of the second volume, *The Gods Resurrected*, was Leonardo da

Vinci.[12] Some of the finest passages deal with the way in which the painter gave thought to how he should render the likeness of Jesus Christ. The novel examines Renaissance artists, preachers and thinkers such as Savonarola and Machiavelli and highlights mankind's relationship with God. But apart from vignettes on Leonardo's painterly musings, the writing has many longueurs. The sharpest chapter depicts a witches' sabbath – Merezhkovski was never one to let his religious devotion get in the way of letting rip with his insalubrious imaginings. The city of Florence is depicted as wild, bustling and unseemly. *The Gods Resurrected* ends with a pedagogical prediction that, after the decline of Rome itself and Byzantium, Russia will become the 'Third Rome'.[13] Merezhkovski had a sermonizing streak. He was declaring that his country alone had the potential to show Europe the way to salvation – and with his millenarian convictions he felt sure that this remained true in the twentieth century.

Nicholas turned keenly to *Peter and Alexei*, the final novel in the *Christ and Antichrist* trilogy.[14] Its focus was on one of the turning points in modern Russian history, the reign of Peter the Great. The content was inflammatory. At the heart of the novel is the terrible relationship between Peter and his son Alexei. Peter is brutal in the extreme. The worst of his abuses is seen in his treatment of the Church, its doctrines and its practices. A sharp contrast is drawn with Tsarevich Alexei, who appears calm, studious and reverent. When father and son fall out, Alexei calls him the Antichrist – this was evidently what Merezhkovski himself thought about Peter. The book closes with a prediction:

> 'One day all things will end in Russia with a terrible revolt, and the autocracy will fall because millions of people will cry out to God against the tsar,' wrote the Hanoverian resident Weber from St Petersburg, announcing the death of the tsarevich.[15]

Published months before the revolutionary emergency of 1905, *Peter and Alexei* came to be seen as a prophecy of the troubles to come, and its popularity continued to rise.

In his diary, Nicholas commented that *Peter and Alexei* was well written and made a 'heavy' impression.[16] The apocalyptic prediction of the Romanov autocracy's collapse must have touched a nerve. So too, probably, did the very name of the tsarevich. Indeed Nicholas seems to have had an obsession about those of his own ancestors who had encountered trouble with the question of succession. There were several such tsars, from Peter the Great in the early eighteenth century through to Alexander I, who reigned from 1801 to 1825. Strict though they could be, the official censors refrained from banning writers from examining the pros and cons of past rulers. Nicholas evidently found some solace in this literature during his own period of trauma. But whereas Peter killed his son Alexei, Nicholas had given up his throne rather than be separated from his own child. The poignant difference can hardly have escaped Nicholas's notice. Everything else we know about him makes it highly likely that he also endorsed Merezhkovski's hostility to Peter's transformation of Russia: Nicholas would have felt a tug of sympathy for the Russian traditions that his ancestor trampled.

After finishing the *Christ and Antichrist* series, he picked up Merezhkovski's novel *Alexander I*. With its unflattering portrait of authoritarian rule, the novel suggests that the country was roughly mishandled during most of the reign. But it also deals fondly with Alexander's wife Elizaveta and his daughter Sofia by his mistress Maria Naryshkina. Merezhkovski portrayed the Romanov family in a gentle light, as when in 1824 young Sofia ponders what is worrying her father:

> She looked him straight in the face. She saw that he was thinking or had just been thinking about something else, something personal – perhaps something as terrible as what was happening to her. But about what? She suddenly remembered: 11 March was the anniversary of the death of Emperor Pavel I. She knew what a day this was for him; she knew that grandfather had not died a natural death and that her father was always thinking about this and being tormented by it even though he never spoke to anyone about it. If she did not know all about it, she could make guesses. How many times she had wanted to talk and ask questions, but she had not dared.[17]

Merezhkovski also wrote kindly of the Decembrist plotters, who sought to bring about radical reform when Alexander died in 1825 and was succeeded by his younger brother Nikolai, as decent men who thought that everything had gone to the bad in Russia. One of them, the poet Kondraty Ryleev, exclaims: 'The children of Russia took Paris and liberated Europe: pray God that they'll liberate Russia!'[18]

Nicholas's fascination with the lives of past tsars continued throughout the summer. These were not the books that he read to his family in the evenings, and there is no sign that he discussed them with

Alexandra, far less with any member of his retinue. But he wanted to sort out his own mind, and Merezhkovski's fevered imaginings about Russian history were his way of achieving this. He kept it all to himself.

Merezhkovski was no admirer of Nicholas and in 1907 had written in a piece that could be published only in France:

> We believe that sooner or later there will arrive the thunderous voice of the Russian revolution in which the Archangel's trumpet will resound over the old European cemetery, announcing the resurrection of the dead.[19]

He declared:

> In the house of the Romanovs, as in the house of the Atreids, a mysterious curse descends from generation to generation. Murder on top of adultery, blood over the mud – 'the fifth act of the tragedy played in a house of tolerance'. Peter kills his son, Alexander I his father, Catherine II her husband . . . God's unction on the Tsar's forehead turned into a curse, into the mark of Cain.[20]

This blustery analysis raised the question of the dynasty's fitness to rule Russia. Nicholas himself looked for an answer in N. K. Shilder's historical monograph about Emperor Paul, who ruled from 1796 until his assassination five years later.[21] The true centrepiece of the work was the reign of Paul's mother, Catherine the Great, who ascended the throne in 1762. Catherine became empress by colluding in the killing of her husband, Peter III, who was Paul's father. Shilder conducted research on all three rulers and concluded that only Catherine deserved any respect despite the nefarious methods used in her accession. But while judging Paul an inadequate successor to his mother, he offered the consoling thought that his reversals of her policies left her basic achievements intact. Paul, he decided, failed to fulfil 'the sacred duties' of the monarchy and treated the Russian people as mere slaves. His assassination by a group of disgruntled ex-army officers was therefore unmourned – in Shilder's telling phrase, he 'thought of building himself an impenetrable court but only made his own grave'.[22] The volume suggested that the only pity was that Paul's son and heir Alexander I also fell short of public expectations, especially when he made the grim martinet Alexei Arakcheev his chief of staff. Arakcheev strove to turn Russia into an armed camp. According to Shilder, this sowed the seeds of the Decembrist Revolt of 1825, seeds which germinated in the humiliation of the Crimean War.[23]

Nicholas in typically clipped fashion commented: 'Very interesting.'[24] There is no sign that he endorsed Shilder's implicit approval of the desirability of some kind of reform. More likely he was intrigued by the saga of intergenerational family conflict and its political implications. His opinions about what should or could be done about the governance of Russia remained unchanged.

When not reading about his Romanov predecessors, he often chose books dealing with the theme of confinement, rescue or escape. Several of them were about the French Revolution. In the winter of 1917–1918 he turned to Victor Hugo's *Quatre-vingt-treize* (*Ninety-Three*), a novel set in the time of a royalist revolt against the Republic in the late 1790s.[25] The leader of the rebels was the Marquis de Lentenac who lands by ship in Brittany. In Paris the government under Maximilien Robespierre sends commander Gauvain against him.[26] Lentenac is captured but escapes, and although Hugo's sympathies were unmistakably with the revolution and against the guillotined Louis XVI, he gives scope for Lentenac and other royalists to appear in a sympathetic light. Gauvain fails to behave strictly in accord with the government's policies and indeed deliberately facilitates Lentenac's flight from captivity. In the crisis that follows, the authorities charge Gauvain with treason and have him executed.[27] While Nicholas must have warmed to Lentenac's selfless heroism, he would surely have been disconcerted by Hugo's picture of the Revolution's objectives. Nicholas himself was a casualty of dreams of liberty, equality and fraternity.

Another book that focused on imprisonment and its traumas was *The Count of Monte Cristo* by Alexandre Dumas, set in the post-Napoleonic era. The leading character, Edmond Dantès, is wrongfully sentenced to imprisonment in the Château d'If. After being driven near to suicide, he succeeds in communicating with a dying fellow prisoner who discloses the whereabouts of a vast, hidden treasure on the island of Monte Cristo. By clambering into the same prisoner's coffin, he gets himself buried alive as a means of escaping the prison. After breaking his way out of the coffin, he secretly regains his freedom. His first task is to find the treasure and make his fortune. Then he returns to France to hunt down those who were responsible for bringing him to court and seeks vengeance against them through a series of complicated schemes involving disguise and other trickery. As Dantès comes to terms with his anger, he often refrains from doing his worst to his potential victims. Dumas's novel is a study in maltreatment, cunning, determination and the futility of revenge. It is doubtful that Nicholas was willing, like Dantès, to forgive his enemies or even to overlook what he regarded as the wrong they had done him. He was perhaps more drawn to the portrait of nobility in conditions of intense stress. Nicholas was determined to face his difficulties with stoicism.

11. KERENSKY'S DILEMMA

The Provisional Government rushed a slim, anonymous biography of Nicholas into print to counteract any public tendency to remember him in a warm light. There was a long charge sheet. Nicholas was depicted as poorly educated and arrogant. It was said that his professional training had been restricted to the armed forces but that his active military service had consisted only in the effort of putting on a uniform. Accordingly, Russia had been turned into 'an armed camp' in 1905, and Nicholas had granted political reforms only to overturn them in 1907 through his unilateral revision of electoral law. The case against him continued with the accusation that he appointed scoundrels as ministers and raised up 'the drunken, filthy, ignorant adventurer Grishka Rasputin'. The booklet also questioned whether he allowed Rasputin and Empress Alexandra to become lovers. It described how Milyukov, Kerensky and Chkheidze had spoken out in the Duma against Nicholas. Nicholas, it was stated, had trained up 'a whole generation of hangmen' and was 'the tyrant of tyrants'. The only surprise was that when he fell from the throne, he failed to put a bullet in his own head. Instead he spent his time planting flowers and walking round the garden while his former subjects eyed him with contempt.[1]

Cabinet ministers and soviet leaders competed to remove the statues and plaques to the Romanov dynasty from public places.[2] Even so, the Bolsheviks and others maintained a polemic against the cabinet's alleged indulgence of Nicholas the Bloody, and dozens of articles and booklets appeared which represented the former emperor as having connived at opening Russia to conquest by Germany.[3] Kerensky was alert to the potential for trouble. He suffered for his pains, being accused of counter-revolutionary objectives. Bolsheviks infiltrated the troops on duty at Tsarskoe Selo and encouraged a paranoid atmosphere. Even small incidents could ratchet up the tension. When a motor vehicle accidentally overran the edge of the park, there was panic that it might be an attempt to transport the former emperor out of his place of confinement. The Tsarskoe Selo garrison had been supportive of the Provisional Government, and the thought was that ministers could be planning to use it in place of the unruly soldiers of Petrograd.[4]

Kerensky had been the rising star of the Provisional Government even before the April crisis when foreign affairs minister Pavel Milyukov was exposed as having sent telegrams to the other Allied governments reaffirming Russia's commitments to the war aims agreed with London and Paris in the secret treaties of 1915. This would have involved Russian acquisition of the Dardanelles. The Petrograd Soviet, led by Mensheviks and Socialist-Revolutionaries, had given support to the cabinet – which had been formed solely because soviets in the capital and elsewhere gave their consent – on condition that ministers maintained a full range of democratic freedoms and confined themselves to a defensive military strategy. Milyukov's initiative shattered the mutual understanding between the cabinet and the Petrograd Soviet, and street demonstrations were organized against him. Since Lenin's return from Switzerland earlier in the same month, the Bolshevik Central Committee had been committed to overthrowing the Provisional Government. Lenin accused the Mensheviks and Socialist-Revolutionaries of a political sell-out to capitalism by agreeing to the existence of the Lvov cabinet, and he adduced the Milyukov telegrams were used as proof that ministers were engaged in an imperialist conspiracy with the Western Allies that was in conflict with the basic interests of working people in Russia and abroad.

The political emergency ended with the resignations of Milyukov and Guchkov and the establishment of a fresh governing coalition that included both Menshevik and Socialist-Revolutionary leaders from the Petrograd Soviet, and the lesson was learned that Russia would be subject to 'dual power' exercised by the Provisional Government and the Soviet. While Lvov remained Chairman, it was Kerensky, promoted to the Ministry of War, who supplied much of the dynamism in decisions about international relations and military operations. The Socialist-Revolutionary leader Viktor Chernov, as Minister of Agriculture, directed agrarian policy increasingly against the interests of the landed gentry; influential Mensheviks Irakli Tsereteli and Matvei Skobelev eased the remaining restraints on the activities of the labour movement. Kerensky pushed for a fresh offensive on the Austro-Hungarian section of the Eastern Front in Ukraine.

Milyukov's successor as Minister of Foreign Affairs was Mikhail

Tereshchenko, a Progressive Party member and wealthy financier, who continued with the plan to send the Romanovs into exile. The original idea of a sea voyage from Murmansk had fallen foul of the probability that the Petrograd Soviet would prevent the Romanovs from using the northern railway to the White Sea. Tereshchenko wondered whether it might be better to move them through Finland in the first instance and get them across the North Sea from a Scandinavian port. He and Ambassador Buchanan held discussions along these lines.[5] Exactly how the Romanovs would cross into Finnish territory was not clear. Although the Duchy of Finland was only thirty miles from Petrograd, the journey would still require use of parts of the Russian rail network subject to scrutiny and control by soviet politicians. If Murmansk was impractical, it is difficult to see why the Russo-Finnish border town of Terijoki would have been easier. But Tereshchenko tried to be positive; he had inherited a tricky legacy from Milyukov and was hoping to dredge something out of the morass.

The British willingness to welcome the Romanovs began to cool after King George V had had time to reflect on the possible implications for himself and the House of Windsor. Initially he had thought of putting his Balmoral residence at his cousin Nicholas's disposal, but second thoughts prevailed. In early June Buchanan came to Tereshchenko in an emotional state. With tears in his eyes, he asked him to read a letter he had received from the Foreign Office's permanent under-secretary, Sir Charles Harding. Essentially, Harding was withdrawing the offer of asylum. He asked how George V could be expected to welcome the former tsar when the Provisional Government itself was casting doubt on his commitment to fighting the Germans.[6] This snuffed out all planning for foreign exile except for when the Danish government made an offer to the dowager empress and her daughters. Maria Fëdorovna turned it down in the light of Grand Duchess Olga's pregnancy. Like most people, the Romanovs had little idea of the growing threat to their physical survival.[7]

Tereshchenko passed the asylum news to Lvov and Kerensky. The Provisional Government put the matter on its agenda but the question was thought so sensitive that the discussion was held without a minute-taker. The gist of it was the ministers believed that if the Romanovs could not go to the United Kingdom, they should be at least moved out of Tsarskoe Selo. Kerensky was put in charge of resolving the question, and at first he contemplated transferring Nicholas and his family to one of the estates of their relatives Mikhail Alexandrovich and Nikolai Mikhailovich. On further thought, he dropped the idea. He recognized the dangers in transporting the family through territory where workers and peasants detested them. It would have been equally perilous to try to move them to Crimea, where the dowager empress had taken up residence.[8]

The Russian armies achieved success on the Eastern Front until the Germans rushed reinforcements from the north and the Central Powers occupied more Ukrainian territory than ever – and the Bolsheviks organized a demonstration against both the Provisional Government, including its Menshevik and Socialist-Revolutionary ministers. Aiming to prevent the growth of Bolshevik influence, the Mensheviks and Socialist-Revolutionaries took part in the demonstration and tried to turn it into one of support of their policies. As news of the failure of the June military offensive percolated from the Eastern Front, the Bolsheviks organized a further anti-governmental demonstration. The cabinet could see that this might be a cover for an attempted coup d'état and banned activities on the capital's streets. Its own internal unity disintegrated after Kadet ministers walked out in protest against projected concessions to Ukrainian demands for self-rule. Petrograd by mid-July was in turmoil, and loyal troops were introduced to disperse the Bolshevik-led demonstration. Files were released that indicated that the Bolsheviks had been in receipt of a financial subsidy from the Germans. A warrant was issued for the arrest of Lenin and other Bolshevik leaders.

Nicholas learned with horror about the emergency in nearby Petrograd, confiding to his diary on 18 July:

> It rained all morning but brightened up before 2 p.m.; it got cooler towards evening. Spent the day as usual. In Petrograd there have been days of disorder including shootings. A lot of sailors and soldiers arrived from Kronstadt yesterday to move against the Provisional Gov[ernment]. Complete confusion! But where are the people who could take a hold over this movement and stop the nonsense and bloodshed? The seed of all the evil lies in Petrograd and not everywhere in Russia.[9]

He continued in his belief that leadership and repressive measures could always countervail against protests on the streets. He also assumed that Petrograd was the source of all the country's woes: it never occurred to him that the grievances that the demonstrators had expressed were shared by a growing number of people in the provinces. In fact, the revolutionary crisis was an all-Russia one.

The Provisional Government survived only at the expense of Lvov's resignation and the promotion of Kerensky to minister-chairman. Kerensky continued the previous coalition's economic and social policies but his cabinet had to operate without the participation of Mensheviks and Socialist-Revolutionaries, who gave priority to enhancing their position in the soviets. Though he too was a Socialist-Revolutionary, Kerensky aimed to impose the Provisional Government's authority on all socialist parties; he also reintroduced the death penalty in the armed forces and liaised with General Kornilov, whom he appointed supreme commander-in-chief, about how to use troops to bring political order to the capital.

Alongside his many huge problems, Kerensky could not afford to ignore the Romanov question because the brush-off from London about the foreign exile project did not absolve the Provisional Government from a duty of care. The British remained Russia's allies, and the fact that many people in the United Kingdom hated Nicholas as a bloody tyrant did not diminish the clamour of others about the fate of the Romanovs. Newspapers kept up a barrage of reports and rumours about their conditions of confinement. Kerensky, who was desperately in need of Western financial credits and strategic collaboration, had to demonstrate that Russia was capable of maintaining lawful procedures while it fought for victory on the Eastern Front. He had become Nicholas's involuntary keeper and knew that he and the cabinet would pay heavily if anything dreadful happened to the family. The recent turmoil in Petrograd showed that he could no longer guarantee the imperial family's safety at the Alexander Palace. If there was a recurrence of trouble on the streets, the bloodshed could spread to nearby Tsarskoe Selo. Hostility to Nicholas remained widespread and intense, and it was clear to Kerensky that it could prove all too easy for an unruly military detachment to storm the Alexander Palace.

Kerensky decided that he had to find a new place of confinement for them. The extended Romanov family was living quietly in various parts of the country. Nicholas's brother Mikhail had retired to his nearby Gatchina residence after renouncing the throne, and the Provisional Government left him in peace in the belief that he was politically harmless.

Their mother, Dowager Empress Maria Fëdorovna, hoped to stay in Kiev, but the cabinet disliked the idea of any Romanov becoming a focus for agitation in a big city, and it was thought best for her to go south to Ai-Todor in Crimea, where she had a residence. Grand Duke Nikolai Nikolaevich went to live in the vicinity after losing his military post in the February Revolution.[10] The Crimean peninsula was turning into a Romanov depository and Grand Duke Mikhail dreamed of moving there after Easter. The thought of this cheered his spirits, as he told his mother: 'I think that in Ai-Todor you'll find it easier to cope with everything that has happened.' But at the same time he urged her to give serious consideration to going into exile and recommended Denmark as a desirable destination.[11] Meanwhile, Crimea became a base for the self-styled Party of 33 and other active monarchist groups who had access to the telegraph office in Chaira. If Nicholas were to move there, his presence would inevitably give further animation to them. The potential for trouble induced the Sevastopol administration to dispatch an armed investigative commission to Yalta. As a result, it was decided to cut the Romanovs from all phone and telegraph lines. Tsarist agitation nonetheless continued under the auspices of the self-styled Central Committee of the 'Forward for the Tsar and Holy Russia' Society, and Crimea remained an area of official concern.[12]

The ultimate decision would lie with the Provisional Government – the time was long past when the Romanovs could do as they pleased. Kerensky himself had to act with caution and had no intention of letting Nicholas and his family make their way abroad, even in the unlikely contingency that loyal military units and railway personnel could be found to transport them to Murmansk and a British naval vessel. He had his hands full dealing with Bolshevik accusations that he was the Russian Napoleon who was betraying the revolutionary cause, and they would have exploited every opportunity to castigate him for any indulgence shown towards the former ruling dynasty. At the same time Kerensky could not afford to let Nicholas, Alexandra and their children move to Crimea. The Provisional Government had to remain their custodian, and Ai-Todor was much too far away from Petrograd at a time when communications, transport and administrative control were falling apart. But where to send them?

12. DISTANT TRANSFER

As Kerensky considered the politics and geography of the matter, he consulted the Tobolsk provincial commissar, V. N. Pignatti, who came to the capital for a conference of all such commissars. The town of Tobolsk in west Siberia was small, quiet and remote and little affected by the tumult in the great cities. The town seemed an ideal place for the detention of the leading Romanovs.[1] First, though, Kerensky took the precaution of commissioning an inspection of the local conditions by ex-Duma deputy Vasili Vershinin and the Socialist-Revolutionary engineer Pavel Makarov. As soon as Kerensky received a reassuring report from them, he gave the go-ahead for the family's transfer to Tobolsk.[2]

He knew there could be trouble about the armed escort that would take the Romanovs to Tobolsk. The Tsarskoe Selo troops distrusted Kobylinski, and appointed their own commissar – an Armenian ensign called Domodzyants – to oversee how the Romanovs were managed. Kobylinski, who thought him uncouth, could do nothing to reverse the decision. Domodzyants was forever appearing in the park when the imperial family were there. He also tried to inveigle his way into the palace. Moreover, he was rude to the Romanovs and followed the precedent of his military comrades by refusing to shake hands with Nicholas. When the Soviet chairman informed Kerensky of Domodzyants's appointment, Kerensky exclaimed: 'Yes, I know. But surely you could have elected someone other than this lout, idiot and scoundrel.' But Kerensky was just as powerless as Kobylinski to sack Domodzyants. Power at Tsarskoe Selo rested with the Soviet. Domodzyants told the troops to reject the emperor's persistent attempts to talk with them on guard duty. This agitated Kobylinski enough to ask Nicholas to desist from greeting any soldiers, and Nicholas obeyed the request. Kobylinski and Nicholas were agreed on the need to keep a sense of calm in and around the palace.[3]

Kerensky asked Kobylinski to take over as military commander in

Tobolsk and arranged for both of them to talk to the Tsarskoe Selo Soviet chairman and its military section leader. After swearing everyone to silence, Kerensky revealed the intention to transfer the Romanovs the following week escorted by Kobylinski. Kerensky talked to the other two individuals separately: he wanted to make sure that all the local 'democratic organizations' continued to support the Provisional Government. Although he trusted Kobylinski to carry out instructions to the letter, his time in office had taught him to act with caution, and he refused to tell even Kobylinski as yet where the Romanovs were being sent. The whole project was shrouded in mystery. All that Kerensky would say as the day of departure approached was that everyone should make sure they took warm clothing.[4]

A couple of days before the departure Kerensky ordered Kobylinski to choose the officers for the trip. Kobylinski knew this was quite impractical. Though he theoretically could pick anyone from the three regiments at Tsarskoe Selo, the time had passed when he could opt for whomever he wanted. No regimental commander could give orders to his troops any longer. Power lay with the soldiers' committees. So Kobylinski thought of a compromise. Of the five officers assigned to each company, permission would be given for the committees to select two of them.[5] The committee of 4th Regiment told him that they had already chosen Ensign Dekonski, who had led the opposition to the garrison's deployment to the front; they also appeared to know where the Romanovs would be travelling. They obviously had confidential sources. This was altogether too much for Kobylinski, who went and asked Kerensky to choose between him and Dekonski. Kerensky lost his temper and Dekonski was removed from the list, but only at the price of many troops refusing to be part of the detachment – and their replacements, at least in Kobylinski's opinion, were of inferior quality.[6]

While Kobylinski would command the military personnel, the Socialist-Revolutionary Pavel Makarov was appointed as the Provisional Government's commissar – Kerensky did not want to leave Kobylinski unsupervised or keep only Makarov as his eyes and ears. He therefore assigned Vershinin to accompany him. Makarov's presence provoked laughter from Count Ilya Tatishchev, Nicholas's confidant, who was tickled at finding that Makarov was a Socialist-Revolutionary.[7] This was the solitary light moment of a sombre occasion (and Tatishchev never explained why he found things so comical). Kerensky confirmed that Dr Botkin would accompany Nicholas as his personal physician while Dr Vladimir Derevenko would serve as doctor for the troops.[8] It was at this point that Kobylinski learned that they were going to the Siberian town of Tobolsk, but he was not allowed to tell the imperial family. Nicholas was studiedly patient. His only request was for the Standard of the Holy Mother icon to be placed on the train so that they could use it on Alexei's birthday – and even this small favour had to be submitted for approval by the troops.[9]

Kerensky told the emperor to get ready for travel to a new site of residence, asking him to recognize that this would be for the good of his family, adding: 'Do you believe me?' Nicholas replied: 'I believe.'[10] By now there was a growing rapport between Kerensky and Nicholas, who told Baroness Buxhoeveden: 'His political views of course are not mine. He always was a socialist and made no pretence at being anything else, but he's a patriot and loves Russia.'[11]

Even so, Kerensky was cautious about what he said to Nicholas and he refrained from revealing the destination for fear that the news should leak out to enemies of the monarchy who might mount some kind of attack. (He obviously had no concerns about a possible rescue attempt by monarchists.) He assured Nicholas that there were no reasons for concern on his part. Nicholas was his stoical self: 'I'm not worried. We trust you. If you say we need to move, that means it's necessary. We trust you.'[12] Nicholas consoled himself with the thought that once the Constituent Assembly elections happened and the political situation calmed down, he would be able to return to Tsarskoe Selo or settle somewhere else that they might prefer.[13] Three or four days before the departure, Kerensky advised the Romanovs to take more warm clothes with them because he did not like the idea of them suffering in the cold weather ahead.[14] This led to speculation that they were being sent to somewhere in Siberia – and, of course, they were right.

Nicholas, on Kerensky's advice, trimmed the size of his retinue and released some leading courtiers from their service. Elizaveta Naryshkina, suffering from inflammation of the lungs, was too ill to make a long trip. The elderly Pavel Benkendorf had served him loyally for years but was physically ailing – and his wife was also poorly. Nicholas decided to replace Benkendorf with Ilya Tatishchev. The invitation was relayed to Tatishchev through Kerensky and Pavel Makarov: 'This surprised me: after all, I wasn't a courtier. But once the Sovereign conceived such a desire, I didn't have a moment's doubt that it was my duty to fulfil the will of my Sovereign.'[15] Tatishchev did not know that Nicholas's first choice had been Kirill Naryshkin, but after Naryshkin had asked for twenty-four hours to consider the request, Nicholas had decided to approach someone less hesitant. Tatishchev's only query was about whether the idea came from Nicholas or Kerensky. On hearing that it was Nicholas's initiative, he immediately accepted.[16]

The plan was for the Romanovs to leave Tsarskoe Selo at dead of night, at eleven o'clock on 13 August. Kerensky addressed the military contingent that Kobylinski had assembled. He spoke with his usual emotional intensity:

> You have been in charge of guarding the imperial family here. Now you have to take over the guarding in Tobolsk, where the imperial family is being transferred by decree of the Council of Ministers. Remember: nobody hits a man when he's down on the ground. Behave decently and not outrageously. Supplies will be issued at the Petrograd district rate. Tobacco and soap will be provided to you in person. You'll be paid on a daily basis.

Kerensky, who had so many other preoccupations, declined to visit all the regiments that contributed troops. Some of these regiments were worse equipped in matters of uniform than others, and Kobylinski noted that some of the men had grown careless in looking after their appearance and displayed low morale. He regretted Kerensky's inattentiveness to this process, and he later contended that this was to have consequences in the months after departure from Tsarskoe Selo.[17]

Nicholas's brother Mikhail arrived at the palace to bid them farewell. He had heard only by chance about the planned departure and hurried to see what was happening. There was a rumour that Kerensky had Kostroma in mind as the destination.[18] When Kerensky turned up at midnight, he prohibited Mikhail from meeting his brother.[19] But he soon relented and gave permission, taking the sole precaution of staying in the room along with his ensign and giving the order: 'Talk to each other!'[20] The Tsarevich meanwhile positioned himself behind the door to catch what his Uncle Mimi and his father were saying.[21] The conversation lasted ten minutes and was mainly about health matters.[22] Nicholas later told Sophie Buxhoeveden about this:

> Imagine, Kerensky had only just arrived with Misha. We were so emotional that we couldn't get things off our chests. Kerensky, covering his ears with his hands, sat at the end of my office. My brother said quietly, 'You've understood me.' I didn't understand his actions but what was there to say to him at that point? So I said: 'God keep you.' We embraced.[23]

The experience at any rate convinced Mikhail that he had been right since March to favour foreign exile for his mother: things were getting tighter for the Romanovs and the future looked bleak.[24]

The family was beset with nerves, and Dr Botkin took it upon himself to go round with a bottle of pills to calm them.[25] The retinue made their way to the railway station but nobody else arrived from the Alexander Palace for several hours. Provisions for five days were loaded on to the train, and the imperial party guessed that Siberia must be the destination.[26] The first sign of action came at six in the morning with the appearance of a limousine carrying Kerensky and Kobylinski. Kobylinski carried a piece of paper that stated: 'Obey the orders of Colonel Kobylinski like my own. Alexander Kerensky.'[27] Also in his possession was a substantial sum of money for the employment and upkeep of the imperial family and retinue: Kerensky intended them to live in comfort at their destination.[28]

A unit of troops stood with their rifles at the ready. Otherwise the station was deserted, for the transfer of the Romanovs was being kept a secret. Kerensky behaved with complete propriety, as if there had been no February Revolution. To Nicholas, he said simply: 'Goodbye, Your Highness.' As he always did, he kissed Alexandra's hand.[29] Accompanying the family on the way to the platform were Dolgorukov, Benkendorf and a group of dedicated officers. There were two trains, with the Romanovs together in the first. Vershinin boarded to act as Kerensky's eyes and ears. Also present was Ensign Efimov for the Tsarskoe Selo garrison – Kerensky had to cover himself against any suspicion of doing something against the interests of the revolution.[30] A separate compartment was reserved for each Romanov as well as for each of their retainers, and there was a special dining car.[31] It was already light on 14 August when steam was built up in the engines and a start could be made. The hours of waiting were over and the Romanovs began to relax and look forward to peace and quiet at their destination.

The trains headed in the direction of Perm in the Urals. The leading engine, in a bizarre attempt to deflect notice, was draped with a Japanese flag. This only excited untoward attention. Railwaymen's Union activists boarded the train and made a fuss until Vershinin waved a copy of Kerensky's orders at them.[32] There were stops at tiny stations on the line where, in daytime, the Romanovs were allowed out of their compartment to stretch their legs. But no halting was allowed in towns and cities.[33] En route the former empress insisted on taking her meals alone with the tsarevich in her coupé.[34] The rest of the family were more open to making the best of the experience, an experience of life in the depths of Russia that was new to all of them. When Sydney Gibbes in the following weeks asked Anastasia to compose an account in English, she wrote about how the train came to a stop mid-journey near a small house and a little boy approached the Romanov carriage and asked her for a newspaper. He addressed her as 'uncle'. Anastasia sweetly replied that she had no newspaper; she pointed out that she was an aunty, not an uncle. Then she remembered that she had had her hair cut and looked less obviously feminine than usual – the encounter caused a ripple of mirth among the soldiers standing nearby.[35]

In the evening of 17 August the train pulled in to Tyumen.[36] The Romanov party alighted and transferred, still under escort, to two ferries, the *Rus* and the *Kormilets*. The former was the more comfortable, and it was this vessel that carried the imperial family down the river to Tobolsk. On the way north, the ship passed the little settlement of Pokrovskoe. This drew forth a wistful recollection from the empress: 'This is where Grigori Efimovich [Rasputin] lived. It was on this river that he used to catch fish and sometimes he brought them to us in Tsarskoe Selo.'[37]

On 19 August, when the steamer reached the quayside at Tobolsk, Makarov and Vershinin took Alexei Volkov from the retinue and went off to inspect Governor's House, which could provide the space, comfort and seclusion that Kerensky wished to secure for the imperial family. Before the February Revolution it had been occupied by Nikolai Ordovski-Tanaevski as governor of the province. Across the road was a large town house belonging to a merchant called Kornilov, and it was there that most members of the Romanov retinue were intended to live.[38] Makarov and his companions found that next to no preparations had been made for the arrival of the Romanov party and that the building was a dirty mess. Volkov asked for substantial refurbishment before the Romanovs moved in. Makarov and Vershinin agreed and the Romanovs were permitted to stay on board the steamer for a week until the work was completed.[39] The town's inhabitants crowded the quayside in the hope of getting a sighting of the celebrities.[40] Kerensky continued to keep the Romanovs in mind. He ordered Makarov and Vershinin to ensure that lady-in-waiting Margarita Khitrovo got nowhere near Governor's House. Other visitors from Petrograd should also be stopped.[41]

Administrative correctness was observed and Nicholas was required to sign an affidavit that everything had been properly handled through to the point of arrival in Tobolsk.[42] Most of the family walked without difficulty from the boat on to the dockside; the exceptions were the empress and Alexei, both of whom were in a frail condition and had to be carried.[43] A limousine then took Nicholas and his daughter Tatyana as an advance party to the house where they would spend the next six months. The rest of the family were transported soon afterwards.[44]

13. DESTINATION TOBOLSK

When Nicholas checked in his old diaries, he was surprised to find that he had paid Tobolsk a visit on his trip through Siberia in 1891. He had stayed in the town just a few hours and could remember nothing about it. It had been at a time, he discovered from his notes, when a French squadron was anchoring off Kronstadt.[1]

Although Kerensky had never been to Tobolsk, he knew it to have the advantages of a provincial capital with good telegraph links while remaining small, quiet and remote. With only a little over 20,000 inhabitants, it was a place where everyone knew what the neighbours were doing. Tobolsk had an appeal precisely because it was so distant from the big centres of population. Overlooked when the plans were drawn for the route of the Trans-Siberian Railway, it lay over 150 miles to the north of the nearest station, which was in Tyumen. This was a definite advantage in the eyes of Kerensky, who wanted to eliminate the risk of a successful rescue. While cities like Ekaterinburg and Chelyabinsk had swollen with people and industry almost as soon as the first tracks of the Trans-Siberian Railway were laid in the early 1890s, Tobolsk was much like the market town that it had become after Yermak and his Cossack force began the conquest of Siberia three centuries earlier. The great changes in economy and culture that were transforming key regions of the old empire had yet to make themselves felt there.[2]

The few foreigners who travelled to Tobolsk found it less than picturesque and less than comfortable. It had only two proper hotels. The streets were unpaved and the sewage system was primitive; when it rained, people had to use wooden boardwalks to avoid the mud.[3] But in its old-fashioned way the town had a certain splendour, its cathedral rising high above the residential and commercial streets. There were more than twenty other churches with their neat, whitewashed walls and golden cupolas. Traders and priests bustled about. The age-old annual fur fair continued to be held as trappers brought their pelts to

market and merchants haggled over prices. (Even so, there was growing competition from Tyumen to the south – and Tyumen had the
advantage of being on the railway line.) The province had a settled
population with scant contact with the wider world. The only newcomers were the 25,000 peasants who had trekked out from Russia and
Ukraine under Prime Minister Pëtr Stolypin's pre-war scheme to allow
each of them to clear forty acres of forest or scrub land and start farm-
steads without paying rent to landlords as they had done in their
provinces of origin. They quickly built huts and sold fur, nuts and
artisanal products while they built up their agricultural enterprises.[4]

There was no industry in the province because nobody had yet
discovered any of the valuable minerals that were being mined elsewhere in Siberia. Agriculture was conducted in much the same way as
in earlier centuries. The notable exception was the innovation in dairy
production. The first butter factory was established in 1894 and by the
start of the Great War there were 1,200 of them.[5]

The local authorities occasionally pondered how to bring the world
to the town. Two of Russia's mightiest rivers, the Irtysh and Tobol, met
below the town's great hill, from which point the waters flowed north-
ward as the expanded River Irtysh until they reached the Arctic Ocean.
The British had pioneered trading routes into northern Siberia from
the late nineteenth century, and the steamer Louisa had arrived from
Hull in 1876 with a shipment of iron, sugar and olive oil.[6] Tobolsk's
elders had hoped that this would end the town's isolation and enable
economic modernization and growth. No one could doubt that the
province's forests would give stern competition to Swedish timber on
the world market if only transport facilities could be established. The
same was possible with livestock and fish catches. Iron was being found
in the province's southern parts around Tyumen, and the long-term
economic prospects for west Siberia looked bright.[7]

Unfortunately for Tobolsk, the imperial government ignored the
pleas of the Tobolsk authorities for help to enable vessels to steam
down from the north and connect the province with Europe. Few
ships apart from some Norwegian steamers plied regularly southwards
to Tobolsk after the Louisa's voyage – there was too little freight or
passenger traffic to encourage other foreign companies to follow the
precedent. Tobolsk remained almost unknown to the world outside
Russia and its trade was overwhelmingly local or with other Russian
towns, although the building of the Trans-Siberian Railway did at least
lead to an increase in the movement of goods and people between

Tobolsk and Tyumen. The rivers, however, remained the fastest mode of transport, as they had been for centuries. Climatic conditions in so northerly a latitude, however, made travel by boat impractical from November to the end of April, during which period the waters were vast sheets of ice. Throughout the long Siberian winter, Tobolsk was a snow-sealed municipality that could be reached only by horse-drawn sleigh or cart along the rutted north bank of the Tobol.[8]

The long, harsh winters and geographical isolation had made the town a perfect site for one of the Russian Empire's largest prisons. Tobolsk Central was a depository for those convicted of revolutionary activity, and after the loss of Sakhalin Island in the Russo-Japanese war of 1904–1905 it teemed with the additional prisoners who could no longer be held in detention off the Pacific coast.[9] The prison visually dominated the main square along with the 'five-headed' cathedral and the local treasury. Inside the penal-labour facilities, discipline was ultra-strict and punishments were severe. Few inmates succeeded in escaping because multiple layers of high walling separated the cell blocks from the white outside walls.[10] The harshness of conditions at Tobolsk Central increased after the 1905–1906 revolutionary emergency, and prison director Ivan Mogilëv gained a grim reputation for the penalties he meted out to prisoners who in any way defied him. Repeated lashings were the norm. After one collective protest he sentenced sixteen men to be hanged and buried in the prison. Tobolsk Central became notorious even by tsarist standards in the decade before the February 1917 Revolution as knowledge about the protests of inmates became known outside its walls.[11]

The town was also one of the traditional places of administrative exile.[12] Indeed, many exiles chose to stay in Tobolsk even when their terms came to an end. Poles had been sent there in large numbers after the suppression of the national revolt in 1867, and the town retained a substantial Polish minority.[13]

When Nicholas II fell from power, the Provisional Government decreed amnesty for all political prisoners; common criminals too were released. Local jailers and policemen fled the area in panic. There were urban disturbances before calm was restored and the town returned to a more settled condition. Yet everyone remembered its penal history, and Kerensky understood that if Nicholas went to Tobolsk, it would look like his just desserts for the isolation and detention he had meted out to the enemies of the old order. This would be a political bonus for Kerensky, who could not afford to appear to be indulgent to the Romanovs. Even so, there was no intention of putting them in jail, far less to subject them to penal labour. On the contrary, the idea was to keep them in dignified circumstances, albeit not at the high level of the Alexander Palace. And they were to be protected from physical harm. This was why Tsarskoe Selo was no longer appropriate as a place of confinement. Kerensky knew from the report made by Vershinin and Makarov that Tobolsk was unusually quiet for a Russian town in the summer of 1917. Its only brush with ructious behaviour had been in earlier years when Rasputin, taking a break from the capital, had paid an extended visit. He got thunderously drunk night after night and propositioned a string of local women. He also secured the acceptance of a district overseer as a priest of the Orthodox Church; he even obtained the promotion of a Tobolsk ne'er-do-well called Varnava to a bishopric.[14]

This had come to seem like ancient history and the local political leaders were seeking to dissociate the town from Rasputin. The urban administration continued to function. Economically, Tobolsk was largely cut off from the rest of Russia, and its inhabitants were suffering less than people in Petrograd, Moscow and the other big industrial centres whose food supplies were depleted. Farmers brought their produce to the markets, troops were more orderly than they were elsewhere and the law was treated with respect. A soviet had been elected, but Bolsheviks were a negligible presence and Socialist-Revolutionaries and Mensheviks headed the labour movement in the town.

The Provisional Government had sound reason to believe that it had made a good choice when sending the Romanovs to Tobolsk. It is true that labour organizations outside Tobolsk distrusted Kerensky's arrangements. Already on 18 August, when the family was on board the Tyumen–Tobolsk steamer, the Ekaterinburg District Soviet – not yet dominated by Bolsheviks – was expressing concern about the transfer. In a message to the Central Executive Committee of the Congress of Soviets in Petrograd, its leaders reported the spread of rumours that the Romanovs were really bound for Harbin across the Chinese border. The same soviet cabled other soviets along the Trans-Siberian Railway asking them to investigate the rumours and take whatever precautions were necessary.[15] Ekaterinburg's socialist leadership was hopelessly misinformed about the family's whereabouts and direction of movement. But its message of complaint was a harbinger of later developments when regional soviets in both western Siberia and the

Urals decided that Tobolsk could not be left to itself and intervened in the interests of the revolutionary security.

Kerensky was well aware that agencies of the labour movement 'in the localities' were capable of taking affairs into their own hands and flouting the prerogatives of his government. The Tsaritsyn Soviet, in the Volga region, declared itself an independent republic and called on other cities to challenge the cabinet in Petrograd. The Russian economy was in free fall as bank credit dried up, factories closed and peasants refused to release their grain stocks to the official procurement bodies. The normal apparatus of state power was disintegrating. The police no longer existed and desertions from the armed forces at the Eastern Front were becoming commonplace. Kerensky remained committed to the Allied cause – his fate was inextricably linked to an early defeat of Germany even if it was going to have to be achieved in northern France rather than Poland or Ukraine. For the moment he hoped that he had solved at least one of his problems by transporting Nicholas and his family to a distant provincial capital in western Siberia.

14. PLENIPOTENTIARY PANKRATOV

After weeks of dithering, Kerensky appointed the plenipotentiary commissar he wanted to take charge of the imperial family in Tobolsk. His choice had fallen upon the veteran revolutionary Vasili Pankratov, whom he summoned for interview. Pankratov at first declined but after an appeal to his sense of duty, he yielded. He selected his own deputy – Alexander Nikolski, a Socialist-Revolutionary who like himself had served time in Siberian exile.[1] Their orders were to supervise the 'detachment of special purpose to guard the former Emperor and his family'. This detachment, which held 337 soldiers and seven officers recruited by Kobylinski from the 1st, 2nd and 4th Guards Riflemen's Regiments, had already reached Tobolsk. Pankratov was to take over duties from Vershinin and Makarov and cable a biweekly report to Kerensky.[2]

Kerensky had found a diamond of a man, but this was not immediately obvious to anyone else since Pankratov had no military experience, only a record of devotion to the revolutionary cause. Kobylinski did not feel reassured. What he found still more disturbing was the story that Pankratov as a young man had murdered a policeman in a dispute over a woman.[3] The truth had nothing to do with sexual rivalry. In fact Pankratov as a young political activist had been caught in a trap by police hunting down members of People's Freedom, an organization responsible for the assassination of Alexander II in 1881. He had taken no part in the killing, but he was known to have sympathies with the aims of the conspiracy and was on the list for arrest on sight. When, three years later, the police caught up with him, a bloody shoot-out took place, and a policeman was fatally wounded by a shot from Pankratov's weapon. The court showed no mercy, sentencing Pankratov to fourteen years in the Shlisselburg prison followed by twenty-seven years in Siberian administrative exile.

In prison, he devoted himself to filling in the gaps in his education. Although he had received only a rudimentary schooling, he was an eager autodidact. His literary skills blossomed and it was not long before he was contributing handwritten pieces to an unofficial prisoners' journal under the pseudonym Plebeian. Drawing on his own years as a turner at the Semyannikov factory, he produced a powerful denunciation of the abuses suffered by apprentices.[4] When he came to the end of his Shlisselburg term, he was transferred to exile in Vilyuisk in Yakutsk province, where he was allowed to train as a geologist despite his status as a convicted murderer. The dynasty's overthrow freed him to travel wherever he wanted but he had grown to love the Siberian ice, snow, tundra and reindeer and savoured the taste of nature and near-freedom after his long time behind bars. A decent, tired man who was feeling his years, Pankratov still wanted to do things that fulfilled him, but it was with obvious reluctance that he had agreed to supervise the very man who had presided over a system against which he had fought so hard.[5]

Having accepted the job, Pankratov left Petrograd for Tobolsk with Nikolski. They took the train to Tyumen and then caught a steamer to Tobolsk, where they arrived on the quayside on 14 September 1917.[6] Nobody in Tobolsk, least of all the Romanovs, could know what to expect. Gilliard disdained Pankratov as an old convict and surmised that Kerensky was seeking to humiliate the emperor.[7] Neither Pankratov nor Nikolski felt the need to ingratiate himself with the Romanovs. They were veteran revolutionaries who had suffered heavily under the tsarist administration, and the first impression that Pankratov made on Nicholas was not of the best: 'Pankratov, the Provisional Government's new commissar, arrived and settled in the retinue's house along with his assistant who is some bedraggled ensign. [Pankratov] looks like a worker or a poverty-stricken teacher. He's going to act as censor of our correspondence.'[8]

Pankratov and Nikolski started as they meant to go on by requisitioning rooms in the house across the road from the Romanovs, which had belonged to the local Kornilov family. The Romanovs had expected the worst and were finding their fears realized. They had grown accustomed to courtesy at Kobylinski's hands, and it looked as if Kerensky's newly arrived commissar would only blight their lives.

Pankratov proved to have a more complex character than they foresaw; for although he spoke to the family's retainers with a soldier's cigarette in his mouth, he made an exception for the emperor, not by refraining from smoking but by holding it in his hand during the conversation. This tiny difference signalled a desire for a workable relationship with Nicholas.[9] But whereas Pankratov was even-tempered and affable, Nikolski was consistently brusque: 'How on earth is it that [the retinue] come and go so freely?' Nikolski ordered all of them to be photographed and issued with cards to carry on entry to the house.[10] More than that, he insisted that the Romanovs too should supply mugshots. Though they loved taking photos of each other, they bridled at Nikolski's demand. His reaction was a blunt one: 'We were once forced to do this and now it's their turn.'[11] He told off Alexei for peeking through a gap in the garden fence, and when Alexei objected, Nikolski left him in no doubt that he was now the master and would tolerate no pressure from a family which no longer had the rights of their ancestors. Times had changed.[12]

The Romanovs could see little to commend in Nikolski. Even so, they underestimated the part he played in quietening the general situation in the town. Nikolski skilfully calmed the tempers of the troops. After the Bolshevik seizure of power it was also essential to prevent the Tobolsk Soviet from interfering at Governor's House if Pankratov and Nikolski wanted to maintain control, and it was Nikolski who held the necessary consultations. Nikolski was more of a diplomat than the imperial family could know.[13]

After telling Kobylinski to assemble the guard detachment, Pankratov explained the orders from Petrograd. He spoke about the importance of decent behaviour and emphasized that they were not to regard themselves as judges set over Nicholas II. The detachment's duties, he announced, would last until the election of a Constituent Assembly, which alone could take a definitive decision about the Romanov family's future.[14] The troops warmed to Pankratov, and he to them. Nearly all of them were soldiers with battle experience, not just garrison training and service. Housing was not initially available, and many had to live down at the wharves but they accepted their situation without complaint. Pankratov threw himself into doing his best for them. He organized schooling for the many who had received no basic education. He gave talks at the People's House on public affairs as well as on natural history, geography and cultural history while Nikolski taught them accountancy.[15] Pankratov and Nikolski embodied an old Russian political tradition that revolutions would fail unless the people who supported them could read and write. The tasks of political transformation had to be supplemented by cultural advance.

This initiative was at first well received among the troops, but by November it was running into difficulty as most of the participants left

as soon as they thought they had learned enough for their own purposes. The rest of the detachment aimed jibes at those who stayed on
to study geometry.[16]

Pankratov also had to cope with a problem of a slightly unexpected
nature when the Provisional Government arranged for the transport of
furniture, carpets and other possessions from Tsarskoe Selo.[17] Tatyana
Nikolaevna wrote to Margarita Khitrovo on 17 October 1917 about
how the carpets made the whole house so much cosier.[18] But there was
a difficulty about other items in the baggage. Some of the trunks
contained bottles of expensive wine. While they were on the train,
there was no problem, but when one of the trunks was dropped while
being loaded on to the Tyumen steamer, causing bottles to be broken,
everyone could smell the alcohol. A soldier on board passed on the
information to his comrades. There had already been trouble in the
town when troops broke into a wine cellar and made off with the contents. The fresh and unheralded consignment of expensive wine had
the potential to spark street disturbances. Tempers were already
rising.[19]

Pankratov sought guidance from the Provisional Government.
The guard detachment, he explained, was in an agitated state about
the freight and he doubted that Kerensky had approved its delivery to
Tobolsk. Pankratov particularly questioned the wisdom of shipping
quantities of alcohol, whose arrival had already put officers and men at
loggerheads.[20]

In the absence of directives from Petrograd, he assigned troops to
guard the unloaded consignment and issued a reprimand to the soldier
who had divulged the news from the steamer. The rumours about the
wine's arrival spread around the town from the garrison. A protesting
crowd swiftly formed and the cry went up: 'We've spilled our blood at
the front!' Pankratov sent for the mayor and head of the town militia.
The Tobolsk Soviet chairman, Dr Varnakov, also turned up. Pankratov
announced his wish for the militia to take the wine into safe keeping.
The militia chief scoffed at the idea, presumably on the grounds that he
did not trust his own men. Pankratov's other suggestion was to distrib-
ute the bottles to local hospitals. When this too met with ridicule, he
concluded that he himself had to take personal charge using soldiers
from the Governor's House detachment. The crowd, however, refused
to be cowed and Pankratov sensed that violence was in the offing. The
choice, he concluded, was 'between the annihilation of wine and the

annihilation of people'. His solution was to order Nikolski to tip all the alcohol into the river.[21]

Bystanders were appalled at the waste of vintage fine wine. People shouted: 'Look how much good stuff is being dumped into the Irtysh at a commissar's caprice!' Some contended that the consignment had really been intended exclusively for officers. There was a dispute about this, and the crowd demanded proof of Petrograd's instructions. Threats were made to take Kobylinski hostage and mount an attack on Governor's House. But Pankratov was made of strong metal. Standing his ground, he insisted that his order be obeyed. The wine that had travelled from Tsarskoe Selo was diluted in the cold, deep waters of west Siberia. The crowd's anger subsided. Pankratov had got his way.[22]

The imperial family were in the dark as this situation came to its climax.[23] If consulted, they would probably have minded little about losing the wine because they were abstemious when it came to alcohol. The retinue, however, had a different attitude. Fine reds and whites were one of the few perks remaining to them in the course of their service, and they heard the news with dismay. Yet another small treat had been swept away. Such was their antipathy towards Nikolski that they immediately assumed that it was he rather than Pankratov who was responsible for the decision – and Nikolski in their view had acted out of sheer malice.[24] Pankratov meanwhile stayed a firm favourite with everyone. The Romanovs had already learned to trust Kobylinski. Now Nicholas also felt a growing confidence in Pankratov, and it was reassuring to him that Kobylinski and Pankratov found that they could work together without undue friction. Pankratov was even-tempered and open to persuasion. Although he had grounds for bearing a grudge against the family after his prison experiences, he was proving himself a noble soul.

Nicholas took advantage of the atmosphere by asking for Tatishchev to be allowed to join him in Tobolsk. Kerensky immediately gave his consent after receiving Pankratov's assurances. But Kerensky was displeased to discover that Margarita Khitrovo too had made her way to the town in late August. Khitrovo made contact with Anastasia Gendrikova, who was one of the children's tutors, and Dr Botkin and, with Kobylinski's permission, passed on presents for the imperial family, mainly sweets and miniature icons. But she had always been highly strung and soon she was telling people that Kobylinski was plotting a dastardly fate for the Romanovs. Her hysterical outbursts induced the authorities to conduct a search of her hotel room and put her under arrest. She was then deported to Moscow.[25] Around this time there was also information that ten unnamed monarchists were planning to arrive from Pyatigorsk in the north Caucasus with the aim of making contact with Nicholas. There was little doubt that their ultimate purpose was to liberate the imperial family. Although Kerensky set up an investigation, there were no serious consequences because the party never arrived at its destination.[26]

Kerensky was confident enough to agree to Nicholas's request for permission to take a stroll around Tobolsk.[27] But Pankratov unexpectedly refused to comply. When Nicholas asked whether he was worried about a possible escape attempt, Pankratov said no and explained that he was merely working to the government's orders. He also mentioned the proliferation of rumours in the press. Was Nicholas having an affair with another woman? Had he divorced Alexandra? Was he entering a monastery? Rumours of this kind were flying round the country and reaching the Eastern Front, and those who hated the monarchy wanted to end what they saw as the indulgence of the Romanovs – Pankratov had had to telegram the Petrograd newspapers to refute the false reports. But army units at the front had still threatened to send a contingent to kill the Romanovs and their protector Pankratov. At the labour club in Tobolsk, too, there were calls to treat Nicholas and Alexandra as criminals and throw them into prison. Pankratov knew the local situation better than the Provisional Government and overruled Kerensky's decision.[28]

Nicholas, abetted by Botkin and Dolgorukov, continued to enquire as to when the Romanovs could take a walk outside the grounds.[29] Botkin wrote directly to Kerensky. Towards the end of September, the family's spirits rose when the doctor received a reply sanctioning a drive by car to the town's outskirts. Pankratov again quashed the idea. He explained to Nicholas that he could not guarantee the family's security; at the same time he wrote back to Kerensky explaining that he lacked a suitable car and would anyway require too many horse-cabs for the accompanying guard unit.[30] But Nicholas did not give up hoping. One of his other ideas was to see whether Kerensky might allow the Romanovs to move to the nearby Ivanovski monastery some miles outside Tobolsk. Alexei Volkov was sent off to inspect the place. In his interview with the abbess, he explained the family's daily requirements. The abbess approved the project and made an offer of a suitable house in the grounds. Pankratov then came out on a visit. The

idea had never appealed to him and the scheme was quietly abandoned.[31]

The Romanovs were cheered, however, by Pankratov's consent to
their attending a Tobolsk church service for the first time on 14 October.[32] They were all excited and woke early to get themselves ready.
The plan was for them to walk to the nearby Church of the Annunciation, but at the last moment the empress called for a wheelchair
because of her sore legs. Nicholas spoke gently in French with his
daughters and son as they assembled in the garden. They were thrilled
at the prospect of what for them was now a kind of freedom. It was
no more than 500 paces to the church, and a line of troops stood on
guard all the way. The glamour of the daughters' black fox-fur coats
impressed the bystanders. People shouted for permission to join in
the service. Pankratov point-blank refused. The family could only
celebrate the Mass if they were strictly by themselves.[33] Nevertheless,
as Nicholas wrote to his sister Xenia, the excitement was intense and
as the Romanovs approached the church, the soldiers themselves
broke ranks and gathered around them. Nicholas likened it to being
the quarry of a hunting party, but he also felt buoyed up to the point
of laughter.[34]

As he and the others made their way back to their house of confinement, the clergy organized a peal of bells in an obvious gesture of
support for the Romanovs. While Pankratov had done everything to
dull the occasion, Father Alexei Vasilev had his own way of sharing his
delight with like-minded inhabitants of Tobolsk.[35] Nicholas's mood
rose to new heights. He had always believed that he was more popular
than his enemies contended, and the experience of walking to and
from the church reinforced this feeling.

Pankratov had more painful thoughts about the occasion. As he
watched the servants carrying Alexandra in her chair over the garden
step, he could not help contrasting her conditions of confinement with
those which he had experienced in the Peter-Paul Fortress in St Petersburg. His cell in the Trubetskoi Tower had been dark and clammy, and
for years he had been able to glimpse the sky only through the barred
frame of a frosted window. While being transferred to Shlisselburg
prison, he had been thrilled by the sudden sight of trees, bushes, snow
and the full expanse of the heavens. He had moved along as if in a
trance. The very trees seemed to be escorting him and he began to
hallucinate that their branches were animate beings that were curious
about him. He had walked with difficulty because of the shackles on

his ankles and wrists. Although Pankratov never forgot his long years of imprisonment, he kept his thoughts to himself that day in Tobolsk, and he had the magnanimity to feel pity for the life that the Romanovs now had to lead.[36]

15. THE OCTOBER REVOLUTION

While the Romanovs adjusted to their circumstances in Tobolsk, the revolutionary crisis elsewhere was deepening. Petrograd was in a state of unrelieved tension and Kerensky decided that a drastic imposition of the Provisional Government's authority over the soviets and the army garrisons was essential.

With this in mind he came to an agreement with General Kornilov to deploy reliable troops from the Eastern Front to the capital. Kornilov, commander-in-chief since July, had become the favourite of army officers and the political right. In Moscow in late August, at the State Conference of all parties and public organizations to the right of the Bolsheviks, he was fêted as a potential dictator who alone might restore order. Kerensky no longer enjoyed widespread popularity as economic and military difficulties increased. As he arrived with his bodyguard, an army officer asked him why he needed such protection. When Kerensky expressed surprise at the question, the officer impertinently explained that it was usual only for a coffin to be surrounded by so large a guard.[1] Moreover, a Cossack colonel was said to have riled him by saying: 'Don't think, Mr Minister, that it's anything like a matter of indifference to the Cossacks as to who occupies the Winter Palace, whether it's Alexandra Fëdorovna with a sceptre in her hands or Alexander Fëdorovich with a syringe!' This was a reference to Kerensky's alleged use of morphine to ease his troubled mind.[2] Although the story was probably apocryphal, the fact that people were spreading it was a sign of Kerensky's weakening popularity.

Kerensky nonetheless remained confident in Kornilov until exchanges via the Hughes apparatus drew him to conclude that Kornilov was plotting a coup d'état using the transferred troops to carry it out. On 9 September he fired Kornilov as commander-in-chief and called off the deployment. At this point Kornilov went into open rebellion. Socialist parties, including the Bolsheviks, sped out to trains already bound for Petrograd and persuaded the soldiers to return to their bases. Kornilov and his military backers were locked up in Bykhov prison. He denied that he had ever had dictatorial ambitions; he claimed to have been loyally carrying out Kerensky's orders until the moment when he received the order to halt the transfer. What is undeniable is that if Kornilov had arrived in full force, many Kadets and right-wing elements would have prodded him into assuming a political role. What is more, Kerensky's victory over him had the curious result of weakening the Provisional Government. Without assistance from the soviets, he could not have turned back the trains, and for the rest of the month his authority ebbed away as Mensheviks, Socialist-Revolutionaries and now even Bolsheviks strengthened their position in the capital.

Nicholas had for weeks been in a state of growing concern, and he was cheered by the news that Kornilov planned to transport forces to Petrograd and suppress the Bolsheviks.[3] But the former emperor was clutching at straws if he thought that his own fortunes were about to improve. Kornilov made no attempt to advocate the monarchist cause. Far from it: he was to put on record his belief that the dynasty was responsible for bringing fateful trouble to Russia.[4] In his appeals to the Russian people, he focused on the mortal danger currently facing the Motherland and warned of the inadequacy of the Provisional Government to deal with the situation.[5] Nicholas could at least agree with this part of Kornilov's case.

On the afternoon of 11 September, Nicholas read telegrams to the effect that Kornilov had risen in revolt and been removed as commander-in-chief.[6] The terms of confinement continued to allow him access to news, and on 18 September he wrote in his diary:

> Telegrams arrive here twice a day; many are formulated so unclearly that it is difficult to trust them. Obvious there is great confusion in Petrograd and another change in the composition of the government. Apparently nothing came of General Kornilov's enterprise. He himself and the generals and officers who supported him have in large part been arrested, and the army units that headed for Petrograd are being turned back. The weather is wonderful, hot.[7]

This was the last time that he referred to events in the capital for some weeks as he gave himself up to settling the family and their entourage in Tobolsk. Reading books and sawing wood became his daytime routine, and in the evenings he tried to cheer up his wife and their children. But this did not mean that he ceased to care about the country's fate. He worried endlessly about the military situation and always the newspapers gave grounds for pessimism.

Food supplies to most cities were diminishing by the week, and the army squads that Kerensky sent into the countryside to requisition grain and vegetable stocks failed to redress the situation. Peasants increasingly refused to pay rent to gentry landowners; in rural Russia, it was the peasantry's land communes rather than the official administration that exercised power. Meanwhile, the urban diet markedly deteriorated. Industrial enterprises began to close as their supplies of raw materials and financial credits dried up. Some large factories closed down entirely. Strained relations between employers and the workforces had been exacerbated by the effects of rampant inflation. Even where an owner yielded to trade union pressure to raise wages, workers experienced a collapse in their standard of living. The industrialist Pavel Ryabushinski had put it starkly: 'It will take the bony finger of hunger and national destitution to grab the throat of these false friends of the people, these members of various committees and soviets, before they will come to their senses.'[8] This kind of remark enabled the Bolshevik Party to claim that the entire propertied elite sought to inflict terrible conditions on 'the people'. As soviets, trade unions and factory-workshop committees underwent re-election, Bolsheviks made gains at the expense of Mensheviks and Socialist-Revolutionaries. Steadily the Bolshevik Party rose to leadership in soviet executive committees.

As awareness grew of the likelihood that peasants would seize the gentry's estates, conscripts at the front and in the garrisons became restless. Officers had long since lost control of their men, and desertions became a mass phenomenon. The German high command saw its chance to break through the defences along the Baltic coast and occupy Riga. A line of trenches that had stayed more or less the same since mid-1915 was broken, and the Russian armed forces lost their military effectives. The Western Allies looked askance at Kerensky's request for financial assistance. Germany, Austria-Hungary, France, the United Kingdom and the United States took it for granted that unless a remarkable political transformation occurred in Petrograd, Russia was on the point of decisive defeat.

Lenin had called for exactly this to happen at the start of the Great War, reasoning that socialist internationalists in the combatant countries had a duty to encourage the demise of their imperialist government. On return from Switzerland, he had rallied the support of those Bolsheviks who favoured the overthrow of the Provisional Government and the establishment of a socialist administration based on 'soviet power'. Such an administration, he contended, would maintain popular support by withdrawing the army from the war, transferring the agricultural land to the peasantry's control, nationalizing the banks and large industrial companies, implementing 'workers' control' in factories and mines and offering the right of self-determination to national minorities. Once he had his growing party's consent, the only question was about when and how to realize his revolutionary project. The Bolshevik Central Committee proved reluctant to implement the recommendations he sent from his hiding place in Finland. Impatient for action, he returned to Petrograd and cajoled the Central Committee to seize power at the earliest opportunity, and Trotsky, who had been a Bolshevik only since the summer, devised a strategy for insurrection which would coincide with the opening of the second All-Russia Congress of Soviets.

The strategy was put into effect on 7 November 1917 (or 25 October, according to the old calendar) by use of garrison troops and Red Guards obedient to the Petrograd Soviet. Kerensky fled the Winter Palace and the Provisional Government ceased to exist. Power was declared to lie in the hands of the soviets. The new Council of People's Commissars – or Sovnarkom – was chosen with Lenin as its chairman and Trotsky as People's Commissar for Foreign Affairs. Decrees were issued on peace and on land. Soviets elsewhere in the former Russian Empire were called upon to eject the old administration and exercise their own governmental authority. In the countryside, where few soviets yet existed, peasants were told to make revolution in their own way and show allegiance to Sovnarkom. Although the Bolsheviks as a party did not have a majority at the congress, the Mensheviks and Socialist-Revolutionaries did them a favour by walking out of the proceedings in protest. Talks were held about forming a coalition government with Mensheviks and Socialist-Revolutionaries. Lenin and Trotsky could not stop the Bolshevik Central Committee from exploring this possibility since it probably constituted the rationale in the minds of most Bolsheviks and their supporters for overthrowing Kerensky. When the talks broke down, the Bolsheviks were left to rule alone.

They increasingly called themselves 'communists' to differentiate themselves from the Mensheviks and Socialist-Revolutionaries as well as to emphasize their ultimate objective of founding a society without a government, a bureaucracy or an army. The fact that they were installing dictatorial rule in order to achieve this objective did not appear to them as a contradiction. They were people who believed that doctrinal and logical nicety mattered less than revolutionary action. Unlike Mensheviks and Socialist-Revolutionaries, they felt confident that where Russia led, the countries of central and Western Europe would quickly follow. Bolsheviks predicted a rapid end to the Great War, brought about by working-class revolutions which would overturn the 'bourgeois' system of rule. Soon, they thought, the workers rather than the capitalist class would dominate politics. Disciplined organization and sheer weight of numbers were forecast to become a decisive obstacle against a successful counter-revolution. The era of human history projected by Karl Marx and Friedrich Engels since the mid-nineteenth century was at last expected – at least by fervent Bolsheviks – to be realizable. Lenin and his comrades lived and breathed the idea that communism, so often derided as a utopian dream, was about to be established in practice; and most of them assumed that this would be accomplished in their own lifetimes.

The diaries of Nicholas and Alexandra initially showed little awareness of the extraordinary events in the capital. On the day when the Bolsheviks seized power, Nicholas sawed wood and had a consultation with his dentist Sergei Kostritski, who was about to depart for Crimea; he wrote about how much he enjoyed the air outside: 'Another excellent day with a light frost.' Alexandra noted the temperature (−6° Centigrade) and recorded: 'The sun is shining bright.'[9]

But the Bolshevik seizure of power in Petrograd had caused confusion in Tobolsk. Newspapers arrived only patchily from the capital, and the information in them was contradictory and depended heavily on each paper's political line. Pankratov and Kobylinski were put into an invidious position. Appointed by Kerensky, they had no links with the new government led by Lenin and Trotsky, and Sovnarkom made no attempt to communicate with them.[10] Events were swirling in the capital. Although Kerensky had departed the Winter Palace, he re-emerged a few days later on the Pulkovo Heights at the head of a force of Cossacks and other volunteers. Overthrown as minister-chairman, he aimed to reverse what Lenin and Trotsky had accomplished. Soldiers and Red Guards loyal to Sovnarkom beat them back and Lenin consolidated the Bolshevik grip on power. Nicholas desisted from recording his thinking about this turn of events. He barely referred to the October Revolution, making only the following record more than a fortnight later:

> A lot of snow has fallen. For a long time there have been no newspapers from Petrograd; likewise telegrams. This is sickening at such a heavy time. Our daughters have played on sledges and leapt from them into a pile of snow. At nine o'clock there were vespers.[11]

For nearly four weeks he confined comments in his diary to matters of the daily routine: books that he was reading, outdoor tasks, letters that he wrote and the worsening weather.

But he spoke of his horror to the retinue. As Sydney Gibbes recollected:

> As soon as the struggle [in Petrograd] began, Tobolsk was cut off from the world and no newspapers were received for quite a long time. Then suddenly a large bundle of newspapers were received all together and the full details of all the terrible details were revealed. I had never seen the emperor so shaken. For the moment he was completely incapable of saying or doing anything, nobody dared to say a word.[12]

The Provisional Government had behaved without undue harshness, but the Bolsheviks were a volatile and terrifying phenomenon.

On 1 December, Nicholas's diary contained his first direct entry about Soviet policy:

> The incredible news has arrived that three parliamentarians of our Vth Army had travelled to meet the Germans beyond Dvinsk and signed provisional truce terms with them. I never foresaw such a nightmare. How ever did those Bolshevik scoundrels summon up the sheer nerve to fulfil their own cherished dream of offering to conclude peace with the enemy without consulting the people's opinion at a time when the adversary has occupied a great swathe of the country?[13]

He was writing from the heart and it does not seem to have occurred to him that neither he nor his ancestors had behaved any differently from Lenin and Trotsky as regards consulting and abiding by the expressed wishes of the people. His thinking was unadulterated by self-knowledge. Nor did he see the illogicality in accusing the Bolsheviks of the sin of doing precisely what they had for months said they aimed to do: calling a halt to the carnage on the Eastern Front and transforming global politics by action and example. What those same Bolsheviks omitted to add was that if peace and 'European socialist revolution' failed to follow from their truce negotiations, their next option was to start a 'revolutionary war' in central Europe.

16. THE ROMANOV DISPERSAL

Although Nicholas and his family lived comfortably on the Provisional Government's subsidy, his relatives faced shakier conditions. Grand Duke Georgi Mikhailovich retired to his Finnish estate at Ritierve. Finland had been an autonomous region under Russian rule since 1809, and although Helsinki and other cities experienced revolutionary disturbances as Finns demanded independence, the countryside was quiet enough for Georgi Mikhailovich to imagine that he could escape the Petrograd turmoil.

He quickly experienced the effects of the general economic collapse and was no longer able to run the estate in the old way. As his finances went into the red, he had to fire his many servants in order to balance the books. He felt bad about this, but his conscience was clear, he said, because he had simply run out of funds. The servants themselves returned to their home villages in the hope of lasting out the turbulent conditions. Georgi kept his head down. He had always thought – like Nicholas in March 1917 – that the best option would be to obtain a place of refuge in England, and he discreetly explored the possibilities over several months. His daughter Xenia was already living there, in Worthing, where by chance she had found herself at the start of the war. They kept up an affectionate correspondence – he poured his passion into his concern for her. At the same time he denounced the 'scoundrels' in the British government who refused him a visa – he reserved his greatest contempt for Ambassador Buchanan, whom he accused of mischievously thwarting his method of using the services of a friendly Norwegian diplomat to send his letters to the United Kingdom.[1]

On 11 July 1917, Grand Duke Georgi Mikhailovich offered his daughter an analysis of Russia's ills that was as crude as it was simple-minded:

> The Yids established the revolution and the Russians thought they
> would fix up things decently but of course they have quickly failed

to fix things up at all well. In the first place, because they cast 'God's Anointed' down from the throne, and this is a great sin. The Lord God will of course punish all of them severely for this, I don't doubt this for a moment. They have completely forgotten God, and God will punish them for this.[2]

Here was the quintessence of the Romanov family outlook: anti-Semitism mixed with Christian monarchism, expressed in language that combined racialist slang and pious pomposity. Soon after the February Revolution Grand Duke Nikolai Mikhailovich in a letter to the dowager empress traced all the country's troubles to people in the schools and universities – and Jews were the ones he held most culpable.[3] As for Grand Duke Georgi Mikhailovich, no one would claim him as the most thoughtful member of Nicholas's extended family and the revolutionary turmoil did nothing to turn his mind towards deep reflection. He was a leaf blown in the wind, and he wished that the gusts would carry him to his daughter in Worthing.[4]

Three days after the Bolsheviks seized power in Petrograd, Georgi Mikhailovich wrote to the dowager empress in Crimea deploring the October Revolution. He noted, incorrectly, that Kerensky's father had adopted Lenin as a young boy. (Kerensky senior had merely been the headmaster at Lenin's secondary school.) As he got into his rant, he claimed that two Jews, Lenin and Trotsky, headed the new 'Maximalist' regime. (Lenin's grandfather had been a lapsed Jew but Lenin was brought up in the Russian Orthodox Church.) The Grand Duke predicted that 'this escapade won't last long'; he fervently hoped for its speedy liquidation; for he was convinced that 'the Jews' – for once he omitted to use the more pejorative word – were running everything in Russia on the orders of an active network of German agents. Sovnarkom was nothing less than a 'government of traitors'. He could only put his trust in Generals Alexei Kaledin and Lavr Kornilov to restore order to the country – he welcomed reports that the Don Cossacks had proclaimed Kaledin dictator. He himself had long ago decided that Kerensky was a dead loss. In Georgi Mikhailovich's opinion, Kerensky had betrayed Russia as early as May 1917, when accepting Socialist-Revolutionary Viktor Chernov as a fellow minister.[5]

Nicholas had written to his mother from Tobolsk on 19 September 1917. He told her something about the chaotic conditions in the capital before the family's departure. He wrote also about the journey to Siberia. But he had no news about what had happened to his brother

Mikhail since their meeting in the Alexander Palace. Nicholas seldom complained about anything, but he did describe the living conditions at Governor's House as 'impossible' until after it was refurbished.[6]

His sister Xenia wrote to Nicholas on 19 December. By then she was living with their mother on the Ai-Todor estate in Crimea under surveillance by the same Vasili Vershinin who had checked out Tobolsk for Kerensky. Xenia called him 'a very sweet and kindly person'. But the Bolshevik seizure of power had robbed him of any true authority, and he had to defer to the Sevastopol Soviet. Times had changed in a fundamental fashion. For Xenia it was a source of satisfaction that their guards agreed to address each of them by the familiar Russian word for 'you'; she said she found some of them 'sympathetic'. As regards conditions in the country, she commented: 'So a truce has been declared [on the Eastern Front] . . . Hour by hour it gets no easier. Everyone is receiving distressing news about their estates; everything is being snatched, nobody dare utter a peep about it: we're all going to be destitute. We're thinking about how we're going to live and earn our bread. We've decided to open a hotel and have already divided up the jobs amongst us.' Xenia, for one, planned to become a housemaid.[7]

Nicholas in his reply expressed approval for the idea of a working hotel. He passed his own days best when he could perform some manual tasks, but he found the nights easier, when he could sink into oblivion.[8] This was the nearest he got to admitting to despair – and perhaps he could only write like this to Xenia: he never seems to have dropped his guard among the inmates of Governor's House.

As for the dowager empress, Xenia reported that she was up and walking at Ai-Todor after a bout of flu. She noted that the communists had arrested their brother Mikhail, who had nearly acceded to the throne in the February Revolution, and brought him to Petrograd. But Xenia rightly speculated that Mikhail had by then been allowed to return to his Gatchina residence. The October Revolution horrified her. Like Nicholas, she was stunned by the pillaging of the wine cellars under the Winter Palace. While the entire country was racked by violence and political conflict, it was this one example of popular delinquency that offended her sensibility, and she explained to Nicholas that she would have preferred to hear that the Germans rather than the Russians had perpetrated such a 'wild outrage'.[9] Xenia's younger sister Olga was equally distraught about the vandalism and wrote to Nicholas that it would never have happened under the Provisional Government: she was very upset about the destruction of magnificent pictures by

Valentin Serov.[10] On 14 February 1918, Xenia told Nicholas that they had been isolated at Ai-Todor for three and a half months, meaning that she could not leave and nobody was allowed to visit. From the newspapers she learned about the violence against officers. She mentioned 'a real massacre' in Sevastopol, saying that the trouble had spread to Yalta, where corpses had been tossed into the sea.[11]

Xenia and their mother were about to be regarded as the lucky Romanovs if only because distance from Petrograd gave them some protection. The rest of the wider family experienced worsened treatment after the fall of the Provisional Government. The Bolsheviks were determined to tighten the conditions of confinement for all of them who fell into their custody.

Grand Duke Mikhail felt especially insecure. Just before Kerensky's overthrow, Mikhail wrote to his mother on 24 October reporting on his problems with an ulcer and commenting that the chances of moving abroad had fallen away for him.[12] At the start of the October Revolution he wrote again to say: 'What a terrible time that everyone has to endure.' He prayed that God should give her the strength to deal with the trauma. While hoping for better times for 'tormented Russia', he desperately wanted to leave the country.[13] But his already slim chances vanished when the Bolsheviks seized power. On 18 November 1917 he informed his mother that the Military-Revolutionary Committee of the Petrograd Soviet had ordered his transfer back to the capital. Sailors from Helsinki oversaw his daily routine, but their attitude was unthreatening. Mikhail consoled himself with the hope that things would improve when the Constituent Assembly was elected and the family could at last go into foreign exile. He had given up dreaming that the Romanovs had any future in Russia.[14]

17. FREEDOM HOUSE

Freedom House, as Governor's House was renamed in accord with the revolutionary times, would have been big enough by itself if the Romanovs had taken only their cooks and domestic servants from Tsarskoe Selo. But they had made only a marginal reduction of the entourage, and at first, Pierre Gilliard was the sole senior retainer who was given a room in the residence.[1] All the others received accommodation across the road in the Kornilov house – each day they walked over to perform their services for the family. Pankratov and Kobylinski were the only other people permitted to enter the premises. The guard detachment, as had been the case at Tsarskoe Selo, was required to stay outside. On most days, the residence was busy with people and activity until bedtime and the Romanovs tried to behave as they had always done. Status and dignity remained important even though Sydney Gibbes, with his eye for custom and propriety, noticed that some retainers were engaging in a greater degree of eye contact with the imperial family than had once been acceptable, but otherwise the old etiquette was preserved. He admired how the Romanovs achieved at least a semblance of normality in the changed circumstances.[2]

It was a claustrophobic existence and tiffs amongst the entourage became frequent as the isolation made itself felt. Ilya Tatishchev tried to keep the peace: 'One mustn't be petty, one mustn't be petty!'[3] The obvious solution was to find indoor pursuits that might lighten the gloom. Gibbes and Gilliard usefully distracted Nicholas's children by teaching them lessons and setting homework. The garden provided another outlet for pent-up energies. Then there were the theatrical performances. On one occasion Nicholas joined in, taking the leading role in Anton Chekhov's *The Bear*.[4] Nicholas himself adapted the text to enable Olga and Maria to take part.[5] The Romanovs took photographs of each other and had them developed and printed locally.[6] Games of bezique whiled away the evening hours.[7]

On 23 September 1917 Maria Nikolaevna wrote to the dowager empress – her grandmother – to assure her about the situation. She expressed delight about their little garden and the hens, ducks and four piglets that the family were looking after.[8] There were also turkeys which the younger Romanovs, including Alexei, enjoyed looking after. The garden had its own tennis court, albeit that it lacked a net. Anastasia Nikolaevna wrote to her friend Ekaterina Zborovskaya: 'It is not too bad, but we spend most of the time searching for balls in the ditch and similar places. We sit on the window sills and entertain ourselves watching the public passing by.'[9] Kolya Derevenko, the doctor's son, visited to play with Alexei on designated days.[10] Alexei wrote brightly to his 'dear Granny' on 5 November 1917: 'In the daytime Papa saws wood with my sisters or clears the pathways. I hope you've recovered from your illness. We all send a big kiss and always remember you.'[11] As had been true at Tsarskoe Selo, Nicholas was also partnered in his outdoor labours by Dolgorukov, Tatishchev, Gilliard or one of his daughters; he was determined to keep himself in physical trim. Alexandra continued to spend the days in her chair reading or sewing. The daughters continued to use their cameras, and Kobylinski felt that the atmosphere was less strained than it had been at the Alexander Palace.[12]

Looking from the balcony windows down on to the street, the Romanovs tried to acquaint themselves with Tobolsk. Anastasia recorded some of the things that impressed her as different from what she had seen elsewhere. The post, she noticed, arrived not by carriage as at Tsarskoe Selo but in a sleigh with jingling bells. The peasants in the winter went about their business in long fur coats which, quaintly, they and the town's inhabitants called their 'geese'. And whereas most Russians wore dull-coloured winter boots in snowy weather, the peasantry of Tobolsk province had theirs dyed crimson.[13] The family obviously had a genuine curiosity about those parts of Nicholas's former domains with which they had only a fleeting acquaintance. But the Romanov detainees were not just forbidden to take walks in the street: they were also prohibited from communicating with the urban population. This meant that they had to gather local information mainly from what the retainers, who could go into town whenever they liked, told them.[14]

Freedom House was comfortable despite being somewhat cold and draughty – Tatyana Nikolaevna wrote to her friend Margarita Khitrovo that the rooms occupied by her father and brother were the only ones that were kept properly warm.[15] This was an early indication of the family's need to manage its budget more economically than at the Alexander Palace. Nicholas and Alexandra had little acquaintance with the practical requirements and simply signed invoices from Nicholas's own funds supplemented by a subsidy from the government. Meals were still provided in plenty. Breakfast was a two-course affair and there was morning coffee with a *zakuska*. Lunch ran to three courses, followed by afternoon tea and pastries and sweet-cakes.[16] The Romanovs began to dine at the same table as Botkin, Ilya Tatishchev, Vasili Dolgorukov, Anastasia Gendrikova, Ekaterina Shneider, Pierre Gilliard and Sydney Gibbes. Retainers at lower levels fared less well but could nevertheless eat their fill and take bags of food back to their families in the town. Freedom House itself had an impact on the local economy as the Romanovs' staff bought up scarce provisions. Hearing of criticism in the town, Pankratov stopped everyone from carrying food off the premises. This annoyed the servants, who complained that their pay was inadequate to look after their families. Pankratov replied that they should take the matter up with Nicholas.[17]

But the family's finances were not in fact as buoyant as most people in Tobolsk assumed, and soon after the move from Tsarskoe Selo there arose difficulties in balancing the accounts at Freedom House. Nicholas had lost access to any personal bank account, and the household had to obtain its supplies on credit in the absence of adequate finance from the Soviet authorities in the capital. Debts were growing inexorably. Kobylinski recognized that such a situation could not continue for much longer. When he applied for assistance at the Tobolsk branch of the State Bank, the advice was to approach a businessman called Yanushkevich and ask for a loan. Yanushkevich, who still had much of his wealth, handed over 20,000 rubles on condition that Evgeni Kobylinski, Vasili Dolgorukov and Ilya Tatishchev stood as guarantors of repayment – and the three of them assented. Nothing was disclosed to Nicholas about this arrangement.[18] It was an arrangement that could only put off the evil day when the last ruble dribbled out, and the retinue's leading members were nervously aware that the Romanovs were living well beyond their means.

Alexandra was never one to spend a kopek more than she absolutely had to, but her understanding of the financial situation was less than perfect. Like the rest of the family, she had always been insulated from the circumstances that daily faced others in society. In Tobolsk, they were more cut off than ever.

The only chance for the Romanovs to obtain a glimpse of life outside Freedom House occurred when they attended Mass at the Church of the Annunciation.[19] Father Alexei Vasilev inadvertently made this difficult for them from 25 December 1917 by offering the traditional prayer for the health and long life of the emperor and his family.[20] This was his way of expressing displeasure at Pankratov's refusal to allow him to teach scripture to the Romanov youngsters.[21] Vasilev was a figure of importance in the town who had joined the town duma in a bloc with the Kadet Party; he also gave religious instruction at the boys' high school.[22] His prayer was a conscious provocation because he was repeating words that had been the official tradition before the February Revolution.[23] The soldiers on duty raised a fuss (Kobylinski had permitted many of the older servicemen to stand inside the church to keep warm). There were shouts of threats to shoot the priest. Bishop Germogen resolved the trouble by banishing Vasilev to a monastery, and Kobylinski refrained from punishing the military troublemakers. Germogen was a major figure in the Russian Orthodox Church who had publicly resigned from the Holy Synod in 1912 rather than accept Rasputin's growing influence. Though he did not court controversy, he did not flinch in the face of trouble.[24] He was also a monarchist, and when he removed Vasilev, his purpose was to save him and the rest of the clergy from retaliation by the Soviet authorities.

A new priest, Father Vladimir Khlynov, was appointed who behaved with more discretion than Vasilev. Nonetheless, the soldiers decided that the Romanovs should be banned from attending church and should have Mass said for them in Freedom House. Kobylinski managed to achieve a compromise whereby the family could go to church but not with the same regularity.[25] Even so, the Tobolsk clergy's sympathy for the Romanovs continued to agitate the guards, who insisted on being present at the services held in Freedom House. Nerves were strained when a prayer was offered to St Alexandra. One of the soldiers, on hearing the name Alexandra, assumed that this meant the empress. Their suspicion was that a prayer was being offered in the names of the deposed dynasty. There was the usual fuss until someone got hold of an ecclesiastical calendar and could prove that there was a saint of the same name.[26] The family was being given a lesson that even if they behaved as they were asked, it was not enough: everyone had to conform to the wishes of those who sympathized with the Soviet government – and no one could predict what they might decide from day to day.

18. LEARNING FROM OTHERS

The Romanovs became fascinated with Commissar Pankratov and his gentle, firm and knowledgeable management at Freedom House. When their favourite dentist, Kostritski, arrived from Crimea to check their teeth, he came across a copy of Pankratov's reminiscences about Siberian exile. The very existence of such a book might have widened the gap between Pankratov and the inmates of Freedom House. Instead, as the dentist told Nicholas, the contents revealed a man who bore no grudges. The Romanovs meanwhile learned the details of the killing that had led to Pankratov's arrest. 'Why,' Alexandra asked the dentist, 'doesn't he like gendarmes?' Alexandra could make no sense of his early life. Pankratov seemed so gentle and unobjectionable. The empress could hardly believe that he had ever served time in one of her husband's prisons. She joined the rest of the family in respecting Kerensky's commissar.[1]

As Pankratov himself scrutinized Nicholas, he acquired a deepened understanding of his limitations. The commissar told the emperor to his face that the outbursts of popular wrath throughout his long reign were no accident. Millions of Nicholas's subjects, Pankratov exclaimed, had been aggrieved about how they were treated. There had been trouble during the Japanese war of 1904–1905. There had been outbreaks of violence in Barnaul and Kuznetsk in summer 1914 when the mobilization papers arrived – Pankratov himself had witnessed this in Siberian exile and seen how people ransacked the vodka stores. He suggested that the disturbances in Petrograd in February and March 1917 had their origins in the same feelings of resentment. Pankratov asked Nicholas to bend his mind as to why Germany and Austria had avoided the same chaos when they had gone to war. He argued that despotisms were always taken by surprise when the people finally decided that enough was enough. This failed to convince Nicholas, who thought for a moment before asking: 'But why wreck a palace?

Why not put a stop to the mob? . . . Why allow robberies and the destruction of treasures?'[2]

The two men, however, found they could commune about Siberia. Pankratov was becoming an exceptional figure in Nicholas's life. Until Rasputin, no one who queried the emperor's basic thinking was allowed into his circle. After Rasputin's death, in Tsarskoe Selo and Tobolsk, no one was left in the retinue who dared to contradict him. Nicholas lived inside a cocoon of his own making which was even more insulating than those which enveloped rival monarchies abroad. Pankratov set about picking it open. As an ex-prisoner of a Siberian labour colony, he had intimate experience of everyday Siberian conditions; he had exceptional acquaintance with the ethnic groups in the frozen north. Pierre Gilliard overheard a conversation that lasted over an hour in which Pankratov recounted his explorations in the Lena river basin. Nicholas and Pankratov loved to talk together – and Nicholas, forgetting about why Pankratov had found himself in Siberian parts, encouraged his companion to tell his stories. They were united in their confidence about the great future that lay in store for Russia in the depths of tundra and taiga. The ex-emperor and his ex-convict were at one in their patriotic enthusiasm.[3]

Alexandra did not share her husband's admiration for Pankratov, and when she had to communicate with him, she preferred to use Dr Botkin as an intermediary. Botkin was happy to oblige. He deeply sympathized with her plight and helped in whatever way she wanted – and he regularly relayed her requests to the authorities.[4]

Pankratov himself never took to the empress. Her glacial self-control whenever he was in the vicinity was hardly endearing, and she refrained from showing the slightest gratitude for the small indulgences he succeeded in contriving for the family. Despite his personal generosity of spirit, he felt a growing contempt for her demeanour. This was not just because he was a populist revolutionary hostile to the old ruling dynasty. Soon after taking over his duties in Tobolsk on behalf of the Provisional Government, he agreed to head the local commission that collected voluntary contributions for Russia's war effort against Germany. People soon complained to him about how miserly the Romanovs were. He dealt with this by handing over the contribution request form to Tatishchev and waiting to see what happened. He did not really believe the stories of Romanov stinginess until he found that the imperial family had given only 300 rubles. 'Was this miserliness or lack of attentiveness?' he asked. 'Or was it a sign of vengefulness?'

Pankratov thought it no accident that it had been the Empress who signed the cheque.[5]

The rest of the family were a different matter, and Pankratov warmed to the way that Nicholas and his daughters were eager to saw timber for the fire and clear snow from the paths. The revolutionary had expected them to behave as the pampered beneficiaries of privilege. Their pleasure in physical work came as a surprise. Even so, Pankratov continued to believe that the entire family had always been artificially isolated from ordinary life in the country they had ruled. In his opinion, moreover, their upbringing had served to stunt their personal development. Nicholas and Alexandra had enclosed their family with rules of etiquette, and power and dynastic pride had given them a narrow and unrealistic outlook on life. Yet Pankratov never ceased to be an optimist. He had seen enough to believe in their constructive potential as fellow citizens and he concluded that it was not too late for them to make a start on changing themselves. (Admittedly, he could hardly believe this possible in the case of the stony-faced empress.)[6]

He noted Nicholas's less than successful attempts to secure his offspring's educational progress. Nicholas took on the teaching of Russian history, going through a book on Peter the Great's reign with Alexei – this was probably the popular textbook by S. A. Chistyakov, which was later found among the Romanov possessions.[7] He boasted by letter to his mother in Kiev: 'I work with Alexei on Russian history, which I love and – I can say – know about.'[8] Pankratov did not share this high opinion and doubted that Nicholas knew much apart from about Russian armies and Russia's wars – and Nicholas himself made no secret of the fact that the military past was his abiding interest.[9]

Even so, Nicholas recognized a need to make changes in the teaching staff and turned to Pankratov for advice. Pankratov had a poor opinion of Anastasia Gendrikova and Ekaterina Shneider, who had been tutoring the youngsters. He recommended Klavdia Bitner, a woman with eight years' experience at a Tsarskoe Selo school. (Pankratov forbore to mention that she was Kobylinski's lover.) The emperor liked the idea and said he would consult the empress, who readily agreed.[10] Bitner had arrived in Tobolsk on the same steamer as Pankratov and Nikolski. While picking up her relationship with Kobylinski, she had aimed to obtain employment at the lycée as a French teacher. The Romanov daughters, according to Dr Botkin, intervened to support the idea of her becoming their tutor. Miss Bitner quickly returned to Tsarskoe Selo to terminate her school contract there before returning to Tobolsk in the company of fellow teacher Sydney Gibbes. She was a woman who knew her own mind, and she informed Pankratov that she wished to discuss her terms of employment alone with the empress. Nicholas and his daughters welcomed her into his office. Nicholas explained simply: 'My wife is waiting for you.' In the conversation that followed, Alexandra was so courteous and enthusiastic that Bitner decided to accept the invitation.[11]

She was pleasantly surprised by how kindly the empress could be in their daily contact. When Alexandra enquired out of sheer human curiosity whether the teacher was remitting money to her mother, Bitner explained that she was short of cash – and Alexandra insisted on giving her some of her own.[12] Bitner was equally impressed by Nicholas. With his impeccable manners, he usually made a favourable impact on those who had not already decided against him. Bitner noticed that whenever she had to take time off for illness, he always enquired how she was on her return. She came to want to do something nice for him.[13] But she held him and his Alexandra culpable for what she saw as their children's cultural deprivation. In her estimation, they were shockingly ignorant of Russian literature, history and geography. In poetry they knew little Pushkin and less Lermontov and had not even heard of Nekrasov.[14] It was scarcely a surprise that Nekrasov, a revered anti-tsarist writer among revolutionaries but not really a first-class poet, had failed to impinge on their consciousness. Impishly, Pankratov urged Bitner to read some of his poems aloud to her pupils. When she did so, she chose 'Russian Women' and 'Red Nose Frost'. She reported back to Pankratov that the Romanov daughters were delighted. 'Why weren't we ever told,' they had asked, 'that we had such a wonderful poet?'[15]

Alexei, meanwhile, was some way short of being a model pupil, and Bitner was disappointed by his preference to have everything read out to him. She accepted that his illness might have made him like this. The empress doted on her son but was less forgiving in this particular instance, comparing him unfavourably with his father, who had read voraciously as a boy.[16] In every other respect, in any case, Alexei won Bitner's heart. The tsarevich was a sweet-natured and brave young lad who hated to ask for help unless he absolutely could not manage without it. Bitner often said to him, 'Alexei Nikolaevich, your leg is hurting.' He would typically reply: 'No, it's not hurting.' She would remonstrate: 'But I can see it for myself.' But the lad was stubborn: 'You always see how it's hurting, but in fact it's not hurting.' Both of them knew the truth, and on one memorable occasion he shared his concerns with her: 'What do you think, will this [illness] ever leave me alone?'[17]

At the age of thirteen, he was growing into someone with ideas of his own. Waste of any kind annoyed him. Although he did not share all his family's culinary preferences, he stoically forbore to ask for something different to eat. He also believed that family expenditure ought to be kept to a minimum. He looked after his personal possessions with care.[18] Oddly, he preferred Tobolsk to Tsarskoe Selo, stating: 'It's better here. They deceived me there. They terribly deceived me,'[19] although he apparently never explained what he was complaining about. It was not long before he had his suspicions about life in Freedom House, too, as some of the family's retainers began to take liberties. One day the tsarevich asked Bitner: 'Tell me, Klavdia Mikhailovna, why everyone is deceiving us.' Bitner replied: 'How are you being deceived? Who is deceiving you?' Alexei explained that Dr Derevenko had told him to take a bath. The order was given for this and Alexei sat and waited to hear that the water was ready. After a long time he was told that the plumbing system was defective. But next day he learned that Maria Tutelberg, one of the chambermaids, had used the bath instead. Court etiquette was on the slide and the former heir to the throne was quick to sense this for himself.[20]

19. TIME ON THEIR HANDS

Nicholas and Alexandra had become intensive readers after the February Revolution. In her effort to pass on her religious understanding to their son, Alexandra studied Nikolai Gogol's *Meditations on the Divine Liturgy*;[1] and for her own edification she examined a general history of Christianity.[2] Whereas Alexandra had packed her luggage with care, Nicholas had omitted to bring a supply of literature from Tsarskoe Selo. Luckily for him, Pankratov allowed him to request books from the Tobolsk lycée library. Nicholas looked at K. Golodnikov's *Tobolsk and its Surroundings*.[3] He also devoured Oskar Jäger's *World History*.[4] Sydney Gibbes lent him his copy of J. R. Greene's *A Short History of the English People*. (Gibbes carried it around with him in case he found himself under arrest.) The book purveyed a cheerful analysis of England's centuries of development and had sold well in multiple London editions. As Gibbes told the story, Nicholas went off with it after breakfast and finished the whole thing by 11 a.m. In fact, according to Nicholas's diary, he took twelve days to get through it. When he returned the book to Gibbes, he said that he had looked at several such works in his youth and was grateful for the chance to refresh his acquaintance.[5]

He reserved most of his time, however, for the Russian nineteenth-century literary classics. They had not been part of his upbringing because his father, Alexander III, a cultural blockhead, thought that the arts might corrupt him. From 26 September 1917, Nicholas enjoyed filling the gaps in his education by reading stories by Nikolai Leskov.[6] Such was his delight that on 16 October he read Leskov's 'The Robbery' aloud to his family;[7] and he followed this with Nikolai Gogol's *The Wedding*.[8] Later he went through Bram Stoker's *Dracula* with them;[9] for his own personal edification, he went back to the Russian canon and in March 1918 read Leo Tolstoy's *Anna Karenina* for the first time. He admitted to being entirely distracted by the experience.[10] From this he moved on to Mikhail Lermontov.[11] And then on to the novels of Vsevolod Solovëv.[12] For the family he meanwhile selected Ivan

Turgenev's *A Huntsman's Notebooks*, followed by his novels *On The Eve*, *Smoke* and *Spring Torrents*.[13]

He also read aloud Scarlet Pimpernel stories by Baroness Orczy for the evening distraction.[14] Set in the time of the French Revolution, they expressed deep sympathy for royalty and aristocracy and utter contempt for the Parisian poor. The opening tale set the tone on page one:

> A surging, seething, murmuring crowd, of beings that are human only in name, for to the eye and ear they seem naught but savage creatures, animated by vile passions and by the lust of vengeance and of hate . . . During the greater part of the day the guillotine had been kept busy at its ghastly work: all that France had boasted of in the past centuries, of ancient names, and blue blood, had paid toll to her desire for liberty and for fraternity.[15]

Orczy's hero was the tall, blue-eyed Sir Percy Blakeney, who slipped across the Channel on covert missions to rescue 'aristos'. The stories always depicted aristocrats, both English and French, as strongly built and generous of spirit whereas she dismissed revolutionaries such as Maximilien Robespierre and Jean-Paul Marat as mediocrities eaten up with murderous intent. When English men and women of the lower social orders put in an appearance, unlike the French, they knew their place and were loyal and patriotic – and tended to be comical in their mannerisms.

Orczy's reactionary outlook must surely have enhanced her appeal to Nicholas and his family. She had been a best-selling author since 1903, when her original play *The Scarlet Pimpernel* reached the London stage. Nicholas had long been an admirer and in 1917 read all five of the then so-far-published novels.[16] The former emperor himself was a man living under conditions of confinement. He did not face – or did not think he faced – a threat of execution. But he and his family evidently obtained a degree of psychological relief in Orczy's tales. They warmed to her reactionary political outlook. (Orczy, a typical Hungarian conservative, consistently described Jews as dirty, snivelling, scheming and untrustworthy, and when she had Sir Percy Blakeney disguising himself as a Jewish trader, he performed entirely in accordance with the stereotype.)[17] Kobylinski was to recall that Nicholas just 'didn't like Jews' and usually referred to them as *zhidy* ('Yids').[18] Nicholas summarized his feelings in a letter to his mother: 'One thing is clear: it is that as long as the Yids remain in charge, everything will continue to get worse – what does Russia mean to them?'[19]

In November 1917 he wrote to his sister Xenia with a list of left-wing revolutionaries who had adopted pseudonyms to disguise their Jewish origins:

Lenin – Ulyanov (Tsederblyum)
Steklov – Nakhamkes
Zinoviev – Apfelbaum
Kamenev – Rozenfeld
Gorev – Goldman
Mekhovski – Goldenberg
Martov – Tsederbaum
Sukhanov – Gimmer
Zagorski – Krakhman
Meshkovski – Gollender[20]

He got both Lenin and others on the list wrong. Although one of Lenin's grandfathers had been Jewish, there was no one called Tsederblyum among his forebears. But Nicholas was not bothered about exactitude. Rather, he was trying to make the point that Jews were capable of any subterfuge to win power – this, indeed, is what he thought had come to fulfilment in Russia since his fall from the throne.

It is true that Jewish militants were over-represented at every level of the Bolshevik leadership in comparison with the percentage of Jews in the imperial population. They were also prominent in the Menshevik and Socialist-Revolutionary parties, and even the Constitutional-Democrats and other liberal organizations contained influential members who were Jewish. Other national and ethnic groups, too, supplied many activists who had positions of authority in the revolutionary movement, including the Bolsheviks – Georgians, Latvians and Poles were prominent among them. But it was the purest fantasy to believe, as Nicholas did, that Russia's Jews in particular had set up a centralized political-religious conspiracy. Nicholas, moreover, was overlooking the part that he himself had played in attracting hostility from many of his Jewish subjects who were politically active: he had not exactly kept secret his enthusiasm for the Union of the Russian People and other far-right organizations which helped to instigate the pre-war pogroms against Jews, and it would have been surprising if the widespread memory of this violence had been forgotten or forgiven. His name had long been a byword for religious intolerance in the lands he once had ruled.

Nicholas himself sought solace in his Christian devotions, and by March 1918 he had made up his mind to read the entire Bible from start to finish, a plan he quickly dropped in favour of other books on his shelves.[21] One volume he devoured was one of the foulest works that has ever gone into print, Sergei Nilus's *The Imminent Coming of the Antichrist and the Realm of the Devil on Earth*.[22]

Published by the Russian Orthodox Church in 1917, it was the expanded edition of a book that had first appeared twelve years earlier. Nilus was a priest, a self-styled mystic and a fanatical anti-Semite. His chapters reproduced, word for word, the notorious 'Protocols of the Elders of Zion' that had circulated in Russia and abroad since the early 1900s and which purported to supply the transcript of an international Jewish convention that was held in Paris to organize a plot for Jews to bring the entire world under their rule. The 'protocols' were in fact a forgery of multiple obscure origins. Nilus had publicized them as a way of turning Russians away from socialism by fomenting hatred of Jewish people as being the cause of all the Russian Empire's ills. In the political free-for-all after the February Revolution, the Orthodox hierarchy had no compunction about playing the anti-Semitic card by making their publishing house available to him. The fact that they were a fabrication had been established by an inquiry which Stolypin had set up in 1906, and Nicholas himself was said to have concluded: 'Abandon the protocols. The sacred cannot be defended by dirty methods.'[23]

Even so, Nicholas returned to the book in Tobolsk as if the Stolypin inquiry had never happened. From the evening of 9 April 1918, indeed, he chose it for reading aloud to his wife and children. He alternated it with passages from the Gospels because it was the season of Lent and the Romanovs were studying the works of the Evangelists. But Nilus had become a preoccupation for Nicholas, who chose *The Imminent Coming* as the main text for him to present to the family on Good Friday and Easter Sunday; he continued reading it to them in the days that followed until he reached the final page.[24] He liked the denunciations of both Freemasons and Jews; it was, he concluded, 'a very timely reading'.[25] Like Nilus, Nicholas accused the Jews of thirsting for mastery in Russia. He thought of Russians as a 'good, fine, soft people'. At least this is what Bitner concluded from her observations, believing that he assumed that once the revolutionary tide subsided, his people would return to their old governable ways – as Nicholas saw things, the current state of affairs was only temporary. Bitner concurred with Kobylinski when he commented that the emperor believed that Jews had come to exercise dominance over the Russians and led them on to a revolutionary path.[26]

Nicholas evidently endorsed the idea that leading adherents of the Jewish faith had concocted an international plot for the downfall of civilization. *The Imminent Coming* impregnated the core of his thinking, and he wanted Alexandra and the rest of the family to listen to every word and share his repugnance at this alleged global conspiracy.

20. 'OCTOBER' IN JANUARY

As the months passed, Nicholas tried to keep abreast of events and began again to receive the London *Times* and the Paris *Journal des Débats* while Alexandra read the London *Daily Graphic.*[1] His entourage continued to pass on anything they discovered on trips into town. Tobolsk, like every place in the country, was awash with talk and rumour, and people had their opinions about Sovnarkom. But precise information was in short supply. The Soviet remained, as had been the case since the February Revolution, in the hands of Mensheviks and Socialist-Revolutionaries. While industrial cities in Russia were succumbing to the Bolshevik political advance, Tobolsk stayed the same as it had been under the Provisional Government, and although Kerensky had fallen from power, his appointees continued to exercise authority there. Pankratov and Kobylinski in particular were under no threat of replacement. Sovnarkom had far too many crises to resolve in Petrograd to bother itself with a quiet provincial outpost such as Tobolsk. So long as the Romanovs were kept under firm control and there appeared no danger of their trying to escape, Lenin and the Bolshevik leadership saw no point in making changes to the guarding personnel. For the first time in his life, Nicholas was of no great interest to the Russian government.

On hearing on 31 November 1917 that the Bolsheviks had signed a truce with the Germans, he wrote in his diary: 'I in no way expected such a nightmare. How did those Bolshevik scoundrels have the foulness to fulfil their sworn dream of proposing to conclude a peace with the enemy without asking the opinion of the people – and at a time when a big swathe of the country is occupied by the foe?'[2] He rarely overheated the language in this fashion in things he wrote for himself. Perhaps he was hoping that people would one day read his words.

Sovnarkom was determined to end the fighting on the Eastern Front and set about demobilizing the old Russian Army. Troops in the older age cohorts were the first to receive their papers to return to their homes and families, but the Freedom House detachment could not safely be reduced in number. The replacements for the demobbed veterans tended to be younger and more impatient, and the revolutionary militants in the town were finding them easier to manipulate.[3] Discipline was ever harder to achieve. When the Romanovs built a snow mountain in the garden, the men on guard took it down on the grounds that someone might shoot a weapon at them from the street – and the soldiers would be held to blame.[4] Pankratov and Kobylinski could never take obedience for granted: it always had to be negotiated. As he had done in Tsarskoe Selo, Nicholas tried to get to know the troops. He especially liked and enjoyed talking to Ensign Tur and Sergeant Grishchenko. He played chess with some of the other soldiers. As the contingent's personnel changed, it was not unknown for departing soldiers to creep upstairs and kiss his hand in farewell.[5] But the departures disconcerted him, and when he asked about who was going to be guarding the family next, no one in the detachment could answer him.[6]

The men of the detachment in Tobolsk were unhappy about being kept on to guard the Romanovs and continually asked why they were being required to stay with their regiments. Meanwhile, other men arrived from the German and Austrian fronts and prowled the streets; soon there were 2,000 of them. Their ill-discipline became notorious. The sight of greatcoats scared many residents and agitated the authorities in charge of security at Freedom House, for these troops talked of wanting to spill blood. The physical security of the Romanovs was put in growing jeopardy for the first time since the transfer from Tsarskoe Selo. People sent threatening letters to Nicholas, which Pankratov and his assistants intercepted and burned. Pornographic messages arriving for the Romanov daughters were dealt with likewise. When the imperial retinue complained about the rigours of confinement, it was pointed out to them that only the 'detachment of special purpose' stood between them and a possible violent attack. Pankratov spelled this out in unambiguous terms to Dr Botkin and asked him to impress it on Nicholas for the good of the entire family.[7]

In myriad ways, great and small, the Romanovs were put on notice that they could no longer count on privileged treatment. Nicholas received a ration card that recorded his full name and address and noted his social status as 'ex-Emperor' (eks-Imperator). Even he had to have such a card to buy staples such as flour, cooking oil, salt, candles, sugar, soap, groats and oats. Card holders were allowed to make purchases either at the official town store or from the Self-Awareness Cooperative.[8]

Nicholas was appalled by the unrest that had continued in every Russian city since his abdication. The Romanovs were never in much danger from the citizens of Tobolsk, and Kobylinski was probably right in claiming that many people were pleased to see them but were too frightened to show this in public.[9] In fact there were plenty of people who were delighted to see them on their way to church and some residents even sent delicacies from their own kitchens as a token of their best wishes. Freedom House was never short of treats in the last months of 1917.[10] But the tension was mounting even in Tobolsk, especially among soldiers and ex-soldiers. Nicholas observed these developments with anxiety. Whereas he despised democratic institutions and procedures, he surprised himself by beginning to pin his hopes on the long-awaited Constituent Assembly. He frequently asked Pankratov when it would meet in Petrograd. Unfortunately, Pankratov had no better idea than anyone else.[11]

Letters to and from the Romanovs continued to be examined before being passed on, and the imperial family took steps to protect their confidentiality. Alexandra sometimes gave messages for Anna Vyrubova written in Church Slavonic to a former medical orderly at Tsarskoe Selo named Zhuk.[12] She also used Sydney Gibbes and the maid, Anna Utkina, to take correspondence to the post office.[13] Anastasia got her friend Ekaterina Zborovskaya to write to the Romanov servant Anna Demidova, the idea being Demidova would be under less stringent scrutiny. Anastasia also sent off some of her own letters without submitting them to Pankratov.[14] She made little attempt to conceal from the outside world where the Romanovs were being confined – earlier, she had even written to Zborovskaya naming Governor's House, indicating the rooms they occupied and including a photo of the building as seen from the road.[15] She could hardly have done more to explain the practical requirements for a rescue attempt – the Romanovs were trying to keep all their options open.

Nicholas appreciated the ways that Pankratov contained the troubles that arose from the guard detachment. This was an uphill task and both Pankratov and Kobylinski were disconcerted by the decline in discipline and order. Soldiers frequently complained about the standard of canteen cooking. They noticed that the Romanovs often left meat on their plates – and they did not see why 'Nikolashka', as they called the emperor, should receive such indulgence. They objected to having to sleep on boards whereas he had a comfortable bed. They were also upset about the fact that they were paid less well than they had been before coming to Tobolsk. When the financial guarantees given to them in August 1917 were rendered obsolete by the October Revolution, they threatened to go out and rob the local shops. Kobylinski prudently increased their pay and improved their meals.[16] Although this calmed things down for a while, the resentment soon returned. Some of the soldiers just for fun carved lewd words on to the swings used by the Romanov daughters.[17]

Meanwhile, political agitation was on the increase in the detachment as the Socialist-Revolutionaries, who had always been active, experienced a challenge from a veteran political exile called Pisarevski who edited the Social-Democratic newspaper *Rabochaya pravda* and was chairman of the Tobolsk Soviet. Kobylinski, failing to appreciate that the Bolshevik–Menshevik split meant little in Tobolsk, wrongly designated him an out-and-out Bolshevik. Pisarevski gave credence to stories that the Romanovs were trying to escape. Politics in the region were in turmoil, and the Bolshevik-led West Siberian Regional Soviet Executive Committee in Omsk repeatedly demanded that the imperial family should be consigned to prison. Tobolsk itself had yet to fall under the exclusive power of the soviets and still had the provincial governor appointed by the Provisional Government. Pisarevski, if not a Bolshevik, was sympathetic to Sovnarkom and took it upon himself to assert 'soviet power'. He went to Freedom House to demand to see the emperor after hearing a story to the effect that he had fled or escaped the night before. This was pure fantasy – as Pankratov firmly pointed out, all the Romanovs in Tobolsk had attended church that morning.[18]

Pisarevski, however, refused to give up. Although he accepted that the Romanovs were still in place, he was convinced that Pankratov was not to be trusted. In one of his discourses to the detachment, he denounced him as a 'counter-revolutionary'.[19]

Olga and Tatyana went down with fever on 14 January – New Year's Day in the old Russian calendar. The doctors suspected German measles and the family walked to Mass at the Church of the Annunciation without the two young women. The diagnosis was confirmed next day even though they both felt somewhat better twenty-four hours later. Alexei caught the infection on 16 January, as did Maria twenty-four hours later. Nicholas was stoical about this turn of events. He was much more shaken by growing signs of rudeness in the 2nd Riflemen's

Regiment – the troops of the 4th Regiment appeared more agreeable.[20] They were calling for a daily vodka and a pay rise, and such were the worries about the potential for disobedience that the authorities promised to increase their salary to 400 rubles a month.[21]

News came from Petrograd that Sovnarkom had abruptly closed down the Constituent Assembly on 19 January. Elections had duly taken place in November and the result was a drastic disappointment for the Bolshevik and Left Socialist-Revolutionary coalition, which polled no more than a quarter of the votes. The Socialist-Revolutionaries won more seats than any rival party. Bolsheviks pointed out that the candidates' lists had been drawn up before the organizational breakaway of the Left Socialist-Revolutionaries. This meant that the Socialist-Revolutionaries were better represented in the Assembly than they deserved. It was also the case that Sovnarkom's decrees on peace and land had yet to register their full impact before the ballot was completed. Nonetheless, these were freely contested elections on the basis of universal adult suffrage – and they had happened under supervision by Soviet officials. When the Constituent Assembly met on 18 January, the Socialist-Revolutionary leader Viktor Chernov claimed the right to form a government, and a public demonstration was arranged in support. Next day Sovnarkom ordered the termination of the proceedings. This was done by sailors from the Kronstadt naval base whose anarchist leader, Anatoli Zheleznyakov, brusquely announced: 'The guard is tired!'

Lacking the troops and weapons to resist, Chernov and other Socialist-Revolutionary leaders decamped to Samara in the Volga region and established an alternative government styled as the Committee of Members of the Constituent Assembly (or Komuch in its Russian acronym). As they set up an administration and assembled their own People's Army, they aimed to seize power from Sovnarkom and reclaim the rights of elected Assembly deputies. From Samara they and their forces spread out to other Volga cities. Chernov chased out the Bolsheviks before realizing his plan to advance on the Russian capital. In the first months of 1918 this was the main threat to 'soviet power', a threat that was headed by socialists who challenged the legitimacy of the October Revolution.

As Pankratov was aware, such a sequence of events undermined his entire standing at Freedom House in Tobolsk. He had agreed to be commissar only until such time as the Constituent Assembly met in the capital. Sovnarkom had dispersed the Assembly and abolished all bodies associated with the Provisional Government. Since it had been Kerensky who appointed him, Pankratov concluded that his duties and usefulness were at their end.[22] His logic was confirmed when the Tobolsk deputies to the Assembly returned from Petrograd. Inside the guard detachment, moves were initiated to elect new commanders as well as a new soldiers' committee. The Soviet authorities in the capital gave their own stimulus. They had never felt complacent about Tobolsk since it was almost a town without Bolsheviks. This was why they empowered the West Siberian Regional Soviet Executive Committee in Omsk to oversee the situation. Omsk was formally in charge of the whole region inside the Soviet organizational hierarchy and Sovnarkom was asking it to bring the town under regular control with particular attention to Freedom House.

But in revolutionary conditions nothing could ever be quite so simple. Some of the detachment's units were all too eager to see the back of Pankratov whereas others hoped to persuade him to stay on. This sharp dispute, however, only strengthened Pankratov's determination. It was time, he believed, to leave.[23]

He therefore handed over his resignation to the soldiers' committee on 24 January 1918, stating that he knew that there would be more trouble if he stayed. Committee chairman Kireev confirmed his agreement with Pankratov's reasoning in an official affidavit.[24] Pankratov had spent most of his life subject to the arbitrary will of authority. If anything untoward happened to the imperial family, he wanted proof that it was not his fault. As soon as he had resigned, he went to take his leave of Nicholas.[25] Both he and Nicholas knew the consequences would be unhelpful for the Romanovs. Nicholas wrote confidentially and in English to his mother: 'The man who was over us has at last been removed away by our soldiers. We have only got our dear colonel [Kobylinski], who came here with us. He does not read our letters nor those that we get from you; he always brings them himself to pretend before others that things go on as they used to.'[26] This was less than crystal-clear English, perhaps because it was meant to keep the contents secret from prying Bolsheviks if they happened to intercept the letter. Probably Nicholas also wanted to lay down a suitable record for posterity.

It was a day of raucous change as the soldiers' committee flexed its authority by ordering Sophie Buxhoeveden out of the Kornilov house.[27] Buxhoeveden was unpopular with the troops. A bout of appendicitis had originally prevented her from accompanying the

Romanovs to Tobolsk. After her operation, she made the trip alone on a train that was full of unruly soldiers, some of whom wandered down the corridors of her carriage shouting 'Death to the bourgeois!' When she presented herself in Tobolsk on 5 January 1918, the guard unit on duty for a while refused to let her in. Apparently the troops objected to her fine apparel, especially her grey overcoat.[28] She had no choice but to move into lodgings with a Miss Mather, a friend of her mother's in the town.[29]

The soldiers' committee also lost no time in ordering Pankratov and Nikolski out of the Kornilov house.[30] The two men were flummoxed by this peremptory behaviour. Tatyana Botkina overheard Nikolski saying: 'We never thought that we'd be leaving before you did.' Nikolski was carrying a small suitcase and wearing a 'grandiose, shaggy black high hat that made him look more than ever like a robber'. He was not in a good mood. When asked where he and Pankratov were heading, he replied: 'We don't know. We'll be looking for some little corner to tend to our feelings of resentment!'[31] Pankratov and Nikolski stayed in Tobolsk for another month before making for Chita, where they arrived in March 1918.[32] The Romanovs put a brave face on the situation. They appreciated the fact that there was more light in the Tobolsk winter than they had had in Tsarskoe Selo, and Alexei built tunnels in the snow and played at crawling through them.[33] All they could do was hope for the best.

On 28 January, Ensign Pavel Matveev and the leader of the soldiers' committee, Kireev, an NCO in the 1st Riflemen's Regiment, decided to impose the guard detachment's authority on the situation. Kireev moved his bed into Freedom House itself and set himself up in comfort in the meeting room there. This disturbed and affronted the Romanovs. Their bow-legged stoker Georgi, known to everyone as Zhorzhik, loosed a volley of curses at Kireev and threatened to throw both him and his bed out on to the street. The real power, however, lay with the soldiers. For them, Kireev had broken with the democratic spirit of the times. If they had to rough it in the adjacent garrison, why should he be any different?[34] They replaced him with Matveev alone, who took a room across the road at the Kornilov house and put up a sign that said: 'Quaters of comrade Pavel Matveevich Matveev'. Someone must have pointed out that he had misspelled the word 'quarters', and soon a modest sign appeared stating simply 'Citizen P. M. Matveev'. Later, when he secured promotion, he tried to improve his education by buying a globe and some books and by taking lessons with local teachers.[35]

The guard detachment sought guidance from Moscow and sent a telegram requesting the dispatch of a Bolshevik commissar. Meanwhile it placed additional restrictions on the family's right to take the air unsupervised. The soldiers themselves soon grew tired with enforcing the order, and the Romanovs were formally permitted to exercise for two hours twice a week without military surveillance.[36] But attendance at church was banned at the same time and the family was no longer permitted its walks to the Church of the Annunciation.[37] The Romanovs knew that the conditions of their captivity were likely to worsen, and the entire family shared a sense of growing danger.[38]

Sovnarkom held one of its rare discussions of the Romanov question on 29 January 1918.[1] It entirely omitted, though, to add to its recent instructions about Tobolsk. Pankratov's unilateral decision to resign had no impact on the central authorities, who felt they had already done enough by prescribing a stricter regime at Freedom House and handing oversight to the West Siberian Regional Soviet Executive Committee in Omsk. This still left Sovnarkom with the problem of deciding what to do in the longer term. The agreed preference was to bring Nicholas to the capital and put him on public trial. Sovnarkom's idea was to use the judicial proceedings as a way of exposing the abuses of power and privilege under the tsarist order. Nicholas had been the fount of all political authority. The Constituent Assembly elections had shown that a majority of men and women in Russia and its borderlands rejected Bolshevism. Sovnarkom obviously had to popularize its purposes to greater effect, and Nicholas's trial was intended as a means to this end. Lenin and his fellow people's commissars badly needed to publicize the rationale for their seizure of power and rally support for the socialist order that they intended to extend all over Russia and then on to Europe.

Despite projecting subversion and revolutionary war in Germany, however, Sovnarkom had to comply with the terms of their negotiations with the Central Powers. Once the armistice had come into force on the Eastern Front, the next stage was to exchange diplomatic representatives between Petrograd and Berlin. Both sides found this distasteful. The Soviet authorities despised the German elite as imperialists; Germany's ministers and commanders regarded Bolsheviks as the revolutionary scum of the earth. But Lenin glimpsed a chance to propagate the Marxist cause by sending a mission to Berlin, and Erich Ludendorff, Germany's de facto military leader, sought to ensure that Russia fell under his control while he tackled the Allied armies on the Western Front. Diplomatic missions from Germany and Austria-

Hungary reached Petrograd in the night of 28–29 December 1917 and stayed at three of the city's finest hotels. Their fellow residents included the British, French and American officials who were attached to their own countries' diplomatic missions.[2] While the Germans strove to browbeat the Soviet government into signing a separate peace on the Eastern Front, Allied emissaries were arguing that Russia's interests lay in resuming operations against the German armies. With the outcome of the Great War at stake, the belligerent powers allowed the Romanov question to fall off their agenda for action.

Sovnarkom meanwhile recognized that their Romanov plan might go awry. Though few people in spring 1917 had lamented the monarchy's overthrow, Lenin and others knew that this could easily change. Rural households in particular might object to Nicholas being subjected to cross-examination, and it was quite possible that there would be a surge of sympathy for the ex-emperor. Sovnarkom also saw the possibility of controversy about whatever sentence might be imposed. If millions of peasants were capable of feeling sorry for Nicholas, caution had to be exercised about his future treatment. Was he to be executed or imprisoned? And if imprisoned, for how long? Only Sovnarkom could take these decisions, but Lenin saw no necessity for swift action. This was a time when the governing coalition of Bolsheviks and Left Socialist-Revolutionaries was debating whether or not to sign a separate peace with Germany in the Great War. Lenin was in favour of signature but he was in the minority both in Sovnarkom and in the Bolshevik Central Committee. The question of war or peace predictably took priority over the Romanov question. Sovnarkom resolved only to make a start by getting Nikolai Alexeev, the Left Socialist-Revolutionary who served as Deputy People's Commissar of Agriculture, to provide it with the resolutions that had been passed about the imperial family at the recent All-Russia Congress of Peasants' Deputies. Sovnarkom wanted to take soundings of rural opinion.[3]

Alexeev reported back on 20 February 1918 when the Romanov question was top of the agenda and he was accompanied by Moisei Uritski, who headed the Petrograd branch of the new political police known as the Cheka. After further discussion, Sovnarkom resolved to require the People's Commissariat of Justice and two representatives from the Congress of Soviets of Peasants' Deputies to prepare investigative material on Nicholas. The timing of Nicholas's transfer from Tobolsk was still postponed until such time as Sovnarkom reviewed the entire question, but the process was at last picking up speed and urgency in the central Soviet leadership.[4]

For the time being, nothing much ensued except for a budgetary order by People's Commissar for State Property and Left Socialist-Revolutionary Vladimir Karelin, who telegrammed on 23 February 1918 to the effect that Sovnarkom could no longer afford to keep the Romanovs in their current comfort. From then onwards the state subsidy would be fixed at a monthly rate of 600 rubles per person. No allowance would be made for the retinue. Nicholas had to choose between firing some of his retainers and drawing on his own funds to continue to pay them, and he asked Tatishchev, Dolgorukov and Gilliard to work out how to deal with the situation. After a painful discussion they concluded that there was no alternative to a numerical reduction of the retinue. The emperor gave his consent, and it was decided that those who lacked private means or could not be kept on his payroll would have to leave the house.[5] The change was planned to start on 1 March.[6] Gilliard would never forget the time when butter and coffee became household luxuries.[7] The emperor got rid of twelve of his staff; he also reduced the pay of all those who remained.[8]

The dismissed individuals reacted with a bout of heavy drinking – there was still plenty of alcohol at Freedom House. Some of the servants got so drunk that they crawled on all fours past the imperial family's quarters to get to their own rooms, where they collapsed in a stupor.[9] It was yet another stage in the degradation of morale. Until then the retinue had stuck to traditional standards of behaviour, but if their services were no longer required, they saw no obligation to defer to such expectations.

Alexandra hoped to ease the problems of unemployment for departing servants by paying them for a further three months. When she looked at the accounts, however, it was clear that she lacked the funds for this. Her solution was to reduce the salaries of the retained staff by a third over the same period and to use what was left over to pay the individuals who were being fired, and at the same time she aimed to make further economies to compensate for the losses suffered by those who remained with the family.[10] As she and Gilliard examined the books, they discovered that the holes in the budget were deeper than she had imagined.[11] She implored Gilliard to explain the situation to the other retainers. Inevitably, he met with a storm of discontent. The staff were furious about the cutting of their salaries, even though they were still being well fed and still had a roof over their heads in a comfortable residence.[12] Loyalty to the imperial family was being eroded. Tatyana Botkina noted that several people in the retinue began to submit improbable expense claims and take their pick from food parcels intended for the Romanovs.[13]

Supporters outside Freedom House secretly helped to prop up Nicholas's budget. Vladimir Shtein, the former vice-governor of Mogilëv, had been out to Tobolsk in January 1918 and returned to Moscow telling monarchists about Nicholas's financial distress. Shtein collected 250,000 rubles before going back to Tobolsk and handing over the money to Tatishchev and Dolgorukov.[14] Nicholas caught a glimpse of him on the street outside. He wrote gratefully in his diary on 26 March 1918 about 'a decent sum from the good people of our acquaintance'. Shtein also brought tea and books for use by the Romanovs.[15]

The family had no information about what was being planned for them in the longer term. They did, though, know about one discussion in the capital that would affect everybody. On 23 February 1918 the Bolshevik Central Committee at last assented to Lenin's argument that a separate peace was the only practical way to save the October Revolution.[16] Since December, Lenin had led a minority of its members in advocating acceptance of German terms for Russian withdrawal from the war. He met with resistance from the majority. For these, there was no point in being Bolsheviks if it meant signing a deal with Europe's most rapacious military and economic power. Many of them could see plainly enough that Russia was on the brink of inevitable defeat on the Eastern Front. Indeed, the old Russian Army had voted with its feet and left the trenches. There was no real front any longer, and the Germans could rampage on Petrograd whenever they wanted. Such was the danger that it had been decided to transfer the capital to Moscow, and arrangements were made for trains to transport the Soviet government and most of its leaders as a matter of urgency.

The treaty was signed on 3 March at Brest-Litovsk, near to the Eastern Front. Lenin secured a 'breathing space' for Sovnarkom, but it came at the price of driving the Left Socialist-Revolutionaries out of the governing coalition and splitting the Bolsheviks in two. Under the treaty's terms, Sovnarkom gave up all claims of sovereignty over the western borderlands of the former Russian Empire. The Germans surged into Ukraine and beyond, occupying Crimea, the Don province and the North Caucasus. They marched even into Rostov in southern Russia.

The Romanovs were not taken by surprise, despite the fact that *Pravda* was not one of the newspapers that they read. When Lenin had seemed enveloped in a hopeless struggle against the odds to persuade the Bolsheviks about the benefits of a separate peace, Alexandra felt instinctively that he would eventually get his way. She wrote: 'The Germans are at Pskov. Peace will be concluded on the most terrible, shameful, ruinous terms for Russia.'[17] She had never been good at political prediction. This time, for once, she was proved absolutely right. Nicholas recalled that Alexandra had often been accused of conspiring against the country's interests. Now he himself asked: 'Who exactly is it who's the traitor?' The Brest-Litovsk treaty appeared to him a disgrace for Russia and a betrayal of the Western Allies. After dinner on 19 March he exclaimed: 'It's such a shame on Russia and the equivalent of suicide! I would never have believed that Kaiser Wilhelm and the German government could stretch out their hands to these wretches who have betrayed their country!'

Nicholas's distress was obvious to everyone. Gilliard later recalled: 'The Brest-Litovsk treaty deeply affected him and so depressed him that it had an effect on his physical well-being. From that moment onwards he aged a great deal. All of us observed in Tobolsk how he had a fearful pallor and big pockets below his eyes and his beard turned sharply grey.'[18]

Alexandra felt the same about Brest-Litovsk; she felt that only divine intervention could remedy the situation. On 19 March 1918 she wrote to Madame Syroboyarskaya:

> What times are these? What lies ahead? It's a shameful peace. It's a total horror what has been reached in a single year. Their sole achievement is to have destroyed everything. The army is being annihilated at full tilt, so how to resist the enemy? A humiliating peace. But God is higher than everything and perhaps He will do something about it where people are simply incapable. Something will happen to save things. Being under the yoke of the Germans is worse than [under] the Tartar yoke. No, the Lord won't permit such injustice and will put everything to rights.[19]

Alexandra was focusing on the future for Russia. It did not yet occur to her or Nicholas that the treaty might have consequences for the entire Romanov family. Sovnarkom's relations with Germany were in fact about to affect every aspect of Russian public affairs. When Bolshevik leaders came back to what to do about the Romanovs, the German factor was always going to be to the fore in their considerations. And, very quietly, the danger was increasing.

22. RESCUE PLANS

Monarchist organizations had been astonished and demoralized by the fall of the dynasty, and the tide of events in the year 1917 moved in a direction entirely opposite to their purposes. They recognized that any attempt at rescuing the Romanovs from the Alexander Palace in Tsarskoe Selo would have been suicidal because of the large local garrison that was full of soldiers who hated Nikolashka. The Petrograd Soviet would have mobilized them to catch and arrest the family and their liberators. No group of conspirators was readying itself to make a move. Monarchism was an idea and not yet a movement.

The transfer of the Romanovs to Tobolsk, followed by the October Revolution, had stirred a handful of monarchists out of their months of passivity. But although they itched to do something decisive, it was never clear how they imagined that they would carry out a rescue of the imperial family. The risks were enormous. If ever they penetrated Freedom House, the guard detachment would resist and there would be much bloodshed. Pursuit, furthermore, would be inevitable in the event that the rescuers managed to make off with the imperial family. There was no chance of using river transport north to the Arctic Ocean or south to Tyumen until the spring thaw. In the winter months the sole travel option was by horse-drawn carriage or sleigh. If the party took the roads to either Tyumen or Omsk, Red forces would easily intercept them as soon as the Tobolsk Soviet raised the alarm about what was happening. The other possibility was for any rescue party to head for the forests across the river to the west of the town, but if they were to take this option, they would still have to decide where to go next. Cities and towns were full of enemies. Escape from Freedom House would be just the start of the difficulties.

The most active figure in the monarchy's cause after the February Revolution was Nikolai E. Markov, widely known as Markov-II, who had headed the Union of the Russian People before 1917 and had been a Duma deputy since 1907. Bulky of girth and long-haired, he cut a striking figure. A virulent anti-Semite, he jokingly used 'Goy' as his pseudonym in newspaper articles. Markov-II was a fanatical believer in autocracy, and his chief criticism of Nicholas in power was that he yielded too many times to liberal political opinion; he refused to accept that the February Revolution was irreversible. He saw Nicholas's rescue and restoration to power as an urgent requirement.

The banker and sugar manufacturer Karl Yaroshinski seems to have supplied a sum of 175,000 rubles for the schemes that were being concocted by monarchist groups.[1] Yaroshinski was a dynamic financier who accrued a vast fortune in time of war. He owned the controlling shares in five big banks and became acquainted with the imperial family through his funding of the convalescent hospitals where Alexandra and her daughters worked as nurses until the February Revolution.[2] When Kerensky became minister-chairman, Yaroshinski approached him with a projected initiative for the restoration of the country's depleted finances. He offered to provide assistance from his own resources, doubtless with an eye to making a future profit for himself while doing his best for Russia. Kerensky passed on the project for scrutiny in the Ministry of Finances, which quickly rejected it – and Yaroshinski disappeared from public view.[3] When the Bolsheviks seized power in Petrograd, he allowed Markov-II to bend his ear about his schemes to liberate the Romanovs.

Markov-II had written to the empress in the Tsarskoe Selo days using Alexandra's confidante Yulia Den as a courier. When the Romanovs were transferred to Tobolsk, he sent a trusted officer from the Crimean Regiment to seek them out with a view to organizing a rescue. His hope was to involve Anna Vyrubova but she declined to cooperate with him and objected to the fact that Markov-II had already sent an army officer to west Siberia. Vyrubova thought Markov-II was complicating her own efforts to secure the release of the Romanovs; and Boris Solovëv, who headed her operation based in Tyumen, took steps that prevented Markov-II's emissary from moving on to Tobolsk.[4]

Solovëv, an army officer, was twenty-eight years old in 1918 and had the reputation of being a fervent monarchist. A tempestuous man, he had come close to physical blows with the Provisional Government's deputy Minister of Trade and Industry, Pëtr Palchinski, who annoyed him by talking of the arbitrariness of rule under Nicholas II.[5] Rather than return to his regiment, he began to work for Yaroshinski, whom he and others persuaded to subsidize a mission to Tobolsk.[6] Solovëv, however, was not just a professed enthusiast for the defunct monarchy but also a past follower of Grigori Rasputin. Through his acquaintance with Rasputin he courted and married his daughter Matrёna. For Nicholas and Alexandra, this was a wonderful recommendation. Many Russian monarchists still felt very differently about Rasputin; but in the political disruptions of 1917, when few were bold enough to speak up for Nicholas, Solovёv had gained some acceptance as a man who had the Romanovs' interests at heart. He also had the military training to carry out hazardous projects which daunted former members of the imperial court. Young and energetic, Solovёv appeared ready to sacrifice his personal security for the salvation of Nicholas and his family.

On 20 January 1918 he left Petrograd on a journey to Tobolsk that took him via Ekaterinburg and Tyumen with baggage containing money, chocolate, perfumes, linen and presents from people who knew the Romanovs; he also took three packets of letters from Anna Vyrubova and Vladimir and Evgenia Voeikov – the Voeikovs had belonged to the imperial retinue before the February Revolution, he as court commandant and she as a lady-in-waiting.[7] Solovёv carefully disguised his identity and while in Tyumen lived under the alias Stanislav Korzhenevski.[8]

He was later to claim that he passed the money he had received for the Romanovs to the valet Alexei Volkov who handed it over to the empress.[9] Pleased by the gift, she started a correspondence with Solovёv.[10] Volkov brought out a message from her advising him to liaise with Father Alexei Vasilev.[11] It was probably to Solovёv that Alexandra made the following request on 6 February 1918: 'Let me know what you think about our situation. Our common desire is to achieve the possibility of living quietly, like an ordinary family, outside politics, fighting and intrigues. Write frankly because I will accept your letter with belief in your sincerity.'[12] Solovёv refused to show undue optimism: 'I'm deeply grateful for your expression of feelings and trust . . . Generally, the situation is very difficult and could become critical. I am convinced that what is needed is assistance from devoted friends, or a miracle, so that all may end well and that your desire for a quiet life may be fulfilled. Your sincerely devoted B[oris].'[13]

Around this time, Solovёv decided to walk past Freedom House in the daylight hours. As he had intended, he was spotted by the Romanovs – Anastasia, Maria and Tatyana were standing by a window at that moment and looking down on the street. The empress wrote him a note which a maid passed on to him. His previous message to her had been obscure about the prospects of rescue and Alexandra could see no hope of escape except by divine intervention:

You have confirmed my fears: I thank you for your honesty and courage. Friends are either somewhere distant and unknown or else they do not exist, and I pray tirelessly to the Lord and put my hopes in Him alone. You talk of a miracle, but isn't it a miracle that the Lord has sent you here to us. May God keep you – gratefully, A.[14]

Alexandra had never met Solovëv but followed her instincts and placed her trust in him. She was desperate. Solovëv was one of the few people outside the court retinue who had succeeded in breaking the cordon around the family's life and circumstances. In her eyes, he was the perfect knight, willing to sacrifice himself for the dynastic cause and the Christian faith.

A number of people in Tobolsk and elsewhere judged Solovëv less benignly. Even his wife objected to him. It was always a difficult marriage and Matrëna suffered frequent beatings.[15] She also complained about his attitude to money. In her diary on 2 March 1918 she mentioned Yaroshinski as one of her husband's financial donors: 'I know how much money that Yeroshinski [sic] gave to Borya [i.e. Boris] but he doesn't want to give me any money. He believes that his money belongs to him alone and my money is his as well.'[16] Solovëv was almost certainly pocketing some of the funds being sent to relieve or rescue the Romanovs. He seems to have delivered only 35,000 rubles, a small proportion of Yaroshinski's 175,000 rubles, to the empress.[17] In later years Yaroshinski testified that he had had no direct dealings with Solovëv. Yaroshinski, of course, may not have been privy to knowledge of the exact chain of financial transfers after the money left Petrograd; and it is not known whether it was transferred in a lump sum or in separate tranches. Even so, he was regarded as a swindler by those of the imperial family's well-wishers who observed at close range the operation that he and Father Alexei Vasilev established in Tobolsk.

Solovëv was not a man who liked to be crossed. He was also devious, and whenever any of his military recruits challenged his authority, he covertly denounced them on spurious grounds to the Tobolsk Soviet, which was happy to take them into custody.[18] Tatyana Botkina despised him and had no higher opinion of Vasilev, a man of the cloth who seemed more interested in making money than in achieving freedom for the Romanovs; she surmised that Vasilev probably also manoeuvred so as to leave himself in a good enough light to benefit if ever Nicholas returned to the throne.[19]

It was usual for Solovëv and Vasilev to exaggerate the size and potential of their 'organization' – and Vasilev, a heavy drinker, talked in his cups of a plan to liberate the family.[20] The two of them claimed to have infiltrated 300 ex-officers into Tobolsk. While accepting that some such recruits existed in the town, Tatyana Botkina questioned whether there really were as many well-trained men as Solovëv and Vasilev reported.[21] In her opinion, Solovëv and Vasilev were no better than liars and fantasists. When she encountered one of their recruits, he told about how he had arrived in Tyumen and was living disguised as a manual labourer.[22] Botkina thought it significant that he never reached Tobolsk, and she concluded that the imperial family's hopes were being artificially boosted. It was her belief that Count Yakov Rostovtsev was the only financial backer who successfully enabled one of his men to travel north from Tyumen and transmit 80,000 roubles to Dolgorukov via Dr Botkin. (This appears to have been the sum of money that Dolgorukov would take with him to Ekaterinburg in April.) The Botkins also became acquainted with an active monarchist who lived for several months in Tobolsk; but it turned out that he belonged to a group that had completely omitted to formulate a serious plan to rescue the Romanovs.[23] Indeed, there was a growing suspicion that Solovëv was not merely a swindler but an agent working for the Germans. Proof was unforthcoming until 1919 when he was found in possession of German intelligence papers, and Botkina came to the conclusion that he had been aiming to destroy the imperial family.[24]

Nor did Solovëv or Vasilev make a good impression on a young ensign, Konstantin Melnik, who stayed in Tobolsk in September 1917 and again in May 1918. He formed the opinion that their 'organization' was a sham. As far as he could see, they held back much of the money intended for the Romanovs and did nothing to arrange for their liberation. Reportedly, Vasilev asked for and received 14,000 rubles for purposes that were not disclosed to Melnik, but Melnik felt sure that Vasilev was up to no good.[25]

Sergei Markov was another young member of the armed forces who put himself at Markov-II's disposal in service of the monarchist cause. In the last days before the abdication, he had inveigled his way into the Alexander Palace at Tsarskoe Selo and asked the empress how he could help her.[26] As a proud officer in the Crimean Cavalry, he regarded the mutinies in the February Revolution as treason.[27] Markov set off for Tobolsk in March 1918 under the false identity of a merchant by name of Marchenko to formulate a proper rescue plan.[28] He ignored a warning from his group's leader, Markov-II, that funds were very stretched for any such venture. In Tyumen he searched out Solovëv, who had already established contact with the Romanovs. Everything that he heard from Solovëv convinced him that he could pull off his assignment. By a relay of horse-drawn sleighs he arrived in Tobolsk and took rooms in an almost empty hotel close to the centre, where Bolsheviks were his main co-residents. While they worked for the destruction of private commerce in Russia, he pretended to be a simple trader: he had to be careful about how he behaved.[29]

Markov quietly introduced himself to Sophie Buxhoeveden and showed her the packages he had brought from Petrograd. Buxhoeveden passed them to the valet Volkov, who took them into Freedom House.[30] Markov introduced himself to the local diocesan, Bishop Germogen, the day after attending a church service and explained his purposes in Tobolsk. Germogen told him: 'God will reward you for this.'[31] Markov also contacted Father Alexei at the Abalak monastery, who had the Romanov servant Kirpichnikov lodging with him.[32]

Kirpichnikov was one of the lowliest figures in the entourage; he skivvied in the kitchen and looked after the pigs that the Romanovs bought after coming to Tobolsk. (He kept pigs of his own and marked out a piece of the yard for them.) A dishevelled man of exceptional strength, he was loved for his loyalty, but the residents hated the fact that he cooked for the family and the animals using the same pots and pans. Kirpichnikov was oblivious of what other people thought, but some days the smell became quite overpowering, and the Romanovs and their retinue fled upstairs to the first-floor rooms, closing the doors behind them. Gibbes, a fastidious man, could not bear to stay in Freedom House when Kirpichnikov was preparing food for the pigs – rather than put up with the pungent fumes, he would claim to be suffering from the flu and take to his room, sitting for whole wintry days with the windows open. But the guard detachment soldiers trusted Kirpichnikov, and he was able to bring letters and sweets into Freedom House for the Romanovs.[33]

The empress had vivid memories of Markov and responded gaily to his letter and books. She sent him a gift through Father Alexei: 'To Little M., many thanks from the Chief and a present from their Highnesses, a big ivory pipe.' The priest explained that Alexandra had not known what to give him but hoped that he would remember her whenever he lit up.[34] Alexandra soon also indicated her concerns for Markov's safety, since he was likely to be recognized by both Kobylinski and Bitner who had seen him in Tsarskoe Selo and might decide to inform on him. Although Kobylinski was helpful to the Romanovs, he was one of the Provisional Government's appointees and ultimately – in Alexandra's opinion – not to be trusted. Her advice to Markov was to return to Solovëv, who by then was living in Pokrovskoe.[35] But caution was alien to Markov. Having swapped messages with the empress, he strolled for a while outside Freedom House so that the Romanovs might see him. By chance Alexandra, standing at the balcony, spotted him. On 25 March 1918 she wrote in her diary: 'Saw my ex-Crimean Markov pass and Shtein too.'[36]

Yet this was as near as Markov got to a rescue attempt. Bishop Germogen was not surprised because he had already concluded that monarchism in Russia remained poorly organized, having been blown to the winds by the revolution that had swept the Romanovs from power.[37] Markov was bold, even brazen, but he could do no more than prance about in the street outside Freedom House.

Irritated by the inactivity of fellow monarchists, Markov continually planned for the liberation of the Romanovs. As he saw it, there were several possibilities. One was to assemble as many cavalry officers as Markov-II could make available and move them at top speed to Tobolsk. He reasoned that the town's geographical isolation would work in his favour, and he counted on help from monarchists based in Tyumen. There were also sympathizers in the Red armed forces whom Markov thought he could organize to carry out a raid on Freedom House. Another idea was to foment a fictitious peasant uprising against the Bolsheviks outside Tobolsk and exploit the ensuing emergency by bringing an armed force into the town and taking charge of the imperial family. Markov believed he could prepare for this by enabling monarchists to desert the Red Army and slip into hiding in Tobolsk until the critical moment. The point was to concentrate a decisive armed core near Freedom House.[38]

Nicholas, too, was looking for reasons to stay optimistic. He had a strong instinct that Kobylinski wished him well and put on a display of severity when under the eyes of the detachment guards.[39] The two of them got on well, for which Nicholas gave thanks in his diary: 'Kobylinski is my best friend.'[40] Tatyana Botkina surmised that support for the Romanovs was much more widely felt in Tobolsk than anyone dared to show; she told intimates of her confidence that Nicholas would find plenty of soldiers and ferrymen to help him if ever he undertook a practical attempt to escape captivity.[41] There was even a rumour that a group of riflemen under Ensign Malyshev had let Kobylinski know that if a rescue mission were to be organized while they were on guard duty, they would not intervene.[42] Alexandra drew on such suggestions, assuring family and retinue that the Freedom House detachment contained NCOs who were quietly sympathetic towards Nicholas and harboured a sense of guilt for what had been done to him. She pointed to the fact that they were secretly continuing to leave gifts of unleavened bread or flowers for the family.[43]

How, indeed, was this to be explained if everyone hated the Romanovs? But Alexandra was overlooking the fact that the former empire was a divided society and that many millions of citizens continued to detest Nicholas the Bloody or, at best, were indifferent to his fate. It was natural for the family to try to comfort itself with the idea that they were loved by most ordinary Russians. But their thoughts were out of touch with reality in revolutionary Russia.

23. THE RUSSIAN FUTURE

Throughout his time in captivity, Nicholas expressed no regrets about how he had ruled his lands. He and Alexandra passionately believed that Russia's military and political troubles were entirely the product of malign alien forces. In Nicholas's eyes, the February 1917 Revolution was an unmitigated national woe, and if ever he thought he could have behaved differently to prevent it, he kept such ideas to himself and instead took pride in having discharged his duty, as he explained to Gilliard: 'I swore at my accession to guard intact the form of government that I received from my father and to hand it on as such to my successor.'[1] After leaving Tsarskoe Selo, he never mentioned the abdication crisis again. The same was not true of Alexandra, who constantly had raw feelings about it and was convinced that he would not have relinquished the throne if she had been staying with him in Mogilëv rather than with the family. But she did not hold this against her husband. What had happened, had happened, and it was her responsibility to cope with things as they had turned out; her love for Nicholas remained as undiluted as her need for his love.

The Romanovs hated everything about the October Revolution and when they learned that the Soviet government had changed the calendar from the Julian to the Gregorian version in use across the rest of Europe, Nicholas was aghast. He woke up on 1 February only to find that it was already almost two weeks later. He disliked the idea of losing thirteen whole days and predicted: 'There'll be no end to misunderstandings and confusions.'[2]

Nicholas, however, was not moved to comment on any of the Soviet government's other new policies on politics and economics. It was a different matter when it came to questions about Germany, the war and Russian armed forces. On 20 February 1918 he wrote: 'Judging by the telegrams, war with Germany is resumed since the truce has run out of time; but it seems that we've nothing left at the front, the army has been demobilized, weapons and supplies have been tossed before the mercy of fate and the attacking enemy: shame and horror!'[3]

Nicholas shared the patriotic pain of military defeat; he could never imagine that anyone might not want to resist the Germans. His was a do-or-die mentality. Russia's honour, from his viewpoint, had been traduced. On 25 February he added: 'Today there arrived telegrams that announced that the Bolsheviks, or Sovnarkom as they call themselves, have to agree to peace on the humiliating terms of the German gov[ernment] in view of the fact that enemy forces are advancing and there's nothing to stop them. It's a nightmare.'[4]

But how did Nicholas or Alexandra explain Russia's disintegration? When talking to Gilliard, Nicholas blamed Kerensky for the army's collapse, even though Kerensky had not willed it to happen. He took a much darker view of Lenin and Trotsky, whom he saw as conscious traitors who had received large sums of money for their work for the Germans.[5] For him, the Brest-Litovsk treaty was a disgrace for Russia and a betrayal of the Western Allies. Nicholas, as the months passed, was oppressed by searing thoughts about military collapse, territorial disintegration and diplomatic humiliation. The army's dissolution in 1917 had given him as much grief as thoughts about his personal trauma. But he had never dreamed that a Russian government would sign a peace like the one that Lenin had insisted on – even Lenin called it 'obscene'.

Nicholas and Alexandra had utter contempt for Wilhelm, who they thought had placed himself outside the bounds of respectable behaviour.[6] There were some things that were indefensible even in the heat of war. Before 1917, Alexandra had said to the valet Volkov, 'He's an actor, an outstanding comic turn, a false person.' After the Brest-Litovsk treaty, she exclaimed: 'I know about his petty nature but I never thought he could sink down as far as coming to terms with the Bolsheviks. What a disgrace!'[7] As a native-born princess of Hesse, she had never had much time for the Hohenzollerns. Bitner witnessed her Tobolsk tirades against the Kaiser and his Germany. Alexandra explained to Kobylinski: 'People accuse me of loving the Germans. Nobody knows how much I hate Wilhelm for all the evil that he has brought upon my Motherland!' She stressed that she was referring to Russia and not to the country of her birth. The empress predicted that Germany too would soon fall apart as Russia had done – and she spoke with more than a touch of Schadenfreude. She wrote to General Alexander Syroboyarski, her ex-patient in the hospital at Tsarskoe Selo: 'In my opinion, this "contagious disease" will spread to Germany but will be much more dangerous and worse there, and I see in this the sole salvation for Russia.'[8]

When on 19 March Nicholas heard from Vasili Dolgorukov of a press report that the Germans were demanding guarantees of the health and safety of the Romanovs, he exploded: 'If this isn't a man-oeuvre to discredit me, it is still an injury that is being done to me!'[9] The whole family dissociated themselves from everything German. The daughters even gave away the presents that Kaiser Wilhelm had given them on a yachting trip.[10]

The Romanovs comforted themselves with fantasies about Russia's soldiery. Alexandra wrote to Anna Vyrubova:

> There's a strangeness in the Russian character – a person soon becomes foul, bad, cruel and irrational, but at the same time that person can become something else. It's called lack of character. Essentially they are big, uneducated children. It's well-known that in times of long wars all the passions become more accentuated. It's horrible what's being done as they kill, lie, steal and imprison – but one has to endure, cleanse oneself and be reborn.[11]

After the Omsk Red Guards rioted, Klavdia Bitner lost patience when Alexandra declared that if only the officers showed some initia-tive, troops would obey.[12] Alexandra added: 'People say they're bad. But they're good. Just look at them. They look around and they smile. They're good.'[13] For Bitner, this was gibberish and she told Alexandra that she was out of touch with reality and had no idea about what the soldiers really thought about her. The fact that they behaved respectfully in the family's hearing meant nothing of importance. Whereas Alexandra believed that Russian soldiers were 'fine, simple, good', Bitner insisted that these same soldiers were treating their officers appallingly.[14]

Nobody, indeed, had spoken to Alexandra so forcefully since she came to Russia in 1894, and she could not hold back the tears. She bridled in particular at Bitner's claim that she was cut off from reality. Alexandra exclaimed that she knew what others said about her. They were talking in fiery generalities. As often happens in any dispute, neither woman was being entirely clear in her arguments. When she had time to reflect on what was said, Bitner assumed that Alexandra assumed that Bitner was criticizing her relationship with the late Ras-putin. This was obviously still a sore point for Alexandra.[15] In fact, Bitner was focusing on what had been happening in the armed forces.

She wanted to get her own point across once and for all by telling the empress that she had no comprehension of the difficulties that the army had experienced in the Great War. In Bitner's view, it was senseless to accentuate the contrast between officers and soldiers. On and on they argued and neither of them would give an inch. Upset and exhausted, they parted on bad terms that day, and Bitner declined to join the rest for dinner, pleading a headache. Alexandra sent a note asking her not to be angry with her: she had at last met her match.[16]

But the empress was never going to change her ways and simply could not stop talking, whatever the topic, as if she knew best. On religion, she was firm and demanding. The rest of the retinue understood this and suspended the Sunday night playlets – the 'spectacles', as they were called – at the start of Lent, and Gibbes dismantled the lighting arrangements.[17] The family began to fast in anticipation of Easter, and Alexandra expected everyone in the house to follow suit. Bitner, however, usually waited until Passion Week and explained that this remained her intention. Alexandra's displeasure was plain for all to see. But Bitner was no more willing to change her ways than Alexandra was.[18]

Bitner had a warmer opinion of Nicholas. From what she saw and heard in Freedom House, the emperor's prime objective was to live as a husband and father in the bosom of his family. In Bitner's view, he yearned for a quiet life and would never have agreed to return to the throne.[19] Gilliard was to counter that, at least for a while, Nicholas and Alexandra continued to hope that they would eventually rule again. This may have been why they abandoned their original aspiration to go into foreign exile, or perhaps they simply recognized that the Soviet leadership was never going to let them go. Nicholas often told Kobylinski of his horror that he and the family might be dispatched abroad.[20] The imperial couple were constant in their will to endure whatever fate inflicted on them, and it would appear that Alexandra confided in Gilliard: 'Our friend [Rasputin] had predicted all these sufferings, but said that after this whole Calvary there would follow a long and prosperous period of rest.'[21] The daughters, moreover, frequently talked about returning to Tsarskoe Selo. Olga was the exception; she seemed to sense that such dreams were unrealistic – and her father appeared to agree. In his heart of hearts Nicholas recognized that his days as monarch were over.[22]

This question interested Bitner, who quizzed young Alexei: 'What if you come to the throne?' Quick as a flash, he said: 'No, all that's finished!' Bitner asked: 'But what if it were to come to pass again that you were to be ruling?' Alexei gave an interesting reply: 'It will then be necessary to arrange things so that I know more of what is being done around me.' Had he heard his mother talking about how people had tricked his father? Was this the glimmering of his potential to be a more demanding – and more effective – ruler than Nicholas had been? Bitner thought so. In her opinion, Alexei already had ideas of his own. She asked what he would do with her if he became tsar. He said he would build a hospital for her to run and would keep everything in order.[23] Bitner also believed that he did not share the family's reverence for Rasputin. This was her conclusion after a minor incident when she taught Alexei at his bedside at a time of illness. On the table there usually stood a small framed picture of the holy man. It fell off one day and Bitner made to pick it up. Alexei told her not to bother. It obviously meant little to him, and she detected a hint of irony in his voice.[24]

If Alexei indeed no longer shared his parents' admiration for Rasputin, Nicholas and Alexandra themselves stuck firmly to the attitudes they had held for years. Nothing that had happened since March 1917 seemed to them to justify the end of tsarist rule. Being too proud to feel sorry for themselves, they prepared themselves to endure whatever life had in store for them.

24. COMRADES ON THE MARCH

Even the slimmest chance of liberation vanished on 26 March 1918, when, completely without warning, a 250-strong Red Guard detachment turned up in Tobolsk sent by the West Siberian Regional Soviet Executive Committee in Omsk.[1] Pierre Gilliard feared the worst. The Omsk troops were noisy and obstreperous, and their hatred of the dynasty was expressed in rowdy behaviour.[2] Alexandra refused to see things quite as bleakly as Gilliard and persuaded herself that some of new arrivals were monarchist officers in disguise, but this was speculation based on nothing more than hope: Gilliard was the one with an eye for hard reality.[3]

For hundreds of miles around Tobolsk, Omsk and Ekaterinburg were the two citadels of Bolshevism. Omsk was capital of the west Siberian region while Ekaterinburg was regional centre for the Urals, and there was much rivalry between them about the Romanov question.[4] The central authorities had devolved authority in these matters to Omsk for the simple reason that Tobolsk was in the west Siberia region, but Ekaterinburg prided itself on having greater revolutionary élan and wanted to take charge of the situation. The Bolsheviks in both cities did, however, agree that the current situation was intolerable. From their point of view, Tobolsk was enemy territory. It still had a soviet headed by Socialist-Revolutionaries and Mensheviks. The military detachment guarding the Romanovs had been put together from regiments that had served in Tsarskoe Selo. Kobylinski was an appointee of Kerensky and remained in post after Pankratov's departure.[5] Rumours were rife that the imperial family hoped to escape along the Trans-Siberian Railway to Japan. Their worry was that nobody in Tobolsk could be depended upon to stop them.[6]

While Ekaterinburg was debating about what to do, Omsk acted.[7] The detachment's head, Commissar V. D. Dutsman, arrived two days in advance of the main party and commandeered a room in the Kornilov house.[8] He had not been expected or invited. A tall man with grey-blue eyes and an inscrutable countenance, he had the demeanour of someone who knew how to be ruthless in the revolutionary cause (and indeed it was apparently he who later signed the death warrant of Bishop Germogen).[9] The other residents, moreover, looked askance at the fact that he was of Latvian-Jewish descent.[10] In the ensuing days he totally failed to restrain the Red Guards who had followed him from Omsk under the command of Commissar A. D. Demyanov and his deputy, Degtyarëv. Demyanov was an expellee from an Orthodox Church seminary; Degtyarëv had once been a cavalry ensign and, in his time at St Petersburg University, had belonged to the arch-reactionary Union of Archangel Michael.[11] Dutsman, Demyanov and Degtyarëv were a law unto themselves. A town that had avoided the turmoil of the big urban centres was plunged into chaos as the men from Omsk ran amok.

On 29 March 1918, they marched to Freedom House and confronted the guard detachment. At the risk of sparking an outbreak of violence, they demanded to enter the building.[12] Nobody knew how to cope with them. Talks between the two detachments brought some calm to the situation but the atmosphere remained volatile.

It was a relief to the Freedom House inmates when Dutsman indicated that his main immediate priority was to bring the Tobolsk Soviet under Bolshevik control and place it at the apex of power in the town. All the other public institutions were to be either abolished or else subordinated to 'soviet power'. Demyanov announced the closure of the old agencies of local government such as the town duma and the creation of a 'council of the people's economy'. It would not be enough to transform politics. Sleepy Tobolsk had to undergo the economic revolution that had started months earlier in other Russian urban centres.[13] While this was happening, Dutsman saw no point in disrupting the work of Kobylinski. Instead, he got himself made secretary of the town soviet, where he spent nearly all his time. Kobylinski observed developments from a distance, though he, too, was not without traces of anti-Semitism and he later complained that Bolshevization served to hand dominant authority to Jews.[14] But Dutsman left him alone, and Kobylinski did what he could to maintain a degree of tranquillity at Freedom House and shield the Romanovs from worrying as much as he himself did about the worsening situation.

Vladimir Kosarev, chairman of the West Siberian Regional Soviet Executive Committee, wrote to Lenin and Trotsky on 28 March 1918 from Omsk. It had been nearly two months since Sovnarkom had given him the duty to oversee Tobolsk politics. He had had his own local difficulties to resolve in Omsk before feeling able to dispatch a military detachment to Tobolsk, 400 miles away. Kosarev was a typical Bolshevik chieftain, brimming with revolutionary zeal and initiative, but Omsk's Red Guards were now in charge of the town, and Kosarev kept in touch with Dutsman, Demyanov and Degtyarëv by telegraph. What he learned was enough to convince him that Lenin and Sverdlov had underestimated the dangers of the situation. Sovnarkom had demobilized the imperial army before deciding what was to take its place. The guard detachment at Freedom House were from that old army, and Kosarev's solution was to replace it with troops from Omsk. He asked Lenin and Sverdlov to empower him to appoint fresh commissars and to inform those in post in Tobolsk to this effect.[15]

The scene in Tobolsk was even more turbulent than Kosarev could know from such a distance. More or less at the same time as his Omsk Red Guards burst into the town, fifty Red Guards came north from Tyumen. Nicholas was horrified, describing them as 'robber-Bolsheviks'. The Tyumen armed unit travelled in fifteen troikas bedecked with bells. Wherever they went, they caused a tremendous fuss and noise. The Tyumenites clearly had yet to learn habits of military discipline. If the Omsk Red Guards were disruptive, these newcomers created sheer pandemonium.[16] Kobylinski asked the empress to stop sitting out on the balcony for three days. There was a provisional discussion about moving the family to the safety of a church building on the town's main hill.[17] The news was increasingly alarming. Although Nicholas could not observe much from inside Freedom House, he could all too easily hear riflemen singing to their balalaikas till five o'clock in the morning.[18] The Tyumen Red Guards had pushed their way into the grounds and demanded the right to free victualling. The Omsk troops were no less alarmed than the men under Kobylinski's control; they united to throw out the intruders and the trouble subsided.[19] A week after arriving in Tobolsk, to everyone's satisfaction, the Tyumen Red Guards went back home.[20]

The Urals Regional Soviet Executive Committee had for weeks believed that it too should play a part. Kosarev had done too little since receiving responsibility from Sovnarkom, and the dangers in Tobolsk were ever-increasing. Alexander Beloborodov, in later years, said that there was a fear in Ekaterinburg that the Germans might exert pressure on Lenin to secure the imperial family's release. The Urals leaders set their face against any such outcome and were determined, if the need arose, to 'liquidate' Nicholas.[21] Already in February 1918, they were planning to govern Tobolsk through a troika under their deputy chairman, Boris Didkovski. The Ekaterinburg communists were sending one of their most accomplished figures. Didkovski was a former emigrant and a trained geologist who combined revolutionary fervour with a knowledge of the world outside Russia. After the October 1917 Revolution he held posts in the gold and platinum industry and was responsible for many of the economic nationalizations in Ekaterinburg – he used the city's telephone directory as an aid when deciding which enterprises to take into the state's hands.[22] The brief that he received in Ekaterinburg was to bring Tobolsk under control in collaboration with the West Siberian Regional Soviet Executive Committee in Omsk.[23]

And so, just days after the Omsk Red Guards appeared in Tobolsk, a 400-strong Red Guard detachment moved on the town from Ekaterinburg.[24] Beloborodov and Didkovski had put them under the command of Pavel Khokhryakov, who made the trip disguised as a merchant because the enemies of Bolshevism were many in western Siberia. Khokhryakov feigned that he was the fiancé of an Ekaterinburg Bolshevik woman whose mother lived in the neighbouring district of Yalutorovsk.[25] In reality Khokhryakov came from Vyatka peasant stock. As a young man he had served as a stoker on battleships in the imperial navy. Calm, steady and not given to boastfulness, he became one of the leading Bolsheviks in Ekaterinburg. He was one of those revolutionaries who got on with the practical tasks assigned to him. Although he was no orator, he inspired loyalty. Khokhryakov spoke softly but was harder than he seemed. The story was told that he later personally shot counter-revolutionaries brought to Ekaterinburg from Tobolsk and Omsk. Among them, it was said, was a priest who was the brother of Bishop Germogen. When the priest pleaded for his life and asked for the sentence to be commuted to hard labour, Khokhryakov's soothing words were: 'Don't be worried, old man. We aren't going to torture you. We'll shoot you and that will be it. Without any unnecessary suffering.'[26]

Khokhryakov had three deputies who arrived separately: Semën Zaslavski, Alexander Avdeev and Ivan Loginov. Avdeev – slim, short, ill-kempt and long-haired – was a lathe-turner in his late twenties who had worked at the same factory in Zlokazovo as Loginov. He claimed to have been imprisoned four times in Kresty prison.[27] Zaslavski was a Petrograd metalworker sent by the Central Committee to strengthen political work in the Urals, where he soon headed the Nadezhdin

Soviet.[28] A small troop of Red Guards was sent to them in early April. They too refrained from making the journey en masse: Tobolsk and its environs were enemy territory, and it would seem that Khokhryakov and his comrades were far from being comforted by what they found in the town. Indeed, Khokhryakov sent reports back to Ekaterinburg expressing his alarm about their first experiences.[29] The three leaders aimed to get rid of Omsk's influence and impose a chain of command stretching back to Ekaterinburg. Khokhryakov focused on winning authority in the Tobolsk Soviet. Avdeev's task was to gain trust among officials at Freedom House. Zaslavski was to concentrate his efforts on planning how to transfer Nicholas to Ekaterinburg and put him under the Urals leadership's control.[30] It was not going to be easy to realize these ambitions, and Zaslavski reported a cold reception both from Kobylinski and from the Tobolsk Soviet.[31]

But the Ekaterinburg team were bent on making a success of their mission and checks were carried out on everyone travelling out of Tobolsk.[32] They wanted to eliminate any possibility that Nicholas might escape northwards down the River Ob. An armed five-man unit was therefore sent to the district centre at Berëzov to set up traffic blocks. Other units were ordered to Golyshmanovo and to the routes that led to Omsk. The instruction was direct and unambiguous: anyone caught answering the description of the former emperor was to be shot. As often with decisions taken in Ekaterinburg, the implementation was somewhat dishevelled. The Berëzov unit was put under arrest by local authorities after making the long trip northwards. Meanwhile the Golyshmanovo unit was found to include men who, after they left Ekaterinburg, boasted that their task was simply to 'kill the Tsar'; they too were arrested. Wealthy merchants in both places took action against the suspicious interlopers.[33] The truth came home to Beloborodov and his comrades that if Tobolsk had nests of anti-Bolshevik activists, the surrounding area was even more dangerous. The idea of leaving the imperial family in that province made less and less sense.

Another account, it ought to be added, puts it a lot more violently. Two armed groups supposedly left Ekaterinburg to patrol the routes out of Tobolsk. The first one was indeed taken into custody in Berëzov. A second was sent by the Urals Regional Executive Committee to the south of Tobolsk, and it soon arrived in the tiny village of Goloputovskoe. Local residents killed them after discovering in whose name they acted.[34]

Tobolsk itself was seething with armed detachments from other towns even after the departure of the Red Guards of Tyumen, and Kobylinski was to admit that he could not keep pace with all the comings and goings.[35] Tensions between one armed detachment and another started to build again. Kobylinski's men felt under equal threat from both the Omsk and Ekaterinburg contingents, and the Omsk troops resented the Ekaterinburg Red Guards as troublemaking interlopers who had no right to lord it in western Siberia. Kobylinski felt himself to be piggy in the middle. Three Tobolsk Soviet deputies visited Freedom House to find out what was happening. This merely served to heighten the tension. There were also ructions over the Omsk detachment's pretensions to take charge of guarding the Romanovs.[36] At the same time, Dutsman and the other Omsk Red Guard leaders believed that they had every sanction from Sovnarkom to exert control. Fractious encounters occurred across the town as Bolshevik military units confronted each other. When Khokhryakov confronted the leaders from Omsk, they physically seized him and accused him of anti-revolutionary 'provocation'. Only after liaising on the direct line with the Urals Regional Soviet Executive Committee did his captors agree to release rather than execute him.[37]

There was talk among the Red Guard leadership about transferring the Romanovs to Tobolsk prison, and this became the Urals Soviet's policy. Kobylinski went post-haste to remonstrate with the Red Guards. When they rejected his claim that the Moscow authorities alone could take such a decision, he pointed out that they were anyway being impractical. If the imperial family were to be moved to the prison, the entire guard would have to be billeted there.[38]

Throughout this time, the Romanovs were trying to keep up with the news but found that the best antidote to the worsening situation was to get on with their lives in the way they had established. The breakfast and lunch menu cards at Freedom House included turkey galantine, wild duck, veal escalopes and roast beef alongside the pasta that the former empress liked.[39] Alexandra had never been keen on meat and frequently asked the servant Ivan Sednëv to prepare her favourite dish of macaroni cheese, which he did over a traveller's spirit stove.[40] The rest of the family preferred their usual cuisine. Things settled down a little after the disruptions of recent days, and there was hope that the process would continue uninterrupted by a fresh Red Guard disturbance. The family took exercise, read books and played entertaining games, and when he was not labouring on his outdoor chores, Nicholas sat quietly with his favourite volumes in his favourite spot on the roof of the orangery.[41] Nicholas wrote in his diary on 1 April: 'Learned from our ceaseless informant Alexander Kirpichnikov a lot of things of interest about the Bolsheviks who have arrived from Omsk.'[42]

But there was nothing that the family could do as the result of what Kirpichnikov told them. The news was always bad for them, and only ever seemed to get worse.

25. TOBOLSK AND MOSCOW

After the peace treaty, stories began to spread in Tobolsk about the extent of German and Japanese military penetration.[1] The Menshevik press continued to function in the town, maintaining a barrage of criticism of Bolshevik social and economic policies;[2] it also denounced the treaty as being contrary to the interests of the working class.[3] This happened at a time when people were re-electing their soviets and overturning Bolshevik majorities. Tobolsk was one of those small towns which would have given no special concern to the Soviet government if only it had not been hosting the former emperor.[4] The troops who guarded him were consumed with anger at being neglected by Sovnarkom while the situation in west Siberia continued to deteriorate. Tobolsk had been in chaos throughout the month and the detachment at Freedom House decided to dispatch two of its men, Pavel Matveev and a delegate named Lukin, to Moscow to make representations on their behalf. Matveev and Lukin hastened to Tyumen, where they caught the next train bound for the new capital.[5]

On 1 April 1918 Lukin was able to make an opening report at the offices of Sovnarkom, detailing the recent disturbances at and near Freedom House. He testified that many of his own comrades had already run off from the detachment and that the remainder were aggrieved about the non-payment of their wages. Lukin talked with the passion of a serving soldier. If the central Soviet authorities wished to keep the Romanovs securely confined, he made clear, they had to transform the set-up at Freedom House. Vladimir Bonch-Bruevich, Lenin's chief of staff, heard enough to convince him that urgent action was required. Contacting officials at the Central Executive Committee of the Congress of Soviets, he was emphatic in saying: 'It's a serious matter.' Under the informal division of duties between Lenin and Sverdlov, it was Sverdlov as chairman of the Central Executive Committee who dealt with Romanov business. Sverdlov immediately called for Lukin to come and see him because he wanted to hear his report in person.[6]

The Central Executive Committee Presidium met on the same day with Sverdlov in the chair. As well as Bolsheviks, the Left Socialist-Revolutionaries Spiridonova and Proshyan were in attendance. Everyone approved of the case for reforms in Tobolsk. Moscow would appoint its own commissar who would take an entirely fresh detachment to Tobolsk consisting of 200 men – including thirty from the Central Executive Committee's own Partisan Detachment and twenty from the Left Socialist-Revolutionaries. The regime at Freedom House was to be changed in such a way that all residents, including Dolgorukov, Tatishchev and Gendrikova, would be treated as prisoners like Nicholas and his family, while Gibbes would be allowed to choose between living there on the same terms and staying outside and having no contact with the Romanovs. Sverdlov offered a guarantee of the necessary finance. These arrangements would be merely temporary, for Sverdlov stressed that the plan was to transfer the entire arrested group to Moscow as soon as it became a practical possibility. A ban was placed on any publicity. Having heard about the troubles in west Siberia, Sverdlov wanted to deal with the Romanov question in the strictest secrecy.[7]

This nonetheless failed to stop the rumours. For some time there had been stories that Trotsky himself would be coming to Tobolsk as commissar, and the fact that some members of the Romanov entourage took them seriously shows how little they understood the workings of the Bolshevik Central Committee.[8] Trotsky might just as well have resigned from the leadership if he had gone to distant Tobolsk. Instead he focused his energies on his new post as People's Commissar for Military Affairs. Perhaps the Freedom House occupants could be forgiven for getting this so wrong. They did not read newspapers like *Pravda*. They knew nobody who had close acquaintance with Sovnarkom discussions. They themselves heard the emperor talking about his hope of returning one day to the Russian throne. From this it was but a short step to exaggerate the importance of the fate of the Romanovs to Bolshevik leaders in Moscow.

The Presidium returned to Tobolsk matters on 6 April and made a further revision to the plan for dealing with the Romanovs. After changing the guards at Freedom House, the new commissar, who had yet to be appointed, should make speedy arrangements for the family's transfer to the Urals. Tobolsk had ceased to be trusted as a site of detention and Ekaterinburg replaced Omsk as the favoured locus of authority until such time as Nicholas was put on trial in Moscow. Sverdlov undertook to inform the Soviet regional authorities in Ekaterinburg and Omsk; he wanted no repetition of the confusion that had marked proceedings since the end of January. He indicated that he was waiting only for Sovnarkom to grant approval – evidently he needed Lenin to sanction the intended course of action.[9]

By 9 April 1918 Sverdlov had obtained the necessary endorsement from Lenin about next steps to be taken, and Sverdlov could send a telegram to Beloborodov as chairman of the Urals Regional Soviet Executive Committee about the details. Ekaterinburg was told to ready itself to take possession of the Romanovs. Sverdlov indicated that this would be a provisional arrangement. He omitted any mention of the longer-term plan, which remained to bring Nicholas to Moscow for public trial. But Beloborodov would become his chief temporary custodian. Sverdlov appointed the Bolshevik Vasili Yakovlev as the commissar who would oversee the transfer to the Urals. Nicholas and his family would be delivered for safekeeping to either Alexander Beloborodov, chairman of the Regional Soviet Executive Committee, or its military commissar Filipp Goloshchëkin. Sverdlov left it to the Urals Regional Soviet to decide whether they should be held in the prison or in some specially adapted residence. Once the Romanovs reached Ekaterinburg, they were on no account to be moved elsewhere without Moscow's permission, and Sverdlov stressed the priority of guaranteeing their physical security.[10]

Beloborodov and Goloshchëkin were a formidable pairing. Both were Bolshevik veterans. It took Beloborodov no time at all – he had arrived in Ekaterinburg only in January 1918 – to impress the rest of the leadership and become elected chairman of the Urals Regional Soviet Executive Committee.[11] He was of average height, thin, pale and with a trim moustache and beard.[12] Born the son of a worker in 1891 in the Urals mining settlement of Solikamsk, he trained as an electrician. Beloborodov joined the Bolshevik faction as a youth and experienced lengthy terms of imprisonment. Unlike his better-off comrades, he never emigrated and his rootedness in the region around Perm gave him a sharp awareness of practical conditions. His friend Goloshchëkin was 'about forty, above average in height, portly, curly haired and with a short moustache'.[13] His alias in the revolutionary underground was Filipp, and this was how he was generally known in Ekaterinburg. He never sat down if he had the choice. This was a result of his prison experience: he tried to keep fit by staying on the move. On his travels, he became the main link between the Urals and the capital after the October Revolution and twice went on missions to liaise with Lenin and Sverdlov in early 1918. His trips took place in late February and in the first half of March. He was the Urals delegate at the party congress in March.[14]

Whoever conducted Nicholas from Tobolsk had to be able to gain the confidence of the Freedom House detachment. The Ekaterinburg men had already shown their complete 'tactlessness'. The troops from Omsk were no better. In fact they were much worse. There was a need for 'a neutral person' to cope with the tasks of transfer.[15] In addition, it would seem, Sverdlov sent a telegram to the Tobolsk Soviet putting it in charge of Freedom House until such time as Yakovlev arrived. If he did not entirely trust the Urals leaders, he also had concerns about the guard detachment.[16] But the detachment would nevertheless have to remain in charge for several days, and on 11 April 1918, after Matveev and Lukin returned from Moscow, an emergency meeting of the sol- diers' committee was called to hear their news. They themselves had received military promotion in Moscow in recognition of their timely alert about what was happening in west Siberia.[17]

Lukin reported on the forthcoming arrival of a new commissar and passed on the news that troops would soon be replaced by an entirely fresh detachment from outside Tobolsk. The detachment vigorously enforced the orders from the capital and set about putting Freedom House into the same quarantine as had been imposed on the Alexander Palace at Tsarskoe Selo.[18] Matveev chaired the discussion, to which he had invited Dutsman, Demyanov and Zaslavski. A fiery discussion followed as the outsiders from Ekaterinburg and Omsk demanded the transfer of the Romanovs to their custody: they had never trusted Kobylinski or the Freedom House detachment, and they wanted to take full control before Yakovlev reached Tobolsk. Matveev was having none of this. He and the detachment had guarded the family safely since the previous summer and had seen off every threat; they were offended at this latest external challenge to their authority. Dutsman, Demyanov and Zaslavski were furious. As they left, they uttered dire threats about what would happen if Matveev had not reversed the decision within thirty-six hours. If he continued to defy them, there would be violence.[19] Matveev and the detachment held their collective nerve. Knowing what Moscow wanted, they got ready to face whatever the Ekaterinburg or Omsk troops tried to do against them. Threats had been common throughout March. Matveev and Lukin put Kobylinski in the picture about the intended changes so as to organize a united front at Freedom House.

Next day Kobylinski acquainted Nicholas with Moscow's written orders. Rooms were prepared so that the designated retainers could be transferred from the Kornilov house.[20] Furniture and suitcases were moved across the street.[21] With seven newcomers to accommodate, the house soon felt overcrowded, at least by the standards of a ruling monarchy. Nicholas speculated that the guard detachment hoped to impress the new commissar, who had yet to arrive, with their firmness.[22]

The orders, however, did not go down at all well with the Urals Soviet leadership, and on 13 April 1918 Boris Didkovski sent a telegram to Lenin and Sverdlov warning of a continuing and growing danger that the Romanovs might escape by sea or land – it could not be discounted that they could reach China. He argued for Khokhryakov, assisted by Zaslavski and Avdeev, to receive supreme authority in Tobolsk, where the situation was running out of control because the Omsk Red Guards refused to submit to the town soviet. Didkovski warned of the imminent possibility of an armed clash involving troops from Ekaterinburg, the Omsk units and the Freedom House detachment. He offered the services of his men to transport the Romanovs to wherever Sverdlov might require.[23] There was only one way to interpret his telegram: Didkovski did not like the idea of an outsider such as Yakovlev being imposed on the Urals comrades. But he was not rebelling. He was asking Sverdlov to alter Moscow's plan in the light of what he reported about Tobolsk.

Meanwhile there were further restrictions at Freedom House, where the guard detachment carried out a search on 15 April. Nicholas was wearing his *cherkesska*, a traditional Caucasian belted overgarment, at the time. When the guards spotted that he was also carrying the traditional dagger, they demanded to search the entire family for weapons. Kobylinski, as usual, had to calm everybody down. Nicholas was upset and angry but handed over his dagger, and Dolgorukov and Gilliard gave up their ceremonial swords after Kobylinski assured everyone that this was the only way to calm the troops down.[24]

Although Kobylinski kept the peace at moments of disturbance, his own nerves were later shaken when his detachment tore off his epaulettes. Deprived of the last visual sign of his authority, he went straight to the emperor with the intention of resigning. Nicholas, with tears in his eyes, put an arm round his back and said: 'Evgeni Stepanovich, I beg you on behalf of myself, my wife and the children to stay. You can see that we are being patient. You need to be patient too.'[25] They embraced and kissed in the Russian manner, and Kobylinski stayed on, but his troubles with the soldiers worsened. Nicholas liked to wear his military uniform, and when their committee announced the intention of stripping the emperor of his epaulettes in the same fashion, Kobylinski warned that Nicholas might put up physical resistance and that there could be consequences if his British cousin George V learned of any violence. He advised the committee to seek Moscow's opinion. This bought time for Kobylinski to discuss the situation with Nicholas. The upshot was that Nicholas decided to wear his black short-coat when walking in the grounds outside. He did, though, continue to don his full military tunic inside the house.[26]

Things elsewhere in the town were also on the boil. The Urals Red Guards were failing to keep control despite the fact that Khokhryakov had become chairman of the Tobolsk Soviet. On 20 April, Khokhryakov reported on his difficulties to Didkovski in Ekaterinburg, and next day, when Goloshchëkin heard about this, he telegrammed a stern rebuke. Khokhryakov in his view had fallen down in his duties. Goloshchëkin said that he would send a further three units under Pëtr Guzakov to strengthen the force from Ekaterinburg. In the meantime he ordered Khokhryakov to make a public announcement that if there was even the slightest resistance to Yakovlev, artillery would be used to crush 'the nest of counter-revolution'.[27] Although the Urals leaders resented Moscow's recent orders, they would brook no trouble from anyone in Omsk or Tobolsk. But there were also tensions between the leadership in Ekaterinburg and their emissaries in Tobolsk. It was a volatile situation that would test the capability of the much-awaited commissar.

26. COMMISSAR YAKOVLEV

Commissar Vasili Yakovlev was in fact the pseudonym of Konstantin Myachin, a friend and comrade of Sverdlov since their years spent working together for the Bolsheviks before the Great War. Yakovlev and Sverdlov used the Russian familiar form of 'you' with each other – and Sverdlov knew Yakovlev as 'Anton', yet another of his aliases.[1] Yakovlev was dark-eyed, thin and muscular. He trimmed his moustache in the English fashion and attracted attention by constantly flicking back his bushy hair. His jerky way of talking left no doubt that he expected to be obeyed: he had a commanding presence.[2]

Although he did not belong to the Urals communist elite that formed in the year after Nicholas's fall from power, Yakovlev had known the Urals since childhood. Born in 1886 and raised in Orenburg province, Yakovlev had crammed a multitude of experiences into his short life. He briefly attended parochial school until being apprenticed first to a watchmaker and then to a cobbler. He ran away from the harsh working conditions and made a new life for himself as a fitter in a metallurgical factory, where he joined the Russian Social-Democratic Workers' Party and aligned himself with the Bolshevik faction. He became a valued militant in the Urals combat groups that Bolsheviks organized to assault political authorities as well as to carry out robberies – the Bolsheviks had no scruples about increasing their factional treasury by such means. Tough and confident, Yakovlev was supremely calm in the face of danger. There was hardly a Urals town where he did not operate as an armed Bolshevik 'expropriator' at a time when Lenin sought finance for the faction's political purposes. Yakovlev's last heist took place in 1909 in an attack on the Miass postal agency to the west of Chelyabinsk.[3]

The robberies helped to pay for the party school that the novelist Maxim Gorky was organizing on the island of Capri off the south Italian coast. Yakovlev himself took refuge abroad to escape pursuit by Russian police. With no private means to fall back on, he got a job as an electrician, working in Liège and Brussels, where he learned French while remaining in touch with the party. Not until after the February 1917 Revolution was it safe for him to return to Russia. (Like Lenin, he did this under the auspices of the German authorities.) He headed for Ufa and found employment at the Sim Works in the Urals while he promoted the Bolshevik cause. The Ufa Soviet sent him as one of the delegates to the Second Congress of Soviets in Petrograd in the autumn. He stayed there to help with the founding of the Cheka before putting in a request to go back to the Urals for some recuperation after his exertions. The central authorities suggested that he should become the military commissar in Ekaterinburg. On arrival he found that someone else, none other than Filipp Goloshchëkin, was already in post. A brief dispute ensued and, rather than prolong it, Yakovlev went back to Ufa where he made a huge collection of grain for transport to starving Petrograd – and Ufa in return received finance and weaponry.[4]

He moved to Moscow when the capital was transferred from Petrograd, and Sverdlov asked him to take personal charge of the delivery of the Romanovs to the Urals.[5] Sverdlov thought that Yakovlev exactly the man to sort out the disarray in Tobolsk. Yakovlev had a shell of revolutionary toughness; he was also already one of the godfathers of the Soviet security service. Sverdlov, knowing that tempers were running high, selected an individual who knew the Urals well and had no reason to indulge the same Ekaterinburg leaders who had given him a frosty reception only a few weeks earlier. Sverdlov had confidence in Yakovlev's capacity to navigate the stormy wrangles at both destinations.

Despite Sverdlov's allocation of troops from Moscow, Yakovlev had to make arrangements of his own to complete his military detachment. He made first for his native Ufa, where he knew people whom he could trust. Goloshchëkin of the Urals Regional Soviet Executive Committee was there at the time and the two of them talked at length about Yakovlev's mission and achieved a degree of mutual confidence: it made sense for Yakovlev to obtain Ekaterinburg's cooperation. From Ufa he travelled on to Chelyabinsk and picked up volunteers for a mounted unit at the nearby Minyar plant. He initiated nobody into his exact purposes as he led the detachment via Chelyabinsk to Ekaterinburg, where he held discussions with the Urals leaders before heading by train for Tyumen. By then he had told his men about the plan and the excitement mounted. The Urals Regional Soviet Executive Committee sent word to Tobolsk ordering its people to submit to

Yakovlev's authority. Everything proceeded harmoniously as Alexander Avdeev came down from Tobolsk to meet him in Tyumen and accompany him on the last leg of the trip north.

Yakovlev brought his own telegraph operator and nurse – both apparently from Ufa like Yakovlev himself. If an awkward situation arose, he needed to have reliable contact with the capital, and he foresaw that there might be times when medical assistance was unavailable. Together with Galkin the telegraph operator, whom he used as a kind of adjutant, he was ready to impose himself at his destination.

On reaching Tobolsk with his contingent in the evening of 22 April, he learned of the trouble caused by Dutsman, Demyanov and Zaslavski. This added urgency to his need to assume personal control. He put the word out to the Ekaterinburg and Omsk forces in town that he would tolerate no interference and immediately spoke to the soldiers' committee. Then he called a general meeting of the entire guard detachment. Brandishing his mandates signed by Lenin, Sverdlov and Secretary of the Central Executive Committee of the Congress of Soviets V. A. Avanesov, he made it clear that he – and nobody else – was charged with full authority to deal with the Romanovs. He revealed that he had already promised the soldiers' committee that he would resolve the payment grievances within the next day or two. Then he spoke about terms of service. With the demobilization of the old army, Yakovlev said, every soldier in the detachment was free to go or stay. He asked that the process should be an orderly one. He claimed that tensions with the other armed detachments in Tobolsk had been resolved. He had told them what he wanted, and he expected to be obeyed.[6]

Pavel Matveev in the chair gave his support and described the many difficulties that had faced the guard detachment after Pankratov's departure. Dutsman, Demyanov and Zaslavski had caused nothing but trouble, frequently issuing direct physical threats.[7] Zaslavski, who was present at the meeting, tried to shift the blame on to Demyanov; he defended his own actions as having been entirely in accordance with the Urals Regional Soviet Executive Committee's instruction to improve security at Freedom House at a time when the Tobolsk Soviet appeared hopelessly divided. Degtyarëv bridled at this picture and accused Zaslavski of introducing an atmosphere of conspiracy. He gave his own assurance that the local garrison would desist from using force.[8] Yakovlev was winning the debate. When Matveev raised the festering grievance about the non-payment of wages, Yakovlev thanked the troops for their valour and loyalty and promised to tackle the wages question as a matter of urgency. Matveev thanked him for his helpful attitude and looked forward to a lessening of tensions in Tobolsk.[9]

The Romanovs were kept waiting in suspense. The daughters feared yet another search and consigned their letters to the flames in case Yakovlev found something in them that would cause trouble (although quite a lot of their correspondence has survived). Maria and Anastasia even burned their diaries.[10] Tension mounted when Yakovlev sent word of his intention to come to Freedom House next day at 11 a.m.[11]

In fact, he turned up half an hour early, accompanied by Galkin the telegraphist as well as Kobylinski, Matveev, Avdeev and an unnamed duty officer. Alexandra was not ready to see them but Yakovlev went ahead and explained his intentions to Nicholas and three of his daughters. They were relieved by Yakovlev's smile and courteous manner as he enquired whether they had any complaints about the guard detachment or the premises. Nicholas was his usual affable self and replied that the troops were giving him no cause for concern. Yakovlev indicated a need to conduct a comprehensive search of the building before taking any further decisions. A brief moment of unease occurred when Yakovlev asked to see Alexei. Nicholas fended off the request by saying that his son was very poorly. Yakovlev firmly repeated his demand. The daughters said nothing as they watched and listened to the dispute. Eventually Nicholas agreed to Yakovlev entering the room where Alexei was lying. This enabled Yakovlev to confirm that the boy appeared mortally ill; he recorded his conclusion that the disease was the result of a genetic inheritance from the Hesse side of the family.[12]

Yakovlev returned to see Alexandra thirty minutes later, when he also took another look at Alexei.[13] Neither Nicholas nor Alexandra was much impressed by the new Bolshevik commissar, but they agreed that he could have been a lot worse. He was patently no ruffian and his politeness was undeniable. Alexandra expressed pleasant surprise: 'There's no problem: he spoke gently with me.'[14] Gibbes even thought him a decent sort of fellow.[15] Mundel, a senior adjutant who had followed the Romanovs from Tsarskoe Selo, judged him to be an intellectual in his thinking and demeanour, noting his frequent use of French phrases, and Kobylinski offered the same verdict.[16]

Nevertheless, Yakovlev declined to be gentle on the detainees, introducing a number of petty restrictions on their daily routines. He also ordered a narrowing of their diet. Until he arrived, the Romanovs and their retainers had a three-course dinner in the evenings. When

Yakovlev cut out sugar from their diet, they could no longer look forward to a pudding course.[17] He may have acted out of an instinctive sense that the Romanovs had to recognize that he alone was in charge at Freedom House. Or perhaps he simply felt that they had been indulged for too long at a time when most Russians were suffering growing material hardship. In any case, his main concern was not with the Romanov diet but with the military situation in Tobolsk. In the first two full days after his arrival, he worked feverishly to secure control – and he knew that the Ekaterinburg and Omsk Red Guard detachments contained resentful elements. He had his own armed contingent and had won over the guard detachment at Freedom House. But if he wanted to avoid an armed clash in the town, he had to convince everybody that he was a genuine revolutionary radical. Force alone was not enough.

Some people, however, proved unpersuadable. Among them was Semën Zaslavski, who plainly had malign intentions towards the Romanovs, even though he pretended otherwise.[18] Orders from Moscow were to keep the family safe. Zaslavski behaved as if he had no need to obey Sovnarkom or the Central Committee. He was not acting independently: as was to become clear many decades later, he was following the secret course of action that the Urals leadership had approved. Although they preferred to see Nicholas in Ekaterinburg than in Tobolsk, they gave calm consideration to the idea of killing him in transit if 'suitable conditions' were to arise.[19] Zaslavski was under instructions to carry out this plan on the leadership's behalf. His lack of discretion meant that everyone in the town had an inkling about what he was up to.[20] He even suggested to Yakovlev that he should avoid sitting next to Nicholas when Yakovlev took the Romanovs south to Tyumen. He could hardly have dropped a clearer hint that an armed attempt was going to be made to shoot the emperor.[21]

Yakovlev was sufficiently alarmed to instruct Avdeev, Zaslavski's own comrade from Ekaterinburg, to take Zaslavski into custody. Avdeev duly complied and Yakovlev was pleased to have won the trial of strength. But it was only a temporary victory; for Avdeev quickly sent a man to release Zaslavski, who promptly left the town. And nobody knew what Zaslavski might try to do next.[22]

27. THE ORDER TO MOVE

On 24 April 1918 Yakovlev informed Kobylinski about the latest instructions from Moscow: the emperor and his family were to be moved from Tobolsk – without delay. This was shocking news for Kobylinski, who exclaimed: 'But what about Alexei Nikolaevich? He can't travel. He's ill!' Yakovlev cut him short: 'Look, the whole thing comes down to this. I spoke on the direct line to the Central Executive Committee. The order is to leave the entire family here but to transfer the former Sovereign.' With that, he asked Kobylinski to accompany him to a discussion with Nicholas next day after breakfast. Tatishchev told Nicholas of the scheduled meeting.[1]

Nicholas and Alexandra stood waiting for Yakovlev next day at the appointed time. Yakovlev behaved with courtesy, even bowing to Nicholas. But he ignored Alexandra: he obviously had important things on his mind. His message to the imperial couple shocked both of them: 'I have to tell you that I am the extraordinary plenipotentiary of the Central Executive Committee in Moscow, and my powers consist in my duty to take the entire family away from here. But because Alexei Nikolaevich is ill, I have received a follow-up order to depart with you alone.'[2] Nicholas lost patience and exclaimed: 'I'm not going anywhere!' Yakovlev dealt coolly with the challenge and explained the facts of life to the man who was his prisoner:

> I ask you not to act like this. I have to fulfil my instructions. If you refuse to travel, I must either use force or else give up the task that has been laid upon me. In that instance they could send someone else who is a lot less humane than myself. You can remain calm. I answer with my own head for your life. If you don't wish to travel alone, you can travel with whomever you want. Make ready. We'll be departing tomorrow at four [in the morning].

With that he bowed again, turned and left. Nicholas gestured to Kobylinski to return to them after seeing Yakovlev out of the building:

he needed to talk about how to deal with the new order. When Koby-linski returned, he found Nicholas and Alexandra in deep discussion with Dolgorukov and Tatishchev.[3]

Nicholas took a solitary walk in the grounds for a full hour while he considered his options. Alexandra grew frantic. As a mother she wanted to stay behind with her sick son, but as a wife she felt an equal obligation to Nicholas. She found it impossible to sit down despite her frailty and talked intensely with her daughter Tatyana and Pierre Gilliard. At times, though, she held a conversation with herself as if they were not present. She cried out: 'This is the first time in my life that I completely don't know how to behave.' She was tormented by the thought of what would happen to Nicholas if he were to leave alone. She felt sure that the Bolsheviks would put pressure on him to sign an endorsement of the Brest-Litovsk treaty – she speculated that they would threaten to harm the rest of the family if he resisted. She paced around her room, trying to make up her mind. Tatyana and Gilliard implored her to decide. In the end she could stand it no longer and came to the only solution that she could abide. 'Well, it's decided,' she said. 'My duty is to go with him. I can't let him go alone. And you will look after Alexei here.'[4]

When Nicholas returned to the building, she told him: 'I'm going with you. I shan't let you go alone.' He was not going to stop her if she was determined to go on the journey. As Gilliard was to record, Nich-olas's reply was brief and simple: 'It's your decision.' They then switched to English, presumably to avoid letting the Swiss tutor know what they were saying.[5]

Nicholas asked Kobylinski where it was that Yakovlev was planning to take him. Kobylinski said that hints had been dropped about Moscow – this tallied with Yakovlev's remark that he expected the trip to take four to five days. The Romanovs and their entourage had been expecting this for some weeks. Kobylinski added the reassuring com-ment that Yakovlev hoped to return to Tobolsk within a fortnight and pick up the rest of the imperial family. The exact arrangements for travel agitated Nicholas less than how the Bolshevik leadership intended to treat him at the as yet to be disclosed destination: 'Well, what they want is for me to endorse the Brest-Litovsk treaty. But I'd rather cut off my own hand than do that!' Alexandra agreed. She repeated what she had decided, adding that her presence was crucial to her husband's capacity to face down the Bolsheviks: 'I too shall make the trip. Without me, they'll compel him to do anything just as they compelled him once before!' She was referring to what had happened in the February Revolution, which in fact had nothing to do with the Bolsheviks. Looking back at the circumstances of Nicholas's abdication, she continued to hold Mikhail Rodzyanko particularly responsible for having broken her husband's resolve to stay on the throne.[6]

Alexandra agreed that the Bolshevik plan was to force Nicholas to endorse the treaty. She told Volkov the valet: 'I'm leaving Alexei Nikolaevich, so look after him here. I've made up my mind and have to share my fate with the Sovereign.'[7] Yakovlev's ultimatum arrived at a time when young Alexei's legs were giving him much pain. He cried and cried, calling for his mother. Tears streamed down her cheeks as she contemplated leaving him behind. Volkov had never seen her in such a condition.[8] It was only the need to prepare for the trip that kept her from falling apart. She also had to put on a brave face in front of her daughters – Tatyana in particular was in a terrible state and squeezed her hands in fright.[9] When Maria Tutelberg expressed sympathy, Alexandra replied: 'Don't exaggerate my grief, Tutels. This is the heaviest moment for me. You know what my Son means to me. I have to choose between my son and my husband. But I've made my decision and it's necessary to be firm. I must leave the boy and share life or death with my husband.'[10]

Yakovlev could scarcely believe what he witnessed in Alexandra that day. He knew from observation and hearsay how devoted she was to her sick son, and yet suddenly she was planning to abandon him to the care of others. What had happened to her maternal instinct?[11] Her political reasoning made no greater sense. Yakovlev's party had nearly torn itself apart over Brest-Litovsk. Lenin had forced the treaty down his party's throat and the last thing he was now likely to do was to reopen the discussion by seeking an endorsement from the detested former emperor.

Over at the Kornilov house, Yakovlev asked Kobylinski: 'Who is going to be travelling?' He at last conceded that Nicholas could take whomever he wanted with him. The sole restriction would be on the baggage load.[12] Kobylinski hurried back to Freedom House, where Tatishchev told him what had been decided. Nicholas wished to take Alexandra and their daughter Maria on the journey along with Evgeni Botkin, Dolgorukov, the valet Terenti Chemodurov, Ivan Sednëv and Anna Demidova. Kobylinski hurried over again to Yakovlev, who said: 'It's all the same to me!' The important thing for Yakovlev was to get going.[13] His impatience was understandable. Despite his enquiries, it was still the case that nobody could tell him where Zaslavski was or who was with him. Yakovlev was a man of action and wanted to complete the transfer of Nicholas to the Urals capital before any Uralite could stop him. With his usual steadiness he calculated that a swift departure from Tobolsk would wrong-foot those like Zaslavski who might try to thwart him. He pressed everyone in his team to get themselves ready for the journey.

Yakovlev sought last-minute clarity from Moscow about its requirements. A message came through from I. A. Teodorovich in the Central Executive Committee of the Congress of Soviets giving permission for just 'the main part' to be transferred to Ekaterinburg. (Teodorovich, writing in guarded language in case his cable fell into unapproved hands, was endorsing Yakovlev's plan to depart with Nicholas, Alexandra and Maria.) This still left Yakovlev with some concerns, and he asked for information about the Urals leadership. He wanted to know whether it was true that Goloshchëkin had recalled Zaslavski.[14]

On Yakovlev's orders, Kobylinski assembled the guard detachment to announce the plan on terms of strict secrecy. Yakovlev himself addressed the gathering. Accentuating his distaste for the Romanovs, he referred to Nicholas as 'the former Tsar'. He assured the soldiers that Alexei's illness genuinely prevented the family as a whole from travelling. This was why he was taking Nicholas, Alexandra and one of their daughters in the first party, to be followed by the other Romanovs as soon as Alexei was fit enough. Yakovlev, knowing that some soldiers might object, gave warning that anyone refusing to obey orders was liable to be shot. He announced that he had asked Kobylinski to draw up a list of suitable soldiers for the armed escort. There had already been complaints that Kobylinski had included the officers Nabokov and Matveev. Could this be some kind of trick to damage the revolutionary cause? Yakovlev dismissed any such thought – after all, Matveev too was a Bolshevik and a promotee from the soldiers' ranks. He had made his decision and now he expected total compliance.[15]

Kobylinski assumed that Yakovlev aimed to get away before anyone in the Tobolsk Soviet leadership knew what had happened. The problem was that the troops in the existing guard detachment were unhappy with the plan unless they themselves supplied the escort. Yakovlev felt that he could manage better with his own men from Ufa. But he offered to take Matveev, Lukin and others of revolutionary solidity with him. He aimed to reassure everyone that he was not planning any kind of betrayal.[16]

The weather was an important factor. Winter was giving way to spring and the northern rivers were starting to melt. Ice was yielding to mud, but the process had only just begun, which meant that horses and carriages, rather than the steamship, would be required to reach the railway at Tyumen.[17] Whichever mode of transport was used, there could be political complications, for Yakovlev could certainly not assume that he would have no trouble in reaching even the outskirts of Tobolsk with the three Romanovs. He therefore sent his Ufa Bolshevik comrade D. M. Chudinov into town to seek guarantees from the Soviet leadership that nothing untoward was being plotted. Chudinov's other duty was to collect a large number of tarantasses for the cortège – he managed to procure nineteen of them.[18] He also arranged for the drivers to be paid by the mile. Invoice forms were taken, to be given to them en route.[19]

Frantic preparations were made in Freedom House as the servant Fëdor Gorshkov packed four suitcases for the emperor.[20] The three Romanovs prepared for the worst and decided to take camp beds, too.[21]

The imperial family dined alone on the eve of the emperor's departure while the retinue had their meal separately. Everyone was sad and depressed.[22] But the Romanovs had been brought up to show durability in times of adversity. The Soviet authorities could impose whatever conditions they liked and the family would accept the inevitable. With Yakovlev's agreement, the emperor and empress would be accompanied by Dolgorukov, Dr Evgeni Botkin, the emperor's valet Terenti Chemodurov, the empress's maid Anna Demidova and Ivan Sednëv. Yakovlev had also granted the request for the Grand Duchess Maria to accompany her parents. Demidova spoke of her own fears: 'Oh! Mr Gibbes, I am so frightened of the Bolsheviks, I don't know what they will do to us.' Tea was served to all the residents at 11 p.m. It was like a wake. Little was said. There was no pretence at gaiety. Yakovlev then announced that the party would leave under cover of darkness. The retinue went back downstairs to wait for orders, which were finally delivered in the dead of night at 3 a.m. Nicholas and Alexandra descended the stairs and there followed a painful parting with Alexei and the other children. Alexandra and Maria preceded Nicholas. The moment of departure had arrived.[23]

Disagreement flared when Yakovlev indicated that he wanted Nicholas and Alexandra to occupy separate vehicles. Whereas Nicholas had no objection to travelling in a carriage with Yakovlev, Alexandra was horrified at the idea of sitting next to Pavel Matveev. An empress, even an ex-empress, disliked physical proximity to an ill-kempt trooper. She demanded that her daughter should sit by her side. Yakovlev gave way, seeing no point in further dispute. Dolgorukov sat with Botkin, and Chemodurov with Sednëv. Yakovlev moved Matveev to a seat next to Demidova.[24] Looking across at Nicholas, he asked why he was only wearing a greatcoat. Some of the retainers reacted as if questioning Nicholas in this way was an insufferable breach of etiquette – their pomposity was extraordinary. But Yakovlev was sensibly concerned about the cold conditions. Nicholas replied that this was what he always wore for a journey, which Yakovlev thought to be downright silly. Yakovlev called over to the tsarevich's valet Ivanov: 'Bring him something.' Ivanov, however, was used to more decorous forms of address in relation to Nicholas; he asked Yakovlev who it was that he meant. Yakovlev pointed at Nicholas and exclaimed: 'What do you mean, who? I mean *him!*' This at last elicited the necessary action as Ivanov went to fetch a blanket for the former Tsar of All Russia to sit on.[25]

28. SOUTH TO TYUMEN

The convoy was set up with an eye towards being ready for any violence on the way to Tyumen. Yakovlev had received no information about Zaslavski's whereabouts and had to prepare for the worst. And as an ex-bank robber and former denizen of the revolutionary underground, he knew how to make plans. In the first tarantass he seated two rifle-men with guns at the ready; in the second there was a machine-gunner. These three soldiers constituted a vanguard with orders to fire on any attackers. Yakovlev and Nicholas would travel in the fourth tarantass, Alexandra and Maria in the sixth. Dolgorukov and Botkin were allo-cated to the ninth and Tatishchev to the twelfth. Under cover of darkness and with the minimum of noise, the Romanovs' trunks were loaded on to carriages thirteen to fifteen.[1] The tension spread to all involved. When everyone was at last on board, the order was given for the off. The former Emperor of All Russia, his wife and one of his daughters were on their way.

Even at this moment, Yakovlev refused to divulge the destination, and Nicholas and Alexandra continued to fret about the son they were leaving behind. But the weather was sharp and there was little time to brood. As horses and tarantasses passed through the town, there could be no doubt that a party of some size was on the move. Just before the party disappeared from sight, Gibbes took a long-exposure picture of the empress's vehicle.[2] Already in the far distance were the five horse-men whom Yakovlev had sent in advance to spy out each of the planned stages of the route – they were ordered to be ready to report in person as soon as the convoy came in view.[3]

Yakovlev set a rattling pace and refused to stop for tea breaks. If the travellers and their escort wanted a drink, they had to wait for the overnight stop or take a gulp of water as they rode along.[4] The road that took them south was rough and muddy at that time of year, making progress uncomfortable. A biting cold wind had been blowing for hours and the wheels were soon iced up. Each carriage lost a wheel or was otherwise badly damaged at some point. Yakovlev arranged for four changes of horses on the first day before they halted at Ievlevo as dusk fell. The convoy had covered eighty-six miles, which included a difficult crossing of the deep waters of the River Irtysh. The Romanovs and their attendants, stoical but exhausted, were thankful to discover that Yakovlev had found a large, clean house for the night. Not having been to bed for two nights, all three of them were soon fast asleep.[5]

Yakovlev, however, could not afford to rest. Avdeev had followed him to Ievlevo with an armed force on orders from Yakovlev himself to commandeer a train in Tyumen for the onward shipment of the Romanovs.[6] But their encounter at Ievlevo involved angry exchanges with some of Avdeev's men, and Yakovlev decided to take one of them into custody.[7] It had become clear that a plot had been laid to disarm the convoy and seize the Romanovs and that Zaslavski and Khokhryakov were behind it and were getting ready to strike. Yakovlev cabled Didkovski and Goloshchëkin to remonstrate about what he had discovered: 'Take rapid measures or there will be bloodshed. Inform Tyumen in detail. Zaslavski secretly slunk out of Tobolsk; I did not manage to arrest him. I am departing Ievlevo.' Yakovlev asked for Tyumen Soviet chairman, Nemtsov, to prepare everything for the convoy's arrival; he ordered his own units to meet him en route.[8] Instructions were issued for a start to be made at 5 a.m. the following morning. In fact, Yakovlev was so tired that he overslept, and the convoy started later than scheduled.[9]

Nicholas observed what was happening as best he could, but Yakovlev did not tell him much. After interrogating the arrested Ekaterinburg soldier, Yakovlev knew that trouble could still lie ahead. Yakovlev did not want to agitate the Romanovs and kept his thoughts of danger to himself.[10]

The tarantasses and carts moved off with fresh horses on the second day. Everyone had to dismount to cross the River Tobol. Nicholas, sociable as ever, got acquainted with Yakovlev's friend and deputy Pëtr Guzakov in order to discover their current intentions. The weather had changed and it was a bright, warm day, but the going remained severe. It was dusty on the roads and muddy in the woods. The carriages shook the passengers, which gave Nicholas some concern about his wife's health.[11] Seated next to Yakovlev for hours, he could not but engage in some conversation. This led to some surprises for Yakovlev, especially when Nicholas claimed to believe in complete freedom of conscience in matters of religion. Yakovlev at first did not know whether he was joking or pretending. Memories of the persecution of Jews before 1917 came to mind. Nicholas looked at him with such a clear face that Yakovlev reckoned that he meant what he said.[12]

Yakovlev changed the convoy after crossing the Tobol and sat in the same tarantass as his deputy Pëtr Guzakov while Chudinov, who headed the detachment, took Yakovlev's place next to Nicholas. Conversation was next to impossible as they shielded themselves from the violent mud spray as the tarantass pounded along. Nicholas took out his porte-cigare and offered Chudinov a cigarette. Chudinov declined, but when they had a restful moment, Nicholas tried again and asked: 'What military school did your commissar train at?' Chudinov replied: 'As far as I know, he only studied at an electrical technical school in Belgium.' Nicholas remarked: 'Yes, it's obvious that he's seen some sights. He's a commissar with a bit of pepper about him.'[13] Despite the physical demands, the journey was exciting for everyone. Chudinov would recall talking to a grey-bearded peasant on the way at one of the places where they changed the horses:

Peasant: Young fellow, would you kindly tell me in God's name where they're taking our good tsar [*tsar'-batyushka*]? Is it to Moscow?
Chudinov: To Moscow, grandad, to Moscow!

And as they left the same staging post, Chudinov heard someone else say: 'Now, glory be, there is going to be order!'[14] It is not clear whether the bystander wanted Nicholas to be punished or to resume power. This vagueness was not unknown at a time when few Russians had a clear idea about how to bring stability and prosperity to their country.

Changes of horses followed a set procedure. Chudinov called out to the horseman left behind earlier in the village, and the fresh mounts were brought out. Usually this took no more than five minutes.[15] Pokrovskoe was one of the most memorable staging posts. As chance had it, the new horses were hitched up directly outside the Rasputin home. The Romanovs were touched to notice the whole family of their deceased friend watching from indoors. No contact was allowed, and Chudinov aimed his Mauser pistol at the house to ensure compliance. But the story spread that Rasputin's wife and mother had crossed themselves and prayed as the travellers paused nearby. As soon as fresh horses had been hitched, the convoy pressed on at full speed.[16]

Every day was a test of Yakovlev's durability. Sverdlov had given him the task of taking the Romanovs safely to the Urals and yet it was Urals Bolshevik leaders who at every turn were conspiring against his efforts. Yakovlev felt that he was the only official who was fulfilling Moscow's wishes. After crossing the River Irtysh, Yakovlev held a rendezvous with his deputy, Pëtr Guzakov, who had some disturbing news. Guzakov had earlier run into Gusyatski, deputy commander of the Ekaterinburg troops who had left Tobolsk in advance of Yakovlev's party. This time Yakovlev had an especially good reason to worry because Gusyatski had let slip to Guzakov that a plot indeed existed to waylay the convoy and kill Nicholas. This confirmed what Yakovlev had suspected throughout the trip. He was furious, and when he met with Gusyatski, he told him that he would not hesitate to execute him and his entire military unit if they fired so much as a single shot.[17]

This was not the end of the matter. Alexander Nevolin from the Ekaterinburg Red Guards secretly approached him that evening and revealed that the plot remained an active one. According to Nevolin, Gusyatski had told his troops that Yakovlev planned to transport the Romanovs to Moscow and enable them to proceed into foreign exile. Gusyatski's counter-plan was to take Nicholas to Ekaterinburg instead. Some of his troops expressed disquiet when Gusyatski talked about aiming to ambush the Romanov convoy and made plain that he expected to liquidate not only Nicholas but also Yakovlev and his detachment. Nevolin had asked: 'So it is that we're going to be brigands?' A rancorous dispute ensued in which Gusyatski was annoyed to see that Nevolin carried a lot of support, and Nevolin, fearing for his life, crept off to Yakovlev's detachment.[18]

Yakovlev started early next morning, again setting a hectic pace. Kobylinski had given orders for the detachment to keep him informed about progress, and Nabokov telegrammed from Pokrovskoe that everything was going well.[19] This was accurate only in relation to the number of miles covered because the passengers and most of their military escort were reaching the point of exhaustion. At a rutted spot on the road, the tarantass carrying Alexandra and Maria broke down and they took shelter in a nearby hut until a replacement could be fetched.[20] A last change of horses took place at the village of Borki. By then Dr Botkin was suffering from swollen kidneys, which led to a decision to leave him behind to recover before moving on. At Borki, the convoy had tea and some titbits of food at the schoolhouse. For once, Yakovlev was taking his time to organize the eighth and final stage of the journey to Tyumen. With his worries about what might wait ahead, he told his men to be ready for any eventuality and then ordered the long ride into Tyumen. A beautiful moon had risen before the convoy reached the town at 9.15 p.m.[21]

Sixteen cavalrymen of the detachment's advance party were sent ten miles downriver from Tyumen to rendezvous with Yakovlev. Their leader, who was named Permyakov, urged them onward: 'Let the former Tsar see the discipline and might of the Red Army, the freest army in the world!'[22] He spoke with the personal authority of a man who had used troops to disarm the Tyumen Red Guards after a series of robberies.[23] As the convoy and its reinforcements approached the town's outskirts, an additional escort of around fifty men rode out to form a protective chain.[24] Darkness enveloped the scene as the party crossed the Irtysh by a movable bridge and came to the railway station.[25]

Sergei Markov, who had moved to Tyumen after failing to liberate the Romanovs in Tobolsk, believed that if only a determined attempt could be made, there was still a good chance of rescuing the family. Resourceful and optimistic as always, he had infiltrated the Red Army by posing as a Soviet sympathizer, and such was his obvious competence that he received command over seventy military recruits. He certainly had the audacity to chance his arm. And it is even possible that he could have successfully tricked his men into mounting an attack on Yakovlev's convoy. Whether he could have gone on to pull off a rescue is doubtful – and the Romanovs might all too easily have perished in the crossfire. In any case, he was no longer free to act. In early April, the Tobolsk Soviet authorities, suspecting that his true loyalties did not lie with Sovnarkom, threw him into prison. It was from a cell that he learned about Nicholas's arrival.[26] Even so, there was enough uncertainty in the local situation for Yakovlev to continue to act with caution. The anti-Bolshevik Markov might be securely detained, but who was to say that he lacked accomplices still at large? And where, oh where, was the Bolshevik Zaslavski and his men-at-arms?

A train was waiting for Yakovlev and the Romanovs at Tyumen's railway station. There were only four carriages, one first-class and three third-class.[27] The prospective passengers, exhausted by their journey, were thankful to get down from the three tarantasses. Their testing ride was over and they had survived it. They disapproved of the state of the compartments, which nobody had bothered to wipe and sweep clean,[28] but they made no complaint. At least they were not going to be jolted in their seats all day, and they would know where they would sleep that night. At 10 p.m. they sank into their beds.[29]

While this was happening, Yakovlev consulted Moscow on the Hughes apparatus.[30] He left Avdeev on the train with strict orders not to leave it, ostensibly because someone with authority needed to supervise the Romanovs. But Avdeev did not like the idea of Yakovlev talking to Moscow without the presence of a witness. When Avdeev climbed down on to the platform to accompany him, however, Yakovlev's men bodily stopped him. Turning to Guzakov, he asked: 'What, does this mean I'm arrested?' When it was made clear that Yakovlev was to be left alone at the apparatus, Avdeev passed a note through the carriage window to his comrade Ivan Loginov telling him to inform Ekaterinburg about what was happening – something Guzakov in this instance allowed.[31]

Yakovlev begged Sverdlov to sanction a change of plan on the grounds that the Ekaterinburg leadership could not be trusted. Their representatives in Tobolsk had clearly intended to annihilate 'the baggage'; they had even urged him not to sit in a carriage beside any of the Romanovs. Their objective had obviously been to attack the travelling party before it arrived in Tyumen. Yakovlev had thwarted their purpose by deploying troops of his own along the entire route. But the armed units from Ekaterinburg continued to put him under intimidating pressure. He warned that an action of some kind might take place before the train reached Ekaterinburg. According to Yakovlev, Goloshchëkin was the sole Urals leader who did not want to kill 'the baggage'. It would therefore be madness to proceed with the original plan. Instead he requested permission to make for Omsk. From there, he indicated, he would take a westbound train on the southern loop of the rail network through to the River Sim mining district, where he knew that he could find a place of safe confinement. Otherwise he could give no guarantee of safety for his Romanov charges.[32]

Sverdlov, comfortably seated at his Hughes telegraph apparatus in Moscow and laden with countless other tasks, enquired whether his old comrade was not a trifle overanxious. After his experience since Tobolsk, Yakovlev stood by every word of his alert. He was asking not for pity but for common sense to prevail. If he had to stick to the old plan, the consequences could be disastrous. Faced by such determination, Sverdlov sanctioned the change of destination and promised to issue fresh instructions when Yakovlev presented himself to the West Siberian Soviet Regional Executive chairman Viktor Kosarev in Omsk.[33]

1. Nicholas II and his son Alexei enjoy a moment of relaxation near the wartime front.

2. Nicholas II dressed in the old Muscovite-style garb that he sometimes chose for public appearances.

3. Grigori Rasputin, the only person who could settle young Alexei in his bouts of haemophilia.

4. The imperial train where Nicholas II had signed his act of abdication. Times had changed, and people could cluster round the carriage and see how the tsar had liked to travel.

5. General Mikhail Alexeev, Chief of the General Staff: bespectacled, hard-working and exhausted. Alexeev tactfully pressed Nicholas to abdicate.

6. Grand Duke Mikhail, who rejected his brother Nicholas's invitation to succeed him as tsar. A sensible decision.

7. One of the successive drafts of the act of abdication, with suggested amendments in pencil.

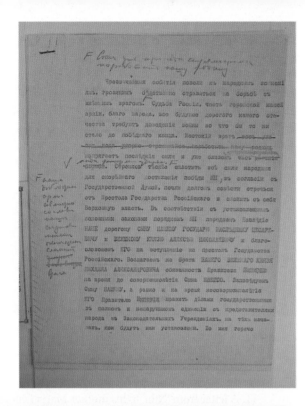

8. Nicholas and Alexandra in happier times with their four daughters and son.

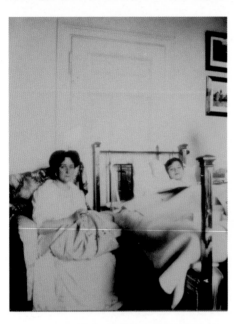

9. A worried Alexandra nursing her son Alexei. Alexandra blamed herself for Alexei's medical condition.

10. The ailing Alexandra in her wheelchair at Tsarskoe Selo.

11. A letter from 'Niki' to his mother Maria Fëdorovna from Tsarskoe Selo, apologizing for his shaky handwriting and recounting that he was teaching Alexei history and geography. He was still using his old notepaper.

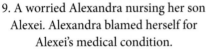

12. Olga Romanova and her mother's unstable confidante Anna Vyrubova. Kerensky ordered Vyrubova's removal from the Alexander Palace.

13. Cousin monarchs, Nicholas II and George V, before the First World War. Two peas in a pod.

14. Alexander Guchkov, Octobrist minister of war
in the first Provisional Government cabinet.

15. Alexander Kerensky, the Socialist-
Revolutionary minister of justice who
became minister-chairman in July 1917.

16. Pavel Milyukov, Constitutional-
Democrat and minister of foreign affairs
after Nicholas's abdication.

17. Sir George Buchanan, UK ambassador to wartime Petrograd.

18. Lavr Kornilov, the Petrograd military commander who rose to commander-in-chief under Kerensky. Kornilov turned against Kerensky in August 1917.

19. Alexander Kerensky among army officers and troops before the October Revolution.

20. Freedom House, Tobolsk, where the Romanovs were held after Tsarskoe Selo.

21. A section of the guard detachment on a snowy day outside Freedom House.

22. Nicholas on their balcony at Freedom House, Tobolsk.

23. Nicholas's letter to his mother, written two days after the October Revolution, lamenting the ban on the family taking a walk around Tobolsk.

Жаль, что города до сихъ
поръ не знаемъ. Наши
господа говорятъ, что
тутъ церкви всѣ старыя и
что имѣется музей съ
интересными историческими
отдѣломъ. Я просматри-
валъ свой дневникъ 1891 г.
и возстановилъ въ памяти
все путешествіе по Сибири;
оказывается, что я провелъ
въ Тобольскѣ нѣсколько
часовъ и то вечеромъ и
потому плохо помню самый
городъ. Это было 10го Іюля
— во то время, это фран-
цузская эскадра посѣтила
Кронштадтъ.

Тобольскъ.   27 Октября
1917 г.

Милая дорогая моя Мама,
На дняхъ Ольга — сестра
написала двумъ моимъ
дочерямъ, что нашъ тебѣ
получены и значитъ моё
письмо дошло до тебя.
Мнѣ это очень отрадно.
Надѣюсь твоё здоровье
совсѣмъ поправилось и
уже больше не безпокоитъ.
Какъ всегда мои мысли
тебя никогда не покидаютъ,
а особенно 17го и 20го Октября.

24. Nicholas and Alexei tending the hens at Freedom House: manual tasks were the family's distraction.

25. Olga Romanova pulling her brother Alexei on a sledge in the grounds of Freedom House.

26. Vasili Pankratov, the ex-prisoner appointed as plenipotentiary to oversee the Romanovs in Tobolsk. He is wearing his favoured Siberian apparel.

27. Evgeni Botkin, the Romanovs' devoted personal physician. Botkin died alongside them in July 1918.

28. Sydney Gibbes, Englishman and tutor to the Romanov children. The fastidious Gibbes disliked intrusions on his privacy in Tobolsk.

29. Baroness Sophie Buxhoeveden, Alexandra's confidante. On arrival in Tobolsk, she quickly annoyed the guards and was ejected from the Kornilov house.

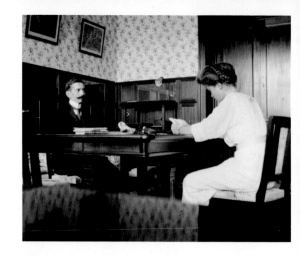

30. Pierre Gilliard, Swiss tutor who helped Alexandra with the family's financial accounts.

31. Ekaterinburg station no. 1, where the crowd was too hostile for Nicholas, Alexandra and Maria to leave the train.

32. The sequestered Ekaterinburg residence of Nikolai Ipatev, where the Romanovs were brought after Tobolsk.

33. Alexander Beloborodov, chairman of the Urals Regional Soviet Executive Committee. Ex-prisoner of the jail in Perm.

34. Filipp Goloshchëkin, military commissar of the Urals Regional Soviet Executive Committee. Goloshchëkin often discussed the Romanov question with Lenin before Nicholas and the family were executed.

35. Yakov Yurovski, last commandant at the Ipatev house and overseer of the execution arrangements in July 1918.

36. Vladimir Lenin, Bolshevik party leader and chairman of Sovnarkom. Lenin did everything to remove the traces of his part in the discussion about killing the Romanovs.

37. Yakov Sverdlov, Bolshevik Central Committee secretary and chairman of the Central Executive Committee of the Congress of Soviets. Close comrade of Lenin in the year after the October Revolution.

38. The blood-stained wall in the Ipatev house cellar after the execution of the Romanovs.

39. Armoured train used by a Czechoslovak fighting unit in 1918. The Czechoslovaks made their locomotives defensible against attack en route by pro-Bolshevik forces.

40. The file of crucial documents from the inquiry into the fate of the Romanovs collected by Nikander Mirolyubov. Mirolyubov retained the status of Procurator of the Kazan Palace of Justice.

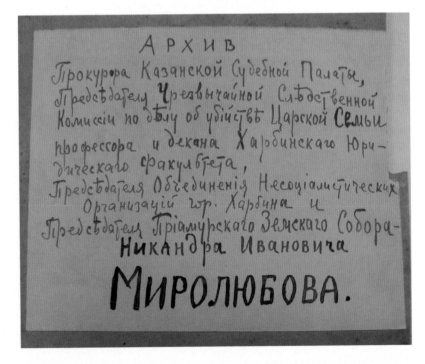

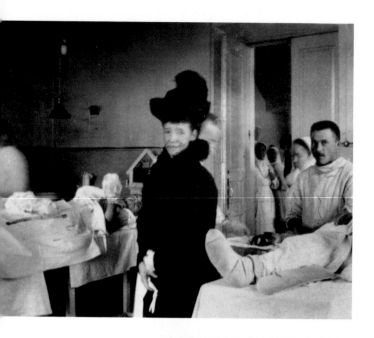

41. Dowager Empress Maria Fëdorovna visiting the wounded in the Tsarskoe Selo hospital in the Great War. After bidding goodbye to Nicholas II in Mogilëv in March 1917, she never saw him again. *Photo © Tallandier / Bridgeman Images*

42. Telegram from Alix (Queen Alexandra) to Minnie (Maria Fëdorovna) on 21 December 1918, pleading with her to come into exile. Maria Fëdorovna felt guilty about leaving the country.

MESSAGE RECEIVED BY WIRELESS TELEGRAPHY FROM THE
ADMIRALTY, LONDON, DATED THE 21st DECEMBER, 1918.
————————————

Following from Queen Alexandra for Empress
Feodorovna, Crimea :—

Darling Minnie,

Have just been informed that it would be
most advisable for you to leave at once before
more complications and horrors, so please make
up your mind before too late to come to me here
in England at once. Bring everyone you wish.
Your loving sister,
A L I X.

————————————

Yakovlev himself sent a cable to Goloshchëkin with an angry complaint about Zaslavski, Khokhryakov and Gusyatski. Trusting in Goloshchëkin's good faith, he expressed doubt that he had been initiated into the mischief being planned by his Urals comrades. Zaslavski, Yakovlev felt sure, was plotting to waylay the train before it reached Ekaterinburg. The plotters had failed to achieve their objective between Tobolsk and Tyumen; they would now make their attempt on the train journey from Tyumen to the Urals capital. Yakovlev told Goloshchëkin that he was determined to resist 'these young boys' by force; he stressed that he was carrying out Sovnarkom's orders, and asked for Goloshchëkin's assistance.[34] He knew that it might not be enough to have written approval from Sverdlov in distant Moscow. If he could, he wanted to get the Urals Regional Soviet Executive Committee to call off Zaslavski's dogs of war. But he still intended to avoid going to Ekaterinburg if he could. Sverdlov had told him to enter consultations on reaching Omsk. For Yakovlev, this was better than being told to go to Ekaterinburg but still not satisfactory. There was still a lot to play for, and he would play as hard as he always had done.

After Yakovlev came back to the train, he told his subordinates: 'We're off to Omsk and from there via Chelyabinsk to the Ust-Katav works in the Sim district.' When Avdeev made objections and refused to go, Yakovlev faced him down. Yakovlev had met tougher men than Avdeev and his physical courage was indisputable. He told Avdeev that Sverdlov himself had laid down that he had to travel. Avdeev made a last effort at resistance by demanding an explanation as to why Yakovlev had confined him to the train. Yakovlev replied simply that someone had to keep the Romanovs under constant surveillance. Only then did Avdeev comply.[35] Not only was party discipline paramount for every Bolshevik, but also Avdeev had no means to consult his comrades in Ekaterinburg. Moscow's orders trumped all other considerations and Yakovlev was playing his cards with his usual panache. For the moment it seemed that it did not matter if the Urals communist leadership disapproved.

29. DESTINATION TO BE CONFIRMED

On 28 April at 5 a.m., just before light dawned, the driver and stoker worked up steam in the locomotive before heading west in the direction of Ekaterinburg – quite the opposite to the plan that Yakovlev had indicated to Avdeev.[1] Russia's trains were slow in comparison with those on many networks in central and northern Europe, and even on main lines it was rare for a Russian train to average more than twenty-five miles an hour. (On branch lines, the usual scheduled speed was lower still.)[2] The trip to the Urals would take most of the day. At least, this was the impression that Yakovlev gave everyone who was standing on the platform in Tyumen. He had already instructed his driver that the real intention was to stop the train at the first little junction, turn the engine round and make for Omsk. Although this would involve passing back through Tyumen, Yakovlev calculated that he would complete the manoeuvre before anyone in the town guessed what he was up to. He was aiming to out-trick those whom he thought were working against him, and in Omsk, he felt sure, he would have the chance to decide exactly what to do next without feeling under threat.[3]

Loginov and Gusyatski in Tyumen, however, duly witnessed what was happening and cabled the Urals Regional Soviet Executive Committee about the train's redirection to Omsk. Their telegram reached Ekaterinburg at 10 a.m. and when it was brought to Beloborodov, he immediately called a meeting of the Soviet Regional Executive Committee to condemn Yakovlev as a traitor to the revolution.[4] Nobody in Ekaterinburg as yet knew that Yakovlev had conferred with Sverdlov and secured his approval. The sole thing that mattered for the Urals leaders was that Yakovlev was deliberately transporting the Romanovs out of their reach. All of Zaslavski's warnings about him seemed to have been confirmed. The Executive Committee also reflected on how respectfully he had talked to Nicholas and arranged life for the family in Tobolsk. Yakovlev's lack of consultation with Ekaterinburg about the changed itinerary gave grounds for deep suspicion, and the Urals leadership felt alarm about the possibility that Yakovlev had no intention of halting in Omsk. Beloborodov and his comrades speculated that Sverdlov's favoured commissar was none other than a secret monarchist who planned to press on to Vladivostok, where he would release Nicholas into foreign exile.

Such a plot would have been anathema to Nicholas since it would mean leaving his son and two of his daughters in grave peril in distant Tobolsk. But the Urals leadership had come to believe the worst of Yakovlev, and some of them supported the idea of killing Nicholas without further ado. These included the Left Socialist-Revolutionaries Khotimski and Polyakov as well as Bolsheviks Boris Didkovski, Georgi Safarov, Ivan Tuntul and Pëtr Voikov. Safarov spoke for them when he complained about the whole transport process since Tobolsk: 'Let the military commissar, comrade Goloshchëkin, tell us,' he demanded, 'how it came about that Tsar Nicholas galloped off to Omsk!' Voikov shouted: 'Scoundrel!'[5] Goloshchëkin, pale and agitated, did his best to explain what had happened but was unable to dispel the growing feeling that he, a known confidant of Yakovlev, had concealed important information from the Executive Committee. The Executive Committee decided to liaise with Moscow at the same time as it wired an alert to every railway station on the line to Omsk: Yakovlev must not be allowed to proceed with his plan to bypass Ekaterinburg. About that, at least, everyone could agree.[6]

Beloborodov angrily informed Sverdlov by telegram that 'his' commissar Yakovlev had tricked everyone by heading against orders to Omsk. Nobody, he stated, knew the train's ultimate destination and Yakovlev's behaviour was treasonous. He revealed that the Urals Regional Soviet had ordered his arrest and transfer along with Nicholas to Ekaterinburg.[7]

In his telegram to railway stations on the Tyumen–Omsk line, Beloborodov accused Yakovlev of disregarding Moscow's orders. The Urals Soviet Regional Executive Committee had concluded that Yakovlev had engaged in a 'betrayal of the revolution' and had placed himself 'outside the ranks of the revolutionaries'. Beloborodov called for Yakovlev to be arrested and, if he showed any resistance, shot on the spot. Yakovlev's entire detachment was also to be taken into custody. Beloborodov expected there to be violence and indicated that the other passengers too could be killed – this would necessarily have included the Romanovs. He asked that nobody should be influenced by any documents that Yakovlev might proffer in self-justification. The Urals regional leaderships of Bolsheviks, Left Socialist-Revolutionaries and far-left Maximalists were in agreement on bringing the 'criminal scheme' to an end.[8] The Urals Regional Soviet ordered a train of its own to travel at full steam to intercept Yakovlev and his party. The hunt for the Romanovs was on.[9]

Yakovlev let the Romanov party off the train to get some air shortly before Ishim, nearly 200 miles to the south-east of Tyumen.[10] He allowed a telegram to be sent to Tobolsk that contained the following message: 'The trip is going well. Christ be with you. How is the little one's health? Yakovlev.'[11] Almost certainly the wording was composed by Nicholas or Alexandra and passed to Yakovlev for approval. Yakovlev wanted the Romanovs to feel comfortable on the way to Omsk. He himself focused on the trip ahead. Despite the many pressures on him and his uncertainty about what the Urals leadership might be doing, he kept calm even though Alexandra was behaving with her usual hauteur. She simply could not help herself. She hated passing people in the corridor on the way to the washroom. Since she could not get rid of Yakovlev's guards and the railway personnel, she took to rising from her bed at four or five in the morning when no one was likely to be around, and if she saw someone, she turned about-face and went back to her compartment.[12]

The Romanovs had felt properly rested when they awoke on their first morning on the train. Looking out at the names of the stations they passed, they could tell that they were moving towards Omsk. But Yakovlev still refused to say where he was taking them, and Nicholas, like Beloborodov, pondered whether it might even be Vladivostok. If this was really true, the only credible plan would be to spirit the imperial couple into foreign exile. Another possibility was that Yakovlev intended to take a sharp turn at the junction with the southern loop of the Trans-Siberian rail line and take them westward to Moscow. They ate a pleasant lunch at Vagai at eleven o'clock, where Yakovlev ordered a halt. Nicholas conceded the querying duties to Maria, who went down to the four riflemen on guard duty at the far end of the carriage. She was unable to elicit any information and possibly they too were in the dark. The Romanovs distracted themselves by peering out of the windows to catch sight of people celebrating Palm Sunday. They went to their beds early after a dinner of cold dishes; they were none the wiser about Yakovlev's intentions.[13]

Avdeev, despite travelling under duress from Yakovlev, continued to discuss his plans with him. Yakovlev told of his commitment to taking the Romanovs through to Moscow – he now made no mention of Ekaterinburg; he reminded Avdeev of their instructions to safeguard the Romanovs and repeated his fear that Zaslavski was lurking somewhere with lethal intent. Appreciating the volatility of the situation, he halted the train again at Lyubino and, leaving the party with strict instructions, commandeered a car to Omsk to find out what was going on.[14] He was hoping for the best. Viktor Kosarev in the West Siberian Regional Soviet Executive Committee was an old party comrade of his. They had attended the Capri party school together and Yakovlev had hopes of securing his help against Ekaterinburg's pretensions.[15]

Kosarev had concerns of his own about Yakovlev's behaviour and had dispatched armed units to the little station at Kulomzino a few miles to the west of Omsk on the Ekaterinburg–Chelyabinsk line. He did this after receiving the telegram from the Urals leaders. He also sent out nearly 2,000 armed men with machine guns and artillery to arrest Yakovlev and the Romanovs. On arriving at Omsk station, which was two miles outside the city, Yakovlev immediately understood that he had to talk on the direct line to Sverdlov. Only Moscow could save him and his imperial captives from disaster.[16] Sverdlov yet again sided with him and telegrammed a message to Kosarev to the effect that Yakovlev deserved 'complete confidence' and was acting entirely according to instructions.[17] Yakovlev meanwhile discovered that Zaslavski, the enemy of all his plans, was somewhere in Omsk. Soon afterwards, it was reported that Zaslavski had disappeared after claiming that he had to return to Ekaterinburg on business. Yakovlev suspected that this was part of an assassination plot. He got on the line to Goloshchëkin and asked whether the Urals leadership had recalled Zaslavski. Goloshchëkin denied that any such order had been given. Yakovlev now knew that dirty work remained afoot and that Zaslavski was behind it.[18]

Sverdlov sent a cable to the Urals Regional Soviet Executive Committee defending Yakovlev against the charge of treachery and stressing that he was obeying Sverdlov's instructions. He warned Beloborodov against undertaking any initiative without Moscow's agreement: 'I repeat: no interference.'[19] The Executive Committee was not best pleased to learn that Sverdlov had engaged in secret consultations with Yakovlev. Sverdlov's behaviour discomfited the Urals leaders, who claimed that it was too late to 'annul' their instruction to Omsk and other cities on the railway line to arrest Yakovlev. This was apparently a bargaining ploy designed to ensure that Yakovlev should be ordered to make immediately for Ekaterinburg. They informed Sverdlov that the entire matter was under discussion at the Bolshevik Regional Party Conference.[20] They complained generally about Sverdlov's failure to keep them abreast of the change in 'Sovnarkom's objectives'. When no answer came from Sverdlov, they contacted Lenin by telegram and asked: 'What do you say to that?' They demanded a 'direct and clear reply'. They repeated that Yakovlev had perpetrated 'a colossal stupidity, with your approval, in driving the "baggage" towards Omsk'. But they ended by offering guarantees of physical safety for the Romanovs 'on condition that this whole business will now be conducted through the Regional Soviet'.[21]

Beloborodov cabled Kosarev to invalidate the content of telegram no. 3507 about how to treat Yakovlev. At the same time he indicated that he had secured the agreement of Lenin and Sverdlov to turn the train with the Romanovs westward along the Omsk–Tyumen line towards Ekaterinburg. He indicated that Moscow was about to inform Yakovlev about the plan.[22] Beloborodov also had to warn off Zaslavski and order him to do nothing to prevent the delivery of the Romanovs alive to Ekaterinburg. He reproduced the text of Sverdlov's respectful enquiry as to whether the Urals leaders would be content with an instruction from Moscow for Yakovlev to proceed to Tyumen and hand over 'the entire baggage' to the Urals Regional Soviet. He appended the expression of consent by Didkovski, Safarov, Khotimski and Preobrazhenski. Beloborodov wanted to leave no doubt in Zaslavski's mind about the fact that a settled policy had been reached between Moscow and Ekaterinburg; he instructed Zaslavski to go instantly to Tyumen. In an attempt to assuage any resentment that Zaslavski might be harbouring, Beloborodov told him to meet up with Yakovlev at the railway station and present his mandate and instructions to escort the three Romanovs, together with Yakovlev, unharmed to the Urals capital.[23] Zaslavski had hitherto acted like an assassin in the shadows; he was now to come into the open and take charge of the so-called baggage. Yakovlev's status was in steep decline.

When Yakovlev next talked on the Hughes apparatus, Sverdlov disappointed him by ordering that he abandon any idea of bringing the Romanovs to Omsk: 'We have agreed things with the Uralites. They have taken measures – they have given guarantees on the basis of the personal responsibility of the regional leaders. Transfer the entire baggage in Tyumen to the representative of the Urals Regional Committee. This is necessary. Go with them yourself, provide assistance to the representative.'[24] Yakovlev himself was to stay on the train until Ekaterinburg and hand over 'the entire baggage' to whoever came to meet him. Sverdlov thanked him for his work: 'You have accomplished the most important thing.'[25] He added that Yakovlev should borrow military reinforcements from Kosarev in Omsk before rejoining the Romanovs. This was an implicit admission that things could still go wrong. The Urals leaders were a recalcitrant bunch, and it could not be excluded that they still had some violent subterfuge in mind.[26]

Shortly after midnight, early on 29 April 1918, Kosarev conferred by the Hughes apparatus with Urals Regional Soviet Executive Committee Presidium member Georgi Safarov. Yakovlev had not yet started back to Lyubino, where he had left the Romanovs; indeed, he too was liaising with Moscow on another such apparatus. Kosarev received Safarov's assurance that the Urals leadership had settled the misunderstandings with Sverdlov and that Yakovlev, like it or not, had to bring 'the baggage' to Ekaterinburg. Safarov wanted to know whether Yakovlev's arrival in Omsk had led to any violence – he obviously had an interest in assembling a charge sheet against him. It was an odd situation; for this exchange happened at the same time as the Ekaterinburg Bolsheviks were depending on Yakovlev to do as Sverdlov had bidden him. Kosarev refused to join in any denigration of Yakovlev. Instead he repeated Sverdlov's demand that the Urals leaders should steer clear of doing anything in contradiction of Moscow's purposes.[27] Kosarev sent a telegram annulling Beloborodov's telegram no. 3507 of the previous day. Emphasizing that Yakovlev had come to Omsk exclusively with the approval of Sverdlov himself, he sought to get all Bolsheviks working well together.[28]

Yakovlev made one last attempt to persuade Sverdlov that the River Sim mining district remained a safer option than Ekaterinburg. This, he argued, would enable the central authorities in due course to bring 'the baggage' to Moscow. He was sceptical about whether this would ever be possible once Nicholas had been handed over to the Urals leadership. He claimed that Guzakov and Avdeev were agreed about the persistent dangers. When Sverdlov refused to change the plan, Yakovlev promised to obey Moscow's instructions, but he stressed that he could no longer take moral responsibility for whatever happened next. He complained about the chaotic conditions of the telegraph and asked that People's Commissar V. I. Nevski should order his people to accept no telegrams with messages that deviated from the plan that

Sverdlov had provided. With that, he promised again to take 'the baggage' to Ekaterinburg.[29]

By then the Urals leadership had sent their own detachment to Kulomzino and were blocking access to the southern loop of the Trans-Siberian Railway that could have taken Yakovlev and the Romanovs back to Chelyabinsk. Yakovlev was politically and geographically cornered. With a heavy heart he took his leave of Kosarev and travelled back to Lyubino, where he gave the order to return to Tyumen. To keep the Romanovs in the dark, he told them that he had been forced to change the plan because a bridge on the line to Omsk had been destroyed.[30]

He also overrode one particular point of his agreement with Sverdlov. Rather than meeting up with Zaslavski, he moved straight through Tyumen at dead of night. Yakovlev's Ekaterinburg adversary Gusyatski, who had stayed in Tyumen, set off in pursuit after learning about this. Nobody could be sure about where Yakovlev was heading, and there arose a concern that he planned to take the branch line to Shadrinsk and disappear with the Romanovs. Gusyatski soon discovered to his relief that Yakovlev was yielding to Goloshchëkin and travelling to Ekaterinburg. When Nicholas himself heard of this, his mood sank. He knew about the severity of the Urals revolutionaries even though he had no clue about the intricacies of their Marxist ideas. He approached Pavel Matveev in the carriage corridor and asked: 'Tell me, has it been definitely decided that we'll be staying in Ekaterinburg?' When Matveev confirmed the news, Nicholas let out a sigh and said: 'I'd rather go anywhere but the Urals.' Matveev tried to reassure him that it made no difference which place was chosen in the zone of Soviet power. Nicholas gloomily remarked that if the local press was to be believed, the Urals workers were fiercely hostile to him.[31]

Yakovlev took his time. After the train moved westward, he twice ordered a halt and allowed the Romanovs to stretch their legs. On the first occasion he insisted that they stayed close to the rail line. On the next he allowed them to walk into the nearby field in his company. Everybody's spirits were lifted.[32] But the halts were only delaying the inevitable for Yakovlev and Romanovs alike. At 8.40 a.m. on 30 April 1918 the train pulled into no. 1 station in Ekaterinburg – Nicholas kept a careful note of this.[33] A crowd had gathered, and Yakovlev held the train short of the platform while he assessed the situation. He lined his men on both sides of the train, threatening to order the machine-gunners to open fire unless people dispersed. Nobody took the slightest notice. Someone yelled: 'Show us that bloodsucker!' They had come to see Nicholas – and perhaps to do him harm.[34] Yakovlev had told Sverdlov that the Ekaterinburg option was fraught with risks. Sverdlov had overruled him, and it appeared that Yakovlev's presentiments were about to be realized.

30. TO THE IPATEV HOUSE

As Yakovlev improvised his itinerary from Tobolsk to Tyumen, Omsk and Ekaterinburg, the Moscow authorities gave the Urals leaders several days to decide how they were going to guard the Romanovs once they at last arrived in the Urals. They needed a site that they could easily keep isolated and impregnable to attack. The most obvious option was the city prison. Beloborodov and Goloshchëkin paid a visit to see whether they might be able to settle Nicholas in a separate wing from the other prisoners. They quickly decided that the architecture of the buildings made this impractical. What also put Beloborodov off was the fact that the director Shechnov, who was in charge of the jail, had been the deputy chief at Perm prison when he himself was a convict there in 1911–1912 – indeed, Shechnov in person had frequently ordered Beloborodov placed in solitary confinement as punishment for his behaviour. Beloborodov accordingly set out with Khotimski, the leading Left Socialist-Revolutionary on the Regional Executive Committee, to reconnoitre other possibilities as they scoured the entire central district for a suitable place of confinement for the Romanovs.[1]

After examining various public buildings, they narrowed their search to wealthy citizens' homes and inspected the house belonging to Dr K. S. Arkhipov, an Ekaterinburg liberal who had cooperated with the Bolsheviks. Whether Beloborodov thought it inappropriate to seize the Arkhipov mansion is unknown, but they eventually chose a residence occupied by the Ipatev family at the corner of Voznesenski Prospekt and Voznesenski Lane.

Nikolai Ipatev was a mining engineer and merchant who had benefited from the city's economic prosperity in the years before and during the Great War. He was a wealthy middle-class notable and his property was judged a suitable target for expropriation, if only on a temporary basis. Ipatev's house was a large stone building of two storeys, one of them being partially below ground level. It was a comfortable mansion for him and his family. The iron roof was painted green and the external walls had been whitewashed. A small garden ran along the side of the lane.[2] On one side it looked down to a broad lake; it also stood on a hill.[3] Both these features made it convenient from the viewpoint of security. It was also close to the centre of the city: the leadership liked the idea of a place that was within range of rapid contact. The sole disadvantage was the fact that the UK consulate was directly opposite on Voznesenski Prospekt.[4] But the Urals leaders aimed to shield the house from British eyes and it would be turned into a prison in all but name.

Their first requirement was to secure vacant possession. On 27 April 1918, already a full day after the former emperor had departed Tobolsk, Nikolai Ipatev received a visit from the Urals housing commissar, A. N. Zhilinski, who ordered the family to quit the premises within forty-eight hours. Written confirmation would be delivered next day. Ipatev was not allowed to know the identity of the new occupants except that they were people 'who won't damage things'. The Ipatevs were thrown into a frenzy as they packed what they could before leaving. In fact, they only had time to gather up small personal possessions. The Urals leaders insisted that the main items of furniture should be left in place. Ipatev took the precaution of locking up the crockery and some carpets, but he was subsequently asked – or rather ordered – to surrender the keys: the authorities intended to put everything at the disposal of the new occupants as soon as they reached Ekaterinburg. Ipatev was displeased and only a little reassured by the arrival of Pavel Bykov, a leading Ekaterinburg Bolshevik and Regional Executive Committee member, to compile an inventory of the house's contents.[5]

As a man of property, Ipatev was anyway about to lose all his civic and personal rights under the proposed new Soviet Constitution. He was a 'bourgeois', a member of the social class detested and persecuted by Soviet authorities. He was a marked man who had to be wary of annoying the Cheka. So he abandoned the house and most of his possessions and lodged with his Golkondski relatives outside Ekaterinburg in the village of Kurinskoe.[6] He could only hope that the Bolsheviks were sincere about looking after the house until he resumed possession. Bykov completed his inventory and put into storage those items that he thought of no use to the Romanovs and their guard detachment.[7] The bigger task was to turn the residence into an urban fortress. Goloshchëkin gave Housing Commissar Zhilinski another forty-eight hours to complete the assignment. Zhilinski recruited a hundred workers to refurbish the interior and organize external security. A double fence was put up to prevent people from entering the house unannounced – the outer one made everything but the upstairs windows invisible to the outside world. Zhilinski drove things at a frenetic pace and the work was finished in time for Nicholas's arrival.[8]

The Urals communist leaders failed to keep the plan a secret and many people in Ekaterinburg heard that the three Romanovs were on the move, and when news came through that their train had left Tyumen bound for the city, a noisy crowd gathered in and around the railway buildings. Crowds frequently gathered at railway stations in early twentieth-century Russia, when the arrival of trains remained the object of public excitement. Talk of the former emperor's expected appearance naturally added greatly to the excitement.[9]

Such was the commotion when the locomotive pulled into station no. 1, however, that Nicholas guessed that yet another dispute had broken out between Yakovlev and the Urals Bolshevik leaders. The truth was that Beloborodov and Goloshchëkin had lost control of the situation in and around the building as more and more people gathered to catch a glimpse of the Romanovs.[10] Some came out of curiosity, others to vent their spleen against Nicholas and his relatives. Tempers flared and threats were shouted: 'They should be done in! They're in our hands at last!' The guards supplied by the Urals Bolsheviks began to shift around nervously on the platform and violence became the likely outcome. Yakovlev at that point stepped down from his carriage and ordered his own soldiers to form a cordon around the train with machine guns at the ready. He was astonished to discover the station commissar himself goading the crowd and shouting: 'Yakovlev! Bring the Romanovs out of the carriage. Let me spit in his filthy face!' An armed stand-off occurred as it became clear that some of the soldiers on the platform supported the station commissar and were brandishing their loaded weapons.[11]

The solution, as Yakovlev saw it, was to move the train and its passengers to station no. 2 on the other side of the city and a couple of miles from the outskirts. Station no. 2 was the one used for commercial traffic and would mean another journey of fifteen minutes, and the hope was that the engine would reach there before any of the crowd did. But Yakovlev had reckoned without the continuing difficulty on the platform at station no. 1. Three further hours of negotiation passed while assurances were given that the Romanovs would be held in strict conditions of custody and that there was no ploy to liberate them. Yakovlev for his part held out for a guarantee that no harm would come to his charges. As he never failed to emphasize, Sverdlov's instructions were to ensure Nicholas's physical security. Having endured threat after threat since Tobolsk, Yakovlev sought a cast-iron guarantee from the Urals leadership. And all this time the crowd refused to disperse. But time took its toll on everyone and an agreement was achieved for the driver to start up the engine.[12]

Not surprisingly, the fracas renewed Yakovlev's concerns about safety. When the train pulled into station no. 2, he delayed the handing over of the captives to Beloborodov and Didkovski. This time there was no calm negotiation, and the Urals leaders, still angry about his management of the journey, bluntly ordered him to fetch the Romanovs from their carriage.[13]

This time there could be no appeal to Moscow. Beloborodov was now the master.[14] Yakovlev's last act of self-assertion was to line up his detachment around the train until he was sure that an orderly transfer was intended. This took a few minutes while he scouted the surroundings. But the delay could not last. With evident reluctance, he led Nicholas, Alexandra and Maria from their carriage, calling out their names when entrusting them to Beloborodov and Didkovski in person.[15] The two Urals leaders presented him with a formal receipt:

> 30 April 1918: I, the undersigned Chairman of the Urals Regional Soviet of Workers', Peasants' and Soldiers' Deputies Alexander Georgievich Beloborodov received from Central Executive Committee Commissar Vasili Vasilevich Yakovlev the delivery of the following from the town of Tobolsk: 1) former tsar Nikolai Alexandrovich Romanov, 2) former tsaritsa Alexandra Fëdorovna Romanova and 3) former Grand Duchess Maria Nikolaevna Romanova to keep them under guard in the city of Ekaterinburg.
>
> A. Beloborodov
>
> B. Didkovski (member of the Urals Regional Soviet)[16]

Administrative tidiness was a hallmark of Bolshevism across the zone of Soviet power. Ekaterinburg was no exception, and the men of the Urals with this bureaucratic chit were teaching Yakovlev that his authority as Sovnarkom's plenipotentiary had reached its term.

Troops walked the Romanovs over to two limousines which were to take them to the Ipatev residence. Three Bolshevik leaders stayed for physical oversight of the process: Didkovski sat at the front of one vehicle with Nicholas and Alexandra in the back seats and Beloborodov and Avdeev occupied the second. The plan was to drive at full pelt for the Ipatev house on Voznesenski Prospekt. There was to be no motorcade. After the palaver at station no. 1, Beloborodov had decided that the fewer people who were directly involved, the easier it would be to slip the Romanovs into the building at the destination. This had not been in the original plan for the day, when Goloshchëkin had made arrangements for a lorry full of Red Guards to shepherd 'the baggage' on its route. Instead it was Didkovski, Beloborodov and Avdeev who constituted the entire escort. They had one revolver each – Didkovski had a Nagant, Beloborodov a Browning and Avdeev a Mauser. If an organized rescue attempt had been made, it would have had a decent chance of success.[17]

Despite these precautions, word had got around and there was already a crowd outside the Ipatev house. Goloshchëkin barked an order and the inquisitive bystanders were dispersed.[18] The Romanovs entered gladly. Their long, exhausting journey was at an end. Although they did not know it, they were entering a house which they would never leave alive.

This was not the end of trouble for Yakovlev and the detachment which he had led from Tobolsk. Once they had handed over the three Romanovs, they themselves were treated as suspects. Yakovlev and his men from Tobolsk were paying for the breakdown of trust between Yakovlev and Beloborodov. It became obvious that the Urals leaders had only accepted Yakovlev's continued oversight of Nicholas from Lyubino because it was the sole practical way of securing their arrival in Ekaterinburg – and they also did not want to fall out with Sverdlov. But now the detachment was to pay a heavy price for their involvement. Instead of being congratulated on carrying out an exhausting mission in difficult circumstances, they were taken into custody in Ekaterinburg. The detachment's soldiers were to claim that they were held in a cellar for three whole days.[19] Nabokov and Lebedev were treated worse than Matveev, who was kept apart from them and somehow managed to communicate with Beloborodov and Goloshchëkin.[20] Matveev as a fellow Bolshevik was angry at the suggestion that he had been abetting a plan for Nicholas to escape.[21]

Yakovlev himself, accompanied by his men, was brought in front of the Urals Regional Soviet Executive Committee, which met in emergency session to sit in judgement about his recent behaviour. It was a noisy affair, as Zaslavski and Avdeev accused him of acting like Nicholas's loyal subject rather than a revolutionary. Angry words were exchanged. Yakovlev refused to be browbeaten. As proof of his right to act as he had done, he produced the tape of his conversations with Sverdlov. Inevitably this showed the extent of his distrust of the Ekaterinburg leadership, but it also revealed how he had asked Sverdlov's consent to take the Romanovs off to the mountains in his native Ufa province. Above all, it showed that Yakovlev had consulted Sverdlov throughout recent days in Tyumen and Omsk. Yakovlev denounced Zaslavski and Avdeev for wanting to kill Nicholas whereas Sverdlov had ordered him to protect all the Romanovs – this alone, he said, was why he had asked Sverdlov's permission to head for Ufa. Although Sverdlov had turned down the idea, he had at least for a while sanctioned the alternative destination of Omsk.[22]

Yakovlev cleared his name, and the Urals Regional Soviet Executive Committee Presidium recognized that he was indeed no traitor. Nonetheless, no love was lost between Beloborodov and Yakovlev. The verdict was less than generous. The session recorded that Yakovlev had displayed excessive nervousness and suspiciousness. No allowance was made for the grounds that the Urals leaders had given for Yakovlev to doubt that they were unanimously committed to obeying Moscow's orders.[23]

Yet there was no further threat to Yakovlev's safety or reputation, and Beloborodov wired to Lenin and Sverdlov that Nicholas, Alexandra and their daughter Maria were held securely in Ekaterinburg. The tensions in internal party relations subsided. Beloborodov told Moscow that he awaited further instructions.[24] The Urals leaders made clear their unwillingness to work again with Yakovlev. Goloshchëkin, with whom he had once shared an understanding, told him: 'Oh, Yakovlev, you've lost your revolutionary spirit!'[25] The Executive Committee packed him off back to Moscow. His soldiers were disarmed, paid off and demobbed; they were free to return to their homes or to Tobolsk. From then onwards, Ekaterinburg Bolsheviks would be responsible for guarding the Romanovs.[26] Yakovlev's first thought was to take all his detachment with him to the capital and have them corroborate what he had experienced since Tobolsk. He had no doubt that Lenin and Sverdlov would be horrified. First, though, Yakovlev returned to Ufa and on 3 May 1918 gave a report to a gathering of two groups of Red Army soldiers. He was still smarting about how the Ekaterinburg Bolsheviks had treated him. He had done his duty as agreed with Sverdlov and met with constant deceit and danger.[27] Only then did he go to Moscow. His soldiers were no longer with him and he went alone.[28]

31. THE URALS AND ITS BOLSHEVIKS

The Romanovs' stopping place, Ekaterinburg, had been chosen because it was a dynamic centre of Bolshevism whose leaders had already made their mark on the entire party. The Bolshevik Central Committee elected in April 1917 included Yakov Sverdlov, who left the Urals to become its secretary. Another Central Committee member from the region was Nikolai Krestinski, and in August, Evgeni Preobrazhenski was added as a deputy member. Other Uralites content to stay on in Ekaterinburg included Beloborodov, Didkovski, Goloshchëkin, Safarov and Zaslavski. Every single one of these was on the radical side in the party's many disputes about policy. Increasingly they were known as Left Communists. They had campaigned against a separate peace with the Central Powers. They had pressed on with fundamental economic change. They were intent on realizing their Marxist dreams without delay and insisted that the whole point of making the October Revolution was to seize the opportunity to establish instant communism. To the rest of the world, Lenin and Trotsky appeared uncompromising radicals while the Left Communists criticized them for undue caution, and the Urals was a crucible for their attempt to put ideas into practice.

Despite having grown into one of the empire's great cities, Ekaterinburg was still classified on maps as a mere district town of Perm province. For months after the October Revolution, Perm had retained the administrative institutions that had served the Provisional Government. The Mensheviks and Socialist-Revolutionaries, moreover, continued to head the Perm Soviet until the winter, whereas the Bolsheviks took power in Ekaterinburg within days of Sovnarkom's establishment in Petrograd.[1]

Industrial activity had expanded exponentially in the Urals since the late nineteenth century and, along with the coming of the Trans-Siberian Railway, was at the core of the city's importance. Modernity and tradition coexisted throughout the region. The old fur trade remained a highlight of the annual fair at Irbit, which, in the entire empire, had been second in size only to the world-renowned fair in Nizhni Novgorod on the banks of the Volga.[2] But it was the mining sector that spurred economic expansion. Coal and iron had been produced near Ekaterinburg for many decades. Russian prospectors swarmed into the Urals and found the world's largest source of platinum – already an important mineral in manufacturing. Chromite was another enticing discovery, and a start was being made on the excavation of copper, manganese and asbestos. An area known colloquially as Magnetic Mountain, south-west of Chelyabinsk, was marked out for exploration and was correctly assumed to contain vast metal resources in global demand.[3]

While the Bolsheviks were proud of having brought a large 'proletarian' centre such as Ekaterinburg under their sway, they knew that the working class was far from conforming to the stereotype laid down in conventional Marxism. Many workers in the Urals retained their ties to the countryside and were the descendants of peasants who had been compelled to labour in the factories and mines since the reign of Peter the Great. It had been a form of industrial serfdom. The peasantry built settlements around the enterprises, and it was common for families to have both a house and garden. Workers were half-peasant, half-proletarian. Families typically worked for the same factory over the generations.

This rural linkage had always made the region a good recruiting ground for the Socialist-Revolutionaries, and their rivalry with the Bolsheviks survived the October Revolution. For some weeks they kept up a comradely relationship. Ekaterinburg's Socialist-Revolutionaries – and even many of its Mensheviks – did not share the hostility to Bolsheviks that was characteristic of the capital. Opinion in the city soviet was already turning in favour of establishing 'soviet power' in early autumn, and when the recently re-elected soviet convened on 7 November, the Bolshevik presence was augmented and approval was given to Lenin's call for the overthrow of the Provisional Government. The Petrograd Soviet's Military-Revolutionary Committee lost no time that day in organizing an uprising and presenting power to the Second Congress of Soviets. The Urals delegates to that congress, whether they were Bolsheviks or not, heartily supported the October Revolution.[4]

The Ekaterinburg Bolsheviks set about lighting their political fire across the entire region. As early as 8 November 1917 the city soviet had declared itself the exclusive authority. The Provisional Government's plenipotentiary was dismissed and the local Kadet newspaper was closed down. Opposition was minimal and when the postal work-ers' union organized a strike that cut the city off from the rest of the country, the effect was to keep the enemies of Bolshevism in quaran-tine. The Bolsheviks set about the task of revolutionary transformation. At first the Mensheviks and Socialist-Revolutionaries collaborated with them by joining the Soviet's Military-Revolutionary Committee on 14 November, but tensions returned among the socialist parties. The revolution of Lenin and Trotsky in the Russian capital was brutal but fragile, and the Mensheviks and Socialist-Revolutionaries steadily moved into outright opposition and maintained their own freedom of manoeuvre.[5] Everything was to play for as the date of the Constituent Assembly election approached, and mutual denunciation became the norm among the parties.

On 6 December, when the results were announced and the scale of the electoral defeat for the Sovnarkom coalition became obvious, the local Bolsheviks repeated their proclamation of the Ekaterinburg Soviet as the sole fount of local power: they were determined to pre-empt the possibility of the Socialist-Revolutionaries forming a new government for the country.[6] On 26 December the city soviet called for the Kadets to be prevented from taking their seats in Petrograd. In Bolshevik eyes, the Kadet Party had put itself beyond the pale by supporting Kornilov's coup attempt in August 1917 and by the armed efforts of Generals Kaledin and Dutov to overthrow Sovnarkom. The Bolshevik deputies to the Constituent Assembly, led by Nikolai Krest-inski and Lev Sosnovski, were instructed to give every support to Lenin's revolutionary decrees.[7] Socialist-Revolutionaries in Ekaterin-burg predictably took the opposite standpoint and demanded obedience to the will of the Constituent Assembly. They were infuri-ated by Sovnarkom's closure on 6 January 1918, and the frail entente among socialists of the Urals collapsed.[8]

The entire Socialist-Revolutionary party network in the city was shut down and leaders were arrested and brought to a public trial designed to expose their supposedly counter-revolutionary activity since the fall of the Romanovs.[9] The Urals Regional Soviet Executive Committee was immediately besieged by citizens demanding their release. Bolsheviks could not afford to ignore opinion on the streets because they had overturned the Provisional Government in the name of the people. Since the Socialist-Revolutionaries retained their repu-tation as genuine revolutionaries, the Ekaterinburg Cheka reluctantly agreed to liberate a number of those incarcerated.[10]

The Bolsheviks went ahead with a general programme of industrial nationalization in January and February 1918,[11] which served only to hasten economic collapse. The monthly production of pig iron fell from 81,000 tons in January 1917 to 34,000 tons in May 1918.[12] With the sharp decline in coal and iron production in the Don basin, the eyes of Sovnarkom turned to the Urals mines as the main supplier. Such a hope was soon disappointed. The region's Bolsheviks were better at nationalizing enterprises than at regenerating production. Industrial activity slowed to a halt in many manufacturing and mining centres. Concern spread among workers that if they stayed unemployed for much longer, they could face starvation. Mensheviks and Socialist-Revolutionaries began to be elected again to seats in the soviets. Bolsheviks reacted in places like Zlatoust by ordering armed units to fire on working-class protesters. Red revolution was growing redder in a way that few had expected. In order to secure their power, Bolshevik leaders everywhere put their own officials and military detachments on privileged wages and food rations.[13]

Anti-Bolshevik army officers had meanwhile gathered in Orenburg under General Alexander Dutov. A battle-hardened cavalryman, Dutov had spent the year 1917 among Cossack military units and became one of their leaders in October. No army officer in the provinces was quite as effective at assembling a force to overturn Sovnarkom. On 15 November he seized control of Orenburg, marking the beginning of civil war in the Urals. Over several months he assembled his own Orenburg Army from volunteers.[14] He was not without a political inclination and had won election to the Constituent Assembly from Orenburg province. After its forcible closure in Petrograd, he offered his services to Komuch while remaining in Orenburg.[15] The Urals Regional Soviet faced the first serious threat to its existence as he swept north in the direction of Ekaterinburg. A financial 'contribution' of 10 million rubles was levied on the middle classes to pay for the new Red Army. In fact only 2 million rubles were collected, but the Bolshevik leaders succeeded in training detachments that could resist Dutov's advance. The first funerals of Red Army soldiers were held on 31 January 1918.[16]

Red Ekaterinburg asserted itself as the supreme power throughout the Urals and a Regional Soviet Executive Committee was created. Even so, the Bolsheviks met with resistance in the city itself. The Urals Pedagogical Union brought teachers out on strike against Soviet power. Beloborodov reacted briskly by closing down the old educational administration and embarking on the establishment of an entirely new one. Teachers sympathetic to Sovnarkom's cause were sought for the schools. But this was no easier than it was to find the money to sustain the region's finances. In November 1917 the Congress of Urals Metal Producers called for funds to be cut off to banks and enterprises. As nationalizations became imminent, there was an outflow of funds as owners strove to place their assets out of the range of Bolshevik expropriators.[17] As banknotes ran short, the Urals leaders printed their own regional currency.[18] They also appealed to Moscow for budgetary assistance. But the economic crisis steadily worsened and the discrepancy between Soviet rhetoric and Soviet practical achievements increased.[19]

In December 1917, when Sovnarkom decreed all banks to be state property, the Urals Bolsheviks broke into safe deposits in Ekaterinburg and seized the contents. At the same time they abolished the traditional judicial system. The old courts were abolished and a revolutionary tribunal began to sit in the city's Upper Iset district theatre – its first case involved the trial of individuals accused of killing a Red Guard. The soldiers' section of the city soviet pressed the Bolsheviks to hurry with the demobilization of the old Russian Army, starting with permission for invalided and evacuated troops to terminate their service; they also demanded the removal of the command staff.[20]

By the start of 1918 it was already obvious to Goloshchëkin that Soviet finances were in a ruinous condition throughout the Urals. He called for greater efficiency among Bolsheviks, who had made next to no preparations to govern. Now power was in their hands and they had to learn to wield it effectively.[21] The call for discipline grew stronger in Bolshevik party committees. The alternative was to remain vulnerable to armed campaigns by Sovnarkom's enemies. The Bolsheviks were famous for endorsing political centralism. They had a single dominant leader, Vladimir Lenin, who was thought to be able to impose whatever he wanted on his party. But the reality was that the party's organizational side was chaotic. It also had prominent veterans who resented the idea of hierarchical control being imposed over other comrades. Safarov, who had returned to Russia with Lenin before moving to Ekaterinburg, warned about the danger of excessive centralization. He reminded everyone about how the German Marxists had taken that path and ended up with policies hostile to genuine revolution.[22] Others objected to centralizing the country's railway administration. The instinct of many Urals Bolsheviks was that local soviets alone were able to achieve the level of responsiveness that the region's workers wanted.[23]

Ekaterinburg's middle classes felt the pinch of revolution as some of them – like Nikolai Ipatev – lost their houses to the new Soviet institutions. Cars, box safes and typewriters were also made liable to confiscation and the process was formalized by the establishment of a Requisition Commission.[24]

The Bolsheviks hoped to retain the services of technical specialists like teachers and doctors, but at the same time they asserted the primacy of working-class interests. The medical profession was among the first to experience the introduction of 'labour duty'. Decrees were issued to require physicians and surgeons to provide care within a framework specified by the city's health commissariat. Bolsheviks laid down that the poor should be accorded priority. Free clinics were established. Night-time medical facilities were made available. Pharmacies were 'municipalized' – this meant that the city administration took them over and expected the pharmacists to agree to work as its employees. A mandatory salary scheme was specified for all doctors. Each was to earn 300 rubles a month, with an additional 50 rubles for each family member. They were to work in line with the commissariat's orders. Health Commissar Nikolai Sakovich – a Left Socialist-Revolutionary and a medical doctor – announced that if he decided to send someone to deal with an outbreak of dysentery in some place or other, complete obedience was expected.[25]

As with other revolutionary changes, the resolutions written on paper were rarely implemented in full or at all. Sakovich hoped to ensure compliance from local doctors at a medical congress he organized in March 1918, but they refused to turn up. He tried again in May, but when he suggested that the healthcare system should be dissociated from political influence, the Urals Bolshevik leadership itself objected. Doctors attended this time, but only for long enough to register their objections to the reforms.[26]

There was a strong feeling in the air by then that 'soviet power' might be about to come to an end. Although professional groups opposed the October Revolution, they were unable to challenge the Red Guards in Ekaterinburg and could only engage in passive resistance such as by withdrawing their labour in the various social and economic agencies of the administration.[27] They walked out and tried to live on their savings. This, however, could merely be a temporary expedient at a time of rampant inflation when the ruble was losing value from day to day and the fiscal demands of the Urals Bolsheviks and their Left Socialist-Revolutionary coalition partners increased.

Food shortages were another difficulty and possession of a ration card became a vital necessity for everyone. Class conflict was lauded by Soviet regional leaders as the guiding principle of the revolution started by Bolsheviks in Petrograd and Ekaterinburg, and the 'bourgeoisie' was deemed full of irremediable enemies of the people.

The Treaty of Brest-Litovsk shattered the governing coalition as the Left Socialist-Revolutionaries resigned their posts in Sovnarkom and denounced the Bolsheviks. In Ekaterinburg, the two parties continued to cooperate even though the partnership became an uneasy one. The Left Socialist-Revolutionaries of the Urals recognized that Beloborodov and his comrades shared their hostility to Lenin's separate peace with Germany. Solidarity with the Ekaterinburg Bolsheviks seemed a desirable objective for Left Socialist-Revolutionaries, and they held on to their premises at the Commercial Assembly building on Ekaterinburg's Voznesenski Prospekt.[28] Together the two parties had weathered the political storms of a long winter. Although military threats, especially from General Dutov, continued to spark into life in places across the region, support for 'soviet power' among industrial workers was falling away. But the Urals Regional Soviet Executive Committee was proud of its achievements and determined to maintain the revolutionary spirit in Ekaterinburg. Beloborodov and his comrades felt that any local difficulties could soon be swept away if only they showed the necessary commitment. Bolsheviks and Left Socialist-Revolutionaries in the city were united in their hatred of the separate peace with Germany; they were eager to pull Sovnarkom back on to the path of unconditional offensives against capitalism and imperialism in Russia and the world.

32. MEANWHILE, IN TOBOLSK

The Urals leadership did not regard the Ipatev house as suitable for most of the retainers who arrived with Nicholas, Alexandra and Maria Nikolaevna. A personal search of Dolgorukov by the Cheka produced a number of suspicious items. It was found that he was carrying a large sum of money as well as two maps of Siberia which highlighted all the waterway routes. This was enough to prompt his dispatch to the Ekaterinburg prison.[1] Tatishchev suffered the same treatment on no such pretext. The fact was that the communists desired to strip the Romanovs of the support of anyone with military or political experience. They also imprisoned Fëdor Gorshkov after Nicholas approved his release from service on grounds of ill-health.[2]

There was a simultaneous tightening of control back in Tobolsk, where the soviet chairman, Pavel Khokhryakov, conducted a campaign of political repression. He was Ekaterinburg's chief emissary to the town, and the Urals Regional Executive Committee's growing influence was confirmed when messages at last reached Tobolsk that Nicholas, Alexandra and Maria had been delivered into its hands. The secret was first revealed on 3 May when Kobylinski at Freedom House received a telegram from Pavel Matveev, who reported on the convoy's adventurous journey. Until then it had been assumed that Moscow was the destination.[3] Now all roads seemed to lead to Ekaterinburg and Khokhryakov was left as the sole man in charge when Moscow designated him by telegram as Yakovlev's successor as its Freedom House commissar – and he paid frequent visits of supervision.[4] Tobolsk as a whole felt the weight of his authority. On 28 April 1918, he ordered the arrest of Bishop Germogen before transporting him to the Urals.[5] Germogen was a tireless opponent of the October Revolution and was implicated in the fitful attempts to rescue the Romanovs. Tobolsk had hardly any native Bolsheviks and there was widespread anti-Bolshevik sentiment in the populace. Khokhryakov aimed to make it secure for

Sovnarkom and he was taking no chances: every enemy of 'soviet power' was to be rounded up and either imprisoned or shot.

As part of his security campaign he conducted a thorough search of Baroness Buxhoeveden and her possessions. The composition of the troops continued to change as some were demobbed and others, including Latvians, arrived for service.[6] Khokhryakov intensified the process, dispensing with what remained of the contingent left behind by Yakovlev and replacing it with his Red Guards from Ekaterinburg.[7] He also called on the Urals leadership to send Rodionov, a Left Socialist-Revolutionary and Regional Soviet Executive Committee member, to Tobolsk and take day-to-day control at Freedom House because the commandant appointed by Yakovlev had taken to drink and was no longer dependable.[8]

Rodionov, like Khokhryakov himself a few weeks earlier, avoided travelling via Tyumen in case of trouble.[9] Arriving in Tobolsk on 6 May, he brought a letter and fresh orders from Beloborodov, who told him that eight of the troops under Yakovlev had been taken into custody because of a mere temporary misunderstanding – he added that everything had been resolved and that they had parted friends. This was an exaggeration of their feelings. Presumably Beloborodov was aware that many of Matveev's comrades remained in Tobolsk and were capable of causing trouble. Beloborodov, having won the struggle with Yakovlev over Nicholas's detention, aimed to keep everything in order in Tobolsk. But he also wanted Bolshevism to triumph and instructed Khokhryakov as the Tobolsk Soviet chairman to levy a special financial 'contribution' from the middle classes and deal ruthlessly with every sign of counter-revolution. Khokhryakov was to continue his repressive campaign and send all serious troublemakers to Ekaterinburg.[10] As it happened, Yakovlev's escort officers, Nabokov and Matveev, arrived from Ekaterinburg on 8 May 1918 along with five comrades.[11] They were inconsequential in the eyes of Khokhryakov and Rodionov, and the fact that they had been on good terms with Yakovlev no longer counted in their favour. Yakovlev too was history.

Rodionov was fit, slim and young with military experience and an abrupt manner. The members of the imperial family and retinue anticipated his arrival with trepidation, but not everyone found him as severe as they expected. Tatishchev recognized him as someone who had served abroad at the same time as he had before the Great War. He mentioned this to Rodionov and asked for his help. According to Gilliard, Rodionov replied: 'I know that you're a good person. You were never contemptuous towards people. I'm ready to help you as much as I can in your current situation.' Tatishchev replied: 'I've only got one request and I'd be grateful if you could fulfil it: it is that you won't separate me from the Sovereign and that I'm allowed to stay with him whatever may happen.' Rodionov, though, could give no such promise. As he explained, he was merely a member of the Regional Committee and was not a free agent. He was willing to be courteous but was not going to make unauthorized concessions.[12]

Kobylinski's authority was already spent – after a fuss made by the troops he even lost the right to enter Freedom House. He began to get the restrictions lifted after appeal to Khokhryakov, but Rodionov's arrival switched everything back. On 11 May he relieved Kobylinski of his responsibilities – and this time there was no reversal of the decision. Rodionov ordered his Latvian troops to bar his entry to the residence. Kobylinski's health worsened under the strain and he took to his bed.[13] The turnover of the old personnel continued. On 17 May 1918 Rodionov dismissed the entire existing guard detachment, replacing it with the force he had brought from Ekaterinburg.[14] In the same days he set about tightening the routines for guarding the Romanovs. Rodionov was concerned about the rumours of plots to rescue them, and he ordered them to sleep with their bedroom doors ajar at night. The Romanov daughters were naturally alarmed about this, but when Alexei Volkov objected on their behalf, Rodionov replied: 'My soldiers aren't going to walk past the open doors. But if you don't comply with my demand, I have full authority to shoot to kill on the spot.' Severity was gradually replacing civility.[15]

The stern treatment increased. Klementi Nagorny, the loyal ex-sailor employed to look after Alexei, was searched at Freedom House on his return from town and found to be carrying a letter to the tsarevich from Dr Derevenko's son. Rodionov told Khokhryakov that this proved the need for a further tightening of conditions. He also confiscated a dagger which had been left with Alexei. When nuns visited Freedom House, the detachment took pleasure in frisking them, and Rodionov placed a guard in the room during religious services. Olga could stand it no longer and said that if she had known in advance, she would have preferred the priest not to come.[16]

It had always been the intention that the young Romanovs who remained in Tobolsk would join their parents as soon as Alexei's health improved. Alexandra sent a message to Tobolsk asking her people to bring as many of the family valuables as possible when they came to

Ekaterinburg. She put this in code, referring to her jewels as medi-cines.[17] In the meantime, dinners at Freedom House continued to follow the settled routine. The menu remained of decent quality – and the Romanov table was even supplied with roast beef.[18] The family's daily requirements were never neglected. Alexei was on the mend and by mid-May, to his sisters' delight, he was feeling a good deal better.[19] The instinct of Tatishchev and Gilliard was to postpone the departure to Ekaterinburg for as long as possible; they felt with some justification that everybody would be safer in Tobolsk. But the three Romanov daughters badly wanted to rejoin their parents, and neither Tatishchev nor Gilliard felt justified in preventing this.[20]

The second Romanov party departed from Tobolsk in the steamer *Rus* at eleven o'clock on 20 May 1918.[21] On board were Olga, Tatyana, Anastasia and Alexei, accompanied by the twenty-six retainers who had stayed behind when Nicholas, Alexandra and Maria departed. Kobylinski remained in Tobolsk. Strictly speaking, as Kerensky's appointee, he did not belong to the retinue, but he had looked after the Romanovs as best he could and was much valued by them, and only illness prevented him from joining them.[22] Rodionov was in charge. He locked Alexei and Nagorny into their cabin – this seemed harsh when he saw no point in doing the same to Alexei's sisters and Alexei was hardly in sprightly shape.[23] Two days later they docked in Tyumen. Rasputin's daughter Maria happened to be at the harbour at the time buying tickets to sail north to Pokrovskoe. She noticed Alexei and Anastasia Gendrikova, his tutor, looking at her through a window of the steamer, and although they had no contact, she recorded: 'They were like angels.'[24] The Romanovs were under strict supervision while being escorted to the railway station, where they took the waiting train to Ekaterinburg. A fourth-class carriage had been reserved for them.[25]

They reached Ekaterinburg by train at two in the morning of 23 May 1918. For the next seven hours the engine pulled them backwards and forwards between the city's two railway stations. This railway carousel was designed to ensure that no crowd gathered to attend the scene.[26] Alexei and his three sisters were the first ones decanted from the train after nine o'clock and taken to the Ipatev house. Tatyana carried her pet dog.[27] When the Bolsheviks returned to the train at around midday, they took Tatishchev, Gendrikova and her fellow tutor Ekaterina Shneider from their carriage. Then they returned to remove the cook Kharitonov, the servant Sednëv, the valet Volkov and the servant Trupp. Sophie Buxhoeveden, perhaps feeling abandoned, moved into the same carriage as Gilliard and others. Eventually, Rodionov told all those of the retinue who remained on board that they 'weren't needed' and were 'free' – the order was then announced that they were required to leave the province altogether and indeed to go back to Tyumen.[28] The guards' duty book at the Ipatev house recorded the arrival of Olga, Tatyana, Anastasia and their brother Alexei together with the handful of retainers they had brought from Tobolsk. Nicholas's family was reunited.[29]

33. ENDURING EKATERINBURG

Nicholas, Alexandra and Maria had arrived at the Ipatev house on the eve of May Day. They could hear birds chirping in the trees next morning before the public celebrations commenced. The Red marching bands were distinctly audible from the building.[1] While listening to them, Nicholas was unaware of the dangerous volatility of the public mood in Ekaterinburg. People at the Upper Iset Works made a move to proclaim a 'day of vengeance' to exact retribution from the imperial family. This so alarmed Beloborodov that he scheduled a presence of Regional Soviet leaders in the Ipatev house for twenty-four hours.[2] His priority was to persuade more workers to sign up for the Red Army at a time when anti-Soviet forces were planning to fight for control of the Urals. Parades were held in the central streets in earshot of people on Voznesenski Prospekt. Banners were waved. Soviet leaders delivered speeches on their urgent plans for the defence of Ekaterinburg. Wealthy middle-class residents were press-ganged to dig trenches. Barricades were erected. Hostages were taken and held in prison under threat of execution.[3]

The Urals communist leadership told the Romanov captives that they would receive no indulgence. Alexandra was affronted by the demand by Didkovski and Avdeev to inspect their possessions – she saw no justification for such a procedure. Avdeev, fresh from Tobolsk and newly appointed as commandant at the Ipatev house, rejected her complaint, arguing that the authorities had to ensure their own security. His remark shattered Nicholas's composure: 'The Devil knows what's up. Until now there has been courteous treatment and decent people everywhere . . . but now?!' Avdeev bluntly explained that Ekaterinburg was not Tsarskoe Selo and that if Nicholas made any trouble, they would isolate him from his family. When Nicholas refused to calm down, Avdeev added that if the former emperor continued to be obstreperous, he would be taken off and put to forced labour.[4] This broke the spirit of resistance in both Nicholas and Alexandra. They could not imagine life apart, either from one another or from their children, four of whom had yet to arrive from Tobolsk.

Avdeev and Didkovski wished to ensure that the Romanovs lived on their state allowances alone and could not subsidize armed resistance. Their enquiries revealed that neither Nicholas nor Alexandra had a single kopek – their daughter Maria was carrying sixteen rubles whereas one of the retainers, Fëdor Gorshkov, kept over 6,000 rubles on his person. The Bolsheviks took most of these monies, leaving their owners with affidavits about the amounts.[5]

Sverdlov on 3 May had cabled fresh instructions. The telegram served to reveal his continuing support for Yakovlev but also to show how events had overtaken the possibility of fine control from Moscow. Sverdlov laid down that Nicholas should be held 'in the strictest fashion' while Yakovlev was to return to Tobolsk and organize the transfer of the Romanovs who remained there.[6] Beloborodov cabled a sharp reply. The Romanovs were already under 'strict arrest' and no outsider was being allowed to visit them. The retinue, including Botkin, were treated as if they had been arrested, and both Dolgorukov and Bishop Germogen were held in prison. Papers found on Dolgorukov had pointed to a potential plan of escape – Beloborodov told Sverdlov not to entertain any complaints about this from other people. The Urals leadership remained unwilling to admit that Yakovlev had had to take precautions to protect 'the baggage' after Tobolsk, and Beloborodov reported that there had been a cold parting between the two sides but that the Executive Committee had absolved him of counter-revolutionary intentions and attributed his behaviour to over-nervousness. Yakovlev, he pointed out, was no longer in Ekaterinburg but at the Asha-Balashev iron works in the Sim River district.[7]

The Executive Committee cut down the size of the retinue. Nicholas blamed Beloborodov. Whenever Beloborodov made his visits of inspection, it was obvious that his was the greatest influence inside the Urals leadership.[8] Nicholas conceived a pronounced dislike for him and asked one of the guards about the religious background of Beloborodov and other leaders. His enquiry was motivated by anti-Semitism, for Nicholas had concluded that Beloborodov must be Jewish. He was surprised when the guard explained that this was not the case and that Beloborodov was a Russian.[9] He nonetheless continued to detest him and the Executive Committee for his misfortunes. He deplored the retinue's treatment. Dolgorukov, Tatishchev and Gorshkov as well as Ivan Sednëv and Klementi Nagorny were under detention in Ekaterinburg prison. On 28 May 1918 Sednëv and Nagorny wrote to Beloborodov asking permission to return to their home provinces; they recognized that their service with the Romanovs had ended, never to be resumed.[10] Eventually, eighteen retainers took a train back to Tyumen, although halfway along the line they were halted at Kamyshlov for ten days.[11]

Goloshchëkin hand-picked a bunch of Bolshevik supporters to serve in a detachment to guard the Romanovs under Avdeev's command.[12] Steadily, the number of guards was expanded. Sergei Mrachkovski, fresh from leading the Red Guards on the 'Dutov front', visited the Sysert factory and recruited thirty workers at 400 rubles a month. A week later Pavel Medvedev, a local ex-miner, returned to the same factory and picked up another twenty volunteers. The Zlokazovo metal factory was another recruiting ground, and Avdeev himself went there in search of volunteers. While most of the new guards were Russian, some were Latvian. These two factories were known as centres of Bolshevik support.[13] It was not hard to tempt people to join the unit. As industrial activity waned, work was hard to find, and guard duties at the Ipatev house were paid well and fed well at a time when incomes and food supplies were in decline. Within a short time the unit acquired over fifty men under arms whose political loyalty could be guaranteed. Goloshchëkin, Mrachkovski and Avdeev had put together a Urals detachment from the local factories. Discipline was strict from the outset. The Executive Committee aimed to avoid the kind of outbursts that had often occurred in Tobolsk.[14]

Avdeev spent every day at the house from nine in the morning to nine at night. His deputy Alexander Moshkin as well as Pavel Medvedev were in permanent residence.[15] The guarding functions were organized in four daily shifts.[16] The guarding work was simple in nature. Medvedev explained to everyone that a guard was expected to stay at his post when on duty and avoid falling asleep.[17] No women were allowed into the building.[18]

The chief solace for the Romanovs was their religious faith, but the Bolsheviks would not allow them to attend church and only a few services were permitted in the Ipatev house. Father Ioann Storozhev ministered to them on 4 May 1918. The next service was delayed for another month. Indeed, there were only four occasions on which the clergy was allowed to minister to the imperial family.[19] Storozhev was to recall a Sunday – it was in fact 2 June – when an ill-kempt, unarmed soldier turned up at his house after early-morning Mass and said: 'You're asked to give a service for Romanov.' To the priest's enquiry as

to exactly whom this was for, the soldier replied: 'Well, for the former
Tsar.' (Troops in Ekaterinburg refused to provide Nicholas with any
lingering status.) Storozhev agreed on condition that his deacon,
Buimirov, could accompany him. Avdeev, however, had stipulated that
Storozhev alone should perform the function. When the priest stood
his ground, the soldier gave way and escorted the two clerics to the
Ipatev house. Avdeev let them in but objected to the idea that the
emperor would receive a communion wafer from Storozhev – the Bolsheviks would permit no chance of anything else being passed by
sleight of hand. Storozhev explained that there could not be even a
short form of the Mass without wafers, and Avdeev gave way.[20]

The imperial family had been eagerly waiting for the service. A
table had been prepared as a makeshift altar, and the sickly Alexei
lay on a bed with his mother sitting in a chair next to him. Led by
Nicholas, all the Romanovs bore up well – or so Storozhev thought,
even though Alexandra seemed physically out of sorts. Nicholas sang
the Lord's Prayer with brio. As the service came to a close, the priest
considered whether or not to offer the cross for the family to kiss.
He and Nicholas glanced at the commandant before doing this, and
the rest of the family followed except for Alexei, whom Storozhev
approached individually.[21]

As regards food, Avdeev had started by insisting that it should
come to the Romanovs and their retinue directly from the nearby
soviet cafeteria and should be heated up on arrival. But after he felt that
he had satisfactory control, he permitted the resident retainers to cook
for the family.[22] The abbess of an Ekaterinburg monastery sent two of
her nuns in lay clothing to the house offering additions to the family's
diet. These included cream, radishes, fish soup, gherkins, sausages and
bread. Avdeev saw no harm in this and even made suggestions about
what he thought might benefit the poorly Alexei.[23] There was cunning
in the seeming attempt to be helpful, for once Avdeev had received the
food supplies, he took what he wanted for himself and the detachment
before releasing the remainder to the Romanovs.[24] There was inadequate provision of cutlery – on one occasion, for example, there were
two spoons too few for the soup course.[25] Sometimes Avdeev, in the
attempt to impose his authority, chose to join the Romanovs for dinner.
He did this with a boorish swagger and once when serving himself
from the common plate, he caught the emperor in the face with his
elbow.[26] Sometimes, too, he was drunk on duty.[27]

Conditions worsened, moreover, on 14 May 1918, when Nicholas learned from Dr Botkin that the family were to be limited to an hour's daily exercise in the grounds. When Nicholas asked the guards for an explanation, he was told: 'So that it should become like a prison regime.'[28] Next day a workman turned up to apply paint to all the windows. The Romanovs were to have no sight of the city street, and when the family took a walk in the garden at 3.15 p.m. they were not even given a full hour before being ordered inside.

Nicholas had diminishing access to news about what was happening in Ekaterinburg or anywhere else in Russia. He no longer had visitors or daily newspapers, and the letters reaching him contained little information about public affairs because his correspondents knew that they had to avoid provoking those who censored the contents. For a man who remained preoccupied about the consequences of the Russian military collapse, the blackout of news was acutely frustrating. And the entire family wanted to hear about what, if anything, Moscow had in mind for their ultimate fate. One of their few sources of reportage was Dr Derevenko, who had lodgings elsewhere in Ekaterinburg. Avdeev saw what was happening and ruled that Derevenko could attend to the Romanovs only under his supervision, and there were days when Avdeev's absence meant that the doctor could not enter the Ipatev house.[29] Until then, the Romanovs had been able to use Derevenko as a two-way conduit of information. With Avdeev looking over his shoulder, the doctor could no longer say or hear anything that might make trouble for Nicholas and Alexandra.[30]

The Romanovs had never known much about internal Bolshevik politics and now they knew even less. Whereas Pankratov, Kobylinski and even Yakovlev had acted as a buffer between them and 'soviet power', all the authorities in the Ipatev house were hostile to the family. It made sense for Nicholas to get hold of the Bolshevik press. When Vorobëv, editor of the regional Bolshevik newspaper, demanded the normal payment for a month's subscription, Nicholas duly complied. He also sought news from the guards. When he asked about how the war was going, Pavel Medvedev replied that the fighting was now between Russians and Russians.[31]

Nicholas liked to ask any soldiers he encountered when they had entered military service, and whenever one of them mentioned a year before 1917 he would refer to him as 'my soldier'. When the answer was 1917 or 1918, he commented that he was a youngster.[32] One day Nicholas asked Medvedev why he was plucking and tearing up burdock. The answer said a lot about economic conditions: Medvedev was using the plant as a tobacco substitute.[33] Nicholas had a touching sympathy with his lot, and even the Bolshevik leaders admitted that the family eschewed many of the accoutrements of luxury. Nicholas wore patched old boots. The Romanov daughters, who lacked their mother's haughtiness, frequently raced to the kitchen to knead the dough and help to prepare the meals.[34] All the Romanov women sewed and knitted to keep busy and Alexei fashioned little chains for his toy soldiers. Nicholas did some outdoor work as at Tsarskoe Selo and Tobolsk, but it was not long before the authorities banned him even from cleaning up the garden.[35] He also suffered a problem with haemorrhoids and had to lie down with a compress to ease the pain, and Dr Botkin arranged for him to have his meals in bed.[36]

Ekaterinburg was meanwhile becoming a magnet for monarchist groups. One was based in the 1st Guards Cavalry Division in Petrograd and called itself the Union of Heavy Artillery. A plan was made for Colonel Kirill Sobolev to scout the possibilities. In May he arrived ostensibly to train at the General Staff Academy but with the intention of planning how to rescue the Romanovs. His survey of the landscape and security precautions around the Ipatev house convinced him that it would be suicidal to attack the premises. Although he remained at the Academy and held discussions with sympathetic fellow officers, he refrained from action.[37]

The hotels of Ekaterinburg continued to greet visitors who petitioned the regional soviet for consent to meet the emperor, and the British consulate across the road erected an observation point from which to follow events at the house.[38] The Urals communist leaders refused every request for an interview with Nicholas. The requests themselves served only to agitate the Bolsheviks, who were acutely worried about the danger of armed conspiracy. Sophie Buxhoeveden, Pierre Gilliard and Sydney Gibbes continually pressed the Western consulates to find a way to secure the release of Nicholas and his family.[39] But there was nothing that the diplomats could do in the situation and they found that their enquiries about the Ipatev house served merely to aggravate the mood of agitation among the Urals communist leadership, and Major Migić, who belonged to the general staff of the Serbian forces and spoke fluent Russian, was especially insistent that he had to discuss the course of the Great War with Nicholas. Other Serbians arrived, including an ensign called Vožetić and a certain Smirnov who served in the Queen of Serbia's entourage. It became clear that they represented Grand Duchess Elena Petrovna, the Serbian wife of

Nicholas's cousin Ioann Konstantinovich, who was in custody in the Urals.[40]

Beloborodov and Goloshchëkin were never going to let a foreign in-law of the house of Romanov enter the Ipatev house, far less discuss the Great War. The imperial family was to remain isolated so that no harm could come to the Soviet cause.[41] In fact, Nicholas was never quite the innocent prisoner that he pretended to be. One of the Cheka officials, I. I. Radzinski, later claimed that Nicholas wrote verses ridiculing the Bolsheviks – supposedly they were found in his bedside drawer.[42] This was the least of his disruptiveness. On one occasion when he wrote to relatives, he tucked a sketch of the Ipatev house into the envelope with indications about who was to be found in each room. This would help assailants if ever they could find a way to break into the building. Nicholas was obviously nursing hopes of a rescue attempt, but he reckoned without Avdeev's scrutiny of every letter.

Avdeev was furious. Instead of talking to Dr Botkin as usual, he summoned Nicholas in person. Nicholas asked for Botkin to be allowed to accompany him. When Avdeev disallowed the request, Nicholas went instead with one of his daughters. Avdeev waved him towards a seat. Nicholas refused, preferring to stay on his feet. If he thought this would give him a psychological edge, he was soon proved wrong. Avdeev began by announcing that a prohibited sketch had been discovered in the latest outgoing letter. Nicholas blustered that this was news to him. Avdeev took no nonsense; he explained that anyone could tell that the handwriting was unmistakably that of the former emperor. Nicholas crumbled, admitting responsibility for the sketch and promising never to repeat the behaviour. He was warned unequivocally that if he failed to keep his word, he would be hauled off by himself to prison. This was enough to break his resolve: he could not bear the idea of being separated from his family, and he reverted to passive acceptance of the current situation.[43]

Pëtr Voikov and I. I. Radzinski tested his sincerity by concocting two provocative letters addressed to Alexandra. Voikov, Regional Commissar for Food Supplies, became involved because he knew French after years working in emigration. He dictated the texts to Radzinski, who wrote them out in red ink and signed them 'Russian Officer'. The aim was to trick the Romanovs into colluding with a conspiracy that did not exist.[44] One of the guards passed a letter to them in late June from someone signing himself this time as 'Officer of the Russian Army' and alerting them to the worsening military situation for the Bolsheviks. Samara, Chelyabinsk and Siberia were now held by their enemies, and the Czechoslovak Legion of ex-POWs, which had risen against Sovnarkom, was only fifty miles from Ekaterinburg. According to the letter, the imminence of military defeat increased the Bolshevik threat to Nicholas and his family. The self-styled officer asked them, in preparation of a rescue attempt, to transmit a sketch of the interior of the Ipatev house.[45] Several exchanges of correspondence followed and the 'officer' instructed the inmates to sleep in their day clothes and be ready to climb from a front window at dead of night. The Romanovs fell for the deceit while asking for a guarantee of no bloodshed, and the Urals leadership acquired confirmation of their feeling that Nicholas would cooperate with any serious effort to liberate them.[46]

Suspicions grew on both sides. On 10 June, the guards ransacked the suitcases stored in the vestibule and removed a lot of items that had accompanied the Romanovs from Tobolsk. No explanation was given. Nicholas felt sure that these things would end up in guards' homes and be lost forever: 'Disgusting!'[47] He noticed a change in the whole demeanour of the guard unit, especially their new reluctance to speak to him. He had the impression that they were worried about something: 'Incomprehensible!'[48] Then on 15 June Dr Derevenko was barred from the residence. He stood outside pleading at least for permission to deliver milk and eggs. Dr Botkin, who lived at the Ipatev house with the Romanovs, made a request to send a letter to the regional soviet asking it to extend outdoor exercise to two hours a day and to get the windows opened.[49] Neither of the doctors was successful. The Romanovs had blotted their already stained reputation in the eyes of the Urals leadership, and no pleas on their behalf stood any chance of fulfilment.

34. A SENSE OF THE WORLD

What sustained the family's morale was their love for each other and their Christian faith. Consequently, if the Soviet authorities had wanted to crush their spirit, the obvious way would have been to separate Nicholas and Alexandra from their children and confiscate their devotional texts. What would equally have unhinged Nicholas would have been a ban on his access to literature. The Urals Soviet authorities refused him permission to request material from a local library as he had done in Tobolsk, and the fact that his senior retainers were barred from the Ipatev house meant that he could no longer borrow volumes from them. Alexandra continued to sink into learned studies of Christianity, and the imperial couple ceased to have the vibrant conversations that had sustained their marriage during their years in power. But Nicholas could still turn to the books that they had brought along from Tobolsk as well as those he found on the shelves of the Ipatev house, and he used them to steady his thoughts.

The first book that Nicholas read was Alexandra's, a copy of Belgian author Maurice Maeterlinck's *Wisdom and Destiny*, in the original French.[1] It was a collection of aphoristic musings that won a wide readership in the pre-war years, and it was on the strength of it that Maeterlinck had won the Nobel Prize for Literature in 1911. Nicholas finished it quickly; he was so impressed that he read it aloud to the family for their evening edification.[2]

With its languorous style and portentous content, *Wisdom and Destiny* has long since lost its admirers. Nicholas never recorded what he liked about it but he was probably encouraged by the pages where Maeterlinck pleaded for sympathy for Louis XVI's difficulties during the French Revolution:

> Let us rather imagine ourselves in his place, in the midst of his doubt and bewilderment, his darkness and difficulties. Now that we know all that happened it is easy enough to declare what

should have been done; but are we ourselves, at this moment, aware of what is our duty? Are we not contending with troubles and doubts of our own? And were it not well that they who one day shall pass judgment upon us should seek out the track that our footsteps have left on the sands of the hillock we climbed, hoping thence to discover the future? Louis XVI was bewildered: do we know what ought to be done? Do we know what we best had abandon, what we best had defend? Are we wiser than he as we waver betwixt the rights of human reason and those that circumstance claims? And when hesitation is conscientious, does it not often possess all the elements of duty?[3]

If any ruler had trudged through a comparable vale of tears, it surely was Nicholas of Russia in March 1917.

Nicholas had tried do the right thing by his own lights, which was precisely what Maeterlinck claimed for Louis XVI:

There is one most important lesson to be learned from the example of this unfortunate king: and it is that when doubt confronts us which in itself is noble and great, it is our duty to march bravely onwards, turning to neither right nor left of us, going infinitely further than seems to be reasonable, practical, just. The idea that we hold today of duty, and justice, and truth, may seem clear to us now, and advanced and unfettered; but how different will it appear a few years, a few centuries later![4]

It is easy to imagine how these words would have comforted a man who had marched 'bravely onwards', convinced that he was carrying out his duty in defiance of hostile political demands.

According to Maeterlinck, moreover, Louis XVI was an early victim of the impact of a new and disturbing set of ideas upon his kingdom:

And is there a thing in this world can be more reassuring, or nearer to us, more profoundly human, than an idea of justice? Louis XVI may well have regretted that this idea, that shattered his peace, should have awakened during his reign; but this was the only reproach he could level at fate, and when we ourselves murmur at fate our complaints have much the same value.[5]

France in the late eighteenth century had been one of the crucibles of the European Enlightenment with its commitment to rationality, science and justice as well as to the removal of nonsensical traditions and oppression from on high. Russia at the start of 1917 suppurated with campaigns to create a more just society. These were not new campaigns but rather had been cultivated for decades by enemies of the tsarist order. Nicholas had always rejected them, and after falling from power, he never queried his assumptions. The likelihood is that he found some consolation, however misplaced, in the sentiments that Maeterlinck expressed.

He may also have been comforted by the author's contention that rulers were not culpable for their lapses in anticipation:

> It is good that the hand should believe that all is expected, foreseen; but good, too, that we should have in us a secret idea, inviolable, incorruptible, that will always remember that whatever is great most often must be unforeseen. It is the unforeseen, the unknown, that fulfil what we never should dare to attempt; but they will not come to our aid if they find not, deep down in our heart, an altar inscribed to their worship. Men of the mightiest will – men like Napoleon – were careful, in their most extraordinary deeds, to leave open a good share to fate.[6]

Maeterlinck painted a picture of politics as an untameable force of nature:

> These feverish hours of history resemble a storm that we see on the ocean; we come from far inland; we rush to the beach, in keen expectation; we eye the enormous waves with curious eagerness, with almost childish intensity. And along comes one that is three times as high and as fierce as the rest.[7]

It is not hard to imagine that a Russian emperor who had made so many avoidable mistakes might have found succour in the idea that history could bring even the mightiest of tsars to his knees.

Maeterlinck stressed that fate plays a big part in human events and that faith in rationality is faith misplaced:

> We shall not become wise through worshipping reason alone, and wisdom means more than perpetual triumph of reason over inferior instincts. Such triumphs can help us but little if our reason be not taught thereby to offer profoundest submission to another and different instinct – that of the soul.[8]

Nicholas, ever the fatalist, had found an author who spoke to his instincts.

After *Wisdom and Destiny*, he turned to Russian literature, and in particular to N. A. Leikin's *Neunyvayushchie rossiyane* (*Undespondent Russians*), not a part of the nineteenth-century classical canon but a lively source of insight into society below the level of the aristocracy and the high command.[9] Something inside Nicholas told him that he knew too little about his people, and perhaps he was at last beginning to recognize that he had been wrong to ignore and despise Russia's merchantry in his years on the throne.[10] Leikin, a friendly rival of Anton Chekhov until his death in 1906, had been famous for his articles about merchants in the *Peterburgskaya gazeta*. His usual focus was on the capital's commercial class, from which he himself was descended. Leikin's tone was humorous and sympathetic towards merchants and professional people of middling achievement, with all their foibles. While affectionately itemizing their clothes, food and manners, he punctured their social snobbery.[11] But beneath his satire, Leikin was a proud Russian. He depicted the towns of Russia as an ethnic melting pot in which Russian culture was peacefully and properly triumphing over its rivals in the empire.[12]

Nicholas also read books that took a grimmer view of Russian society. Engineer Ipatev had left behind the collected works of Mikhail Saltykov-Shchedrin on his shelves, and it was not long before Nicholas was reading *The Golovlëv Family*.[13] This was a novel that offered an unsparing indictment of small-town life and trade. Old man Golovlëv, a penny-pinching merchant, tyrannized his sons and turned them into copies of his own resentful, unimaginative nature. Readers in the nineteenth century took Saltykov-Shchedrin to their hearts as an observer of the stagnant pools that required stirring before Russia could make progress. Nicholas did not record how he reacted to the novel and it is not even certain that he read it to the dispiriting end. (If he did, his resilience under house arrest was truly extraordinary.)

After Saltykov-Shchedrin, he moved on to Tolstoy's *War and Peace*. For educated Russians, this was one of the great national classics, and – if we are to take his diary entries as a guide – he had never looked at it before his detention in Ekaterinburg. Tolstoy, despite his worldwide fame, had continued to suffer restrictions by the censors through to his death in 1910; he had also been excommunicated by the Russian Orthodox Church. But there was something about *War and Peace* that powerfully appealed to Nicholas. The novel dwells on Russia's travails in a time of invasion and defeat by Napoleon's Grande Armée followed by victory. When Nicholas fell from power in early 1917, Russia had not yet been defeated, not by a long way. But it was a moment of gathering crisis and conditions at the front went from bad to worse once he abdicated. Furthermore, the Brest-Litovsk treaty signalled a military and territorial loss to the Germans as grievous as that which had been suffered at French hands in 1812. By the end of the same year, the Russians had exposed the logistical weaknesses in Napoleonic strategy, and the Grande Armée was pushed into a humiliating retreat as Napoleon himself fled to Paris and personal safety.

Such was Nicholas's enthusiasm for *War and Peace* that in the May evenings he read the novel's huge final section to his family.[14] There were searing chapters about the burning of Moscow in 1812 by Russian authorities seeking to deprive the French of the fruits of its military victory. One of the heroes, Pierre Bezukhov, sets out on an abortive personal mission to assassinate Napoleon. Meanwhile, the Russian armies are regrouped for a counter-attack and soon the French are pushed into a humiliating retreat. It is not hard to imagine that the depiction of defeated French armies uplifted the mood of Nicholas and his family – perhaps the same fate awaited the German occupiers. The Romanovs were clinging to remnants of hope.

35. CIVIL WAR

The Romanovs' removal to Ekaterinburg had been planned on the premise that they could be held there more safely than in Tobolsk until such time as Moscow was ready to receive them for a big show trial. The only thing right about this calculation was that Tobolsk was insecure as a place of confinement. The Bolsheviks had never had a strong political base in the vicinity, and Sovnarkom's sovereignty was entirely attributable to the external military agencies from Petrograd, Omsk and Ekaterinburg. Violence as yet was minimal. A Red Guard detachment made yet another sortie to Golyshmanovo in June. When the village priest rang the church bell at their approach, the Red Guards thought he was sounding an alarm for anti-Bolsheviks to escape into hiding. After an exchange of fire, the priest was taken captive and marched off to be executed.[1]

Most of the armed conflicts in the Urals and adjacent regions in the first months of 1918 remained local in nature, having little practical significance for Moscow or Petrograd, and it was the same situation in most other territories of the former Russian Empire. The Bolsheviks, despite frequently talking in 1917 about the potential outbreak of civil war, were remarkably slow to appreciate the scale of the fighting that their seizure of power was likely to bring about. Komuch's People's Army was aiming to move into central Russia as soon as it had enough troops and equipment. When this happened, it would be a war between two left-wing forces, one led by the Socialist-Revolutionaries, the other by the Bolsheviks. But armies were also being formed which adhered to the political right. General Kornilov, after escaping captivity, joined General Alexeev deep in southern Russia, where they were recruiting a volunteer army. Initially it consisted mainly of ex-officers, but Alexeev planned to expand its ranks and, as soon as possible, march on Moscow. Admiral Kolchak was pursuing a similar purpose in mid-Siberia. It was only a matter of time before these military preparations would burst into all-out civil war and compel the Bolsheviks to organize a stern defence of the cities that they held in central Russia.

Lenin himself nevertheless felt sure that the civil war was already over as early as February when the Reds in southern Russia defeated a small Cossack force under Afrikan Bogaevski. As late as April he was still displaying a pronounced military complacency:

> The task of suppressing the resistance of the exploiters was already resolved in the period from 25 October 1917 to (approximately) February 1918 or to the surrender of Bogaevski.
>
> Next on to the agenda there comes . . . the task – the task that is urgent and the peculiarity of the current moment – of organizing the *administering* of Russia.[2]

It remained an article of faith among Bolsheviks that so long as they could hold on to their support among industrial workers, their security would be guaranteed. In February, after having demobilized the old imperial army, they started to form their own Workers' and Peasants' Red Army, but with less than total urgency, and much prejudice against military professionalism remained to the fore throughout the party leadership.

The Bolsheviks and Left Socialist-Revolutionaries in Ekaterinburg focused their military preparations on defence against General Dutov's force. It is estimated that there were 12,375 Red Guards in the Urals in the last winter months and that 3,000 were based in Ekaterinburg alone.[3] The Urals Regional Soviet Executive Committee brought them together in two groups. The first was led by Ivan Malyshev, the second by Sergei Mrachkovski. Malyshev took his people off in early 1918 to Orenburg to confront a force headed by Ataman Dutov. Mrachkovski concentrated on preparing the defences of Ekaterinburg.[4] These volunteers were no match for experienced troops. Local Red Guards were used to doing as they pleased rather than obeying orders. They objected to the instructors who provided weapons training; they also disliked the idea of marching or deploying in formation. Bolshevik leaders only made a bad situation worse. A. Kadomtsev was famous as a veteran of the faction's armed units in the 1905 Revolution. He was proud of Bolshevism's accomplishments without assistance from the detested officer corps of the Russian Army. For him, it was a good thing that each Red Guard unit (or *druzhina*) should act on its own initiative. Preference was given to recruits from the industrial factories. In the early military encounters there were often bursts of ill-aimed fire when the enemy appeared ahead.[5]

But outside the Urals there were other forces that allied themselves with Dutov. Chief among them was the People's Army of Komuch, which radiated out from the Volga region and looked for organized armed formations to challenge Sovnarkom and its local governmental agencies. As yet the Urals Regional Soviet Executive Committee faced no direct menace from Komuch and its allies, but there was an obvious necessity to prepare for any sudden change in the strategic situation, and efforts were made in Ekaterinburg to strengthen the city's military capacity.

The Urals enlistment campaign intensified after the peace treaty with Germany was signed at Brest-Litovsk, and some of the Urals volunteers were to claim – admittedly as prisoners of counter-revolutionary forces, when they might have wanted to appear more patriotic than they really were – that they yearned to fight the Germans and instead were mobilized against Dutov.[6] The Bolshevik regional leadership encouraged all this. Although they could not rip up the peace treaty and continued to believe that Lenin had committed a terrible mistake, they aimed to make the best of a bad job by making military preparations; they also lent their weight against any more concessions being made to imperial Germany.[7] Their hope was that the Party Central Committee would see the error of its ways and proclaim an armed crusade against world capitalism. Recruitment of troops was conducted with a view to being ready for a 'revolutionary war' that would pitch the Reds against Germany and Austria-Hungary, shatter the political regimes in central Europe and install communist administrations throughout the continent. The Urals leadership accepted that it could not start such a war by itself. While it waited on events at the national level, it aimed to bring the Urals under proper control. This above all else required a decisive campaign on the 'Dutov front'; recruits were also deployed to the villages to requisition grain from a reluctant peasantry.[8]

The military situation worsened still further after the transfer of the Romanovs to Ekaterinburg. Although the origins of the process had nothing to do with the Urals, the impact on the region would soon become profound.

Violence reached a new peak of intensity in the Urals with a revolt by the Czechoslovak Legion that exploded in Chelyabinsk, only 140 miles to the south of Ekaterinburg and linked to it by a direct rail line. The Legion was a force consisting of Czech and Slovak POWs travelling in groups to Vladivostok. Their intention was to re-enter the Great

War on the Allied side in Western Europe. After Brest-Litovsk, Trotsky as People's Commissar for Military Affairs sought to keep up a degree of cooperation with the Allies as a counterbalance to the Germans. He and Lenin were aware that the Brest-Litovsk peace might not hold. It was always possible that Germany might suddenly invade Russia and overthrow the Bolsheviks. To guard against a worsening of relations with Berlin, Trotsky continued to talk to British, French and American diplomats and forged working links with Robert Bruce Lockhart, the United Kingdom's leading emissary in Moscow. The permission for the Czechoslovak Legion to leave for abroad was one of Sovnarkom's gestures designed to prove that the Soviet authorities were not yet wholly under Germany's control. There was also the hope that this would dissuade the Allies from dispatching a military expedition against Soviet Russia.

This was always a risky policy, and Trotsky's growing distrust of the Czechoslovak Legion commanders pushed him into issuing an order for the travelling force to be disarmed. In the first clashes in Chelyabinsk, the Red forces were no match for men of the old Austro-Hungarian army who had seen action on the Eastern Front and retained their morale and determination. The Czechoslovaks seized the telegraph facilities and transmitted a call to arms to the groups that were dispersed to the east and west of Chelyabinsk along the Trans-Siberian Railway. At every station on the line they crushed the Red resistance and cabled their news to their comrades elsewhere.

The Czechoslovak plan as it quickly developed was to gather together all their groups and ally with Komuch to overthrow the Bolsheviks. From Chelyabinsk they sent units west to secure a number of mining townships including Miass and Zlatoust in the direction of Ufa. A force of Czechoslovaks also moved north up the Chelyabinsk–Ekaterinburg link, stopping at Kyshtym; they also moved east from Chelyabinsk along the Trans-Siberian Railway and took Shadrinsk and Kurgan. Omsk fell to Czechoslovak troops on 7 June.[9] Their victories encouraged Russian anti-Bolshevik armed detachments to begin operations. Further north, Tyumen fell to an anti-Bolshevik force. Nizhni Tagil followed shortly afterwards. These were heavy losses for the regional administration because Tyumen lay directly to Ekaterinburg's east and Nizhni Tagil to its north. The ring of enemies was near to being closed around Ekaterinburg by early July.[10] They could travel neither to the north nor to the south, and if they wanted to inspect Alapaevsk they had to take the branch line that avoided Nizhni Tagil.

The Urals Regional Soviet Executive Committee had lost almost all authority over the provinces in its region.

Panic spread throughout Ekaterinburg when the news of the fall of Chelyabinsk arrived. As the military emergency intensified, the Ekaterinburg Soviet mobilized a section of its own deputies to bolster the Red Army as it prepared to withstand attack by the Czechoslovak Legion.[11] The railway stations were packed with people.[12] Bolsheviks in Ekaterinburg needed all the voluntary assistance they could find to halt the Czechoslovak advance. They turned to the anarchists, whom they had recently expelled from their political headquarters in the city. The Czechoslovak threat brought them together again, and joint action by Red Guards and anarchist armed groups was established.[13]

The circle of Soviet power was being rapidly constricted. In the middle of June, Omsk fell to assault by Siberian Cossacks, and the advancing Czechoslovaks, who also seized control of the railway close to Tyumen. Red forces and their political leaders conducted a strategic retreat.[14] Workers' uprisings in the Urals against the Bolsheviks were widespread in the early summer.[15] Discontent with Sovnarkom's failure to bring about economic recovery was rife, and resentment of police terror was intense. Lenin and his comrades had promised the moon in the previous year. The disillusionment among even the industrial working class was quick to reach the Urals. Demands were frequent for re-elections to the soviets across the entire region.[16] It could merely be a matter of time before the Czechoslovak Legion would decide to move on Ekaterinburg, and the prospects for the city's defenders were grim. The Bolsheviks had little over a thousand men under arms. These included Red Guards whose discipline was far from dependable. A lot of their weaponry was of poor quality – many of the troops were shouldering only hunting rifles.[17]

Within days almost the entire railway between the Volga and Vladivostok had tumbled out of Soviet control. Well-organized armed forces, however small, were capable of huge military impact if they had sufficient determination. The Bolshevik leadership in the capital was acutely aware of its insecurity. Without the Latvian riflemen in and around the Kremlin, Sovnarkom was in constant danger of being taken by surprise. By the same token it was entirely possible that the Czechoslovaks, no longer able to trust Lenin and Trotsky, might act as the vanguard of an offensive designed to crush the October Revolution.

36. GERMAN MANOEUVRES

The Germans achieved what they wanted with the Brest-Litovsk treaty: the Eastern Front was closed down and German army divisions could be transferred to fight the British and French before they could be reinforced by the Americans. Ukrainian foodstuffs could be secured for German troops and civilians. Germany at last had control over those vast territories to the west of Russia which were so enticing for German entrepreneurs. Russia itself could soon become an economic vassal.

But did Lenin and Trotsky deserve prolonged confidence? It would have been imprudent for Ludendorff and Hindenburg, the real masters in Germany, to take Sovnarkom for granted. Lenin had won the vote for a separate peace in the teeth of opposition from inside the ruling coalition. The Left Socialist-Revolutionary People's Commissars laid down their offices (even though Left Socialist-Revolutionaries continued to serve at lower levels of the administration). Bolshevik opponents of the treaty maintained their objections. Trotsky in particular was suspect because he had accepted the peace only with intense reluctance and did not stop courting the favour of Allied diplomats – he and the British diplomatic emissary Robert Bruce Lockhart spent a lot of time together, and nobody could be sure that Trotsky would not revert towards his preference for war. Many Bolsheviks, indeed, would have applauded him for such a move. Soviet rule itself was facing huge difficulties and it was entirely imaginable that the government would collapse as discontent grew among industrial workers and peasants. For all these reasons, German diplomacy pursued a dual-track policy of collaborating with the Bolshevik leadership while seeking out possibilities for an alliance with pro-German Russians.

This second track was daily becoming more realistic as Russia's anti-Bolshevik groups looked for ways to topple Sovnarkom and became willing to consider enlisting German financial or military assistance. Their reasoning was practical. Having concluded that Russian forces were no longer capable of challenging German power, they predicted defeat for the Allies in the Great War. If Germany was going to rule over Eastern Europe, many Russian patriots considered accommodating themselves to the new reality in hope of obtaining the means to overthrow Bolshevism. They aimed to persuade Berlin that an alternative government in Moscow was infinitely preferable to communism and its anti-monarchical, anti-business and anti-clerical threat to every country in Europe, including Germany itself.

Count von Mirbach took until 26 April 1918 to set up and open the German embassy at 5 Denezhny Pereulok (Money Lane). This was the same street in which the French military mission was ensconced, and the two sets of diplomats sought to get the better of each other. Their official limousines frequently came close to colliding as Denezhny Pereulok was turned into a race track.[1] Mirbach set the tone for his colleagues; he acted as if the Bolsheviks were mere temporary custodians of Russian statehood, and he left little doubt where his basic sympathies lay by paying visits to leading monarchists; he even gained an audience with Nicholas II's sister-in-law Natalya.[2] Nicholas would have been appalled to hear about this since he continued to regard Germany as his country's main enemy. But Mirbach was giving thought to a future Russia where the Germans would remain dominant and the Bolsheviks would be no more. A victorious Kaiser Wilhelm would predictably want to restore the monarchy in some form to Russia. Meanwhile, Mirbach issued a demand for the German businesses confiscated in the years since 1914 to be given back to their owners. Sovnarkom was forced to comply, and made an exception in its drive towards state industrial ownership: all property belonging to Germans was to remain sacrosanct.[3]

Russian monarchists saw their chance to turn to the German embassy and plead for its assistance in getting the Soviet leadership to improve the conditions of detention for the Romanovs.[4] Although Mirbach received requests from former senator Dmitri Neidgart on three occasions, he merely expressed his personal sympathy without offering any prospect of action.[5] Neidgart was understandably dispirited by the experience. Alexander Trepov, who had served briefly as Nicholas's prime minister in late 1916, joined other monarchist activists in trying a different approach. Their idea involved going to Ober-Gofmarshal Count Pavel Benkendorf and persuading him to intercede with Mirbach on the grounds that, after the Brest-Litovsk peace, only the Germans had the authority to guarantee the safety of the Romanov family. Trepov wanted to issue an implicit warning to the

Germans that if anything untoward happened to the Romanovs, he and his friends would tell the world that Germany was to blame.[6] Mirbach, an aristocrat as well as a professional diplomat, received Benkendorf with courtesy but was not much more encouraging than he had been to Neidgart. He argued that Nicholas II's fate should be left in the hands of the Russian people. He would only agree to consider what Germany might be able to do for 'the German princesses'.[7]

There were a few signs that the Germans followed this with some exploratory moves. Sometime in April 1918, Mirbach approached Sverdlov at the behest of the German imperial family and the Spanish queen with a view to getting the Romanovs transferred to Petrograd. Apparently, Sverdlov told him that he would do what he could while emphasizing that the local soviet authorities were hard to handle; he did not want to be held responsible for any unpleasantness in the Urals.[8] Not every embassy official judged that the German side, if it had truly wanted, could not have insisted on securing Nicholas's release from detention as part of the Brest-Litovsk peace settlement. But such diplomats also recognized that the Berlin authorities might stir up opposition from socialists in the Reichstag if any such initiative had been undertaken – and, anyway, Nicholas would be in danger of assassination were he to secure his liberty.[9] Nonetheless, around 15 May 1918, Gilliard's suspicions were aroused when he heard that a Red Cross mission from Germany had recently been in Ekaterinburg, and while he was sitting in a restaurant with Buxhoeveden and Alexandra Teglëva, they spotted some German nurses talking openly in their own language.[10]

There is little sign that the imperial family did anything other than comply with the demands of their captors. But things might have been happening in the shadows. By June, Sergei Markov, the irrepressible would-be rescuer of the family, had decided that salvation for the Romanovs could happen only with Germany's help.[11] He also believed that his own leader, Markov-II, was already collaborating with 'the Germans', which seemed to explain why so few volunteers had arrived in Tyumen earlier in the year – and Markov-II could not afford to annoy the German government by enabling Nicholas to head a movement dedicated to ripping up the Brest-Litovsk treaty. The Germans, they thought, would only endorse an action that was aimed at spiriting the Romanovs abroad.[12] Major-General Vladimir Kislitsyn was to testify in 1919 that he met Sergei Markov in Berlin in December 1918. Markov showed him a letter that he was carrying, purportedly from

Alexandra in Tobolsk to her brother Prince Ernst of Hesse. Though the letter remained sealed, Kislitsyn felt confident that he recognized Alexandra's handwriting on the outside.[13] Like other former Russian Army officers, Markov was being well treated by the Germans. Talking expansively, he claimed that the Kaiser – who by then had fallen from power – had earlier offered to spirit Alexandra and her daughters off to Berlin but that Alexandra had point-blank refused.[14]

Markov never revealed what he thought was in the letter, and the saga has gone to his grave with him. A still more extraordinary story was told by Vasili Golitsyn, the young aristocratic son of a general in the old Russian Army. Golitsyn told of meeting in Ekaterinburg Ensign Praslov, who had spoken to a commissar who had heard from a Red commissar that a German general had made his way to Ekaterinburg and made contact with Nicholas himself in the Ipatev house. Supposedly, when asked to endorse the peace treaty, Nicholas had rebuffed the suggestion. At this, it was claimed, the general warned that he would end up being killed – and Nicholas replied that he was ready to give his life for the Motherland.[15] Whether any such exchange really took place is open to doubt, but it would have been strange if the German intelligence agencies had made no attempt to discover what was happening in the Urals. In such a situation it was hardly surprising that rumours flourished.

Meanwhile, the Germans and Austrians behaved imperiously in those large territories of the former Russian Empire that they occupied. Whenever they took a major city there was a big parade. Troops were lined up on both sides of the central boulevards to keep back the crowds. Every soldier wore a sprig of evergreen in his helmet. Cavalry was given pride of place. Military bands accompanied the marching regiments and movie reels were made of the events. The local residents watched in befuddled silence as the German and Austrian high commands celebrated victory. In following days the shops would be reopened and something like normal life resumed. Puppet administrations were established with willing Ukrainian and Russian collaborators, but little further attempt was made to disguise the reality of German supremacy – even the Austrians walked in their shadow.[16] Ukraine became a place of refuge for people fleeing Soviet rule. German policy had no interest in disturbing the old social order and Russian aristocratic and wealthy families could appear in public without the kind of molestation that had frequently beset them in 1917. Some of them began to judge that if Russia had lost the war on the Eastern Front, imperial Germany might offer a useful instrument to bring down the Bolsheviks.

So whereas Nicholas II remained hostile to any reconciliation with imperial Germany, monarchist officers from the old Russian Army were willing to consider getting German help in mounting a thrust into the Urals and rescuing the Romanovs. Some German military commanders in Kiev favoured this option, but their diplomatic colleagues were less than eager. General A. I. Mosolov, who once had served at the imperial court, asked Ambassador Mumm in the Ukrainian capital for clarity about Berlin's intentions. Mumm bluntly replied that he disagreed 'that the question of saving the Tsar was important for Germany'.[17]

Kadet leader Pavel Milyukov, the passionate advocate of Allied military victory in 1917, was among the first of Russia's public figures to perform a political volte-face and seek German armed assistance. In late May 1918 he travelled secretly across the new Russo-Ukrainian border under the pseudonym Professor Ivanov. Claiming to speak on behalf of the recently formed secret anti-Soviet Right Centre, he made contact with the German occupation authorities. He appealed for Germany's consent to help Russian officers from Alexeev's Volunteer Army to organize a military coup against Sovnarkom in Moscow. German military force would be crucial in sealing off access to the capital and threatening to make a move against the Bolsheviks. Germany, Milyukov hoped, would supply the Volunteer Army with weapons and ammunition.[18]

Milyukov had to be very discreet. If word got out about him going cap in hand to the Germans, the Bolsheviks would create a scandal in Russia and ruin his reputation. In Kiev Milyukov asked N. P. Vasilenko, a Kadet colleague who held ministerial office in the Ukrainian government led by German protégé Pavlo Skoropadskyi, to act as his intermediary with the Germans. It was a delicate business because Milyukov had until recently been a fierce proponent of the case for a crushing victory over Germany, and he excoriated the Brest-Litovsk treaty that the Bolshevik leadership had signed. There was a curious dynastic aspect to Milyukov's Ukrainian trip. Vasilenko's contact in the German military administration was Major Haase, who had important responsibility for foreign and security affairs under General Herman von Eichhorn. Haase was the professional alias of Prince Ernst of Hesse, who was the brother of none other than former Empress Alexandra. Haase was understandably cautious. The Brest-Litovsk treaty had brought benefit to the German cause in the Great War by enabling the transfer of troops from the Eastern Front to northern France. If Milyukov were to come to power, Haase wanted assurance that Germany's war effort would not suffer.[19]

Meeting Haase on 21 June, Milyukov claimed that General Alexeev and the Volunteer Army were no longer averse to recognizing the objective facts of the military situation and were open to the idea of collaborating with Germany. (This was pure fantasy on Milyukov's part, and perhaps he was hoping it could be true.) Prince Ernst pressed him to describe his ideas for Russia's future. Milyukov urged the Germans to moderate their pretensions, and he explained that, although he wanted to see Russia reunited with Ukraine, he envisaged a loose linkage – and he expected Germany to be satisfied by this. Having always desired a constitutional monarchy, he indicated a wish for Grand Duke Mikhail to take the throne. He liked Mikhail's gentle nature and foresaw no difficulty in manipulating him. The obvious snag was that the Bolsheviks were holding him in custody, but Milyukov remained optimistic. For him, the succession was only 'a technical question'. If Mikhail proved unavailable or unamenable, he suggested, the authorities could marry off Grand Duke Dmitri Pavlovich to Nicholas's eldest daughter Olga.[20]

It does not seem to have worried Milyukov that he displayed such extravagant cynicism while parleying about the Prince's own close relatives. Grand Duke Dmitri had been involved in the plot that killed Rasputin, for which Nicholas had punished him by exile to the Persian front. After the February Revolution, like all other Romanovs, he had to leave military service and chose to seek refuge with the British mission in Tehran. This was hardly likely to endear him to the Germans. Moreover, Milyukov's sketch of a future Russian administration excluded the possibility of a return to the throne by Nicholas. This would have untoward consequences for Ernst's own sister, Alexandra. Perhaps Milyukov simply assumed that Ernst recognized that Nicholas had been an unmitigated disaster as a ruler. In any case, a marriage between two first cousins – Dmitri and Olga – was hardly a project that geneticists would have approved. Milyukov was engaged in wild speculation. In despair about the prospects for his country, he was grabbing at straws. In his tactless way he was beseeching the German authorities to identify their interests as lying in dealing with him, a Russian patriot, rather than with fanatical communist internationalists.

Milyukov had failed to appreciate that the Volunteer Army under

Alexeev recruited its officer corps from men trained to regard the Germans as the enemy. It would take a lot to turn them in the direction of favouring Berlin. On 4 July he received a message from Alexeev making it clear that he had no intention of adopting a German 'orientation'.[21] The Western Allies, furthermore, were beginning to offer financial aid to those organizations which were committed to the anti-German struggle.

Milyukov, however, refused to give up. Staying on in Kiev, he met Prince Ernst again on 10 July to press the case for cooperation between Germany and anti-Bolshevik Russians like himself. He argued that the Brest-Litovsk treaty, far from consolidating German supremacy, was a step too far for the Germans if they looked seriously to their national interest – but he did not explain why he thought this. He repeated his commitment to the monarchical principle and insisted that peasants, if not workers, would welcome a new tsar.[22] But without Alexeev's support, his hope to overturn the Bolsheviks in Moscow was a distinctly forlorn one. When leaving Kiev, he had anyway failed to win agreement with the Germans. What made things worse was the decision by his fellow Kadets to walk out of the Right Centre: this was bound to make it more difficult to resume productive links with the Western Allies.[23] Even so, the Bolsheviks would have been shedding their usual concern about possible dangers in international relations if they had not worried that their Russian enemies might strive to do a deal with imperial Germany. The Germans were more than capable of tearing up the Brest-Litovsk treaty and seeking partners in Moscow more malleable than Lenin and Trotsky.

37. LAST DAYS IN THE HOUSE

By May 1918, there was growing evidence of malfeasance inside the guard detachment at the Ipatev house. Avdeev conducted an inquiry at the end of the month and, as a result, sacked his deputy Alexander Moshkin for thieving Romanov property. But Avdeev himself was corrupt. When shortly afterwards he too was found guilty of theft, the Urals Regional Soviet Executive Committee removed him from his duties and he was never seen in the Ipatev house again.[1]

The Chekist Yakov Yurovski was named to take Avdeev's place as commandant and bring order to the guard system. The new commandant was a big, beetroot-cheeked man with a personality to match.[2] Yurovski had worked as a regimental medical orderly in the army's wartime hospitals. After the February Revolution he was elected to the Ekaterinburg Soviet. There was talk that he had started out as a Socialist-Revolutionary.[3] If true, this was hardly an unusual change of stance. The Bolsheviks in 1917 had acted as a magnet for many people who saw them as the sole party capable of taming capitalism and ending the Great War. Like other young militants, Yurovski was proving himself in the fires of the country's turmoil and he rose to the Urals regional Cheka board after the Bolshevik seizure of power and the establishment of Sovnarkom.

The Urals leadership demanded order in the guard detachment. They told Yurovski nothing about what ultimate fate was intended for the Romanovs, and they themselves at this moment knew nothing more than the current Moscow gossip – and the Sovnarkom discussions about putting Nicholas on trial can hardly have escaped the knowledge of the Regional Soviet Executive Committee and trusted officials.[4]

Yurovski's first inspection of the Ipatev house convinced him that management under Avdeev had been incompetent as well as corrupt. He decided to introduce fresh guards even though the old ones had been employed only since the end of April; he brought members of the Ekaterinburg leadership's own special-purpose detachment with him to create a reliable core.[5] Yurovski had a low opinion of the Russian workers Avdeev had recruited from the Urals factories and instead introduced some trusted Latvians. While continuing to allow the Russians to patrol the exterior of the house, he reserved tasks of internal security for his Latvian team. While aiming to strengthen discipline, he may also have seen advantage in having guards who were less than fully fluent in Russian and would be unable to talk informally with the Romanovs.[6] He drastically reorganized the living quarters by allowing the newcomers to monopolize the occupancy of the lower floor of the Ipatev house.[7] Whenever he was on duty, Yurovski signalled that the old laxities were no longer tolerable. As a Cheka officer, he turned the residence into a prison-fortress.

Beloborodov visited to inform Nicholas in person about the change of personnel. The thefts of property were going to be stamped out, and Yurovski together with an assistant drew up an inventory of gold rings and bracelets. They took items off with them for safekeeping, but not before explaining that illicit instances of sales of several items had been detected – and Avdeev had been found guilty. (Nicholas privately thought that Avdeev had been unable to control the unit and felt rather sorry for him.)[8] Yurovski, however, took a different viewpoint. If Avdeev had succumbed to temptation, so too might any of the Latvians. The practicalities in one instance were trickier than he had imagined, and he gave up the attempt to remove a bracelet from the empress when she exclaimed that she had worn it on her wrist for twenty years and would need a key to take it off.[9] He returned next day with a casket containing all the removed valuables and asked the Romanovs to check that nothing was still missing. With that he sealed the casket and handed it to them for safekeeping.[10]

The list of objections to Avdeev grew longer: he had omitted to formulate a plan for evacuation in case of fire; he had allowed some correspondence between the Romanovs and their friends outside the city, and nuns from a nearby monastery were still bringing food into the residence.[11]

Yurovski was severe from the start. He turned down Nicholas's request for permission to clean the garden area.[12] He put the family on the same rations as ordinary Ekaterinburg citizens and stopped outsiders from delivering delicacies that supplemented their diet. He wanted to reduce Nicholas to 'the condition of an average bourgeois'. No case for privileges would be entertained. He rejected a complaint from the cook Kharitonov that he could not prepare a decent dish for the household from a quarter-pound of meat. Yurovski indicated that the Romanovs had to get used to living as prisoners rather than as respected members of the erstwhile imperial dynasty.[13] When the nun Maria Krokhaleva turned up as usual at the outside door with a basket of food, he asked: 'Who gave you permission to bring things?' Krokhaleva explained that Avdeev had allowed the delivery on advice from Dr Derevenko. This failed to reassure Yurovski, who queried where the milk came from. Krokhaleva explained that the cows belonged to the monastery farm. Her patent honesty calmed him down, and he too started to make suggestions about what else the monastery might supply. (Like his predecessor, he was possibly aiming to improve the entire household's diet.)[14]

Although he curtailed the previous illicit practices, however, he did nothing about general standards of behaviour. Chekists like Yurovski aspired to political order and shared the Bolshevik contempt for middle-class prejudices. Whatever background they came from, they cultivated a swaggering vulgarity. One of the guards, Faika Safonov, scrawled 'fuck' and other lewd swearwords on the wall and sang dirty songs. Permission for religious services was less readily granted. Moreover, a shot was fired at Anastasia when she tried to look out on to the street from a window. Yurovski and Nikulin indulged themselves. Seated at the piano in the commandant's room in the evenings, Nikulin struck up some revolutionary songs – and Yurovski was heard joining in. Nikulin also brought his blonde lover into the house.[15]

Reports of trouble at the Ipatev house began to reach Moscow, and Sverdlov remembered the warnings that Yakovlev had constantly given about the Ural leadership and its wildness. He sent a message of concern to Beloborodov, telling him of the kind of stories he had been hearing. Beloborodov assured him that all was well now that Moshkin was under arrest and Yurovski had replaced Avdeev, and the composition of the entire internal guard unit had been renewed. There was, therefore, no reason for Moscow to worry.[16] But rumours were flying around the Urals. One of them had it that the Bolsheviks had slaughtered Nicholas and his family. The French vice-consul, staying at the British consulate in Ekaterinburg, sent out a telegram on 9 July rejecting these stories.[17] As soon as one false story was successfully dismissed, another spread around the city. Ekaterinburg was buzzing with presentiments about the coming approach of the Czechoslovak Legion, and the thoughts of many people turned towards the question of what might lie in store for the imperial family.

Father Ioann Storozhev sensed that the Romanovs were depressed when he conducted a service for them on 14 July. Their desire for spiritual refreshment was almost palpable, and although they were forbidden to talk to him after the service, he thought he could hear one of the daughters saying a quiet thank you. He felt drained by the experience. In the commandant's office afterwards, Yurovski asked: 'Why are you breathing so heavily?' The priest replied: 'I feel sad because I gave so little of a service and I'm weak and sweaty. I'm leaving now and about to get flu.' Yurovski finally found something in common with the clergy and said: 'Well, let's close the window to stop the draught.' Storozhev replied it was time to go home. Yurovski said he could wait a while if he wanted, adding sympathetically: 'Well, look, they've said their prayers and now the heart rests easier.' He added: 'I've never denied the influence of religion and I say that to you in all frankness.' Taken aback by these words, Storozhev thanked him for permitting the service to take place. Yurovski seemed annoyed by the remark and snapped: 'But where do we forbid any of this?' Storozhev sensed that it would be imprudent to prolong the conversation. Yurovski offered his hand. They shook and then parted.[18]

When Storozhev and his deacon, Buimirov, had left the Ipatev house and were by themselves, they reflected on the day's experience. Buimirov gave voice to an instinctive impression: 'You know, Father Priest, something has happened there with them.' Storozhev thought the same but asked him to explain. Buimirov answered that none of the Romanovs had sung during the service. The imperial family were known as lusty singers. Their reticence, he thought, must have some unpleasant meaning.[19]

The Romanovs had, in fact, picked up hints about what was happening militarily in the area near to Ekaterinburg, despite the fact that their guards told them almost nothing and sometimes fed them with misinformation. But they could see and hear enough to know that big changes were afoot, changes that were unlikely to enhance their physical security. As they listened to the noise on the streets, they detected the familiar sound of artillery being trundled. They knew that Austrian former POWs were being prepared for defence against the expected offensive by the Czechs. The irony was not lost on Alexandra, who recorded in her diary on 13 July that both the Austrian and Czech forces were constituted from troops who had once been in Russian captivity.[20] The external disturbances outside Freedom House in Tobolsk were dwarfed by the warfare that was rumbling its way through the Urals and approaching Ekaterinburg. From being on the periphery of the intensifying civil war, the city was set to become one of its main military fronts – and Nicholas and his family could sense that the fighting would almost certainly have adverse consequences for them.

38. THE EKATERINBURG TRAP

Sovnarkom and the Bolshevik Central Committee could provide only intermittent assistance to Ekaterinburg. Communications were patchy and fragile – the cable system became so disrupted that messages between the two centres sometimes had to be routed through Petrograd, which slowed down the exchange of news. The Bolsheviks had advanced their power by fostering a spirit of self-reliance amidst their provincial cadres. Lenin often had to sit back while they furthered the party's cause as they saw fit. Sovnarkom and the Bolshevik Central Committee sent out emissaries whenever possible, but local party committees were always pleading for more of them. The Bolshevik Party had a chronic shortage of personnel. Having achieved exponential growth since spring 1917, it had had no time to train up the number of officials that were essential for a governing party to govern. At times the best that Lenin could do was to issue decrees and call on lower party organizations to show initiative in working out how to implement them. He explained that the decrees themselves were of a 'demonstrative' character rather than detailed legal instructions. He and Sverdlov insisted that this was what things were like in the heat of revolution.[1]

Lenin and Sverdlov remained in close contact with Ekaterinburg, and there were frequent conversations on the Hughes apparatus while Nicholas was on his way between Tobolsk and Ekaterinburg.[2] On 2 May 1918, Sovnarkom discussed the Romanovs for the first time since their arrival in Ekaterinburg three days earlier. Reports from the Urals confirmed that there was no serious danger of successful escape. A public announcement about Nicholas's transfer was required and Sverdlov was asked to compose a suitable concise draft for the Soviet press.[3] Otherwise, little was revealed about what was happening to the Romanovs. An exception was made on 16 May 1918 in *Izvestiya* with an interview of Yakovlev about the trip from Tobolsk. Yakovlev mentioned the conversations he had had with Nicholas and Alexandra. He

spoke of Nicholas without rancour, save that he criticized his 'phenom-
enal limitedness', but he did not hold back about Alexandra, accusing
her of low cunning and pride – and he omitted all reference to the
disputes among Bolsheviks in Tobolsk, Omsk and Ekaterinburg.[4]

On 19 May the Bolshevik Central Committee again put 'Nikolai
Romanov' on its agenda. Sverdlov noted that the Central Executive
Committee Presidium, which he chaired, had recently discussed the
preferred 'fate' of the Romanovs. He reported that Bolshevik leaders in
the Urals were pressing for a ruling on the matter. At Sverdlov's suggestion, it was decided to delay any action while maintaining Nicholas's
physical safety. Sverdlov was to pass on this decision to the men of the
Urals and urge them to understand the increasingly difficult conditions
in Moscow.[5] Nonetheless, the Central Committee kept its focus on
making steady preparations for a show trial. In line with this, on 4 June
1918, the People's Commissariat of Justice put its comrade Bogrov at
Sovnarkom's disposal. Bogrov was to gather the necessary pile of documentation for court proceedings so that the authorities might have a
credible charge sheet against Nicholas.[6] It was the same state of affairs
as in February 1918 when Sovnarkom had first asked the same People's
Commissariat to prepare the case. Now the People's Commissariat was
tossing the task back to Sovnarkom and offering young Bogrov to help
out.

Reports appeared in Moscow newspapers not controlled by the
Bolsheviks that Red Guards had killed Nicholas in Ekaterinburg.[7] The
Soviet government was alarmed by the spread of the story, which had
the potential to upset relations with both the Germans and the Allies.
The Urals leadership, moreover, had a record of pursuing its own line.
It was vital to ascertain the truth. On 20 June Lenin's personal assistant,
Vladimir Bonch-Bruevich, telegrammed to enquire whether there
was any truth in the stories that the Urals leadership had executed
Nicholas. It took three days for the message to reach Ekaterinburg.
Bonch-Bruevich had to repeat his enquiry next day.[8]

Moscow found it difficult to be sure what was happening in Ekaterinburg, and there was a degree of suspicion that Beloborodov and
his comrades were not always providing unbiased information. When
yet another story spread in the capital that the Regional Executive
Committee had killed the Romanovs, Lenin and Sverdlov demanded
an independent testimony one way or another. Reinhold Bērziņš,
the commander-in-chief of the North Urals and Siberian Front, was
ordered to carry out an inspection of the Ipatev house. The Latvian

Bērziņš was trusted in Moscow as a military leader who had no dogs in the fight. He telegrammed his findings to Moscow on 27 June. The story about the emperor's execution, he assured Lenin and Sverdlov, was a simple 'provocation' that lacked all credibility.[9] But the episode showed that if Ekaterinburg had no firm confidence in Moscow, the feeling was reciprocated by Moscow. After all, it hardly enhanced Soviet military preparedness when one of the Red Army's leading commanders was asked to abandon his operational duties and conduct an on-the-spot inquiry about a handful of civilian detainees.

The Urals Regional Soviet Executive Committee, as all its members and rare official outsiders like Bērziņš were only too well aware, was under ever-growing challenge in the city itself. Mikhail Efremov, the city Cheka leader, organized a raid on Kadet offices in May 1918 to seize files and arrest leading activists.[10] Opposition of a more dangerous kind emerged when the Socialist-Revolutionaries began to train armed units in woods on the outskirts. Ten Red Guards were sent to flush them out. The search proved fruitless, and the possibility of an internal military challenge to Bolshevism grew.[11] On 17 May the Red Guards went out to Upper Iset and suppressed a Socialist-Revolutionary uprising, executing thirty captured militants.[12] Anarchists too maintained their own urban force and constantly criticized the Bolsheviks. Their leader, Pëtr Zhebenev, raised a black flag over headquarters that had formerly belonged to an engineer named Zheleznov. The Cheka delivered an ultimatum, telling them to get out or face an assault, and when their cache of machine guns was later discovered, the regional soviet administration was convinced that they had been plotting something untoward.[13]

While control was firm at Voznesenski Prospekt, other parts of the central precincts were less easy to secure. On 12 June 1918 the Bolshevik leaders discovered an apparent attempt at subversion by means of a move to arm the wounded troops who remained in the city. Red intelligence about the movement of Czechoslovak forces in Siberia and the Volga region was terrifying. Omsk had fallen to them only four days earlier. Now it seemed that the anti-Bolsheviks were organizing an internal assault on Soviet power. Preventive measures were taken that included the seizure of businessmen and intellectuals as hostages. If an uprising occurred in Ekaterinburg, these people would immediately be executed.[14]

Since the end of May, Beloborodov had had to prepare for the worst as reports of the relentless movement of trains carrying the

Czechoslovak Legion arrived on his desk. A body of 500 Kronstadt sailors arrived to stiffen revolutionary morale, but they caused trouble, especially after they seized a vodka distillery and its contents.[15] Ekaterinburg had to prepare its own defence and boosted the local recruitment to Red forces. This was becoming an arduous task as the word spread that the troops of the Urals Regional Soviet Executive Committee would soon be fighting an armed contingent which had crushed every body of Soviet soldiers which had been deployed against it. Beloborodov maintained a show of optimism. While anti-Bolsheviks among the city's inhabitants began to pray for rapid success by the Czechoslovaks, he resolved to teach them a lesson in Bolshevik grit and ruthlessness. First, he arrested a bunch of wealthy residents and put them to manual labour. Trenches had to be dug on the outskirts of the city and the Ekaterinburg Soviet administration reversed the conventional social routines in this kind of emergency. Immediately there were objections from the conscripted individuals, several of whom claimed physical incapacitation. Health Commissar Sakovich vetted three of them on behalf of the Urals Regional Soviet – he later claimed that his habit of releasing people from their obligations incurred a threat to mobilize Sakovich himself for digging work.[16]

The Urals Bolsheviks prided themselves on refusing to take the path of compromise that Lenin had taken. They continued to uphold the policies that they had advocated in 1917, and while refraining from direct destabilization of Sovnarkom, they did what they could to ensure that Bolshevik measures became more radical. In Moscow, they assumed, there was a chance that Lenin, the architect of the Brest-Litovsk treaty on the Russian side, might accede to further pressure from Berlin. They obeyed Lenin and his Sovnarkom without trusting him.

The Regional Executive Committee suspected that some nefarious concession might be in motion when an order was issued for a number of prominent aristocrats of the Baltic region to be dispatched from Ekaterinburg to Petrograd. These people had recently arrived in the Urals for use as political hostages. Among them was Count Lieven. Beloborodov and his comrades disliked any idea that Sovnarkom might be caving in to German demands for their liberation.[17] But the Urals Regional Soviet Executive Committee could not just snub its nose at Lenin. As the Czechoslovaks advanced ever nearer, the Bolsheviks of Ekaterinburg needed whatever assistance that Moscow could provide. Beloborodov and Goloshchëkin were in no position to annoy the central party leadership unduly at a time when they hoped for military support and knew that its own forces were inadequate. Ekaterinburg's finances, moreover, were ruinous, and in early May an urgent plea had gone forth for Moscow to bail them out – and Sovnarkom had sent a trainload of banknotes. The Urals Regional Soviet Executive Committee had to ring the central streets with Red Guard units while the crates were delivered from the station.[18]

The Soviet Regional Executive Committee recognized that it could not put together an effective defence of the city, and steps were taken to prepare for a timely evacuation of personnel and finance before the Czechoslovaks arrived. The enemy was approaching unopposed, according to dependable reports, from two directions. As the Czechoslovak Legion moved westward along the Trans-Siberian Railway, another force was approaching from Kuzino.[19] Panic was beginning to grow among sympathizers with Sovnarkom as the Czechoslovaks got nearer. The long-awaited military dénouement was at hand and every Red Guard volunteer was mobilized. Safarov and other leading comrades hurried round the factories in an effort to ensure that all of them turned up for duty; they also strove to recruit new volunteers.[20] Workers were told of the horrors awaiting them if the counter-revolutionary forces proved victorious. But every Urals leader also knew that the Bolsheviks could not resist for long. Priority was given to gathering everything of value and assembling it at the railway station for transport to the west. The next destination could only be Perm.

39. THE MOSCOW FULCRUM

While the situation continued to deteriorate, Bolshevik policy was still focused on a public trial of Nicholas in Moscow as soon as circumstances permitted. The immediate source of anxiety for Lenin and Sverdlov was that the Urals leaders might pre-empt such an outcome by finding a pretext to kill him, and in early July the rumour was sprouting yet again that the Bolsheviks had indeed killed Nicholas in Ekaterinburg, and Trotsky was asked whether it was true. The People's Commissar for Military Affairs dealt insouciantly with the question. As a German diplomat at the Moscow embassy noted, Trotsky simply said, 'I don't know; this is of completely no interest to me. I cannot take interest in the life of an individual Russian citizen.'[1] When he wanted, Trotsky could be as prim as a vicar and impassive as a judge. He liked to stun Germany's ambassadorial personnel, especially those of noble birth, with his nonchalance.

It was all an act. The reality was that behind the scenes there was much discussion on the subject at the top of the Bolshevik Party, and Trotsky had been vociferous about holding a show trial for Nicholas. But events were running too fast and dangerously for Sovnarkom to handle with the necessary stagecraft. At some time earlier in summer 1918 Sverdlov had spoken at a closed meeting of fifty to sixty leaders of the Moscow party organization, where he reported that the Urals Bolsheviks had enquired about how the central authorities would react if they decided to execute the entire imperial family. By his own account, he allowed himself a smile when replying: 'I think I'll reflect our general mood if I reply that this is not a matter of direct concern to us. [We stand for] "All Power to the Localities", and if local comrades find this step necessary for local reasons, they are in their rights to take it; we're not going to protest!'[2] This was the start of efforts by the supreme leadership to distance itself from anything untoward that might happen to the Romanovs. The Soviet government sought to free itself from all potential blame. But as yet the official policy remained intact: Nicholas was to be brought to the capital for judicial proceedings.

On 4 July 1918, when Goloshchëkin arrived in Moscow for the Congress of Soviets and for consultations with the central authorities, he had no presentiment about this. This is what Bolsheviks in Ekaterinburg called 'sending the heavy artillery'.[3] His mission was to discuss future arrangements with Sverdlov and Lenin. Bolshevik leaders in both centres could see the necessity of a proper plan of action. The Czechoslovak offensive against Ekaterinburg was expected within a matter of days, and the Urals Bolsheviks needed to know what help they could expect from the capital. They also had to discuss what was to be done about the Romanov detainees. With Ekaterinburg likely to fall to the Czechoslovaks in the near future, a prolonged stay at the Ipatev house was clearly unsuitable.

Goloshchëkin, Lenin and Sverdlov had no presentiment that the factors underpinning security policy were about to undergo drastic disruption – nor that the transforming events would take place in Moscow and the rest of central Russia rather than in the Urals. The Congress of Soviets opened in a predictable fashion in the capital's Bolshoi Theatre. It was a noisy affair which the foreign missions watched from the height of the best boxes. On one side was Mirbach with his Austrian, Hungarian, Bulgarian and Turkish colleagues – and the head of German intelligence, Rudolph Bauer, was also present. They faced the Allied representatives on the other side of the hall.[4] Lenin spoke for the Brest-Litovsk peace, Trotsky for the Red Army's preparedness. No sliver of disagreement appeared between one Bolshevik commissar and another. Maria Spiridonova and the Left Socialist-Revolutionaries, still operating openly under the regime, denounced Sovnarkom – Boris Kamkov screamed that they were inhuman scoundrels and as he looked up at Mirbach's party the cry went up: 'Down with the assassins!'[5]

This spirit was also reflected behind the scenes. Their Central Committee was secretly plotting nothing less than a campaign of terrorism in Moscow. The idea was not to kill Lenin or Trotsky but to organize a 'provocation' that would wreck the Brest-Litovsk treaty and bring the Bolsheviks back to the path of 'revolutionary war'. They were going to do this by assassinating Ambassador Mirbach, which they believed would force Berlin to break with Moscow.

On 6 July Yakov Blyumkin, an eighteen-year-old Left Socialist-Revolutionary still working for the Cheka, tricked his way into the

German embassy and shot Mirbach. Sovnarkom immediately out-
lawed the entire party and arrested several of its leaders. Dzierżyński
raced off to their party headquarters to impose control. Instead the Left
Socialist Revolutionaries took him into custody, and he was freed only
when the Latvian Riflemen intervened with superior forces. Lenin and
Karl Radek – one of the party's leading experts on German questions
– hastened to the embassy to deliver their formal condolences, hoping
to avert a German military occupation of Moscow.[6] They wanted to
preserve the peace signed at Brest-Litovsk. This was difficult for Radek,
who had been known as a vociferous opponent of the treaty. Lenin was
using him as physical proof that the Soviet leadership was determined
to stand by what had been agreed between Russia and Germany. The
Germans called for the arrest and punishment of the killers and their
'ideological inspirers'; they also demanded the right to dispatch their
own forces into Russia.[7] Frantic to oblige, the Soviet government
ordered the execution of V. A. Alexandrovich, the Left Socialist-
Revolutionary in post as deputy chairman of the Cheka.

Things calmed down and the Germans quietly indicated that they
appreciated the Bolshevik official reaction. Radek joked that jobs had
become vacant for Nicholas II's generals to join the volunteer detachments that would publicly shed crocodile tears in Mirbach's funeral
cortège.[8] Anatoli Lunacharski, the People's Commissar of Enlightenment, assured British and French diplomats that the emergency was
drawing to a close. Like other Bolsheviks, he had concerns that the
Allies might begin a preventive war to save Russia from German occupation.[9]

This was not mere paranoia in the light of efforts made by the
Allies to get rid of the Bolsheviks. The British and French diplomats
and intelligence services encouraged Boris Savinkov with his plans for
an uprising by his Union for the Defence of the Fatherland and Freedom in Yaroslavl, 155 miles north-east of Moscow.[10] The idea was to
foment the resistance to Bolshevism in the cities of northern and central Russia, and Savinkov hoped for support from the so-called White
Army that General Alexeev was raising in the south.[11] The French in
particular gave the impression to Savinkov that the Allies were about
to undertake a full invasion.[12] On 6 July, when the Left Socialist-
Revolutionaries shot Mirbach, Savinkov's armed groups went ahead
with their uprising and occupied Yaroslavl and nearby towns.[13] Savinkov had been deceived by the Allies; he quickly discovered that no

Allied assistance was being made available when the R
against the rebel force.[14]

These events turned politics in Moscow upside dow
was predictable any longer, even though the Germans expressea tnem-
selves content with the Bolshevik reaction to the killing. Nobody in
Sovnarkom yet felt they could trust them. It was conceivable that
Berlin might secretly be planning to overrun Russia and set up a
puppet administration as it had done in Ukraine. The rest of that
summer had to be devoted to placating the German authorities. When
Goloshchëkin had arrived for the congress, it was still the Bolshevik
leadership's intention to ship the former emperor to the capital for a
show trial. But if there was one further thing that would undoubtedly
agitate official opinion in Germany, it was such a trial. The assassination put an end to the plan.

On 9 July the Urals Regional Soviet leadership met in joint session
with the Bolshevik Party Regional Committee leaders to review the
Mirbach shooting and the Left Socialist-Revolutionary revolt. By fifteen votes to zero with five abstentions, they sent a message of
solidarity to Moscow declaring that the Left Socialist-Revolutionaries
had placed themselves 'outside of the Revolution's ranks'. The meeting
left the door open for individual Left Socialist-Revolutionaries in Ekaterinburg to leave their party and join the Bolsheviks.[15] The two parties
in the Urals had once been united in their opposition to the peace
treaty. They had worked in coalition together, and Left Socialist-
Revolutionaries had held responsible jobs at the regional level even
after the Brest-Litovsk treaty was signed. While Lenin ordered the
execution of some of their leaders in Moscow, Beloborodov was still
prepared to greet them with warmth so long as they recognized
Sovnarkom's authority. The evidence of divisions between Moscow and
Ekaterinburg lingered on.

Central leaders maintained a watch over events in the Urals. Lenin
was more directly involved in Moscow–Ekaterinburg exchanges in the
week from 6 July than in previous months. He wanted to finalize
arrangements about three Finns in custody in Ekaterinburg. On 13 July
Safarov assured him that their case was settled.[16] Lenin also received
telegrams in response to his enquiries about his cousins Alexander
and Vladimir Ardashev, who were based in Ekaterinburg, and on
17 July the Urals Cheka was to inform him that Alexander Ardashev,
a Constitutional Democrat, had escaped after organizing a revolt at the
Upper Iset Works – two of his nephews had been taken hostage in

reprisal.[17] The telegraph system worked efficiently but slowly: it usually took three whole days for a message leaving Moscow to reach Ekaterinburg.[18] On 7 July 1918, before Goloshchëkin left Moscow, Lenin gave the order for Beloborodov to be put in direct-line contact with the Kremlin.[19] His own recent experience had convinced him that he and Beloborodov had to have a smoother means to exchange information. Knowing how bad the military situation was in both Moscow and Ekaterinburg, he foresaw that decisions would have to be taken about the Ipatev house detainees. Neither Lenin nor Sverdlov was willing to allow the Urals leaders to take such decisions by themselves.

48. THE MAN WHO WOULD
NOT BE TSAR

In all the other territories under Soviet control, the perils continued to grow for members of the extended Romanov family. The Red Guards snatched Georgi Mikhailovich from Ritierve and deposited him under house arrest in Vologda. The authorities decided that this was not secure enough and by April 1918 he was back in Petrograd under tight supervision.[1] Official Soviet concern about the Romanovs spread to the Urals, where the Regional Executive Committee wanted to be sure that none of them escaped. The Vyatka Provincial Party Conference wanted to be rid of its Romanovs and voted to send them to Ekaterinburg. Grand Dukes Sergei Mikhailovich, Konstantin Konstantinovich, Igor Konstantinovich, Ioann Konstantinovich, Grand Duchess Elizaveta Fëdorovna and Count Vladimir Palei were transported to Alapaevsk, over ninety miles to the north-west of Ekaterinburg.[2] Grand Duchess Elena Petrovna – wife of Grand Duke Ioann – was one of the fortunate ones. She was a member of the Serbian royal family, and at this stage the central party leadership wanted to avoid an unnecessary international incident.

Her blood relatives continued to make pleas for her to live freely. At first she was allowed rooms at the Ataman Hotel in Ekaterinburg, but the Urals Regional Soviet Executive Committee disliked the idea of her wandering around the city and transferred her to Perm and then to Moscow. She was distressed at the Cheka's insistence that she had to leave her husband behind.[3]

But she had no choice and dutifully collected her belongings, consoling herself that she would be near her children, whom she had been forced to leave behind in Petrograd. In fact she was being used as a pawn in Soviet foreign policy: the Bolshevik Central Committee was considering exchanging her for leading communists in prisons abroad. A minor Romanov was surely worth releasing if it meant the liberation of German far-left Marxist leaders such as Karl Liebknecht or Rosa Luxemburg. In fact, the German government remained impervious to any such initiative, and it would not be until the end of the following year that the Bolsheviks could swap Grand Duchess Elena for Béla Kun after the collapse of the Hungarian communist revolution.[4] But the idea was in the air at least in Moscow, which was among the reasons why the Urals Regional Soviet Executive Committee continued to feel uneasy about Lenin's leadership. Beloborodov and his comrades were worried that he might simply release the Romanovs under direct German pressure just as he had succumbed to the Treaty of Brest-Litovsk.

The Executive Committee was aware that its own security requirements had been poorly tended. While it could vouch for conditions in Ekaterinburg, it had responsibilities for the whole Urals Region, and Chekists in some areas were plainly in need of reinforcement. The transfer of so many Romanovs to Alapaevsk called for better organization and communication. In May 1918 the Executive Committee took steps in this direction by merging the Perm and Ekaterinburg Chekas under the command of a new Urals Cheka. Space for offices was taken at the vast American Hotel, and the Ekaterinburg Cheka moved out of its previous accommodation on Officers Street.[5]

Nicholas's brother Mikhail was left behind in Perm. Mikhail, who had spurned the invitation to take the throne in the February Revolution, had lived quietly in the city with his wife since the Soviet authorities had expelled him from Petrograd. The couple had taken his devoted personal secretary Nikolai Johnson with them. They stayed in the imperial suite at one of the best hotels and went about town unmolested. On one occasion, when they spent an evening at the theatre, flowers were thrown in their direction.[6] The well-wishers would have been more sensible to have avoided any such gesture of support. There had always been fewer Bolsheviks in Perm than in Ekaterinburg and they were edgy about their chances of remaining in power. This tended to reinforce their inclination to use violence. They assumed that a demonstration of ruthlessness would help to discourage attempts to dislodge them. Perm's crucial disadvantage from the party's point of view was the scarcity of factories, mines and industrial works. The Bolsheviks compensated for this by maximizing their readiness for combat, and their militarist methods made them a fearsome force. Mikhail's continued residence in a prominent hotel was a challenge to their pretensions. If it was deemed that the other Romanovs should be kept in detention, the question then arose about what should be done with Mikhail.

One of the most influential figures in Bolshevik discussions was the Perm party leader, Gavriil Myasnikov. Headstrong and volatile, Myasnikov swaggered around in his long boots and cut an aggressive appearance with his carefully curled moustache. He did what he liked on party duty and the Motovilikha Bolsheviks, on Perm's outskirts, got used to obeying him. After agreeing to work for the Perm Soviet administration, he went back to the city, where he could expect greater licence to behave as he pleased.

His proposal for resolving the question of Mikhail Romanov was to abduct and kill him. The idea of keeping him in detention some-where did not appeal to Myasnikov, who acted as if he believed that the only good Romanov was a dead Romanov. He prepared the way by getting the Perm Cheka chairman Sorokin to sign the official order. When Sorokin demurred, Myasnikov made an angry fuss. Sorokin eventually succumbed and the way was laid open for Myasnikov to arrange his desired operation. Secrecy was vital to its success. Across the Urals region, a particular method of dispatch had become favoured by the Soviet authorities. Victims, if they were not shot in prison, would be told that they were to be moved elsewhere for safety reasons. Typically they were driven to city outskirts and, when the escort reached a wooded area, told to dismount. Out of public sight, they would be executed – sometimes their corpses would be tossed down one of the Urals' many disused mineshafts.

The problem for Myasnikov was how to induce Mikhail to leave the hotel. Myasnikov took the extreme measure of cutting off the tele-phone cable and locking up all the serving staff in their rooms. This enabled him to march into Mikhail's suite and tell him that he was in danger of being assassinated. Myasnikov, posing as his protector, per-suaded him and Johnson to leave the building in a guarded carriage.[7] The plan worked to perfection. Mikhail and Johnson agreed to be transported and when they reached a forest, they were ordered to get down. Rifles were pointed at them. They stood no chance of escape and were briskly done to death.

Lenin said and wrote absolutely nothing about the nature of his in-volvement in the killing. This was deliberate for the simple reason that he wanted to avoid accusations of personal responsibility. Throughout 1917 he had ensured that no traces should be left for people to connect him to the financial subsidy that the Bolshevik Central Committee received from the German government. There is in fact no indication that Lenin ordered or sanctioned the order for Mikhail's liquidation, and the likelihood is that if Myasnikov in the Urals had consulted him, Myasnikov would have recorded it in his memoirs. Although he and Lenin were opponents in the dispute about war or peace, they shared an insouciance about contemplating the killing of Russian enemies of Sovnarkom. With his demands for dictatorship and terror, Lenin fostered a climate of opinion in which ruthless murders were part and parcel of the duty of committed revolutionaries. He had spoken and written this way in 1917, and his bloodthirsty tirades had increased in the months since the October Revolution. Myasnikov, a Bolshevik veteran, knew that there were few party leaders who harboured compassionate thoughts about how to deal with the Romanovs.

About Lenin's general attitude to the Romanovs, though, there is evidence from someone who belonged to the Cheka squad that executed Mikhail Romanov in Perm. A. V. Markov was the Chekist in question, and later in 1918 he presented himself to Sverdlov in Moscow. Sverdlov took him to see Lenin, who quizzed him about the Perm killing. Markov assured him that the process had been a clean and straightforward one. Lenin did not bother to probe him on the question. (Mikhail's execution had in truth been a gruesome process.) He simply applauded the efforts of Markov and the local Bolsheviks: 'Well, you did well and did it correctly.'[8] This was Lenin's usual attitude, and he fired off angry telegrams to anyone who failed to act with the utmost ruthlessness. The following year he was to rebuke none other than Beloborodov: 'It's necessary not to beat the enemy but to annihilate him. Don't limit yourself to half-measures.'[9]

But in mid-1918, all Russia was caught up in a swirl of rumours. One of them suggested that Mikhail was aiming to take the throne he had refused in the February Revolution. Posters and manifestos started to appear on urban walls purporting to have been signed by him. General Alexeev, who was still assembling a volunteer army on Russian territory north of the Sea of Azov, was disturbed by this. As a monarchist, he had tender feelings for the Romanovs even though he had recommended that Nicholas should abdicate. But he wanted his new force to operate on the basis of known realities. It was a confused situation for him. In June 1918, after making enquiries with due diligence, he concluded that Grand Duke Mikhail had never issued any such poster or manifesto. He was equally sceptical about the story that any of the Romanovs had made it to England.[10] But General Alexeev also knew that his own information was far from comprehensive. He had also heard the claim that the Grand Duke was no more and that the Bolsheviks had killed him. What was the truth? Alexeev had no means of telling. Stuck in southern Russia, he was as baffled as nearly everyone outside high Bolshevik circles in Perm and Ekaterinburg.[11]

On 13 July, Sovnarkom sharpened its measures against the Romanovs by laying down that all property belonging to Nicholas and his family was to become the 'legacy' of the Russian Socialist Federative Soviet Republic. This was to include everything that they owned in Russia and abroad. The decree covered everyone named as a family member in the official genealogical book; it was signed by Lenin and his chief-of-staff Vladimir Bonch-Bruevich.[1] This was kept a secret for several days even though Romanov lands had already been seized through Lenin's Land Decree in the October Revolution, and no Soviet official had been inhibited about confiscating other items of the family's property. It is just possible that Lenin, being aware that the imperial family was about to be executed, wanted to place such seizures on a proper legal foundation. He may have also discussed drastic action in the previous week with Goloshchëkin in Moscow or possibly with Beloborodov by the Hughes apparatus. And perhaps he aimed to preclude any Romanovs who found sanctuary abroad from lodging any claim to Nicholas's property. Lenin was the ultimate legal nihilist and thought constitutions were a 'bourgeois scam'. But he was also a trained lawyer who could see the point of making it difficult for anyone, either in Russia or abroad, to disrupt the affairs of government.

In the second week of July, Lenin and Sverdlov were preoccupied by the Mirbach assassination and the Moscow and Yaroslavl uprisings, and the likelihood is that the capital's leadership had not yet come to a definitive decision on the Romanovs. One thing alone was clear: Moscow at that time was no longer feasible as a place of trial for the former emperor.

But there is another interpretation. The commissar responsible for food-supplies, Pëtr Voikov – according to a memoir published in the West by the defector G. Z. Besedovskii – later asserted that the Urals regional leadership's new policy had once reflected a difference of opinion with Moscow. But Voikov added that Moscow itself was divided, and that whereas Lenin stayed minded to preserve Nicholas's life as a bargaining chip in talks with the Germans, Sverdlov and Krestinski supported the men of the Urals. But supposedly Lenin switched his stance in the capital when he heard of the imminent attack by the Czechoslovak Legion. The Central Committee did, however, warn that the deaths of Alexandra and the Romanov children had to be kept absolutely secret at a time when the German authorities were talking about giving them asylum and there was still an acute fear of irritating Berlin after Mirbach's assassination.[2] This is an entirely credible theory, but it is also completely unprovable. What is more, Voikov might well have been parroting the soon-to-be-agreed official line that the ultimate decision was taken unilaterally in Ekaterinburg. Another possibility is that Lenin and Sverdlov sent Goloshchëkin on his way with a number of approved possibilities while leaving the ultimate choice to the Regional Executive Committee.

Although documentation is slender about Lenin's culpability for the exact decision at this stage, he was certainly responsible for making it easy to proceed with the executions. Throughout the summer, he chided any Bolsheviks he suspected of lacking the necessary mercilessness towards the enemies of the October Revolution. He was creating and endorsing an environment of violence. He had a chance to halt the killings in the Urals after hearing about how Myasnikov had done away with Mikhail Romanov, but in fact he refrained from making any comment of disapproval. Indeed, it is quite possible that Lenin did provide Goloshchëkin with his secret sanction for the same action to be taken against the detainees in the Ipatev house.[3]

On 12 July, after Goloshchëkin returned from his Moscow negotiations, the regional soviet met to consider its own prospects. According to Executive Committee member Pavel Bykov's account a few years later, the first big question put to the military command was simply how long Ekaterinburg could hold out.[4] The answer was obvious. Czechoslovak forces were overrunning every city they reached. Chelyabinsk had become their military hub in the Urals until they decided to send regiments to the Volga region to link up with the People's Army of Komuch while dispatching others under a Russian commander, Lieutenant Colonel Sergei Voitsekhovski, against Ekaterinburg.[5] The Urals communist leadership recognized that the city's defences were inadequate and that the Red forces remained inferior to the new enemy in discipline and experience. This sealed the fate of the captive Romanovs. Any idea of putting them on trial in Ekaterinburg or anywhere else was unrealistic. 'Soviet power' was under threat of extinction throughout the region, and indeed Ekaterinburg and Perm were the only large centres of population still under Bolshevik rule. Rather than move the family westward, the Executive Committee resolved to execute them. This was thought better than to run the risk that the imperial family might fall into the hands of the counter-revolutionaries, and anyhow the Executive Committee contained several individuals who had wanted to kill them much earlier than summer 1918.[6]

An unidentified man had turned up at the house on 9 July 1918. When asked to move on, he responded with verbal abuse. The guards escorted him to Cheka headquarters.[7] In the worsening military situation, no chances were being taken. Nerves were stretched to breaking point. Another odd event that happened in those days was the trip made around town by Dr Arkhipov, whose residence had been spared being requisitioned by Bolsheviks. Arkhipov went to every store where he thought he might find sulphuric acid. Apparently he was shopping for 400 liquid pounds of it – a vast amount for the average doctor, and its lethal purpose was to become obvious only in retrospect.[8]

On 14 July 1918 Goloshchëkin went for a walk with Anuchin, his deputy and the district military commissar in the Urals leadership. Safarov joined them. This was how the Bolsheviks had always met to confer before 1917 when they wanted to avoid the prying eyes of landladies and police, and such was the emergency hanging over Ekaterinburg that the local leaders sought relief from sitting in committee rooms. As they knew, it could be their last chance before fighting began in the approaches to their city. The three men agreed on the urgent requirement to execute all the Romanovs. Others in the group rejected the proposal. Among them was Regional Soviet Executive Committee member Nikolai Ufimtsev, for whom it made more sense to kill only Alexandra – he argued that she bore a special personal guilt for Romanov misrule. Essentially Ufimtsev assumed that the uxorious Nicholas lacked a mind of his own; he also disapproved of any suggestion of slaughtering the young Romanovs. The group of Bolsheviks returned to the city without having resolved the question about who should be killed. Murder was on the leadership's agenda in Ekaterinburg, but the list of intended victims had yet to be established.[9]

On 16 July Yurovski arrived at the Ipatev house at eight in the morning and was joined by Beloborodov. After inspecting the building, they departed for further meetings, leaving Nikulin in charge until

Yurovski's return that evening.[10] Beloborodov had made his decision to have the executions carried out as soon as sanction arrived from Moscow.

The Urals Regional Soviet Executive Committee met later that day in the American Hotel – the Cheka's regional headquarters – to hear Goloshchëkin's account of his Moscow trip. Goloshchëkin by then was living there with the Chekist leadership.[11] Some of those present at the session expressed disappointment at his failure to obtain Sverdlov's unequivocal sanction to kill the Romanov family. Safarov pointedly asked Goloshchëkin how long he expected Ekaterinburg to hold out against the Czechoslovak advance.[12] But how and where should the killings take place and who should be killed? After some debate it was resolved to carry out the task inside the Ipatev house. This meant slaughtering not only the imperial family but also the doctor, cook, lackey, serving maid and kitchen devil who attended them. The rationale was brutal: they had thrown in their lot with the Romanovs and now they had to face the consequences.[13]

But how should the killings be organized? Beloborodov's proposal was to stage a fictitious escape attempt by the Romanovs while the Cheka transported them to woods on the city's outskirts and did them to death. Nicholas himself was to be kept behind. The idea was to carry out a public execution of him after the text of the charges against him had been read out. Goloshchëkin spoke against the proposal on practical grounds; he could not see how it would be possible to put on a credible attempt at escape. His preference was simply to convey the family to the woods, shoot them and throw the bodies down some mineshafts. He wanted to accompany this with a brazen announcement that the Romanovs had been moved to a place of greater security. Voikov had another idea, which was to take the Romanov family to the river, weigh them down and drown them.[14] In the end it was Goloshchëkin's ideas that broadly commended themselves. His plan had the advantage of simplicity as well as being the easiest to disguise from prying eyes.

Yurovski, who was ordered to put it into effect, went back to Voznesenski Prospekt and made arrangements. He told Pavel Medvedev, who was conducting the detachment's routine management, to announce to the guards on duty the plan to execute the imperial family.[15] He also gave an instruction to transfer the young servant boy from the building to the Popov house, where Red Army soldiers were billeted – Yurovski as a fighter for the working class apparently decided that the lad's life should be spared. He also instructed Medvedev to remove all the guards' revolvers. When Medvedev handed them over, Yurovski explained: 'Today we're going to shoot the entire family.' Yurovski had decided to use a select inner group for the firing squad and wanted the best weapons available to him. He told Medvedev to tell the guards not to get agitated when they heard gunfire. He was brisk, concise and committed.[16]

Moscow had to be informed about Ekaterinburg's intentions, and Goloshchëkin and Safarov sent a joint telegram to Zinoviev in Petrograd on 16 July 1918. At the time this had become the surest way to send messages to Moscow, and Zinoviev was meant to relay the contents to Sverdlov, with a copy for Lenin. (Obviously Lenin's order for the Regional Executive Committee to be able to communicate directly with him by cable had not been realized.) The fact that Goloshchëkin and Safarov rather than Beloborodov signed the telegram was of no importance. The city was about to be attacked and the ruling group were dividing their tasks as they got ready for evacuation. The Urals leadership wanted endorsement from Lenin and Sverdlov to kill the Romanovs. Zinoviev immediately recognized the importance of the contents and transmitted his own telegram with the following comment on the contents of the telegram from Ekaterinburg: 'Inform Moscow that the trial agreed with Filipp [Goloshchëkin] cannot because of military circumstances be delayed. If your opinions are negative, please inform with the utmost urgency: Goloshchëkin and Safarov. Contact Ekaterinburg yourselves: Zinoviev.'[17]

The telegram from Petrograd was registered as having arrived in Moscow at 9.22 p.m. on 16 July 1918 – or 11.22 p.m. in the Urals time zone.[18] The contents make no sense except in some agreed code. Just as Sverdlov and Yakovlev in April had referred to the travelling Romanovs as 'the baggage', Goloshchëkin and Safarov were presumably avoiding a word like 'execution' in favour of the more innocuous 'trial'. No Bolshevik leader could ignore the possibility of a Soviet defeat in the civil war, and if any of them happened to be captured by the enemy, pity would be in short measure if their communications showed complicity in the plan to liquidate the Romanovs. The Bolsheviks were anyway wary about popular opinion and did not want to incur disapprobation for killing Nicholas or, more especially, his blameless children. And in the years before the February Revolution they had been masters of coded messages and encryption. After the October Revolution, when they gained control of the telegraph network, they prudently declined to abandon such precautions. Whatever else, Goloshchëkin and Safarov knew that Lenin and Sverdlov would know what they meant since they had agreed how to cable each other.

In the Ipatev house, the firing squad was kept at the ready throughout this time. But Yurovski could do nothing before the Executive Committee leadership heard from the capital and empowered him to proceed.[19] This makes a mockery of the notion that the Urals leadership acted on its own initiative and only informed the Moscow leadership afterwards.

In Moscow there was a spasm of action as Lenin and Sverdlov conferred before handing a message to one of Lenin's bodyguards, A. I. Akimov, who took it by motorbike to the central telegraph building on Sverdlov's orders. Sverdlov told him to act with unusual discretion and bring back the copy and tape of the telegram. When the telegraph operator refused to comply, Akimov pulled out a revolver. Akimov then returned to the Kremlin and resumed his guard duties. The telegram was dispatched to Ekaterinburg by the same roundabout route via Petrograd and then Perm.[20] No trace of it has ever come to light. There is therefore still no verification that Lenin and Sverdlov ordered the death of Nicholas and his family. This was deliberate. The Sovnarkom, Soviet Central Executive Committee and Party Central Committee records were kept as clear as possible of anything that might pin the blame on the Bolshevik leadership in Moscow. In the decades since July 1918 there have been those who denied that the Bolshevik central leadership knew anything about the decision to execute the Romanovs in the Ipatev house. Indeed, it is a belief that continues to be held by many of Lenin's admirers to this day.[21]

42. DEATH IN THE CELLAR

Yurovski had made his preparations but kept his precise plan to himself until the moment for action. He did, though, have to explain to Medvedev that they had to wait for a signal from the Urals Regional Soviet Executive Committee. Nothing could happen until a comrade arrived at the house and uttered the code word 'chimney-sweep'. Yurovski meanwhile divulged the plan to his chosen firing squad, and when giving the details to them, he heard murmurings of dissent. Some of the Latvians were troubled about the idea of killing defenceless young women. Yurovski stood them down rather than proceed with people who lacked a firm commitment to their revolutionary duty.[1] It was going to be a bloody business and he needed ready butchers. Once he had finalized his selection, he told each of them whom to aim at. Then he handed out the Nagant revolvers.[2] Why revolvers rather than rifles? The answer must be that he aimed to take the Romanovs by surprise, and they were unlikely to recognize what was afoot if the soldiers were carrying hand-weapons only.

Amidst all this, the boom of the Czechoslovak artillery could be heard, and it was getting louder.[3] The guard detachment were acutely aware that the ultimate moment of crisis was at hand. Yet nothing could happen inside the Ipatev house until Moscow gave permission and its telegram had been delivered. Guards were told to wait and be patient. On no account were the Romanovs to discover what was in store for them. Outside on the street, unbeknownst to the family inside, the Bolsheviks installed machine guns and blocked access to everyone.[4]

The hours of waiting dug into everyone's nerves as midnight approached, and Yurovski had no idea what was holding things up. The tension mounted. By one o'clock he was distinctly concerned: there was still no signal from the leadership. The more time that passed, the harder it was to keep up morale in the firing squad. Word finally reached him at 1.30 a.m., when a party comrade turned up at the guard point and passed on the 'chimney sweep' instruction. At last Yurovski could take action. The moment had arrived. As a Chekist officer he was ready to do whatever he thought would serve the revolution's interests, and if orders came to kill the hated Romanovs, he was eager to carry them out. But as with everything else that had happened since February 1917, leaders could not assume that they would be obeyed. Luckily for him, he had selected his squad with care and knew that they would do whatever he commanded.[5]

Yurovski himself roused Dr Botkin from his sleep and told him to get dressed. He used the pretext of disturbances in the city that required him to move the Romanovs to a place of greater safety. The same message was repeated to the imperial family, who were told to dress and go down to the cellar. Yurovski deliberately avoided hurrying them so as to maintain a calm atmosphere, and although it was an unusual wholly unheralded command, the family took it equably and washed before presenting themselves to the guards.[6]

At two o'clock, Nicholas carried Alexei in his arms down to the cellar from the upper storey. Yurovski assumed control when everyone was assembled. Before addressing the group, he ordered Alexandra and Alexei to be seated in the two armchairs that had been placed in readiness. The rest were asked to stay standing. Yurovski had Nikulin with him; there were also Pavel Medvedev, Mikhail Medvedev and Pëtr Yermakov and seven Latvians. The twelve men each clasped one of the dozen Nagant revolvers that Yurovski had sequestered earlier.[7] (According to Medvedev's later testimony, Yurovski ordered him to go outside the cellar and listen as to whether the shots were audible,[8] but, as likely as not, he said this in the vain hope of avoiding self-incrimination.) Yurovski then curtly announced the Urals Regional Soviet Executive Committee's order to execute them. Nicholas turned and, astonished, tried to ask a question.[9]

Yurovski repeated his statement and, without hesitation, shouted: 'Fire!' He himself, as had been arranged, took aim and killed Nicholas. Some of the other shootings were chaotic and bullets ricocheted off the walls. Despite the short distance, not all the guards took accurate aim, and some accounts have it that Mikhail Medvedev of the Urals Cheka was Nicholas's killer, having specifically asked for him as his target.[10] Outside the house, arrangements had been made for lorry engines to be revved up to drown out the noise coming from inside the walls. The shooting continued until Yurovski called a halt after establishing that nobody had survived. He then walked across to examine the victims.[11]

It was a sickening sight. The cellar resembled a butcher's cold store, spattered with blood, exposed bone and pieces of ripped flesh. Pavel Medvedev was to testify that all the victims were dead except for Alexei, who was still groaning. Yurovski shot him another two or three times to finish him off. Some members of the squad could no longer stomach the scene, and Yurovski shouted to Pavel Medvedev to go and calm the other guards in the duty room. They had heard the shooting and wanted to learn what had happened. A few of them encountered him before he could say anything. They pointed out to him that he would have to take responsibility for what had been done; they certainly wanted no future blame to attach itself to them. Medvedev ordered them back on duty. When Yurovski learned about their misgivings, he told Medvedev to go back and talk to the guards again. Yurovski had completed the task that the Executive Committee had set him, and he did not want things to unravel because criticisms reached the streets of Ekaterinburg. The guards had to keep their mouths shut about what had taken place.[12]

Yurovski gave instructions to wash down the floors and walls of the cellars.[13] Buckets, mops and brooms were supplied. It was an unpleasant, awkward task as corpses, clothes and the corporeal debris had to be moved aside before the work could commence. Afterwards the guards wanted to go back to their quarters at the Popov house for a rest. Medvedev forbade this out of fear that they would blab the news all over town. Instead, he forced them to sleep in the Ipatev bathhouse.[14]

Meanwhile, the bodies of the Romanovs and their retainers had been heaped into a lorry at the Ipatev house and driven out of Ekaterinburg under the command of Pëtr Yermakov. The intention was to cremate the bodies and dump them down a mineshaft. The road was bumpy and the journey took longer than had been expected. When the lorry reached its destination, Yermakov gave orders for a thorough search of the corpses for jewels and other possessions, and it was found that the Romanovs had hidden all manner of small valuables in their clothes. A pile was made of bodies with dresses and coats to act as tinder, and cans of petrol were poured on top before a match was lit and the flames leapt up to the sky. It was a crude cremation, and Yermakov decided that, in order to leave no traces, it would be wise to move the remains to another nearby mineshaft and soak everything in acid. While Yermakov could not imagine why anyone would want to climb down a disused shaft, he did not want any of the corpses to be recognizable.

Yermakov was acting on orders. The Czechoslovak Legion would be fighting their way into the city within days. Peasants who lived in the vicinity of the mineshafts and who were told to stay away from the lorry were bound to notice the burning pyre and were hardly going to keep what they had seen secret. The Urals communist leadership had not thought through the implications of the plan, and it would not take a genius to work out what might have been happening out in the woods. The Bolsheviks were already planning the Red evacuation of Ekaterinburg: they knew that unless a miracle occurred, the Czechoslovaks and their Russian allies would be the new powers in the city. The British still had a consulate across the road from the Ipatev house. Even if they had been fooled by the revving-up of lorry engines during the killing of the imperial family, they were bound to have suspected something untoward, and Yurovski had already had difficulty in keeping a lid on public information. Moreover, the businessman Ipatev would soon be reclaiming his property and could tell the world about what he discovered there.

Yurovski and his team aimed to reduce the evidence to a minimum. Fire and acid would do their job at the mineshaft; brushes and detergents would complete the task at the Ipatev house. When the Bolshevik leadership departed the Urals capital, they and their misdeeds would simply disappear. They achieved most of what they wanted. Their greatest magic trick had been performed: the captive Romanovs had vanished into the night air.

43. RED EVACUATION

Beloborodov dispatched an urgent coded telegram to Lenin's aide Vladimir Gorbunov at 9 p.m. on 17 July 1918. It consisted of a single sentence: 'Tell Sverdlov the entire family suffered the same fate as its head, officially the family will perish in evacuation.'[1] According to I. I. Radzinski's later account, one of Sverdlov's secretaries – a certain Vinogradskaya – told him that the news took Sverdlov by surprise.[2]

Next day Sverdlov brought the Ekaterinburg telegram to the Central Executive Committee of the Congress of Soviets, where he gained approval for what the Urals leadership had done, and Sverdlov, Sosnovski and Avanesov received the task of drafting an announcement. The plan was to pretend that only Nicholas had been executed. Sverdlov also aimed to publish a series of documents on the Romanovs, including Nicholas's diary.[3] Later that day he delivered the news to a Sovnarkom meeting chaired by Lenin and attended by Trotsky. Sovnarkom merely took note of the news of Nicholas's execution and endorsed the decision, which was attributed to the 'Ekaterinburg Soviet'.[4] This was the origin of the official Soviet line that the initiative for the killing had come exclusively from the Urals city rather than Moscow and that the Ekaterinburg Bolsheviks had acted wholly in reaction to the military threat from the 'Czechoslovak gangs'. Allegedly, moreover, the other Romanovs in the Ipatev house had been taken to a place of safety. The history of the big lie had begun, with Sverdlov its principal author.[5]

The rationale for the Soviet refusal to reveal just how many Romanovs had been killed remained a secret, and no document has yet emerged as to why Sverdlov and Lenin adopted this approach. It is probable that they were aware that the execution of the five Romanov children would cause widespread revulsion at home and abroad. Foreign policy considerations are also likely. The communist leadership in Moscow had to obviate any pretext for a German military intervention. As Alexandra was a princess of Hesse by birth, the Germans had frequently enquired about both her safety and that of her offspring, and Kaiser Wilhelm was quite capable of telling his commanders and diplomats to prioritize the rescue of living Romanovs as well as becoming enraged if he learned that they had been done away with. Better, Lenin and Sverdlov must surely have thought, to make everyone think that only one adult male had perished in the Ipatev house.

After conducting Moscow business, Sverdlov held a conversation with Beloborodov by Hughes telegraph.[6] Sverdlov knew that extraordinary events were happening in the Urals, and asked the regional leadership to supply the latest information. What had happened at Alapaevsk? What had the Cheka been up to? Beloborodov could not or would not always provide full answers. He insisted that all was not lost in Ekaterinburg. Perhaps he was trying to prove he had the true fighting spirit of a true Bolshevik leader. All but the Red forces, he reported, had already been evacuated. The Urals Bolsheviks were going to defend the city. Sverdlov gave permission for Beloborodov to publish the Central Executive Committee's decision; he urged Beloborodov to hold on and promised to send military reinforcements – or at least some hundreds of Petrograd and Moscow workers who would conduct propaganda for the cause. He reminded Beloborodov that what happened in the rear was just as important as the coming conflict at the front.[7]

Beloborodov must have regarded the promise and advice as less than impressive at a moment when trains of fearsome Czechoslovaks were about to advance on Ekaterinburg. If Sverdlov had been able to dispatch an army of weapons-drilled, disciplined troops, it might have been a different matter. But as People's Commissar for Military Affairs, Trotsky was concentrating the Red Army's forces in the Volga region in the front against Komuch. The only consolation that Sverdlov could offer was that war with Germany was no longer likely and that the Germans were no longer insisting on sending one of their army battalions to Moscow, as they had demanded after the assassination of Mirbach.

Fears about the military situation reached a high pitch in Ekaterinburg. Security was maintained as usual at the Ipatev house, and it was not until the afternoon of 17 July 1918 that Filipp Proskuryakov and his fellow guards were told they were free to go off on their own and relax in the city. Yurovski, Nikulin and Medvedev supervised the collection of Romanov possessions. This continued for two whole days after the executions. Those who did the work were calm, and some thought they were tipsy as they packed the suitcases for removal. The guards saw no reason to keep their hands off items of value. Mikhail Letemin took possession of a dog called Jack, which had rather attached itself to him. By the night of 18 July it was decided that the tasks were completed and Pavel Medvedev told the guards about the Ural leadership's plans for the detachment: they were all to leave Ekaterinburg.[8] They were going to be an obvious target for the anti-Bolshevik forces, and half the detachment had departed by the end of the day.[9] If any proof was needed that Beloborodov had no serious intention of fighting for the city, his order to transport reliable troops out of the range of danger provided it. 'Soviet power' was coming to a pitiful end.

The suitcases were brought from the Ipatev house and loaded on to a train. Then Yurovski departed with the Latvian personnel.[10] He had to send a telegram to Beloborodov from Bisert railway station on 20 July explaining that, in his hurry to vacate the Ipatev house, he had left 2,000 rubles on the table; he asked for someone to pick it up for him.[11]

Before they departed the Urals, the leadership felt it prudent to make an announcement at a large public meeting. On 19 July, a vast crowd turned up at the Opera House on Glavny Prospekt to hear Goloshchëkin. Seeking to quash the rumours about the Romanovs, Goloshchëkin gave a fiery speech celebrating the execution of Nicholas the Bloody. Following the version of events concocted in agreement with Sverdlov, he claimed that the rest of the Romanov captives had been removed to another place for their own safety; he also stuck to the story that the decision had been taken by the Urals communists alone – he was protecting Moscow against any suggestion about its complicity. Many in the audience were dissatisfied with Goloshchëkin's report, and they shouted out: 'Show us his body!'[12] But this was the only occasion of public excitement. People in Ekaterinburg had too many problems of their own to bother themselves with the fate of the Romanovs.[13]

The guard detachment's departure was part of the plan that Beloborodov had devised for the evacuation of Soviet officials, Bolsheviks and Red Army units. As trains arrived in the city, they picked up people and cargo and then returned in a westerly direction. The sole avenue of escape by rail was to Perm. Officials and militants received priority. Many wives and children were included in the travelling groups because of fear that the Czechoslovaks would wreak vengeance on them in the absence of their menfolk. Each of these women was issued with 300 rubles for subsistence.[14] (Not everyone received a place in the contingent, and some of the abandoned families were to be quickly arrested and interrogated.) Beloborodov planned to gather up all the available human and material resources that would be crucial for Sovnarkom's eventual military response. This involved ransacking the banks for cash and the pharmacies for medical supplies.[15] Everything that could be of future use to the Soviet authorities was piled on to carts and taken to the railway station. The anti-Bolsheviks were meant to inherit a dearth of useful facilities.

A few guards remained on site until 21 July, when the residence reverted to the possession of its previous owner.[16] The Bolsheviks were alive to the possibility that people in Ekaterinburg might create a disturbance if it was revealed how many of the imperial family had been killed.[17] The slight difficulty was that Yurovski, only two days before the killings, had requested the monastery nuns to bring eggs and milk for the Romanovs. He had also handed over a note from one of the Romanov daughters who had asked for more sewing thread. The nuns turned up on 17 July, just hours after the slaughter. They noticed an unfamiliar car outside but thought nothing of it. What was unusual was the reluctance of anyone to come to the door. When a guard eventually appeared, they asked: 'Where's Yurovski?' They were told that he was still taking his breakfast. After a further delay, another guard came out and announced: 'They don't need more milk. They're ill. Just wait a bit.' He too disappeared and as the nuns strained to listen, they overheard someone asking, 'What should be said to them?' When the door opened again, yet another guard ordered: 'Do you know what, don't bring things any longer. Go away!'[18]

This was a remarkable incident. No one in Ekaterinburg would have rejected a nourishing meal at a time of growing food shortages. It could only mean that the people in the residence did not expect to be there for long. But if the sisters worked out that a murder had taken place, they had the sense not to say anything to the guards. One person who suspected what had happened was Evgenia Poppel, who was Nikolai Ipatev's sister-in-law. Poppel had been keeping an eye on events at Voznesenski Prospekt and on 22 July, after discovering that the last of the Bolsheviks had vacated the premises, she sent a coded telegram to her brother-in-law: 'The occupant has left.'[19]

Conditions in the city prison had changed when commissars ordered those hostages who had a trade, especially tailors or cobblers, to do useful work. They freed many of the petty criminals and then even some of the hostages. But the detainees from the Romanov retinue were denied such treatment. The time came when the Urals Regional Soviet Executive Committee started to transfer prisoners westward – the idea was to prevent them from falling into the hands of the anti-Bolshevik forces. The tutors Anastasia Gendrikova and Ekaterina Shneider were among those moved, along with Alexei Volkov, leaving Volkov's fellow valet Terenti Chemodurov behind in jail. When they asked about the destination, one of the soldiers said it was Moscow. Volkov feared that they were really about to be executed. Once they were outside the prison, he whispered to Gendrikova and Shneider to make a run for it. Both of them refused: they were ill and anyway did not appreciate the danger of the situation. Volkov loyally stayed with them and in fact the little party was delivered from Ekaterinburg to the prison in Perm.[20]

It took until 23 July before *Ural'skii rabochii*, the Bolshevik Party's regional newspaper, announced the murder. In accordance with the official line, only Nicholas's death was mentioned. Safarov's editorial bluntly declared: 'He lived too long, enjoying the indulgence of the revolution, like a crowned murderer.' The decision was ascribed to the Urals Regional Soviet. Safarov declared that the Provisional Government had been filled with monarchists and their sympathizers. The October Revolution had made a start in crystallizing the changes that would improve the lot of working people. But dangers had mounted. The Czechoslovak revolt along the Trans-Siberian Railway had served to unleash pogroms by the same Black Hundreds who had slaughtered Jews in the empire's western borderlands before the Great War. General Alexeev was gathering an armed force to bring back the Romanov monarchy. Safarov expressed alarm about Milyukov's attempt to seek assistance from the Kaiser. In this situation, he declared, Nicholas's life had to be forfeited. Admittedly there had been no judicial process. But Safarov took pride in the Bolshevik willingness to do the necessary thing to preserve the changes made by Sovnarkom since the removal of the Provisional Government.[21]

On the same day, the Third Army's report to Red Army commander-in-chief I. I. Vatsetis in Kazan was grim. No fresh forces were available to stem the enemy's advance on Ekaterinburg. Kuzino was in grave danger.[22] There had until then been only a tiny chance of external assistance to the Urals leadership. When Vatsetis removed all hope, Red Ekaterinburg was doomed.

44. MURDERS, COVER-UPS, PRETENDERS

The carnage in Ekaterinburg was followed twenty-four hours later by an operation in Alapaevsk where, since May, other Romanovs had been held in the Napolnaya school on the outskirts of town. They had been given freer conditions than those endured by Nicholas and his family, being able to walk around the streets and talk to inhabitants. The Latvians who guarded them were not as strict as those at the Ipatev house and allowed the younger grand dukes to play football and skittles with local lads. The Romanovs busied themselves as best they could. They tended the school gardens; they also read works of Russian literature as well as the Old and New Testament.[1] In early July 1918, however, the regime withdrew the right to take strolls in the town, and a barbed-wire fence was erected around the school. A trench was dug to prevent attack or escape. Cheka officials arrived in the little town on 17 July 1918, in the hours when the corpses of the Ipatev house Romanovs were being transported to the wooded place of their ignominious cremation.[2]

On the night of 17–18 July the Chekists, together with some Alapaevsk Soviet leaders, turned up unannounced at the Napolnaya school in several three-horse carriages and informed the detainees that they were to be transferred to a safer place because an attack by anti-Bolshevik forces was imminent. The grand dukes were told to prepare for departure, taking only light baggage. It was promised that their other possessions would be restored to them in due course. Half an hour later, they were on the move. The secret scheme was to take them to a nearby mineshaft where they would be killed. As the carriages left Alapaevsk, gunshots and exploding grenades were heard. This was a Cheka trick to give the impression that the counter-revolutionaries were already assaulting the school – the authorities wanted to be able to claim that others were to blame for the disappearance of the Romanovs in the crossfire. When the carriages arrived at the mine, the detainees were ordered to alight. In a gruesome manoeuvre they were manhandled and thrown down into the shaft. Stones and earth were hurled into the gaping hole. A shot was fired that hit Sergei Mikhailovich in the head, killing him outright. The rest of them remained alive and, among groans of pain, started to sing hymns.[3]

It was butchery without cleavers. The armed men at the top of the shafts heard the howls but could not see their victims gasping for air, water and food, and no medical help was provided. The Romanovs died excruciatingly slowly, their bodies broken by their fall. Even the grisly scenario organized by Yurovski in the Ipatev cellar had been less gruesome.

The Urals Bolshevik newspaper on 20 July 1918, published in Ekaterinburg, carried a report that the Romanov detainees had escaped from the Napolnaya school in the course of an attack by 'bandits', and their current whereabouts were said to be unknown.[4] As the process of evacuation got under way in the city, news about more Romanov deaths had little impact. This time there was no public meeting; no speech by Goloshchëkin or article by Safarov. In any case, the execution of the former emperor was bound to evoke a greater reaction than did the 'disappearance' of members of his extended family. The gruesome massacre outside Alapaevsk was hardly even mentioned again in the Soviet press of the Urals. Indeed, little more news – or fabrications – about the Romanovs was to be found in Moscow newspapers, except for the publication on 19 July of the text of Sovnarkom's decree to confiscate all Romanov property.[5] Lenin and Sverdlov were trying to play down the Ekaterinburg events and bury the news of Alapaevsk entirely. No information was distributed about where Nicholas's wife and children were allegedly being held. They were hoping that the execution of a former emperor was a matter of secondary importance for most Russians at a time when the civil war had reached a high pitch of intensity.

Foreign countries were another matter. Sovnarkom as yet had few official representatives abroad because no Allied government would accept them. Switzerland, Germany and Sweden were the notable exceptions. People's Commissar Mikhail Pokrovski, who had attended the Sovnarkom session on 18 July, wrote to his wife in the Soviet mission in Berne about the experience. Pokrovski was no sentimental politician, but there was a trace of the shock that he felt in his phrase that the former tsar had been done to death 'like a dog'.[6]

Berlin was the international centre of Soviet diplomatic activity. Adolf Ioffe was sent there as head of mission to liaise with the Germans after the signature of the Brest-Litovsk treaty. Ioffe had lived in Vienna for years before the Great War, spoke German fluently and was well educated. For some weeks, however, he was discomfited in carrying out his duties by the rumours about the fate of the Romanovs. On 24 June he had written to Lenin warning of dire consequences if Nicholas II were to be executed. When Richard von Kühlmann, Germany's Secretary of State for Foreign Affairs, broached the matter, Ioffe had replied that he had no information about the Urals but pointed out that the Czechoslovak offensive, coupled with widespread hostility to the Germans, made an outbreak of popular fury possible in Ekaterinburg. This was his way of saying that workers were after Nicholas's blood. Ioffe wanted Lenin to ensure that, whatever happened to the Romanovs, nobody would be able to blame the Moscow communist leadership for any violence; he also demanded to be kept up to date with events.[7] The Germans meanwhile told Sovnarkom to guarantee the safety of Alexandra and the children, but Ioffe still had no message from Moscow about what had occurred, and he pleaded to be kept in the picture so that he could better do his job.[8] He was whistling in the wind. Ioffe was known in leading Bolshevik circles as an upright man, too upright to do what diplomats are said to do: to lie abroad for his country. Lenin took a cynical line. While valuing Ioffe's handling of German politics, he declined to initiate him into the facts of collective butchery.

The Kaiser, however, expressed a personal interest in the fate of his cousin's family and asked his own ministers to make enquiries about what had taken place in Ekaterinburg. Empress Alexandra's brother had the same idea. This only served to make Lenin want to continue to keep Ioffe in the dark when German inquisitiveness was reported to him. In autumn 1918, when Dzierżyński took a break from his Moscow duties and travelled secretly to Berlin on a mission to foment a communist revolution, Lenin told him: 'Don't let Ioffe know anything! That way it will be easier for him to tell lies there in Berlin!'[9] True to form, Ioffe replied to enquiries with a flat denial that any Romanov other than Nicholas had been executed – it was to be another year before Ioffe, who by then had been expelled from Germany, extracted the truth from Dzierżyński.[10]

The secret had never been watertight on the Bolshevik side, where there was a swirling mist of rumour, fabrication and accurate testimony. Much of the confusion was deliberately started by the Urals Bolsheviks. Fëdor Lukoyanov, the Cheka city leader in Ekaterinburg, told his sister that only Nicholas had been shot. She did not believe him, reckoning that he was trying to spare pain to their mother, who was listening to them, and soon another Bolshevik told her the truth that the entire family had perished.[11] Before the evacuation it was widely known among the Bolsheviks that the emperor's family had perished with him in Ekaterinburg.[12] Beloborodov confirmed this in conversation while continuing to discourage debate about the details.[13] And as time passed, Beloborodov saw fit to distance himself from complicity in the decision to kill them, but he could not entirely shrug off responsibility unless he dared to challenge the official line that Ekaterinburg rather than Moscow had been where the essential decision had been taken – and, somewhat lamely, he added that he had been asleep when the executions were taking place.[14]

The official obfuscations led many people to step forward claiming to be one or other of the Romanov family. In the opinion of the earliest anti-Bolshevik investigators, the Cheka leadership actively encouraged the process with the aim of befuddling discussion, and an easy way to do this was to start some gossip about sightings of the Romanovs. The obvious place for this to happen in the first instance was Perm, the city to where the Urals Bolsheviks retreated after leaving Ekaterinburg, and indeed Perm quickly witnessed the emergence of cranks and ne'er-do-wells purporting to have escaped from the Ipatev house. Before summer ended there were more 'Romanovs' than the family had in the last generation. Sovnarkom would have preferred people to stop thinking about what had happened to Nicholas's closest relatives, and the next-best thing was that people received a plethora of conflicting claims. Some of the surviving Romanov retainers, exhausted and disoriented by their experiences, said things that served to reinforce the untruths about the killings in Ekaterinburg. The valet Chemodurov, who made it over to Tyumen by the second half of August 1918, assured everyone that the emperor and his family were still alive. He declared that it had been Dr Botkin, Nagorny and others in the retinue who were killed in the Ipatev house.[15]

Sergei Markov, their would-be rescuer, was taken in. After he was released from prison in Tyumen he went on a brief trip to Ekaterinburg to reconnoitre the situation in person, just as he had done in Tobolsk. He returned to Petrograd the day after Mirbach's murder and was still there when the communiqués were issued about Nicholas's execution. On 22 July he ran the risk of going to the German consulate, where he pleaded for Berlin to intervene and save the lives of the other Romanovs. He had no inkling about the true body count. His idea was to seek help in getting the empress's brother and her sister Irena to facilitate an agreement to liberate those in confinement in the Urals.[16] Markov was not a man to give up at the first obstacle. In August he set off for Kiev on a mission to persuade the German authorities to help him rescue the surviving Romanovs – it never occurred to him that the entire imperial family had been slaughtered.[17]

45. THE CZECHOSLOVAK OCCUPATION

The Czechoslovaks marched unopposed into Ekaterinburg in the early hours of 25 July 1918. The last train convoy of Bolsheviks had left on the previous night. City residents who hated Soviet rule turned up to celebrate their departure and waved flags and banners and tossed flowers into the victory parade two days later. Silver bands added to the festive atmosphere, and nobody seemed to mind that they played German marching melodies. Bells were rung in all churches. A banquet was held in the public gardens. A new Regional Urals Government was installed under Pavel Ivanov, who promised to unite all democratic political groupings. Cries of 'Long live the Constituent Assembly!' were heard.[1]

In the following days the evicted owners returned to repossess their private property, among them Nikolai Ipatev. Fine buildings had been ill-used for months. Businesses were stripped of their assets before the Red evacuation finished. The city's economy lay in ruins. On the plus side, the railway and telegraph still worked, the churches were open and clergy no longer walked in fear. Teachers and other professional people looked forward to an alleviation in their circumstances. But everyone could see that any general improvement was going to take a long time. Across the region a multitude of factories and mines had closed their gates. In those that remained open, production was down, and the returning proprietors had intense difficulty in restarting moribund operations. Hospitals, pharmacies and other medical services had been reduced to a shabby condition. The Urals capital was no longer the vibrant industrial and commercial hub it had been since the 1890s.

The evacuees had not included every member of the Ekaterinburg Soviet administration and the Bolshevik Party. Families sometimes refused to move or else were unable to obtain places on the trains. It had all been a mad scramble, and some people felt sufficiently marginal to Bolshevism to reckon that, however hard life might become in

Ekaterinburg, it would be much worse for refugees in Perm. And the prospect of conscription into the Red Army was not of universal appeal.

Among the conflicting local talk about the fate of the Romanovs, there was already widespread speculation that the entire family had perished on 17 July. Many inhabitants of Ekaterinburg had heard some version of events, even though the details differed from one informant to another.[2] Indeed, it was common talk inside Bolshevik families as individuals in the know sought to get the information off their chests.[3] Voznesenski Prospekt residents, moreover, could recall the experience of their own ears. Viktor Buyvid at no. 47 had been disturbed by fusillades late in the night. Guessing what had happened, he had stayed indoors for fear of being arrested.[4] But the tale lacked unanimous support. The barber Fëdor Ivanov had a lot of Bolshevik customers and had repeatedly asked about what was going on. While clipping the hair of one official, he was assured that 'we're sending Nicholas off today'. Ivanov was left to wonder what really had taken place, and it was only later that he discovered the truth about the killing. Like others, he had little confidence in the official version, but nor did he have reliable contrary information.[5]

Other Ekaterinburg citizens queried whether the emperor had been executed even after the Bolsheviks announced the death.[6] The whole city was talking and guessing. One of the first things that the Czechoslovaks did was to release those political prisoners the Bolsheviks had not taken off with them. Fëdor Gorshkov was among them, but Gorshkov was no wiser about what had happened to the Romanovs and their retainers than anyone else. Indeed, he knew a lot less because he had been locked up in jail for weeks.[7]

The Czechoslovak military authorities began an inquiry in Ekaterinburg as early as 30 July 1918 and appointed Alexei Namëtkin, a 'judge of instruction' in Ekaterinburg, to head it. By then the victorious forces had looked inside the Ipatev house, where the merest glance at the walls and floor of the cellar confirmed that blood had been shed. Bullet holes pocked the cellar walls and much of the debris, which included remnants of clothing and personal possessions, told of a violent event. Unless something completely improbable like a gunfight among the guards had taken place, the obvious explanation was that some – and possibly all – the Romanov detainees had been shot. No one trusted the Bolsheviks' announcements in either the city or Moscow and there was an immediate hunt for corpses, a hunt that intensified after local residents spoke about the strange little convoy that had made its way to nearby mineshafts. But who had been killed? Was it just Nicholas or had more of the family and their retainers perished? Did anyone escape the death marked down for them? Were any of those who now claimed to be family members genuine? Who carried out the execution and who had ordered it – and where had the command originated, in Ekaterinburg or in Moscow?

The Czechoslovaks, however, had more on their mind than the Romanovs. Their original objective was to make their way to Vladivostok for the purpose of onward shipment to join the Allies on the Western Front. The clashes with the Soviets since May 1918 had changed their thinking, and they were encouraged by the Allied emissaries in Russia to stay there and fight the Bolsheviks. They accepted the change of plan as congruent with their interests. Basically, they calculated that if they could help the anti-Bolsheviks to overturn the Soviet government and disrupt the Brest-Litovsk peace, they would win permanent favour with Britain, France and the United States. At the end of the Great War, they believed, this would enable the creation of a new and independent Czechoslovakia out of the ruins of Germany's main military partner Austria-Hungary.

Although the Czechoslovak Legion had marched into Ekaterinburg almost without resistance, the Bolsheviks had not given up all hope of retaking the city. The bulk of the Red forces had only feigned retreat to Perm. Most troops were in fact ordered to hide in the woods around Ekaterinburg and await further instructions. It soon became obvious the Czechoslovaks had left a garrison of only 800 before moving on towards Perm. On 31 July the Reds began a surprise counter-attack. Panic broke out until the arrival of a Serbian force from Chelyabinsk, which quickly dispersed the Red operation. Czechoslovak supremacy was reasserted.[8]

Meanwhile intense fighting took place in the Volga region as Komuch occupied Kazan and plotted an offensive against Moscow. It controlled Samara and Ufa provinces and sizeable tracts of Saratov, Simbirsk, Kazan and Vyatka provinces. The Red Army, poorly led and organized, crumbled before this campaign. Trotsky had no experience beyond his work as a war correspondent in the Balkans in 1912–1913. He did, though, have extraordinary determination, self-confidence and a remarkable ability to adapt. The Socialist-Revolutionaries celebrated countless victories until his arrival outside Kazan. Under Trotsky's impetus, the Red Army acquired a degree of professionalism after he insisted on employing the expertise of willing ex-imperial officers. To each layer of the military hierarchy he attached a political commissar so as to ensure the reliability of his forces. When he spoke to the troops, he spoke proudly and rousingly while also threatening deserters with capital punishment. In his locomotive and specially refurbished carriages, which became known as the Trotsky train, he travelled from one hot spot to another, and by 7 August Kazan had fallen to the Red Army's assault.

Komuch was revealed as being incapable of recruiting either an adequate command staff or a sufficient number of troops. Although peasants voted for the Socialist-Revolutionaries, they proved reluctant to fight for them. It was therefore of much consolation to Komuch that the Czechoslovak Legion offered to join a military coalition against the Red Army. Komuch still held power in Ufa province in the south-west Urals and the Czechoslovaks retained Chelyabinsk and had now occupied Ekaterinburg. The Red capture of Kazan was a blow to Komuch's expectations but the war between Komuch and Sovnarkom was not yet over, a war between two vehemently opposed left-wing political leaderships.

The Bolsheviks' attitude quickly hardened with the intensification of the fighting. Lenin had announced a Food Supplies Dictatorship in May that gave the right and duty to armed units to requisition grain and other agricultural products without regard to the peasantry's wishes. He also endorsed a faster campaign of industrial nationalization – earlier he had urged caution on the Left Communists, including the Urals Regional Soviet Executive Committee, about this. Even so, he had already decreed all banks and many big metallurgical enterprises to be state property, and now his zeal to expropriate private business rivalled anything that Left Communist leaders were demanding.[9] It was a fight to the death. Lenin's only worry was that Bolsheviks might fail to show the necessary ruthlessness. He told the Penza communists to be ruthless to the enemy, especially to the richer peasants known as kulaks:

> The *entire* revolution's interests require this because 'the last decisive battle' with the kulaks is now under way everywhere. An example must be shown:
> 1. Hang (and ensure that the hanging takes place *in the full view of the people*) *no fewer than one hundred* known kulaks, rich men, bloodsuckers.

2. Publish their names.
3. Seize all their grain from them.
4. Designate hostages in accordance with yesterday's telegram.[10]

This was Bolshevism red with the blood of future victims.

On this occasion it was the richer peasants whom he denounced as bloodsuckers. He had called Nicholas by the same name, and for those at the time and in later generations who doubted his willingness to exterminate the Romanov family, the message to Bolsheviks in Penza is an uncomfortable factor. The reality was that he and most of his leading associates had become sure that they would win the civil war only if they could wreak terrible violence at the front and in the rear. Sovnarkom and the Bolshevik Central Committee had yet to centralize and coordinate the Soviet state in all the ways that would be necessary to crush the armies that were massing against them. The Germans continued to consider whether to shrug them aside and occupy Petrograd and Moscow. The Allies landed expeditionary forces: the British took Archangel, the French seized Odessa. Russian former army officers who disdained to enlist in the socialist forces of Komuch were training armies in southern Russia and mid-Siberia. Sovnarkom had never monopolized governmental power in Russia, and the territory under its dominion was smaller in mid-1918 than it had been at the start of the year. The Bolshevik Party and the Red Army refused to give up hope. They aimed to win the civil war and then campaign for communist revolution throughout Europe.

The Czechoslovak Legion refused to be discouraged. Having crushed 'soviet power' between Chelyabinsk and the middle of Siberia, its commanders planned to repulse the Red Army. As part of their efforts, they hoped to receive helpful political support from Namëtkin's investigations in Ekaterinburg. While the war would be won by military means, the fighting would be assisted if it could be shown how brutally the Bolsheviks had behaved in the Soviet zone – and the Ekaterinburg episode became an important element in Czechoslovak calculations. But Namëtkin turned out to be an awkward appointee. Although the Czechoslovaks had provided useful service as the city's liberators, it ought to be Russians who governed in Russia. Namëtkin therefore asked for a local procurator, rather than a foreign occupying force, to confirm his appointment in the conventional fashion. The Czechoslovaks regarded this as prevarication or worse – they suspected him of political hostility. On 7 August, rather than seeking a way to work with Namëtkin, the Czechoslovaks replaced him with Judge Ivan Sergeev.[11] Ekaterinburg had become a temporary Czechoslovak fiefdom after the Red evacuation; it was not until 8 September 1918 that the Russian White forces, which had consolidated their position in Siberia, felt strong enough to take full charge of the city and the 'Czech Commandant' stepped down from office.[12]

Sergeev lasted longer in his post and made progress with the inquiry. Scores of residents of Ekaterinburg were summoned to give testimony, including some who had been guards at the Ipatev house or had family connections to prominent local Bolsheviks, and signed transcripts were made of the interrogations. A detailed registry was collated of items that had once belonged to the Romanovs. Telegrams to and from the Urals communist leadership were copied and, when necessary, decoded. Sergeev and his team supplied abundant evidence that Nikander Mirolyubov, who retained his status as Procurator of the Kazan Palace of Justice after moving to work for the Kolchak administration in Omsk, included in his preliminary report on 12 December 1918. He provided a succinct summary of what had as yet emerged from testimonies and physical searches. Working fast in less than perfect conditions, Mirolyubov arrived at conclusions that were to prove correct in most of their basic details. He was also right in his main point: the Romanov family had been executed in the cellar in the early hours of 17 July 1918 and no one had escaped.[13]

46. ROMANOV SURVIVORS

The announcement of Nicholas's execution increased Western concerns for the safety of those Romanovs who remained alive. The Bolsheviks were indefatigably pursuing everyone associated with the family. In early September 1918, Anastasia Gendrikova, Ekaterina Shneider and Alexei Volkov were at last escorted from Perm prison. The sailor in charge, as they drew near a wood on the outskirts, signalled to Volkov to flee as fast as he could. This time Volkov had no second thoughts. He hurtled off into the trees as three salvoes whistled over his head. Fortunately, nobody bothered to hunt him down. But this time for Gendrikova and Shneider there was no escape and they were shot on the spot.[1]

Dowager Empress Maria and Grand Duchess Xenia were in obvious danger. They had lived quietly at Ai Todor since 1917. When Ukraine and Crimea came under German occupation after the Treaty of Brest-Litovsk, they were left unmolested by the revolutionaries. Bolsheviks remained in Sevastopol and the surrounding area but their activity was limited to preparing for occasional attempts at sabotage of Germany's grip on the main Ukrainian cities. Meanwhile, the Volunteer Army of Generals Kornilov and Alexeev moved into the vacuum of power around Yalta. They had no trouble from the nearby German forces. They in turn found it prudent to avoid antagonizing the occupiers. As leaders of the Russian Army in 1917 they had insisted that every inch of soil should be defended against foreign invasion. Kornilov and Alexeev detested what the Bolsheviks had done at Brest-Litovsk and Sovnarkom replaced Germany as the main enemy. They took the step of assigning cavalry and infantrymen to guard the Romanovs in Crimea as German forces began to withdraw in advance of Germany's defeat on the Western Front. Three hundred Russian officers were based at the palace at Ai Todor. Until the Bolsheviks infiltrated the peninsula, many of them had a lively social life. In addition, two cavalry squadrons patrolled the nearby mountain passes. It was a comfortable deployment for them and the officers took the chance to drink and carouse.[2]

Maria Fëdorovna and Xenia tried to live as normally as they could in the circumstances and they hated the whole idea of abandoning the country. Like Nicholas in his last months, they believed that their duty was to stay rather than flee.

The German military authorities left them alone and treated them with respect. While Germany still had a chance of victory in the Great War, the women were safe at Ai Todor. But their situation became less predictable as the battles on the Western Front turned steadily in favour of the Allies. Princess Marie of Romania, based in Jassy on the Romanian frontier with Ukraine, appreciated the danger. Known to her relatives as Missie, she wrote on 1 September 1918 to the dowager empress – her aunt Minnie – to express her condolences about Nicholas. 'I do not even dare mention,' she added, 'the name of Nicky! Such a tragedy lies around it that one can only fall down on one's knees and beg that God gave him strength.' She deplored the 'comedy of peace' that had followed the Brest-Litovsk treaty.[3] Missie, who became Romania's queen that October, followed this with a plea for the dowager empress to see sense and agree to go abroad. Once the Germans withdrew from the East, she explained, every surviving Romanov would be in mortal danger from the Bolsheviks; she urged her aunt to allow a Canadian, Colonel Boyle – 'a man of extraordinary courage and capability' – to transport her from danger in a Romanian vessel.[4]

Boyle had an astounding reputation. Nobody was more surprised about this than the Canadian authorities, who had initially rejected him for active service because he was already in his fifties. Boyle's feats of derring-do were unmatched in the Allied forces. The reason the Romanian royal family adored him was that in November 1917 he and Captain George Hill of British intelligence had spirited the Romanian crown jewels from Moscow to Jassy after commandeering trains down through Kiev.[5] If anyone could arrange an escape for the two Romanov women, it was Boyle.

As the weeks passed, the Romanian princess's project became more and more convincing to everyone but the dowager empress. Germany's spring 1918 offensive on the Western Front was a last-gasp attempt to achieve victory. German economic resilience was stretched to the limits; popular morale was collapsing in Berlin and other big cities, and signs of political disgruntlement were on the increase. To the consternation of Hindenburg and Ludendorff, the French and British armies put up an effective defence. Through the summer the Allies held their lines and even pushed the Germans back a little. The prospect of newly arrived American forces bolstering the Allied side produced a pall of gloom over Germany's high command. By October the logistical situation was so dire that Hindenburg and Ludendorff, until then fêted as national heroes, resigned their posts. They knew that the Great War was lost, and did not want to take responsibility for accepting the terms that the Allies might impose. German might was on the point of crumbling in northern France. People began to consider what would happen in Russia and Ukraine when Germany's military occupation was lifted.

As the news quickly reached countries in Eastern Europe, the Romanian royal family repeated its efforts to secure the escape of the Romanovs from Crimea. Colonel Boyle was their willing instrument. He immediately volunteered to lead an expedition from the mouth of the Danube to Crimea. Broad-chested and brave to the point of recklessness, he made few demands before embarking. Apart from 200 sailors and oil for the ships' engines, he foresaw the need for plenty of wine so that he could entertain those Bolsheviks he encountered before reaching Ai Todor and whose help he would have to enlist. The Jassy adventure had taught him the value of making friends and bribing acquaintances. He had a style all his own, even taking the Romanian prime minister's limousine on the trip, in which he planned to convey the dowager empress from the palace.[6]

Landing from the sea at Yalta in mid-November, Boyle contacted the Bolshevik leadership and threw a splendid dinner for them. The one thing he did not mention was the purpose of his visit. He knew that the authorities would want to keep their hands on every living Romanov. Next day, he and a Russian guide drove the limousine into the countryside to Maria Fëdorovna. Her staff, which had diminished in the past year, still included a redoubtable English lady called Miss Dane. Boyle immediately noticed that conditions had worsened for them. Their clothes were rather grubby and one of the officers had a leather patch on his boots. The dowager empress, however, refused to move. Though touched by Boyle's invitation, she said: 'I am an old woman now. My life is nearly over. Here I am able to help in organizing some resistance to the Bolsheviki. You cannot take with you all those who have sacrificed everything for me and my family. I cannot abandon them.'[7] Such was her spirit that when the local soviet required her to obtain identity papers before she could receive her sugar ration, she signed herself simply as 'Marie'. The Bolshevik functionary objected to this as being insufficient. She proudly retorted: 'I have been signing "Marie" for fifty years; it isn't sufficient, I can do without the sugar.'[8]

Boyle departed from the Crimean coast in low spirits after his unaccustomed lack of success. While at sea, he spotted the approach of a British naval flotilla on the same mission. This was the first time that the Royal Navy had steamed through the Dardanelles since before the Great War. It could do so now because the Germans had surrendered unconditionally to the Allies on 11 November 1918. The Kaiser had abdicated days earlier and the strategic situation was transformed on both sides of the continent. The Western Allies began to emasculate Germany as a continental power, and the dismantling of its conquests in Ukraine and the Baltic commenced. But they had yet to work out a policy on communist Russia beyond supporting the anti-Bolshevik armies that were still being formed. The Bolsheviks themselves were aiming to pull Ukraine and Crimea under Sovnarkom's control and point their Red Army in the direction of Warsaw and Berlin. Moscow treated the finishing tape of the Great War – or the 'imperialist war', as Bolsheviks called it – as the starting point for a competition for supremacy throughout Europe. The area around Yalta would inevitably become a scene of military action as soon as the Germans left.

Maria Fëdorovna at last began to accept the arguments in favour of evacuation as she recognized the increasing dangers. Boyle ordered his vessel to accompany Vice-Admiral Arthur Calthorpe, Mediter-ranean commander-in-chief, back to Crimea with higher hopes of persuading Maria Fëdorovna than a few days earlier.[9] Calthorpe played his part, writing to her on 19 November 1918 that King George was 'very anxious' about her safety and offering through Comman-der Turle to take her secretly to Constantinople and from there in a battleship to a place of safety in Europe.[10] The king's mother, Queen Alexandra, wrote by telegram from Britain to her sister Maria on 21 December 1918:

Darling Minnie,
     Have just been informed that it would be most advisable for you to leave at once before more complications and horrors, so please make up your mind before it is too late to come to me here in England at once. Bring everyone you wish.
     Your loving sister,
     Alix[11]

Guilt and genuine sympathy were intermingled.

The dowager empress and her daughters felt ill-informed about what was happening in their country. Not trusting the Soviet account of the fate of their family in Ekaterinburg, they dispatched Pavel Buly-gin, a captain in their bodyguard, to Siberia via Odessa and a round-the-world sea trip to ascertain the facts.[12] But information from Petrograd soon became so clear and so shocking as to stiffen Maria Fëdorovna's resolve to leave. Late on 24 January 1919 four Romanovs in custody in the Peter-Paul Fortress prison – Grand Dukes Nikolai Mikhailovich, Pavel Alexandrovich, Dmitri Mikhailovich and Georgi Mikhailovich – were taken from their cells and shot. The ostensible intention was to retaliate against the murder of German far-left Marxist leaders Rosa Luxemburg and Karl Liebknecht in Berlin by anti-socialist paramilitaries. Maria Fëdorovna wrote in her diary: 'The newspapers are announcing the appalling news to the effect that four victims – Paul, Mitya, Nikolai and Georgi – have been shot. I cannot believe in the truth of this news – it's such a barbarous and disgusting act.'[13]

Together with her daughter Xenia and Grand Duke Nikolai Nikolaevich she no longer felt chafed by anxiety about abandoning their country to its fate, and they boarded HMS *Marlborough* and accepted the vice-admiral's hospitality.[14] On 14 April 1919 George V wrote to his aunt, giving thanks that she was crossing the peaceful Mediterranean. Soon she would be in Malta, where she could explain her 'wishes for the future'.[15] On 16 April 1919 Queen Alexandra via the Admiralty sent a telegram to the *Marlborough* expressing relief about Maria's escape from the clutches of the Bolsheviks.[16] On 22 April 1919, after receiving a pitiable message from Maria Fëdorovna, the queen replied that she well understood her 'poor, torn, miserable feelings'.[17] The Romanovs changed ships in Valletta. On 21 April 1919 the King telegrammed again, from Windsor Castle: 'Delighted you have arrived safely and that you have agreed to come in [the] Lord Nelson. Much looking forward to seeing you soon. Best love, George.'[18]

He could have behaved with the same generosity to Nicholas two years earlier but had chosen not to. He could not yet know that, even if he had done so, it is doubtful that Nicholas would have been able to leave. As it was, Nicholas's fate remained on his conscience.

Although the two families – or what remained of them in the case of the Romanovs – were reconciled, only Xenia felt comfortable about spending her exile in the United Kingdom. Nikolai stayed in the south of France; he renounced all claim to the Russian throne – this was prudent since some veterans in eastern Siberia wanted to proclaim him tsar. Maria Fëdorovna stayed for a while with her sister Queen Alexandra but made her mind up to accept an invitation to return to Denmark, the homeland she had left in 1866 when, as Princess Dagmar, she married the future Alexander III. While the Bolsheviks and the Red Army were fighting to retain and expand their control over Russia, the surviving Romanovs resigned themselves to a quiet retirement abroad.

47. THE ANTI-BOLSHEVIK INQUIRY

In November 1918, Siberian politics were transformed when Russian Army officers overthrew the pro-Komuch administration in Omsk and proclaimed Admiral Alexander Kolchak as Supreme Leader of All Russia. He despised the Komuch government and arrested or fired its surviving officials throughout western Siberia – he held them almost as culpable as the Bolsheviks for Russia's disintegration since the February Revolution. Kolchak's White Army immediately gained the valuable allegiance of the Czechoslovak Legion and could ready itself to wage war on the Reds. His forces immediately received financial and logistical support from the Western Allies. Kolchak himself declined to profess the monarchist cause, which he knew would alienate Allied support – and perhaps he understood that he would diminish the pool of potential recruits to his White Army if he announced the intention of restoring the Romanovs to power. Many of his commanders remained devoted to their military oath of allegiance to Nicholas II, and Kolchak encouraged the continuation of the Ekaterinburg massacre inquiry. Whatever was discovered in Ekaterinburg was bound to put the Bolsheviks in a poor light.

After bringing his forces to Ekaterinburg, Kolchak ordered a lightning westward offensive. The rest of the Urals had been in political ferment since mid-summer. The Izhevsk Steel Foundry rose against the Bolsheviks after a re-election of the Izhevsk Soviet in July replaced the Bolshevik majority. The Bolsheviks reacted by deploying Red Guards from Kazan. But it remained an explosive situation, and on 7 August the anti-Bolshevik workers rose against rule by commissar and extirpated every trace of it.[1]

The Reds rushed reinforcements to their Third Army in Perm to stop the Whites in their tracks. By then the Red Army had proved itself in battles by the River Volga. Red commanders warned that Perm would be no easy place to defend. Defences were dug. Troops were rallied and political commissars moved among them explaining that the October Revolution's survival was under threat. Kolchak's White Army, high in morale and well organized, rampaged across every obstacle. Just as the Czechoslovaks had found in the summer, the Bolsheviks did not always put up an effective resistance. A mood of panic seized the minds of party, soviet and Red Army personnel and a desperate mass escape was undertaken after defeat in the battle for the city. Perm was completely abandoned on 25 December 1918 after only the most ineffectual attempt at its defence. The result was a chaotic evacuation involving the relinquishing of vastly more assets than during the planned departure from Ekaterinburg. The Bolshevik Central Committee was horrified. Ekaterinburg had been bad but Perm was massively worse, and if the process were to be repeated, Kolchak would soon be the master in the Kremlin.

As for the Romanov inquiry, the seizure of Perm meant that many questions that had baffled Ivan Sergeev and Nikander Mirolyubov could be addressed by rounding up a group of new potential witnesses. The Whites had captured several Bolsheviks and their sympathizers who had taken part in the detention or execution of the imperial family. Mikhail Letemin had belonged to the guard detachment at the Ipatev house. According to a Soviet source, he was arrested in Ekaterinburg after being spotted taking the Romanov dog he had acquired for a walk. Apparently it had been the valet Chemodurov who recognized the animal.[2] Letemin had refused to enlist in the Red Army and join in the evacuation; indeed, he had shuddered at the idea of doing any fighting: 'I didn't sign up for that – I signed up only for service in the guarding team at the house of special assignment.' He claimed that he had acted to save the dog from dying of hunger. The inquiry noted his evidence but ignored his pleading, and his decision to stay on in Ekaterinburg proved fatal. When Letemin's house was searched, it was found to contain a pile of Nicholas and Alexandra's possessions.[3] Having got out of him the information that they wanted about the Romanovs in the Ipatev house, the Whites killed him.

On 17 January 1919 Admiral Kolchak appointed General Mikhail Diterikhs to head the inquiry. Diterikhs had until recently commanded the military front and had no legal experience, but Kolchak thought that he would bring a fresh urgency to the process. Sergeev had already earned the displeasure of the military command. In Diterikhs's eyes, the judge was drawn to Socialist-Revolutionary ideas and was no patriot. Diterikhs also believed that Sergeev lacked sympathy for Nicholas and the imperial family and showed signs of professional incompetence: he especially held against him that he had interrogated Soviet officials and Red Guard captives so lightly. Worst of all, according to Diterikhs, was the possibility that Sergeev was of Jewish descent – and the fact that he professed the Christian faith made no difference in Diterikhs's opinion. On 25 January, he required Sergeev to hand over the files he had accumulated since the start of the investigation.[4]

Diterikhs brought everything he received to Omsk and looked for ways to invigorate the process. With Sergeev out of the way, he aimed to recruit another investigator with proper legal experience. Diterikhs's choice fell upon a judge in Omsk called Nikolai Sokolov, who was known for his attentiveness to fact and detail. Above all, Sokolov was Russian born and bred, a Christian, a patriot and a monarchist who had none of the alleged softness towards Jewish Bolsheviks such as Trotsky (or Bronstein, as he called him). Sokolov had gone into hiding to evade the Red Guards during a difficult escape from Penza. On 5 February, Kolchak summoned him for interview and asked him what he would need. Sokolov returned to Kolchak next day with a list of his own practical requirements for the task. Kolchak explained that wartime conditions made for less than ideal conditions, and he asked him to take charge of the matter as best he could. Sokolov got down to work with the files that Diterikhs had passed over; he also conducted interrogations of witnesses both in Omsk and through his subordinates elsewhere.[5]

Diterikhs was a passionate nationalist, a believer in the greatness of the 'Christian Russian people' and a rabid anti-Semite.[6] He was always keen to emphasize how many revolutionaries had changed their names and stressed that neither Sverdlov nor Goloshchëkin was Russian.[7]

It was Sokolov, however, who managed the day-to-day work, and Diterikhs let him get on with it without interference. Sokolov deeply sympathized with the murdered monarch, but once he took on his duties, he put aside most of his feelings and concentrated on establishing the verifiable facts. He quickly briefed himself about the considerable progress already made by Alexei Namëtkin and Ivan Sergeev, and threw his team into tracing new witnesses and examining fresh material. He was always fossicking for convincing proof as reports came on to his desk; his subordinates learned to avoid all sloppiness. Everyone could see that Sokolov was a true professional, punctilious about details and reluctant to accept statements at face value. He kept scrupulous records of his interrogations as well as those conducted by his subordinates. (This was not to endear him to his superiors in the longer term, especially Diterikhs, who came to want to monopolize the credit for the investigation and also disliked Sokolov's failure to share his more simplistic assumptions about Russia in revolution.)

Despite having been relieved of his duties, Sergeev submitted his conclusions on 20 February 1919. He knew enough to damp down the rumours that anyone in the emperor's family at the Ipatev house had survived. He also named the retainers who had perished. As for Pavel Medvedev, currently held in captivity, Sergeev was in no doubt that he had given misleading testimony and had taken an active part in the killings in the Ipatev house.[8]

One of the urgent necessities for Sokolov was to check out the many stories that one or more Romanovs had fled the clutches of their captors. Several witnesses had continued to repeat this or that rumour while cheerfully admitting that it was only hearsay.[9] A certain Fëdor Sitnikov testified to having talked to a woman calling herself Grand Duchess Anastasia, but when pressed for corroboration, he added little that might have advanced the investigation.[10] Vivid 'evidence' also came from the military control investigator Alexander Kirsta, who scoured Perm for people who claimed to know about what had happened to the Romanovs. Kirsta was one of the individuals ordered to extend the inquiry to the city after December 1918, when Kolchak had driven out the Perm Soviet administration. He quickly encountered people who said they had come across Anastasia or other female Romanovs, including even the former empress. Natalya Mutnykh, sister of an Ekaterinburg Bolshevik official, reported that she had caught sight of several of them under detention in Perm. In one interrogation she named four daughters, in another she mentioned only three.[11]

Kirsta was not the only person who refused to accept that a Bolshevik firing squad had killed all the Romanov residents of the Ipatev house. Assistant Procurator Tikhomirov was convinced that, after Nicholas's execution, the rest of the family had been spirited off to Perm and then deeper into Soviet-occupied territory. He gave credence to the story of Anastasia's presence in Perm and highlighted evidence that a certain Dr Utkin's prescriptions for her medical condition had been discovered. The problem was that they proved to be written on printed forms that belonged to a Dr Ivanov.[12]

Steadily, Kirsta's professional competence was called into question as were the conditions that other investigators had to contend with, one of whom, V. Iordanski, complained that the military authorities refused to lend him and his colleagues the necessary cooperation and that they sometimes kept information to themselves.[13] As he investigated Kirsta's allegations, moreover, he quickly became sceptical about Utkin's claim to have treated Anastasia in Perm after he failed abysmally to recognize her from photographs. Iordanski could also see no reason to reject the testimony of Pavel Medvedev, who had been in the Ipatev house on the night of 16–17 July, to the effect that all seven Romanovs and their retainers who were present had been slaughtered.[14] Pavel Shamarin, Perm's own district procurator, reported his impressions to higher authority. As he got to know Kirsta face to face, he found him boastful and evasive. Kirsta, according to Shamarin, had been a fool for anyone who told him stories about how one or other Romanov had been seen under conditions of captivity at some place in Perm. Shamarin was shocked by Kirsta's gullibility, especially when the informants were women. Natalya Mutnykh, it was reported to Shamarin, had been adept at befuddling him.[15]

Pretenders were not a new phenomenon. Several individuals had been appearing in Siberia who declared themselves to be Romanovs. Even when the family was under detention in Tobolsk, the London *Daily Graphic* had published a fantastical report that Grand Duchess Tatyana had arrived in America. Imposters vastly increased in number after the Ekaterinburg executions, and usually they were quickly exposed as bogus.[16]

Sokolov, however, felt he had to take Dr Utkin seriously since he was a medical professional and was making big claims. If the inquiry was to have an authoritative status, all the conflicting assertions had to be thoroughly examined. An appointment for interrogation was made, and this time it was Sokolov himself who put the questions. He was not impressed by the doctor, who yet again proved incapable of substantiating his testimony and talked in exactly the same unconvincing fashion as previous investigators had reported. Sokolov drew the obvious conclusion and sided with those calling Kirsta a fool and an incompetent.[17] By 1 April 1919 he already felt able to write out his preliminary conclusions. They were little different in essentials from Sergeev's earlier ones: Sokolov was in no doubt, on the basis of an overwhelming amount of credible evidence, that the imperial family had perished in the Ipatev house along with Dr Botkin, the servant Trupp, the cook Kharitonov and the maid Demidova. He named Yurovski as the killing team's leader, and Nikulin and Medvedev as his main accomplices. He put the time of death between midnight and 3 a.m. His was an exemplary exposition.[18]

Now the civil war was turning against Kolchak. The Red Army as well as the Bolshevik Party and the Soviet government regrouped after losing Perm. Centralization of authority under the party's aegis was agreed at the party congress in March 1919, and the changes were drastic and immediate. The Bolsheviks had always been ruthless enough. Now they added organizational dependability to their armoury, and they were able to conscript from a large demographic pool and to benefit from the industrial warehouse stocks and from control of the railway arteries. In June they retook Ufa in the southern Urals; next month they reoccupied Chelyabinsk. The fighting intensified through-out the summer as Perm and Ekaterinburg fell again to the Reds after Kolchak failed in his attempt to stabilize his front line along the Tobol and Ishim rivers. By November the Whites had to fall back to Omsk. Trotsky and the Red high command were so confident of eventual victory that they were able to redeploy forces to Ukraine and southern Russia against the other great White Army, which had been formed by Alexeev and Kornilov and was commanded by General Anton Denikin after their deaths.

Sokolov kept up the work of interrogating witnesses and sifting the Bolshevik telegrams and Romanov possessions as best he could. A careful inventory was made of testimonies and material remains. Because of the Red Army's successful offensive, he moved east along the Trans-Siberian Railway to Chita. Being no longer able to ask his team to scour Ekaterinburg and its environs for further evidence, he largely had to complete the work with the boxes of transcripts and notes he had brought with him from the Urals. White Ekaterinburg had become Red Ekaterinburg once again. His morale was tested by the uncooperativeness of the military control authority. Indeed, he had enemies among the Whites who made no secret of the fact that they intended to make an attempt on his life. Sokolov overheard some con-spirators discussing their plan in the very next train compartment to his own – with characteristic sang-froid he asked them: 'Not so loud, please, gentlemen, I happen to be next door, you know!' Undeterred, on 7 October 1919 he wrote yet another report, still not a full one but adding important new information. He sent it to Mirolyubov, com-plaining at the same time about the army authorities and regretting that he had been unable to lay hands on Yurovski or Goloshchëkin.

The rest of this latest report indicated the costs of maintenance for the many agents that he had to employ.[19]

The wartime exigencies and rivalry with the military control authority were not the only sources of tension between Sokolov and the army command. Another was the feeling among leading White officers who thought he lacked the necessary outlook of a reliable anti-Bolshevik. Diterikhs hated Jews and had little time for liberals or even moderate conservatives. Being steeped in the Orthodox Christian monarchism of his fellow commanders, he had thought Namëtkin and Sergeev tainted by association with the openness to political compromise that typified the period of rule by the Provisional Government. But Diterikhs retained a degree of confidence in Sokolov and left him to get on with his work until one of Sokolov's security officers, Captain Pavel Bulygin, informed Diterikhs about the physical danger that Sokolov had to deal with. (This was the same Bulygin who had come to Siberia at the behest of the dowager empress.) Bulygin pointed out that if someone tossed a hand grenade at Sokolov, it might simultaneously destroy a pile of inquiry materials. Diterikhs was horrified, but on 19 December 1919, instead of reinforcing Sokolov's protection, he peremptorily requisitioned his boxes. Sokolov could stand it no longer and wrote next day to Procurator Mirolyubov asking to be relieved of his assignment.[20]

As his precious boxes were removed back west along the railway to Verkhne-Udinsk, he was angry and embittered. He was convinced that Diterikhs had acted deliberately to terminate his involvement in the inquiry. In fact, as Bulygin discovered from a personal interview, Diterikhs genuinely believed that he had done the only thing that would guarantee the survival of the primary evidence. The military situation nevertheless continued to worsen for the Whites in Siberia, inducing him to transport the boxes over the Chinese border to Harbin, where the UK consulate agreed to take care of them. At the same time he asked the British to facilitate Sokolov's safe journey to Harbin, return his boxes to him and enable him to travel on with them to Europe. Sokolov, the supreme professional, put aside his feelings of resentment and made his way out of Siberia, eventually becoming reunited with the boxes that he had last seen in Chita. By chance, Pierre Gilliard was already in Harbin, where he witnessed the confusion at the British embassy as officials came and went. Gilliard saw the need for someone to take proper charge of the boxes and concluded that French General Maurice Janin was the only individual currently with sufficient authority to arrange the transport to Vladivostok for onward dispatch to Europe.[21]

Sokolov was naturally reluctant to be separated again from the materials, but in the end he recognized that this was the only realistic way of conveying them safely out of Asia. After his adventures, Sokolov still had just one thing in mind, to finish the work of the inquiry from a West European base. His determination was undimmed by his travails. Even if the Reds were in sight of winning the civil war, there was no reason for them to be allowed to spread without challenge their falsehoods about the Urals executions. Establishing the historical truth became the cause of Sokolov's life.

48. DISPUTE WITHOUT BONES

In March 1919, when the Bolsheviks assembled in Moscow for their party congress, there was still no public clarity about what had happened to the Romanovs. The custom was for delegates to pass their queries to the platform on slips of paper. One of them asked Lenin why there was still a delay in bringing Nicholas to Moscow for a big open trial.[1] Only a poorly informed Bolshevik could have made such an enquiry. *Pravda* and other newspapers had announced the execution eight months earlier, and it is hardly surprising that there is no record that Lenin bothered to give an answer. But however stupid the query was, the Soviet leadership had certainly helped to spread confusion, and the official falsehood that only Nicholas had been executed was maintained. Rumours continued to spread and pretenders still sprang up in villages and provincial towns. The tale that Nicholas's wife and family had been transferred to some unspecified place of safety at a distance from Ekaterinburg gave rise to the obvious question: well, where are they now? The combination of reticence and lies by Soviet authorities opened the ground for other tales to flourish, and White reactionaries put forward a variety of potential dynasts to mount the Romanov throne.[2]

This in itself did not compel a change to the account given in Moscow; indeed, as earlier, a degree of muddle in some ways suited the communist rulers. But their complacency was destroyed in 1920 when White refugees in Istanbul made the first serious attempt to release documentation about the Ipatev house killings. Whereas the communists could control what was printed in Soviet Russia, they could do nothing about foreign publishing houses. This little book, which was disseminated to émigré communities in Europe and elsewhere, contained documentation that offered a fundamental challenge to Moscow's account. It summarized what Alexei Namëtkin and Ivan Sergeev had found in summer 1918. In particular, it described some of the discoveries of jewels and other items belonging to the Romanovs.

It mentioned the interrogations of Fëdor Gorshkov, Pierre Gilliard and Mikhail Letemin, and it told how the peasants had pointed to the strange happenings at the mineshafts. The book also referred to the telegraph traffic between Moscow and Ekaterinburg. The conclusion was unconditional: the Romanov captives in the Ipatev house had all been shot and none escaped.[3]

In the same year a blistering attack on the Bolshevik official fiction appeared in the account by Robert Wilton. Through his acquaintance with both Diterikhs and Sokolov, both of whom he admired, he gained access to the inquiry dossiers, and as a journalist he appreciated the importance of producing his book with all possible speed. But he did not do the best of jobs. This was because Wilton marshalled the evidence in an extremely tendentious fashion in order to put the blame for all the killings on a Jewish conspiracy. Allegedly Sverdlov, who was a Jew, was chief of the plotters, whereas the Russian Lenin was a mere 'dummy', and the authoritative leaders on the spot were purportedly all Jews by origin. Wilton even claimed that the reason Judge Sergeev had refused to mention the Jewish connection in his report was that he himself was a Jew. This was also the reason Wilton saw fit to denigrate the Istanbul book that was published earlier in the year. With poisonous anti-Semitic fervour, he contended that its authors omitted to mention the Judaic origins of the murderers principally because of their own Jewish origins.[4]

Wilton did at least accept, though, that all the Ipatev house detainees had perished, and General Diterikhs gave a boost to this case when, on 27 February 1921, he gave an interview to a newspaper in Vladivostok. The Siberian far east had yet to fall into Red hands, mainly because Lenin was wary of annoying the Japanese, and this meant that the White forces who had been driven from the Urals remained in charge of the city. Diterikhs knew that his communiqué would be immediately relayed abroad.[5]

After explaining how Kolchak had put him in charge of the inquiry, he announced his main findings: 'The whole imperial family and the grand dukes were killed. The first ones in Ekaterinburg, the second group in Alapaevsk sixty kilometres [sic] from Ekaterinburg. The imperial family was killed by decree of the Urals Regional Soviet in the night of the 16–17 April [sic].'[6] Apart from the misdating of the month, this was an announcement that could not easily be ignored at a time when the Soviet leadership was trying to build up commercial and diplomatic ties with foreign countries where the fate of the Romanovs remained controversial. Trade negotiations with the United Kingdom were reaching a climax at the time of Diterikhs's announcement. The Soviet central authorities knew the truth of his basic contention and could expect difficulty in maintaining the fiction that only Nicholas had been shot; for Diterikhs, resuming control of the anti-Bolshevik inquiry boxes, had delivered twenty-nine of them to the British naval vessel *Kent*, which transported them to safety in Western Europe.[7]

Once the lie about the singular killing of Nicholas was exposed, the communist authorities prudently decided to change their story. The alterations were published not in Moscow but in the Urals, when the Ekaterinburg branch of the State Publishing House issued *The Workers' Revolution*. There was still no intention of revealing the full details of the Ipatev house killings, but it was clear that the leadership had to acknowledge how many Romanovs had perished.

The Workers' Revolution opened with a chapter titled 'The Last Days of the Last Tsar' by Pavel Bykov, who had belonged to the Urals Regional Soviet Executive Committee in 1918 and had visited the Ipatev house on its behalf. He knew as much as anyone still working in Ekaterinburg about the fate of the Romanovs. Bykov recounted the transfer of Nicholas and his family from Tsarskoe Selo and then to Tobolsk before their final place of detention in the Ipatev house. He cited the growing danger of a rescue attempt as the reason they were moved to the Urals. Even in Ekaterinburg there were signs of conspiracy. According to Bykov, the Urals Regional Executive Committee alone took the fatal decision to kill the Romanovs living in the territories it controlled. By implication Lenin and Sverdlov had nothing to do with it.[8] Bykov dropped all pretence that only one person had perished in the Ipatev house. As he put it, what had occurred on 17 July 1918 was 'the execution of Nikolai Romanov and all those who were with him'. He bluntly stated that they had all been lined up against a wall and shot. He claimed that the execution squad had contained only four persons.[9] The motives behind this last false numerical detail are unclear, but at least it accompanied an admission that all the Ipatev house captives had been liquidated.[10]

The Last Days of the Last Tsar was the next book on the subject to appear in Russia. Yet again, a provincial publishing house was chosen. Appearing in Tver in 1922, it took the story back to Tobolsk, where there had been 'a concentration of counter-revolutionary elements and a whole sequence of provocational communications about the flight and seizure of the former Tsar'. The book also pointed to the signs of subsequent plots in Ekaterinburg. The arrival of Major Migić of the Serbian general staff as an emissary of the Queen of Serbia had shown that something was afoot. Responsibility for the decision to kill the Romanovs was ascribed to the Urals Regional Soviet Executive Committee. 'Fantasists' proliferated. Details were revealed for the first time, such as that Nicholas and his family had been taken down to the cellar in the Ipatev house before being shot. Truth was mixed with a new untruth; for it was claimed that the corpses were taken to a wood near the Upper Iset Works and the village of Palkina, where they were cremated. The geography was falsified presumably to stop the mineshafts from becoming a place of monarchist pilgrimage. But it was stressed that all the Romanovs held in Ekaterinburg, Perm and Alapaevsk had been executed.[11]

At the same time, the Whites were denounced for spreading the false rumour that Nicholas and his family had not been executed but were instead taken away from Ekaterinburg – a 'rumour' that Soviet authorities themselves had started in the pages of *Pravda*. White publications nonetheless began to be used whenever they corroborated Moscow's new official line, and the recent Vladivostok communiqué by Diterikhs was used in support of the true idea that nobody escaped the Ipatev house cellar alive.[12]

Diterikhs himself repeated this idea in *Murder of the Tsarist Family and Members of the House of Romanov in the Urals*, which he rushed into print in 1922 before he left the territory of the former Russian Empire for China. By then Kolchak was dead, having fallen into the hands of Left Socialist-Revolutionaries in east Siberia who, in February 1920, handed him over to the Bolsheviks. After a short trial by revolutionary tribunal, he was shot and his body was tossed into the icy waters of the Angara River. After Kolchak's army had been routed, Diterikhs was at least free from the political need to avoid saying things that might displease governments in America, France and the United Kingdom. One of his first steps was to wave the monarchist flag, which Kolchak had never been able to do if he wanted to maintain Allied support. Indeed, Diterikhs proclaimed Nikolai Nikolaevich – Nicholas II's cousin – as the new Tsar of All Russia. His own book was a self-aggrandizing account in which he played down the contribution that Namëtkin, Sergeev and Sokolov had made to the inquiry. Diterikhs wore his prejudices on his sleeve. The Bolsheviks to a man and woman, he wrote, were godless fanatics who operated under Jewish leadership.[13]

Nikolai Sokolov meanwhile continued to refine the work on the inquiry that he had had to suspend in Chita. The urgent need was to find himself a place of refuge in Western Europe. On 19 February 1920 he wrote to Sydney Gibbes ('Sidnei Ivanovich') as someone who might offer assistance in enabling him to make the journey. Stranded in Harbin on the Chinese side of the border with Russian Siberia, he worried about the safety of the materials that he had transported from the Urals. There were five large boxes of his own in his luggage, and he worried that Bolshevik agents might make an attempt to seize hold of them as he made his way south across China.[14] After reaching Beijing, he headed for Shanghai from where he took a boat to Europe.[15] When he disembarked in Dubrovnik, he journeyed to Paris and made contact by letter with the Dowager Empress Maria Fëdorovna. He was mortified by her reaction. Maria Fëdorovna was psychologically unready to accept that her son and his family were dead, and she rejected his requests to talk with her and showed him no cooperation beyond granting him a financial subsidy. Grand Duke Nikolai Nikolaevich, too, refused to be interviewed. Sokolov ruefully said that if he had known how his painstaking work would be treated, he would have left his inquiry boxes with Russian peasants in Manchuria rather than provide 'sport for political wire-pullers'.[16]

It hurt him that he was publicly maligned by those fellow émigré monarchists who wanted to believe that some of the Romanovs had survived the Ekaterinburg massacre. But duty conquered the pain, and Sokolov buried himself in his fourteen volumes of working notes. He paid no heed to his assistants who urged him to cease worrying about details and to publish his book without delay. His ambition was to complete an authoritative account appropriate for a judicial process.[17]

In private correspondence Sokolov gave vent to several of the attitudes that were to the fore in what Diterikhs had written. As a monarchist loyal to the memory of Nicholas II, he despised the Russian diplomatic corps left behind by the Provisional Government and still in occupation of embassy buildings in Western Europe. It was Sokolov's crazed belief that men like Ambassador Girs in Rome would soon be working abroad for the Bolsheviks. He blamed the Provisional Government for putting 'the Sovereign' under arrest and thereby laying the path that led to his execution. He felt sure that Rasputin's clique had been linked somehow to the German intelligence network. He noted how many of the individuals who surrounded Rasputin were Jews, and he assumed that such people were bound to lack a sense of patriotism in times of Russian national peril. He saw Germany's hand in the travails that beset Russia after the February Revolution. With justification he pointed to evidence that Boris Solověv, self-styled would-be rescuer in Tobolsk in 1918, might in reality have schemed to wreck the chances of a successful escape. But Sokolov also went further than what he could prove when he claimed that it had been German pressure on Sovnarkom that led to Nicholas's transfer from Tobolsk.[18]

He put aside most of this speculativeness when writing up his *Judicial Inquiry into the Murder of the Russian Imperial Family*, which first appeared in a French edition in 1924.[19] Its careful analysis and quotations from documents, depositions and interrogations gained international notice. Quickly coming out in a Russian émigré edition as well as in English, it became established as the standard Western account.[20] In basic respects its main findings about the killings have been confirmed by later discoveries. Sokolov himself was worn out by his labours and ignored by Russian émigrés; he died in the little town of Salbris in Loir-et-Cher in the same year that his book appeared.

Most of the volumes that were published in the early years after Nicholas's death focused on the last day of his life. Sokolov gave more information than Wilton or Diterikhs about the previous months, but he generally stuck to the task of inquiring into the killings. Memoirs appeared by the hand of former retainers who had made their way to Europe. The first of these was Pierre Gilliard, who in 1921 produced an eyewitness account of his experiences with the imperial family.[21] The doctor's daughter Tatyana Botkina and Sophie Buxhoeveden continued in this vein, and General Alexander Syroboyarski published his correspondence with the empress.[22] The image that they all conveyed was of a family without blemishes: Nicholas as the kindly patriarch; the imperial couple as devoted spouses even though Alexandra could be domineering towards others, including her retainers; the daughters and son as sweet innocents. Sometimes it was allowed that the welcome they had given to Rasputin had had baleful consequences, but generally the memoirists took it for granted that Nicholas the autocrat had the right to rule autocratically. There was little political analysis of his contribution to his own downfall in the February Revolution – and next to nothing about his reaction to events in 1917–1918.

Other Russian refugees were less generous about the dead tsar but none of them, with the fleeting exception of the Provisional Government's Alexander Kerensky, had had direct contact with any of the Romanovs after the February Revolution. As they tried to explain the causes of the dynasty's collapse, they delivered damning verdicts on Nicholas's long reign in regards to politics, economics and social policy. Most of them had scant interest in the emperor as an individual.

Such attitudes were shared by Western commentators except for the unconditional monarchists. Those who welcomed the October Revolution caricatured the emperor as Nicholas the Bloody and spared no pity on his fate, and most writers who deplored the chaos wrought by the Bolsheviks were eager to blame Nicholas for having reduced Russia to conditions that made possible their advance on power. This had the unintended result of permitting monarchists, Russian or foreign, to dominate the discussion of Nicholas's personality and ideas as well as his behaviour towards retainers, supporters, guards and political enemies. From the mid-1920s the debates outside Russia were skewed by the question as to whether a particular woman found in a Berlin mental asylum and known as Anna Anderson was really Grand Duchess Anastasia. Judicial proceedings and an inquiry funded by Alexandra's brother Prince Ernst of Hesse denied the authenticity of her claims, but this only whetted the appetite of newspapers in many countries to sustain her case. The resultant farrago of pseudo-evidence served to concentrate minds on the fateful executions in the Ipatev house.[23]

Nicholas was turned into a cartoon-like version of himself, quite unlike the historical man and ex-ruler. Ironically, it was a Soviet publication, Vasili Pankratov's memoirs, that got closest to a credible depiction of him in the months of his detention by writing of his modest habits, ineffectual attempts at teaching Alexei and enthusiasm for knowledge about Siberia. There was also a worthy documentary publication, *The Fall of the Tsarist Regime*, that appeared in the middle of the 1920s and was the stenographic record of the proceedings of the Provisional Government's Extraordinary Investigative Commission, including testimonies by many of the political figures who either served Nicholas or worked to bring him down. But otherwise the Moscow authorities preferred to draw a curtain across such matters, and whenever the dead emperor was mentioned, he received no fairer treatment than he himself would have accorded to the communists whom he detested.[24]

49. AFTERWORD

The last sixteen months of Nicholas II's life are a lasting object of fascination. Outside Russia, he has characteristically been depicted as a loving husband and father and a butchered ex-ruler. Books have dwelt on his noble qualities during a captivity that grew ever harsher in Tsarskoe Selo, Tobolsk and Ekaterinburg. The stereotype culminated in Robert and Suzanne Massie's *Nicholas and Alexandra*, which became a global best-seller in 1967. The Massies highlighted the ghastly scene of collective execution in the Ipatev house.[1] They touched a nerve with millions of readers who were open to the idea that communism in Russia had been a bloodbath in the first year after the October Revolution – and the imperial couple were represented as entirely innocent of thoughts and actions that might have led to their deposition from power in 1917. A less sentimental portrait of the events leading to the February Revolution was offered in the British Hammer film *Rasputin the Mad Monk*, starring Christopher Lee and accentuating the dark forces that operated behind Nicholas's throne. (The screenplay strangely omitted Nicholas from the cast of characters.) The common thread was that Russia, at the point when the Romanovs lost power, took a disastrous lurch on to a path that exaggerated all the exotic and grotesque tendencies that until then it had been steadily eliminating.[2]

Soviet writers ignored all such trends. From Lenin and Stalin onwards, the official line was always that monarchs made little difference to public affairs but rather were the puppets of robust economic forces. Nicholas was thrust into this analytical mould. The question for official debate was about whether the last tsar devoted himself to defending the interests of the ancestral landowning elite or aligned his administration with the demands of new industrial and financial forces. It was also asked whether the Russian Empire under Nicholas was truly an independent great power or the plaything of foreign imperial states, particularly the United Kingdom and France. No full-scale account of his rulership was approved for publication in the USSR either before or after the Second World War. The grim story of the last days in Ekaterinburg was kept under wraps.

Behind the veil of secrecy, an effort was made in Moscow to gather documents and testimony about the Romanovs in 1917–1918. Nikita Khrushchëv, Stalin's successor as party general secretary, called for the illumination of hidden corners of the Soviet past. His principal objective was to find damning data about Stalin. Khrushchëv's other imperative was to discover uplifting sources for the career of Lenin, who became the single unifying focus for Marxism–Leninism in the USSR. Assiduous efforts were made to excavate each and every item of Leniniana. As regards the killing of Nicholas, those members of the Ipatev killing squad who remained alive were interviewed and those interviews were recorded on tape. One of the official purposes was to prove that Lenin had nothing to do with the order to execute the Romanov family. The interviewees duly complied with what was required of them. But a trace of embarrassment persisted about the Ipatev house butchery, and the sound recordings were consigned to the archives. What is more, there was no serious attempt to produce a focused account of Nicholas's long period as emperor or his fate as captive of the Provisional Government and Sovnarkom. In order to prevent any resurgence of monarchist feelings under Khrushchëv's successor, Leonid Brezhnev, it was decided even to demolish the museum that had once been the Ipatev house in Ekaterinburg.

Western historical writers reacted patchily to Soviet claims, accentuating the theme of escape, and gullibility about successful Romanov refugees from Ekaterinburg was not confined to the case made by 'Anastasia'. In 1976 BBC investigative journalists Anthony Summers and Tom Mangold produced a book, *File on the Tsar*, which claimed to disprove the entire story of the murder of Nicholas and his family. Summers and Mangold argued that one or more members of the family escaped to sanctuary in Perm.[3] The evidence was slim and their attempts at annotation were pitiful. I have worked on the same 'file' (which consists chiefly of the extant set of correspondence received and sent by Nikander I. Mirolyubov, Procurator of the Kazan Palace of Justice) in the Hoover Institution at Stanford University, and note that Summers and Mangold omitted to look at statements in the very same letters that blew a hole in their contention about the reliability of witnesses such as Natalya Mutnykh. The book nonetheless remains in print. Moreover, its basic hypothesis about a collective relocation of Romanovs to Perm or its surroundings has continued to grip the imagination of several writers. Although the British seem to have cornered the market in outlandish narratives about the Romanovs, American authors have started to compete with them. Perhaps the widespread prurience about private lives in the House of Windsor has spawned a credulousness about all reigning dynasties past and present.

Interest in Nicholas II has waned among professional historians, who have been more attracted by earlier Russian emperors such as Peter the Great and Catherine the Great. An exception was the measured biography by Dominic Lieven in 1993, which set the last tsar firmly in the political frame of his times, and Richard Wortman has recently highlighted the symbols and ceremonies developed by Nicholas to disseminate his idea of the kind of Russia he wanted to create.[4] Geoffrey Hosking examined the tense relationship between the tsar and his outstanding conservative prime minister Pëtr Stolypin.[5] Heinz-Dietrich Löwe explored the connections between Nicholas and anti-Semitic organizations and doctrines before 1917.[6] Simon Sebag Montefiore examined his failures as a ruler while showing that the marriage of Nicholas and Alexandra was a coupling of mutual passion and support.[7] Helen Rappaport investigated the local peculiarities of the situation in Ekaterinburg.[8] Such accounts have healthily moved away from the saccharine treatments that once were the standard offering. They have also highlighted why Nicholas is a subject deserving of historical attention.

Nicholas has gained in public respect in Russia since 1991, when the USSR disintegrated and communism was swept from the scene. When President Yeltsin designated the decades since the October Revolution as 'a totalitarian nightmare', the Romanov dynasty began to be seen in a brighter light than had been permitted under communist rule. Even so, Nicholas remained a dark reactionary figure in many accounts and Genrikh Ioffe stuck resolutely to the line that it was the men of Ekaterinburg alone rather than of Moscow who took the ultimate decision to kill the Romanovs.[9] But the stronger trend portrayed Nicholas in a sympathetic fashion and as Lenin's fatal victim. Indeed, the romantic image of the tsar and his family became a staple of popular histories. Prominent in promoting such a portraiture was the playwright Edvard Radzinski.[10]

A host of investigative scholars – V. V. Alexeev, A. N. Avdonin, Vladimir Khrustalëv (together with American historian Mark Steinberg), L. A. Lykova, I. F. Plotnikov and Yuri Zhuk – have meanwhile dug up fresh sources about the Romanovs in captivity through to their deaths. They have sensibly avoided the Western controversies about Anastasia or other so-called Ekaterinburg escapees.[11] They have concentrated on the sources in Russia without being able to give equal attention to complementary material in Western holdings, and have tended to limit themselves to questions about Lenin's culpability and the circumstances of the confinement and execution in the Urals. Some of them also have monarchist sympathies.

The rehabilitation of the Romanovs was furthered by Yeltsin's decision to rebury their remains in St Petersburg's Peter-Paul Cathedral on 17 July 1998, eighty years to the day after their murder. Forensic archaeology was undertaken in and around disused mineshafts outside Ekaterinburg, and the excavated bones were subjected to DNA testing and proved to have a Romanov lineage. Yeltsin himself had been the Communist Party chief who in 1973 had carried out Brezhnev's orders to demolish the former Ipatev house, an action he had come to regret. The Russian Orthodox Church, however, withheld its complete approval because remains of not all the Romanov detainees were found among the fragments of bones and clothing. Predictably, this gave renewed stimulus to those seeking to convince the world that one or more of the family had avoided execution. President Putin, who succeeded Yeltsin in 2000, encouraged continued public respect for the murdered Romanovs. Despite reservations about the recent scientific inquiry, Patriarch Alexi was loyal to the memory of the Romanovs and canonized them as 'passion-bearers' who sought to live by the principles of the Gospels.

Nicholas and his family met a gruesome end in the Ipatev house. The former emperor's dignity in the circumstances of captivity was impressive. He was indeed a devoted husband and father who vacated the throne in the February Revolution mainly because he could not bear the thought of being separated from his haemophiliac son Alexei. What shattered his confidence as monarch was the military high command's withdrawal of support. His competence to oversee the governance of Russia had never been better than average, and his autocratic wilfulness wrecked any chances of a gradual transition to a more balanced constitution. The widespread image of him as a blameless monarch is unconvincing. In power and out of it, he was a nationalist extremist, a deluded nostalgist and a virulent anti-Semite. When held in confinement in Tsarskoe Selo, Tobolsk and Ekaterinburg, he strove to make sense of his experience by reading historical literature on the travails of his dynastic forebears. He also introduced himself to books that told him about those social classes in his empire with which he had negligible acquaintance. The imperial couple continued to cherish an idealized and misleading vision of the Russians as a people. Neither Nicholas nor Alexandra gave adequate thought to the causes of their fall from power, and in so far as Nicholas tried to understand what had happened, he blamed alien forces that had deceived and manipulated his former subjects.

The anti-Bolshevik inquiry of 1918–1919 was focused on the period of detention and execution. It deserves commendation for getting most things right in a difficult environment for investigators. The original interrogation records lie at the foundations of this book. Of course, we now can examine documents and memoirs that were unavailable to Nikolai Sokolov. It is at last possible, as we have seen, to clear up several long-standing controversies: about Yakovlev's choices of route to transfer the Romanovs from Tobolsk; about the Urals leadership's political management in early 1918; about Lenin's part in the setting of policy in the summer; and about the relationship between Moscow and Ekaterinburg.

My own broader purpose has been to look at the tsar after his abdication through to his death from combined political and personal angles and to ascertain how much his attitudes underwent change about Russia, politics, rulership, war and international relations as well as about himself after his abdication. His diaries, recorded conversations and reading habits are revelatory about his thinking when he was no longer at the helm of public affairs. His ultimate purposes before 1917 have given rise to decades of debate, and there is a question about whether he was truly as mentally rigid as his enemies claimed. The evidence suggests that those enemies had a point. In captivity he had the time to recognize any of his mistakes and rectify his basic analysis. In fact he did nothing of the kind. Although he belatedly allowed that if his son, Alexei, had been able to succeed him, a constitutional monarchy of some sort could have been attempted, he never expressed regret that he himself had set his face against any such outcome while he held power.

Nicholas was nonetheless a more complicated person than anyone could easily know because he kept so many of his thoughts secret from ministers, revolutionaries and even retainers. His best chance to commune with others came when he got to know Plenipotentiary Pankratov and Commissar Yakovlev. For Alexandra, the same opportunity occurred through conversations with her children's teacher

Bitner. Nicholas was more willing than Alexandra to pay mind to some of the notions of people with whom he disagreed. Even so, he barely altered a single one of his underlying assumptions. At a psychological level this is hardly surprising. In 1913 he had celebrated the tercentenary of the Romanov dynasty. Four years later he lost power when workers and soldiers joined in political demonstrations against Nicholas the Bloody. Naturally, he was reluctant to accept that he had brought much of the turmoil on his own head and made little effort to comprehend either the February Revolution or the October Revolution of 1917.

After abdicating, he was living in seclusion in a Russia that underwent ceaseless transformation. The Provisional Government altered fundamental features of official policy before being overthrown by the Bolsheviks, who implemented an even more radical set of revolutionary objectives.

The communist leaderships in Moscow and Ekaterinburg hated and despised Nicholas too much to try to understand him and his point of view. Lenin and the Bolshevik Committee, as is clear, were regularly consulted by the Urals regional comrades about what was happening in Ekaterinburg in the weeks before the killing took place in the Ipatev house. Lenin and Sverdlov were deft in the way they erased the traces of responsibility for the order of execution, and they and their comrades wasted no time in expressing pity for the former emperor and his family. For Bolsheviks, it was crystal-clear that the future lay definitively and forever with the revolutionary cause. Until 1991, the official slogan was: 'Lenin lived, Lenin lives, Lenin will live!' Exhumed from the dank depths of a disused Urals mine, Nicholas has enjoyed a tenacious afterlife. As with Lenin, moreover, myths about the last tsar compete fiercely against the demonstrable historical record. This is how it has been since the bloody Urals events of 1918 and how it is likely to continue.

BIBLIOGRAPHY

ARCHIVES

Arkhiv Prezidenta Rossiiskoi Federatsii (Moscow: Archive of the President of the Russian Federation)

Gosudarstvennyi Arkhiv Rossiiskoi Federatsii (Moscow: State Archive of the Russian Federation)

Hoover Institution Archives (Stanford University, CA)
   Mikhail V. Alekseev Papers
   Nikolai de Bazili Papers
   Vera Cattell Papers
   Agnes M. Diterikhs Papers
   Barbara Dolgorouky Papers
   Dmitri I. Fedichkin Papers
   Georgii Mikhailovich, Grand Duke of Russia Papers
   Kseniia Aleksandrovna, Grand Duchess of Russia Papers
   Alexis V. Lapteff Papers
   Robert Bruce Lockhart Papers
   Nikander I. Miroliubov Papers
   Nicholas II Papers
   Boris I. Nicolaevsky Collection
   Ivan I. Serebrennikov Papers
   Serebryakova Papers
   Nadia Shapiro Papers
   Rudolf von Stackelberg Papers
   Nikolai Alekseevich Sokolov Papers
   Lev Sukacev Papers
   Georgi Alexandrovich von Tal Papers
   Alexandre Tarsaidze Papers
   Aleksei B. Tatischev Papers
   Trotsky Collection
   Dmitri Antonovich Volkogonov Papers
   Ekaterina Zborovskaia Papers
   K. Zershchikov Papers

National Archives (Kew)
Oxford University (Oxford)
   Sydney Gibbes Collection (Special Collections, Bodleian Library)
Rossiiskii Gosudarstvennyi Arkhiv Sotsial'no-Politicheskoi Istorii (Russian State
   Archive of Social and Political History: Moscow)

NEWSPAPERS AND JOURNALS

Argumenty i fakty (Moscow)
Evening News (London)
Izvestiya (Moscow)
Komsomol'skaya pravda (Moscow)
Literaturnaya gazeta (Moscow)
Literaturnaya Rossiya (Moscow)
Ogonëk (Moscow)
Peterburgskaya gazeta (St Petersburg)
Peterburgskaya pravda (St Petersburg)
Pravda (Moscow)
Svet (St Petersburg)
The Times (London)
Tobol'skie eparkhal'nye vedomosti (Tobolsk)
Tobol'skii rabochii (Tobolsk)
Ural'skii rabochii (Ekaterinburg)

BOOKS AND ARTICLES

14 mesyatsev vo vlasti bol'shevikov. (Permskie uzhasy) (Ekaterinburg: Russkoe
   byuro pechati, 1919)
R. Abraham, *Alexander Kerensky: The First Love of the Revolution* (New York:
   Columbia University Press, 1987)
E. Acton, V. Yu. Cherniaev and W. G. Rosenberg (eds), *Critical Companion to the
   Russian Revolution* (London: E. Arnold, 1997)
V. V. Alexeev, *Gibel' tsarskoi sem'i: mify i real'nost': novye dokumenty o tragedii na
   Urale* (Ekaterinburg: Bank kul'turnoi informatsii, 1993)
A. D. Avdeev, 'Nikolai Romanov v Tobol'ske i Yekaterinburge', *Krasnaya nov'*, no.
   5 (1928)
A. N. Avdonin, *V zhernovakh revolyutsii: dokumental'nyi ocherk o komissare V. V.
   Yakovleve* (Ekaterinburg: Bank kul'turnoi informatsii, 1995)
H. Azar (ed.), *The Diary of Olga Romanov* (Yardley, PN: Westholme, 2014)
S. Badcock, 'Autocracy in Crisis: Nicholas the Last', in I. Thatcher, ed., *Late
   Imperial Russia: Problems and Prospects* (Manchester: Manchester University
   Press, 2005)
Baedeker's Russia, ed. K. Baedeker (London: T. Fisher Unwin, 1914)

N. de Basily, *Memoirs: Diplomat of Imperial Russia, 1903–1917* (Stanford, CA: Hoover Institution Press, 1973)

D. Beer, 'Vae Victis: Siberian exile as a revolutionary battleground, 1900–1914': St Antony's College (Oxford) history seminar series, 2 March 2015.

D. Beer, *The House of the Dead: Siberian Exile under the Tsars* (London: Allen Lane, 2016)

P. Benkendorf, *Last Days at Tsarskoe Selo* (W. Heinemann: London, 1927)

M. Bernshtam (ed.), *Ural i Prikam'e, noyabr' 1918 – yanvar' 1919: dokumenty i materialy* (Paris: YMCA-Press, 1982)

G. Z. Besedovskii, *Na putyakh k termidoru* (Moscow: Sovremennik, 1997)

A. N. Bokhanov, *Sumerki monarkhii* (Moscow: Nauka, 1993)

K. von Bothmer, *Mit Graf Mirbach in Moskau: Tagebuch-Aufzeichnungen und Aktenstücke vom 19. April bis 24. August 1918* (Tübingen: Osiander'sche Buchhandlung, 1922)

N. M. Bozheryanov (ed.), *Trista let tsarstvovaniya doma Romanovykh* (St Petersburg, 1913)

L. Bryant, *Six Red Months in Russia: An Observer's Account of Russia before and during the Proletarian Dictatorship* (New York: George H. Doran, 1918)

A. D. Bubnov, *V tsarskoi stavke* (New York: Chekhov Publishing House, 1955)

G. Buchanan, *My Mission to Russia and Other Diplomatic Memories*, vol. 2 (London: Cassell and Co., 1923)

P. Bulygin, *The Murder of the Romanovs: the Authentic Account* (London: Hutchinson, 1935)

Yu. A. Buranov and V. M. Khrustalëv, *Gibel' imperatorskogo doma* (Moscow: Progress, 1992)

S. Buxhoeveden, *The Life and Tragedy of Alexandra Feodorovna, Empress of Russia: A Biography* (London: Longman, Green and Co., 1929)

P. Bykov, 'Poslednie dni poslednego tsarya' and 'Yekaterinburgskii Sovet', in N. I. Nikolaev (ed.), *Rabochaya revolyutsiya na Urale: epizody i fakty* (Ekaterinburg: Gosizdat, Ural'skoe Oblastnoe Upravlenie, 1921)

P. M. Bykov, *Poslednie dni Romanovykh* (Sverdlovsk: Izdatel'stvo 'Ural'skiĭ rabochiĭ', 1990)

G. V. Chicherin, *Vneshnyaya politika Sovetskoi Rossii za dva goda* (Moscow: Gosizdat, 1920)

N. Cohn, *Warrant for Genocide: The Myth of the Jewish World-Conspiracy and the Protocols of the Elders of Zion* (London: Eyre and Spottiswood, 1967)

A. Cook, *To Kill Rasputin: The Life and Death of Grigori Rasputin* (Stroud: Tempus, 2005)

A. Cook, *The Murder of the Romanovs* (Stroud: Amberley, 2011)

D. Crawford, *The Last Tsar, Emperor Michael II* (Edinburgh: Murray McLellan, 2012)

R. Crawford and D. Crawford, *Michael and Natasha: The Life and Love of the Last Tsar of Russia* (London: Weidenfeld and Nicolson, 1997)

R. Day and M. M. Gorinov, *The Preobrazhensky Papers: Archival Documents and Materials*, vol. 1: *1886–1920* (Chicago: Haymarket, 2015)

L. Dehn, *The Real Tsaritsa* (London: Butterworth, 1922)

'Dioneo' (V. I. Shklovsky), *Russia under the Bolsheviks* (London: Russian Liberation Committee, 1919)

M. K. Diterikhs, *Ubiistvo tsarskoi sem'i i chlenov doma Romanovykh na Urale*, part 1 (Vladivostok: Voennaya Akademiya, 1922)

Dnevniki imperatora Nikolaya II, 1894–1918, vol. 2, part 2, ed. S. V. Mironenko and Z. I. Peregudova (Moscow: Rosspen, 2013)

V. V. Dublënnykh, *Belaya armiya na Urale: istoricheskie spravki chastei i soedinenii* (Ekaterinburg: Izd. Ural'skogo Universiteta, 2008)

V. Fic, *The Revolutionary War for Independence and the Russian Question* (New Delhi: Abhinav Publications, 1977)

V. M. Fic, *The Bolsheviks and the Czechoslovak Legion: The Origin of their Armed Conflict, March – May 1918* (New Delhi: Abhinav Publications, 1978)

J. T. Fuhrman (ed.), *The Complete Wartime Correspondence of Tsar Nicholas II and the Empress Alexandra, April 1914 – March 1917* (Westport, CT: Greenwood Press, 1999)

W. C. Fuller, Jr, *The Foe Within: Fantasies of Treason and the End of Imperial Russia* (Ithaca, NY: Cornell University Press, 2006)

N. V. Galushkin, *Sobstvennyi Ego Imperatorskogo Velichestva Konvoi* (Moscow: Reittar, 2004)

R. Giardina, *Complotto reale: l'ascesa dei Coburgo alla conquista d'Europa* (Milan: Bompiani, 2001)

P. Gilliard, *Le tragique destin de Nicolas II et de sa famille* (Paris: Payot, 1921)

M. Golubykh, *Ural'skie partizany: pokhod otryadov Blyukhera-Kashirina v 1918 godu* (Ekaterinburg: Uralkniga, 1924)

F. Grenard, *La révolution russe* (Paris: Armand Colin, 1933)

J. Hanbury-Williams, *The Emperor Nicholas II as I Knew Him* (London: A. L. Humphreys, 1922)

J. R. Harris, *The Great Urals: Regionalism and the Evolution of the Soviet System* (Ithaca, NY: Cornell University Press, 1999)

T. Hasegawa, *The February Revolution: Petrograd, 1917* (Seattle: University of Washington Press, 1981)

G. A. Hill, *Go Spy the Land* (London: Cassell, 1932)

G. Hosking, *The Russian Constitutional Experiment: Government and Duma, 1907–1914* (Cambridge: Cambridge University Press, 1973).

V. Hugo, *Quatrevingt-treize* (New York: William R. Jenkins, 1896)

G. Z. Ioffe, *Revolyutsiya i sud'ba Romanovykh* (Moscow: Respublika, 1992)

G. Ioffe, *Revolyutsiya i sem'ya Romanovykh* (Moscow: Algoritm, 2012)

M. P. Iroshnikov, *Sozdanie sovetskogo tsentral'nogo apparata: Sovet narodnykh komissarov i narodnye komissariaty, oktyabr' 1917 g. – yanvar' 1918 g.* (Moscow/Leningrad: Nauka, 1966)

R. L. Jefferson, *Roughing it in Siberia, With Some Account of the Trans-Siberian Railway, and the Gold-Mining Industry of Asiatic Russia* (London: Sampson, Low, Marston and Co., 1897)

S. Kallistov, *Tobol'skii Tsentral* (Moscow: Vsesoyuznoe obshchestvo politkat-orzhan I ss-poselentsev, 1925)

N. I. Kanishcheva et al. (eds), *Dnevnik P. N. Milyukova, 1918–1921* (Moscow: Rosspen, 2015)

Princess Kantakuzen, *Revolutionary Days: Recollections of Romanoffs and Bol-sheviki, 1914–1917* (London: Chapman and Hall, 1920)

L. A. Kasso, *Rossiya na Dunae i obrazovanie Bessarabskoi oblasti* (Moscow: A. Snegirëva, 1913)

G. Kennan, *Siberia and the Exile System*, vol. 2 (New York: The Century Co., 1891)

M. Kheifets, *Tsareubiistvo v 1918 godu: versiya prestupleniya i fal'tsifitsirovannogo sledstviya* (Moscow: Festival, 1992)

V. M. Khrustalëv, 'Taina "missii" chrezvychainogo komissara Yakovleva', *Rossiyane*, no. 10 (1993)

V. M. Khrustalëv, *Alapaevsk: zhertvy i palachi* (Moscow: Dostoinstvo, 2010)

V. M. Khrustalëv, *Petrograd: rasstrel Velikikh knyazei* (Moscow: Dostoinstvo, 2011)

V. M. Khrustalëv (ed.), *Dnevniki Nikolaya II i imperatritsy Aleksandry Fëdorovny, 1917–1918*, vols 1–2 (Moscow: Vagrius, 2008)

V. M. Khrustalëv and M. D. Steinberg (eds), *Skorbnyi put' Romanovykh 1917–1918 gg.: gibel' tsarskoi sem'i: sbornik dokumentov i materialov* (Moscow: Rosspen, 2001)

G. King and P. Wilson, *The Fate of the Romanovs* (Hoboken, NJ: John Wiley and Sons, 2003)

J. Klier and H. Mingay, *The Quest for Anastasia: Solving the Mystery of the Lost Romanovs* (Edgware: Smith Gryphon, 1997).

D. Koenker, *Moscow Workers and the 1917 Revolution* (Princeton, NJ: Princeton University Press, 1981)

B. I. Kolonitski, *Simvoly vlasti i bor'ba za vlast': k izucheniyu politicheskoi kul'tury Rossiiskoi revolyutsii 1917 goda* (St Petersburg: Dmitrii Bulanin, 2001)

B. I. Kolonitskii, *'Tragicheskaya erotika': obrazy imperatorskoi sem'i v gody pervoi mirovoi voiny* (St Petersburg: Novoe Literaturnoe Obozrenie, 2010)

A. N. Kuropatkin, *Zadachi russkoi armii* (St Petersburg: V. A. Berezovskii, 1910), vols. 1–3

The Last Diary of Tsaritsa Alexandra, ed. V. A. Kozlov and V. M. Khrustalëv (New Haven, CT: Yale University Press, 1997)

R. S. Latimer, *Dr. Baedeker and his Apostolic Work in Russia* (London: Morgan and Scott, 1907)

N. A. Leikin, *Neunyvayushchie Rossiyane: Rasskazy i kartinki s natury*, 2nd revised edn (St Petersburg: M. A. Khan, 1881)

M. K. Lemke, *250 dnei v tsarskoi stavke: 25 sent. 1915 – 2 iyulya 1916* (Petersburg [sic]: Gosizdat, 1920)

V. I. Lenin, *Biograficheskaya khronika*, vol. 5 (Moscow: Gosudarstvennoe izdatel'stvo, 1974)

D. Lieven, *Nicholas II: Emperor of all the Russias* (London: John Murray, 1993)

D. Lieven, 'Nicholas II', in E. Acton, V. Yu. Cherniaev and W. G. Rosenberg (eds), *Critical Companion to the Russian Revolution* (London: E. Arnold, 1997)

D. Lieven, *Towards the Flame: Empire, War and the End of Tsarist Russia* (London: Allen Lane, 2015)

H.-D. Löwe, *The Tsars and the Jews: Reform, Reaction and Antisemitism in Imperial Russia, 1772–1917* (Reading: Harwood Academic Publishers, 1993)

S. Lyandres, 'Progressive Bloc Politics on the Eve of the Revolution: Revisiting P. N. Miliukov's "Stupidity of Treason" Speech of 1 November 1916', *Russian History*, no. 4 (2004), pp. 447–64

S. Lyandres, 'Conspiracy and Ambition in Russian Politics before the February Revolution of 1917: The Case of Prince Georgii Evgen'evich L'vov', *Journal of Modern Russian History and Historiography*, no. 8 (2015), pp. 99–133

S. Lyandres (ed.), *The Fall of Tsarism: Untold Stories of the February 1917 Revolution* (Oxford: Oxford University Press, 2013)

L. A. Lykova, 'V. I. Lenin i sud'ba tsarskoi sem'i', *Istoricheskii arkhiv*, no. 5 (2005)

L. A. Lykova, *Perm': taina gibeli Mikhaila Romanova* (Moscow: Dostoinstvo, 2010)

L. A. Lykova (ed.), *Sledstvie po delu ob ubiistve Rossiiskoi imperatorskoi sem'i* (Moscow: Rosspen, 2007)

M. Maeterlinck, *Wisdom and Destiny* (London: George Allen, 1898)

S. Markov, *Pokinutaya tsarskaya sem'ya* (Vienna: Amalthea, 1928)

R. Massie and S. Massie, *Nicholas and Alexandra* (New York: Atheneum, 1967)

A. Maylunas and S. Mironenko, *A Lifelong Passion: Nicholas and Alexandra, Their Own Story* (London: Weidenfeld and Nicolson, 1996)

L. McReynolds, *The News Under Russia's Old Regime: The Development of a Mass-Circulation Press* (Princeton, NJ: Princeton University Press, 1991)

T. E. Mel'nik-Botkina, *Vospominaniya o tsarskoi sem'e i eë zhizni do i posle revolyutsii* (Belgrade: M. I. Stefanovich, 1921; repr. Moscow: Ankor, 1993)

D. Mérejkowsky, 'Préface' and 'Religion et Révolution', in D. Mérejkowsky, Z. Hippius and Dm. Philosophoff, *Le Tsar et la Révolution* (Paris: Société du Mercure de France, 1907)

D. S. Merezhkovskii, *Khristos i Antikhrist*, vol. 1: *Smert' bogov. Yulian otstupnik*; vol. 2: *Voskresshie bogi. Leonardo da-Vinchi*; vol. 3: *Antikhrist. Pëtr i Aleksei* (St Petersburg: M. V. Pirozhkov, 1907).

D. S. Merezhkovskii, *Aleksandr I*, vol. 6, in *Polnoe sobranie sochinenii*, 24 vols (Moscow: I. D. Sytin, 1914)

S. S. Montefiore, *The Romanovs* (London: Weidenfeld and Nicolson, 2016)

A. A. Mosolov, *Pri dvore poslednego Rossiiskogo imperatora* (Paris: Poslednie Novosti, 1934)

S. Mstislavskii, *Pyat' dnei: nachalo i konets fevral'skoi revolyutsii* (Moscow: Z. I. Grzhebin, 1922)

B. Mueggenberg, *The Czecho-Slovak Struggle for Independence, 1914–1920* (Jefferson, NC: McFarland and Co., 2014)

P. V. Mul'tatuli, *Vneshnyaya politika Imperatora Nikolaya II (1894–1917)* (Moscow: FIV, 2012)

Neobkhodimost' otkrytiya porto-franko v ust'yakh rek Obi i Yeniseya (Tobolsk: Gubernskaya Tipografia, 1907)

N. I. Nikolaev (ed.), *Rabochaya revolyutsiya na Urale: epizody i fakty* (Ekaterinburg: Gosizdat, Ural'skoe Oblastnoe Upravlenie, 1921)

Nikolai II-oi Romanov: ego zhizn' i deyatel'nost, 1894–1917 g.g., po inostrannym i russkim istochnikam (Petrograd: Gosudarstvennaya Tipografia, 1917)

M. Occleshaw, *The Romanov Conspiracies: The Romanovs and the House of Windsor* (London: Chapmans, 1993)

M. Occleshaw, *Dances in Shadows: The Clandestine War in Russia, 1917–1920* (New York: Carroll and Graf, 2006)

A. Olano-Eren'ya, 'Ispanskii korol' i politika spaseniya sem'i Nikolaya II', *Novaya i noveishaya istoriya*, no. 5 (1993), pp. 152–65

Baroness Orczy, *The Scarlet Pimpernel* (London: Hodder and Stoughton, 1960)

Otrechenie Nikolai II: vospominaniya ochevidtsev, dokumenty, ed. P. Ye. Shchegolev, 2nd expanded edn (Leningrad: Krasnaya gazeta, 1927)

M. Paléologue, *La Russie des tsars pendant la Grande Guerre*, vol. 3 (Paris: Plon, 1922)

V. Pankratov, *So tsarëm v Tobol'ske: iz vospominanii* (Leningrad: Kooperativnoe izdatel'skoe t-vo 'Byloe', 1925)

E. Pantazzi, *Roumania in Light and Shadow* (London: T. F. Unwin, 1921)

Pis'ma svyatykh tsarstvennykh muchennikov iz zatocheniya, ed. E. E. Alfer'evym, D. S. Tatishchev and S. P. Andolenko (St Petersburg: Spaso-Preobrazhenskii Valaamskii monastyr', 1996)

I. F. Plotnikov, *Pravda Istorii: gibel' tsarskoi sem'i* (Ekaterinburg: Sverdlovskaya regional'naya obshchestvennaya organizatsiya, 2002)

Poslednie dni poslednego tsarya: inochtozhenie dinastii Romanovykh (Tver: Tverskoe izdatel'stvo, 1922)

T. H. Preston, *Before the Curtain* (London: John Murray, 1950)

Protokoly Tsentral'nogo Komiteta RSDRP(b), avgust 1917 – fevral' 1918 (Moscow: Gosudarstvennoe izdatel'stvo politicheskoi literatury, 1958)

E. Radzinskii, 'Gospodi – spasi i usmiri Rossiyu': Nikolai II, zhizn' i smert' (Moscow: Vagrius, 1993)

H. Rappaport, *Ekaterinburg: The Last Days of the Romanovs* (London: Windmill Books, 2009)

H. Rappaport, *Four Sisters: The Lost Lives of the Romanov Grand Duchesses* (London: Macmillan, 2014)

Rasputin the Mad Monk (Hammer Films UK: dir. D. Sharp, 1966)

D. Rayfield, *Anton Chekhov: A Life* (Evanston, IL: North-Western University Press, 1997)

P. Robinson, *Grand Duke Nikolai Nikolaevich: Supreme Commander of the Russian Army* (DeKalb: Northern Illinois University Press, 2014)

K. Rose, *George V* (London: Weidenfeld and Nicolson, 1983)

L. P. Roshchevskaya and V. K. Beloborodov, *Tobol'skii Sever Glazami politicheskikh ssyl'nykh XIX – nachala XX veka* (Ekaterinburg: Sredne-Ural'skoe knizhnoe izdatel'stvo, 1998)

N. Ross, *Gibel' tsarskoi sem'i: materialy sledstviya po delu ob ubiistve tsarskoi sem'i, avgust 1918 – fevral' 1920* (Frankfurt am Main: Posev, 1986)

C. A. Ruud and S. Stepanov, *Fontanka 16: The Tsars' Secret Police* (Stroud: Sutton, 1999)

J. Sadoul, *Notes sur la révolution bolchévique, octobre 1917 – janvier 1919* (Paris: Sirène, 1920)

R. Service, *The Bolshevik Party in Revolution: A Study in Organisational Change* (London: Macmillan, 1979)

R. Service, *Lenin: A Biography* (London: Macmillan, 1998)

G. N. Sevastyanov et al. (eds), *Delo generala Kornilova: materialy Chrezvychainoi komissii po rassledovaniyu dela o byvshem Verkhovnom glavno komanduyush-chem generale L. G. Kornilove i ego souchastnikakh, avgust 1917 g. – iyun' 1918 g.*, 2 vols (Moscow: Materik, 2003)

P. E. Shchegolev (ed.), *Padenie tsarskogo rezhima: stenograficheskie otchëty doprosov i pokazanii, dannykh v 1917 g. v Chrezvychainoi sledstvennoi komis-sii Vremennogo pravitel'stva*, 7 vols. (Leningrad-Moscow: Gosudarstvennoe izdatel'stvo, 1924–7)

N. K. Shil'der, *Imperator Pavel Pervyi. Istoriko-biograficheskii ocherk* (St Petersburg: A. S. Suvorin, 1901)

Skorbnaya pamyatka, ed. A. V. Syroboyarskii (New York: Kassa Pomoshchi Blizh-nim v Pamyat' o Tsarskoi Sem'e, 1928)

W. Slater, *The Many Deaths of Tsar Nicholas II* (London: Routledge, 2007)

D. Smith, *Rasputin: Faith, Power, and the Twilight of the Romanovs* (London: Macmillan, 2016)

J. P. Smythe, *Rescuing the Czar: Two Authentic Diaries Arranged and Translated* (San Francisco: California Printing Co., 1920)

J. Snodgrass, *Bureau of Foreign and Domestic Commerce: Russia: A Handbook on Commercial and Industrial Conditions* (Washington, DC: Government Printing Office, 1913)

N. Sokoloff, *Enquête judiciaire sur l'assassinat de la famille impériale russe, avec les preuves, les interrogatoires et les dépositions des témoins et des accusés* (Paris: Payot, 1924)

N. Sokolov, *Ubiistvo tsarskoi sem'i* (Berlin: Slovo, 1925)

M. D. Steinberg and V. M. Khrustalëv, *The Fall of the Romanovs: Political Dreams and Personal Struggles in a Time of Revolution* (New Haven, CT: Yale University Press, 1995)

N. Stone, *The Eastern Front, 1914–1917* (London: Hodder and Stoughton, 1975)

A. Summers and T. Mangold, *File on the Tsar* (London: Gollancz, 1976)

I. Thatcher (ed.), *Late Imperial Russia: Problems and Prospects* (Manchester: Manchester University Press, 2005)

N. M. Tikhmenev, *Iz vospominanii o poslednikh dnyakh prebyvaniya Imperatora Nikolaya II v Stavke* (Nice: Kruzhok Revnitelei Russkogo Proshlogo, 1925)

D. W. Treadgold, *The Great Siberian Migration: Government and Peasant in Resettlement from Emancipation to the First World War* (Princeton, NJ: Princeton University Press, 1957)

Ubiistvo tsarskoi sem'i i eë svity: offitsial'nye dokumenty (Constantinople: Russkaya Mysl', 1920)

F. I. Uspenskii, *Istoriya vizantiiskoi imperii*, vols. 1–2 (St Petersburg: Brokgauz-Efron, 1913)

V. N. Voeikov, *S tsarëm i bez tsarya* (Helsinki: Oy. Littera, 1936)

A. A. Volkov, *Okolo tsarskoi sem'i* (Paris: Moscow, 1928)

P. V. Volobuev (ed.), *Petrogradskii Sovet rabochikh i soldatskikh deputatov v 1917 godu*, 5 vols (Nauka: Leningrad/St Petersburg, 1991–2003)

A. Vyrubova, *Memories of the Russian Court* (London: Macmillan, 1923)

A. Vyrubova, *Souvenirs de ma vie: avec 52 photographies hors-texte et 39 lettres inédites adressées à Anna Viroubova par le tsar, la tsarina, le tsarévitch et les grandes duchesses, durant leur captivité* (Paris: Payot, 1927)

P. Waldron, *Between Two Revolutions: Stolypin and the Politics of Renewal* (London: UCL Press, 1999)

F. Welch, *The Romanovs and Mr Gibbes* (London: Short, 2002)

R. Wilton, *The Last Days of the Romanovs, from 15th March 1917* (London: Thornton Butterworth, 1920)

R. Wortman, *Scenarios of Power: Myth and Ceremony in the Russian Monarchy from Peter the Great to the Abdication of Nicholas II* (Princeton, NJ: Princeton University Press, 2006)

R. Wortman, *Imperial Encounters in Russian History: Russian Monarchy: Representation and Rule* (Boston, MA: Academic Studies Press, 2013)

Yu. Zhuk, *Yekaterinburg: prizrak Ipat'evskogo doma* (Moscow: Dostoinstvo, 2010)

Yu. Zhuk, *Voprositel'nye znaki v 'tsarskom dele'* (St Petersburg: BkhV-Peterburg, 2013)

NOTES

ABBREVIATIONS

AMDP   Agnes M. Diterikhs Papers

DAVP   Dmitri Antonovich Volkogonov Papers

DNIIAF   V. M. Khrustalëv (ed.), *Dnevniki Nikolaya II i imperatritsy Aleksandry Fëdorovny, 1917–1918*, vol. 1 (Moscow: Vagrius, 2008)

DINII   *Dnevniki imperatora Nikolaya II, 1894–1918*, ed. S. V. Mironenko and Z. I. Peregudova (Moscow: Rosspen, 2013)

GARF   Gosudarstvennyi Arkhiv Rossiiskoi Federatsii

GTSMS   N. Ross, *Gibel' tsarskoi sem'i: materialy sledstviya po delu ob ubiistve tsarskoi sem'i, avgust 1918 – fevral' 1920* (Frankfurt am Main: Posev, 1986)

HIA   Hoover Institution Archives

KAGDRP   Kseniia Aleksandrovna, Grand Duchess of Russia Papers

NABP   Nikolai Aleksandrovich de Bazili Papers

PIGTS   I. F. Plotnikov, *Pravda Istorii: gibel' tsarskoi sem'i* (Ekaterinburg: Sverdlovskaya regional'naya obshchestvennaya organizatsiya, 2002)

PTR   *Padenie tsarskogo rezhima: stenograficheskie otchëty doprosov i pokazanii, dannykh v 1917 g. v Chrezvychainoi sledstvennoi komissii Vremennogo pravitel'stva* (Leningrad/Moscow: Gosudarstvennoe izdatel'stvo, 1924–7)

RGASPI   Rossiiskii Gosudarstvennyi Arkhiv Sotsial'no-Politicheskoi Istorii

SCBLOU   Special Collections, Bodleian Library, Oxford University

SGC   Sydney Gibbes Collection

SPR   V. M. Khrustalëv and M. D. Steinberg (eds), *Skorbnyi put' Romanovykh 1917–1918 gg.: gibel' tsarskoi sem'i: sbornik dokumentov i materialov* (Moscow: Rosspen, 2001)

VZR   A. N. Avdonin, *V zhernovakh revolyutsii: dokumental'nyi ocherk o komissare V. V. Yakovleve* (Ekaterinburg: Bank kul'turnoi informatsii, 1995)

1: TSAR OF ALL RUSSIA

1. N. M. Bozheryanov (ed.), *Trista let tsarstvovaniya doma Romanovykh* (St Petersburg, 1913).
2. I. I. Serebrennikov, 'Moi vospominaniya', vol. 3: Ivan I. Serebrennikov Papers, Hoover Institution Archives (hereafter HIA), box 10, pp. 92–3.
3. S. K. Buksgevden [i.e. Sophie Buxhoeveden], 'Gosudar' Imperator Nikolai II: iz vospominanii', part 1: Nikolai Aleksandrovich de Bazili Papers (hereafter NABP), HIA, box 23, folder 1, p. 4.
4. Ye. S. Kobylinskii (inquiry testimony), 6–10 April 1919: Agnes M. Diterikhs Papers (hereafter AMDP), HIA, box 1, folder 8, p. 754; A. A. Volkov (inquiry testimony), 20–23 August 1919: ibid., box 1, folder 9, p. 1119.
5. Father Nicholas (S. Gibbes), untitled memoir (typescript): Sydney Gibbes Collection (hereafter SGC), Special Collections, Bodleian Library, Oxford University (hereafter SCBLOU), box 1, MS Facs c. 106, p. 4.
6. S. K. Buksgevden (sic), 'Gosudar' Imperator Nikolai II: iz vospominanii', part 1: NABP, HIA, box 23, folder 1, p. 4.
7. Ye. S. Kobylinskii (inquiry testimony), 6–10 April 1919: AMDP, HIA, box 1, folder 8, p. 754; A. A. Volkov (inquiry testimony), 20–23 August 1919: ibid., box 1, folder 9, p. 1119.
8. A. A. Mosolov, *Pri dvore poslednego Rossiiskogo imperatora* (Paris: Poslednie Novosti, 1934), p. 27.
9. Ibid., pp. 28–9.
10. Ibid., p. 29.
11. Ibid., p. 28.
12. S. K. Buksgevden (sic), 'Gosudar' Imperator Nikolai II: iz vospominanii', part 1: NABP, HIA, box 23, folder 1, p. 23.
13. N. de Basily, 'Note sur l'Empereur et l'Impératrice': NABP, HIA, box 23, folder 1, p. 2. 'Nicolas de Basily' was how Nikolai Bazili (or Nikolai de Bazili) was known abroad after the October 1917 Revolution; his materials are held in the Hoover Institution Archives in the Nikolai Aleksandrovich de Bazili Papers.
14. Father Nicholas (S. Gibbes), untitled memoir (typescript): SGC, SCBLOU, box 1, MS Facs c. 106, p. 2.
15. S. Gibbes, 'Ten Years with the Russian Imperial Family' (typescript): SGC, SCBLOU, box 1, p. 7.
16. See S. S. Montefiore, *The Romanovs* (London: Weidenfeld and Nicolson, 2016), pp. 496–7.
17. A. F. Romanova to N. A. Romanov, 14 December 1916 (OS): J. T. Fuhrman (ed.), *The Complete Wartime Correspondence of Tsar Nicholas II and the Empress Alexandra, April 1914 – March 1917* (Westport, CT: Greenwood Press, 1999), p. 675.
18. Mosolov, *Pri dvore poslednego Rossiiskogo imperatora*, p. 231.
19. V. B. Frederikhs (Extraordinary Investigative Commission testimony), 2 June 1917 (OS): P. E. Shchegolev (ed.), *Padenie tsarskogo rezhima: stenograficheskie*

otchëty doprosov i pokazanii, dannykh v 1917 g. v Chrezvychainoi sledstvennoi komissii Vremennogo pravitel'stva, 7 vols. (Leningrad-Moscow: Gosudarstvennoe izdatel'stvo, 1924–7) (hereafter *PTR*), vol. 5, p. 33.

20. Ye. S. Kobylinskii (inquiry testimony), 6–10 April 1919: AMDP, HIA, box 1, folder 8, pp. 754 and 758. See R. Wortman, *Scenarios of Power: Myth and Ceremony in the Russian Monarchy from Peter the Great to the Abdication of Nicholas II* (Princeton, NJ: Princeton University Press, 2006), p. 317.

21. See H.-D. Löwe, *The Tsars and the Jews: Reform, Reaction and Antisemitism in Imperial Russia, 1772–1917* (Reading: Harwood Academic Publishers, 1993), pp. 221–7.

22. See R. Wortman, 'Nicholas II and the Revolution of 1905', in *Imperial Encounters in Russian History: Russian Monarchy: Representation and Rule* (Boston, MA: Academic Studies Press, 2013), p. 207.

23. A. F. Romanova to N. A. Romanov, 14 December 1916 (OS): Fuhrman (ed.), *Complete Wartime Correspondence*, p. 675.

24. P. Gilliard to N. de Basily, 29 April 1934 (notes): NABP, HIA, box 2, folder 62, p. 1.

25. S. K. Buksgevden (sic), 'Gosudar' Imperator Nikolai II: iz vospominanii', part 1: NABP, HIA, box 23, folder 1, p. 11.

2: AT GHQ

1. *Baedeker's Russia*, ed. K. Baedeker (London: T. Fisher Unwin, 1914), pp. 257–8.

2. See N. Stone, *The Eastern Front, 1914–1917* (London: Hodder and Stoughton, 1975), pp. 191–3.

3. A. D. Bubnov, *V tsarskoi stavke* (New York: Chekhov Publishing House, 1955), p. 179; N. M. Tikhmenev, *Iz vospominanii o poslednikh dnyakh prebyvaniya Imperatora Nikolaya II v Stavke* (Nice: Kruzhok Revnitelei Russkogo Proshlogo, 1925), p. 10.

4. Bubnov, *V tsarskoi stavke*, pp. 179–81; Tikhmenev, *Iz vospominanii*, pp. 12–13.

5. See S. Lyandres, 'Progressive Bloc Politics on the Eve of the Revolution: Revisiting P. N. Miliukov's "Stupidity of Treason" Speech of November 1, 1916', *Russian History*, no. 4 (2004), pp. 447–64, at 456–60.

6. Tikhmenev, *Iz vospominanii*, p. 14.

7. S. K. Buksgevden (sic), 'Gosudar' Imperator Nikolai II: iz vospominanii', part 1: NABP, HIA, box 23, folder 1, p. 20.

8. Bubnov, *V tsarskoi stavke*, p. 190.

9. See Stone, *The Eastern Front*, p. 187.

10. Ibid., pp. 191–3.

11. R. von Stackelberg, untitled memoirs (typescript): Rudolf von Stackelberg Papers, HIA, p. 47.

12. See Stone, *The Eastern Front*, pp. 191–3.

13. See S. Lyandres, 'Conspiracy and Ambition in Russian Politics before the February Revolution of 1917: The Case of Prince Georgii Evgen'evich L'vov', *Journal of Modern Russian History and Historiography*, no. 8 (2015), pp. 99–133, at 102–12.
14. Bubnov, *V tsarskoi stavke*, pp. 182–3.
15. Ibid., pp. 183–4; see also the cogent argument of Lyandres, 'Progressive Bloc Politics on the Eve of the Revolution', pp. 454–7.
16. Bubnov, *V tsarskoi stavke*, pp. 183–4.
17. Mosolov, *Pri dvore poslednego Rossiiskogo imperatora*, p. 226.

3: THE FEBRUARY REVOLUTION

1. S. K. Buksgevden (sic), 'Gosudar' Imperator Nikolai II: iz vospominanii', part 1: NABP, HIA, box 23, folder 1, p. 20.
2. Ibid.
3. A. F. Romanova (diary), 21 February 1917 (OS): V. M. Khrustalëv (ed.), *Dnevniki Nikolaya II i imperatritsy Aleksandry Fëdorovny, 1917–1918*, vol. 1 (Moscow: Vagrius, 2008) (hereafter *DNIIAF*), p. 162.
4. S. K. Buksgevden (sic), 'Gosudar' Imperator Nikolai II: iz vospominanii', part 1: NABP, HIA, box 23, folder 1, p. 21.
5. A. A. Volkov (inquiry testimony), 20–23 August 1919: AMDP, HIA, box 1, folder 9, p. 1096.
6. S. K. Buksgevden (sic), 'Gosudar' Imperator Nikolai II: iz vospominanii', part 1: NABP, HIA, box 23, folder 1, p. 21.
7. Colonel K. Zershchikov, 'Sobstvennyi ego velichestva konvoi v dni revolyutsii' p. 6: K. Zershchikov Papers, HIA.
8. S. Markov, *Pokinutaya tsarskaya sem'ya* (Vienna: Amalthea, 1928), p. 116.
9. Ibid., p. 117.
10. M. G. Tutelberg (inquiry testimony), 1919: AMDP, HIA, box 1, folder 8, p. 975.
11. M. V. Rodzyanko (oral testimony from the Polievktov Collection): S. Lyandres (ed.), *The Fall of Tsarism: Untold Stories of the February 1917 Revolution* (Oxford: Oxford University Press, 2013), p. 109.
12. N. de Basily, 'End of the Monarchy' draft chapter (in French): NABP, HIA, box 24, p. 10.
13. Ibid.
14. See T. Hasegawa, *The February Revolution: Petrograd, 1917* (Seattle: University of Washington Press, 1981), pp. 326–32 and 379.

4: ABDICATION

1. N. de Basily, 'End of the Monarchy' draft chapter (in French): NABP, HIA, box 24, p. 11.

2. Ibid., p. 23.

3. Ibid.

4. N. de Basily, *Memoirs: Diplomat of Imperial Russia, 1903–1917* (Stanford, CA: Hoover Institution Press, 1973), pp. 116–17.

5. M. V. Alexeev to N. A. Romanov (telegram), 2 March 1917: V. M. Khrustalëv and M. D. Steinberg (eds), *Skorbnyi put' Romanovykh 1917–1918 gg.: gibel' tsarskoi sem'i: sbornik dokumentov i materialov* (Moscow: Rosspen, 2001) (hereafter *SPR*), pp. 40–1.

6. Ibid., p. 121.

7. Mosolov, *Pri dvore poslednego Rossiiskogo imperatora*, p. 226.

8. *Otrechenie Nikolai II: vospominaniya ochevidtsev, dokumenty*, ed. P. Ye. Shchegolev, 2nd expanded edn (Leningrad: *Krasnaya gazeta*, 1927), pp. 107–8.

9. A. A. Mordvinov, 'Poslednie dni imperatora': ibid., p. 110. The conversation was unwitnessed, but as he left the emperor's carriage at four o'clock, Fëdorov breached etiquette by revealing its content to a group of military personnel.

10. De Basily, *Memoirs*, p. 138.

11. S. K. Buksgevden (sic), 'Gosudar' Imperator Nikolai II: iz vospominanii', part 1: NABP, HIA, box 23, folder 1, p. 23.

12. Draft abdication manifesto: Hoover Safe, HIA; de Basily, *Memoirs*, pp. 122 and 125.

13. Ibid., pp. 125–6.

14. Ibid., p. 119.

15. See Lyandres (ed.), *The Fall of Tsarism*, p. 83, note 12.

16. V. Shulgin, 'Podrobnosti otrecheniya', *Rech'*, 21 March 1917.

17. M. I. Skobelev (oral testimony from the Polievktov Collection): Lyandres (ed.), *The Fall of Tsarism*, pp. 186–7.

18. See Hasegawa, *The February Revolution*, pp. 519–24.

19. A. I. Guchkov (Extraordinary Investigative Commission testimony), 2 August 1917 (OS): *PTR*, vol. 7, p. 263.

20. V. Shulgin, 'Podrobnosti otrecheniya', *Rech'*, 21 March 1917; A. I. Guchkov (Extraordinary Investigative Commission testimony), 2 August 1917 (OS): *PTR*, vol. 7, p. 263.

21. A. I. Guchkov, 'Otrechenie Gosudarya' (typescript): NABP, HIA, box 24, pp. 1–3; A. I. Guchkov (Extraordinary Investigative Commission testimony), 2 August 1917 (OS): *PTR*, vol. 7, p. 264; minutes of meeting of A. I. Guchkov and V. V. Shulgin with N. A. Romanov, 15 March 1917: *SPR*, pp. 45–6.

22. Ibid.

23. Conversation between N. de Basily and A. I. Guchkov, 9 November 1932: NABP, HIA, box 22, pp. 16–17. This was also the impression given some days later at Tsarskoe Selo: P. Benkendorf, *Last Days at Tsarskoe Selo* (W. Heinemann: London, 1927), p. 48.

24. Conversation between N. de Basily and A. I. Guchkov, 9 November 1932: NABP, HIA, box 22, pp. 9–11.

25. Ibid., pp. 12–13.
26. Minutes of meeting of A. I. Guchkov and V. V. Shulgin with N. A. Romanov, 15 March 1917: *SPR*, p. 46.
27. Conversation between N. de Basily and A. I. Guchkov, 9 November 1932: NABP, HIA, box 22, p. 12.
28. Minutes of meeting of A. I. Guchkov and V. V. Shulgin with N. A. Romanov, 15 March 1917: *SPR*, p. 47.
29. A. I. Guchkov, 'Otrechenie Gosudarya' (typescript): NABP, HIA, box 24, p. 4; A. I. Guchkov (Extraordinary Investigative Commission testimony), 2 August 1917 (OS): *PTR*, vol. 7, p. 265.
30. Minutes of meeting of A. I. Guchkov and V. V. Shulgin with N. A. Romanov, 15 March 1917: *SPR*, p. 47.
31. G. A. von Tal, 'Memuary ob otrechenii ot prestola Rossiiskogo Gosudarya Imperatora Nikolaya II' (manuscript): Georgi Alexandrovich von Tal Papers, HIA, p. 54.
32. V. V. Shulgin to A. I. Guchkov, June 1928, in G. Ioffe, *Revolyutsiya i sem'ya Romanovykh* (Moscow: Algoritm, 2012), p. 77.
33. A. I. Guchkov, 'Otrechenie Gosudarya' (typescript): NABP, HIA, box 24, p. 4; A. I. Guchkov (Extraordinary Investigative Commission testimony), 2 August 1917 (OS): *PTR*, vol. 7, p. 265; minutes of meeting of A. I. Guchkov and V. V. Shulgin with N. A. Romanov, 15 March 1917: *SPR*, p. 47.
34. A. I. Guchkov, 'Otrechenie Gosudarya' (typescript): NABP, HIA, box 24, p. 4; A. I. Guchkov (Extraordinary Investigative Commission testimony), 2 August 1917 (OS): *PTR*, vol. 7, p. 265.
35. A. F. Kerenskii (inquiry testimony), 14–20 August 1920: Dmitri Antonovich Volkogonov Papers (hereafter DAVP), HIA, box 22, p. 106a.
36. G. A. von Tal, 'Memuary ob otrechenii ot prestola Rossiiskogo Gosudarya Imperatora Nikolaya II' (manuscript): Georgi Alexandrovich von Tal Papers, HIA, p. 57.
37. V. Shulgin, 'Podrobnosti otrecheniya', *Rech'*, 21 March 1917.
38. De Basily, *Memoirs*, pp. 125–6.
39. N. de Basily, 'End of the Monarchy' draft chapter (in French): NABP, HIA, box 24, pp. 26–7.
40. De Basily, *Memoirs*, p. 137.
41. N. A. Romanov (diary), 3 March 1917 (OS): *Dnevniki imperatora Nikolaya II, 1894–1918*, ed. S. V. Mironenko and Z. I. Peregudova (Moscow: Rosspen, 2013) (hereafter *DINII*), vol. 2, part 2, p. 296; de Basily, *Memoirs*, pp. 139–40.
42. N. de Basily, 'End of the Monarchy' draft chapter (in French), p. 51 and attached notelet, quoting draft memoir by A. I. Guchkov: NABP, HIA, box 24.
43. Ibid., pp. 51–2.
44. N. de Basily, 'End of the Monarchy' draft chapter (in French), pp. 52–3 and attached notelet, quoting draft memoir by A. I. Guchkov: NABP, HIA, box 24. For Mikhail's abdication manifesto, see Nicholas II Papers, Hoover Safe, HIA.
45. N. de Basily, 'End of the Monarchy' draft chapter (in French): NABP, HIA,

box 24, p. 54; M. A. Romanov, abdication manifesto, 16 March 1917: *SPR*, p. 51.

46. Benkendorf, *Last Days at Tsarskoe Selo*, pp. 16–17.
47. S. K. Buksgevden (sic), 'Gosudar' Imperator Nikolai II: iz vospominanii', part 1: NABP, HIA, box 23, folder 1, p. 23.
48. N. A. Romanov (diary), 3 March 1917 (OS): *DINII*, vol. 2, part 2, p. 296.
49. J. Hanbury-Williams, *The Emperor Nicholas II as I Knew Him* (London: A. L. Humphreys, 1922), p. 167: diary (19 March 1917).
50. Ibid., pp. 168–9: diary (19 March 1917).
51. Ibid., p. 170: diary (20 March 1917).
52. Ibid., p. 174: diary (21 March 1917).

5: TSARSKOE SELO

1. A. A. Volkov (inquiry testimony), 20–23 August 1919: AMDP, HIA, box 1, folder 9, p. 1098.
2. Ye. S. Kobylinskii (inquiry testimony), 6–10 April 1919: ibid., box 1, folder 8, p. 744.
3. T. H. Preston, *Before the Curtain* (London: John Murray, 1950), pp. 226–7.
4. S. Gibbes (diary), 26 July 1916: SGC, SCBLOU, box 1.
5. Colonel K. Zershchikov, 'Sobstvennyi ego velichestva konvoi v dni revolyutsii': K. Zershchikov Papers, HIA, p. 3.
6. Ibid., pp. 4–5.
7. P. A. (sic) Gilliard (inquiry testimony), 5–6 March 1919 (OS): AMDP, HIA, box 1, folder 7, p. 456.
8. A. F. Romanova to N. A. Romanov, 17 March 1917: A. Maylunas and S. Mironenko, *A Lifelong Passion: Nicholas and Alexandra, Their Own Story* (London: Weidenfeld and Nicolson, 1996), pp. 552–4.
9. Executive Committee meeting, 16 March 1917: *Petrogradskii Sovet rabochikh i soldatskikh deputatov*, ed. P. V. Volobuev (Nauka: Leningrad/St Petersburg, 1991–2003), vol. 1, p. 9.
10. Executive Committee meeting, 19 March 1917: ibid., pp. 16–17.
11. Cabinet meeting, 20 March 1917: *SPR*, p. 57; interview of A. F. Kerenskii, 14–20 August 1920: DAVP, HIA, box 22, p. 105.
12. See R. Abraham, *Alexander Kerensky: The First Love of the Revolution* (New York: Columbia University Press, 1987), pp. 156–7.
13. Provisional Government session, 20 March 1917: Maylunas and Mironenko, *A Lifelong Passion*, pp. 554–5.
14. Hanbury-Williams, *The Emperor Nicholas II as I Knew Him*, p. 173: diary (20 March 1917).
15. V. M. Vershinin, report to Provisional Government (n.d. but no earlier than 22 March 1917): *SPR*, pp. 65–6.
16. Colonel K. Zershchikov, 'Sobstvennyi ego velichestva konvoi v dni revolyutsii': K. Zershchikov Papers, HIA, p. 33.

17. Ibid.
18. De Basily, *Memoirs*, pp. 141–2.
19. Colonel K. Zershchikov, 'Sobstvennyi ego velichestva konvoi v dni revolyutsii': K. Zershchikov Papers, HIA, p. 35.
20. V. M. Vershinin, report to Provisional Government (n.d. but no earlier than 22 March 1917): *SPR*, p. 66.
21. Ibid.
22. A. F. Romanova (diary), 8 March 1917 (OS): *DNIIAF*, p. 340; Captain N. N. Krasnov, memoir dictated to M. A. Polievktov, 5 June 1917 (OS): http://rarebooks.library.nd.edu/exhibits/polievktov/ssrr.shtml. Semion Lyandres kindly alerted me to Krasnov's testimony about the Kornilov visit.
23. Markov, *Pokinutaya tsarskaya sem'ya*, p. 114.
24. Ye. S. Kobylinskii (inquiry testimony), 6–10 April 1919: AMDP, HIA, box 1, folder 8, pp. 710–11.
25. Ibid., pp. 709–10.
26. Ibid.
27. Markov, *Pokinutaya tsarskaya sem'ya*, pp. 169–70.
28. Ibid., p. 170.
29. Ye. S. Kobylinskii (inquiry testimony), 6–10 April 1919: AMDP, HIA, box 1, folder 8, p. 714.
30. A. A. Volkov (inquiry testimony), 20–23 August 1919: ibid., box 1, folder 9, p. 1098.
31. Ibid.
32. P. Gilliard (inquiry testimony), 5–6 March 1919: ibid., box 1, p. 452.
33. N. A. Romanov (diary), 9 March 1917 (OS): *DINII*, vol. 2, part 2, p. 297.
34. Markov, *Pokinutaya tsarskaya sem'ya*, p. 116.
35. N. A. Romanov (diary), 9 March 1917 (OS): *DINII*, vol. 2, part 2, p. 297.
36. Ye. S. Kobylinskii (inquiry testimony), 6–10 April 1919: AMDP, HIA, box 1, folder 8, p. 711.
37. S. K. Buksgevden (sic), 'Gosudar' Imperator Nikolai II: iz vospominanii', part 1: NABP, HIA, box 23, folder 1, p. 22.
38. Hanbury-Williams, *The Emperor Nicholas II as I Knew Him*, pp. 180–1: diary (24 March 1917).
39. Ibid.
40. A. A. Volkov (inquiry testimony), 20–23 August 1919: AMDP, HIA, box 1, folder 9, p. 1100.
41. Ibid.
42. Colonel K. Zershchikov, 'Sobstvennyi ego velichestva konvoi v dni revolyutsii': K. Zershchikov Papers, HIA, pp. 38–9.
43. Ye. S. Kobylinskii (inquiry testimony), 6–10 April 1919: ibid., box 1, folder 8, pp. 712–13.
44. Ibid., p. 713.
45. N. Lavrova, 'Rasputin's Pyre is Russia's Revenge', *San Francisco Examiner*, 7 October 1923: Nadia Shapiro Papers, HIA, box 5, folder 18.

6: FAMILY LIFE

1. Father Nicholas (S. Gibbes), untitled memoir (typescript): SGC, SCBLOU, box 1, MS Facs c. 106, p. 6.
2. A. F. Romanova to N. A. Romanov, 22 February 1917 (OS): *SPR*, p. 24.
3. S. K. Buksgevden (sic), 'Gosudar' Imperator Nikolai II: iz vospominanii', part 1: NABP, HIA, box 23, folder 1, pp. 6–7.
4. For her strident recommendations about ministerial appointments, see A. F. Romanova to N. A. Romanov, 14 December 1916 (OS): Fuhrman (ed.), *Complete Wartime Correspondence*, p. 675.
5. Ye. S. Kobylinskii (inquiry testimony), 6–10 April 1919: AMDP, HIA, box 1, folder 8, p. 755.
6. N. de Basily, 'Note sur l'Empereur et l'Impératrice': NABP, HIA, box 23, folder 1, p. 2.
7. S. K. Buksgevden (sic), 'Gosudar' Imperator Nikolai II: iz vospominanii', typescript, part 1: NABP, HIA, box 23, folder 1, p. 3.
8. K. M. Bitner (inquiry testimony), July 1919: AMDP, HIA, box 1, folder 8, p. 1022.
9. S. K. Buksgevden (sic), 'Gosudar' Imperator Nikolai II: iz vospominanii', typescript, part 1: NABP, HIA, box 23, folder 1, p. 3.
10. Ibid.
11. Ibid., p. 4.
12. Ibid.
13. Ibid., p. 6.
14. Diary notes: Princess Barbara Dolgorouky Memoirs, HIA, box 1, p. 78.
15. P. A. (sic) Gilliard (inquiry testimony), 27 August 1919: AMDP, HIA, box 1, folder 9, p. 1128.
16. Ye. S. Kobylinskii (inquiry testimony), 6–10 April 1919: ibid., box 1, folder 8, p. 756.
17. S. K. Buksgevden (sic), 'Gosudar' Imperator Nikolai II: iz vospominanii', part 1: NABP, HIA, box 23, folder 1, p. 10.
18. N. de Basily, 'Note sur l'Empereur et l'Impératrice': NABP, HIA, box 23, folder 1, p. 2.
19. M. G. Tutelberg (inquiry testimony), 1919: AMDP, HIA, box 1, folder 8, p. 974.
20. P. A. (sic) Gilliard (inquiry testimony), 27 August 1919: ibid., box 1, folder 9, p. 1129.
21. Ibid.
22. S. Gibbes (diary), 1–4 March 1917: SGC, SCBLOU, box 1.
23. K. M. Bitner (inquiry testimony), July 1919: AMDP, HIA, box 1, folder 8, p. 1019.
24. Ibid.
25. S. Gibbes (diary), 8 and 13 October 1916: SGC, SCBLOU, box 1.

26. S. I. Ivanov (inquiry testimony), 19 July 1919: AMDP, HIA, box 1, folder 8, p. 952.
27. Ye. S. Kobylinskii (inquiry testimony), 6–10 April 1919: ibid., box 1, folder 8, p. 758.
28. P. A. (sic) Gilliard (inquiry testimony), 5–6 March 1919 (OS): ibid., box 1, folder 7, p. 456; Ye. S. Kobylinskii (inquiry testimony), 6–10 April 1919: ibid., box 1, folder 8, p. 712.
29. Ye. S. Kobylinskii (inquiry testimony), 6–10 April 1919: ibid., box 1, folder 8, p. 756.
30. Ibid., p. 757.
31. Ibid.
32. K. M. Bitner (inquiry testimony), July 1919: ibid., box 1, folder 8, p. 1017.
33. Ye. S. Kobylinskii (inquiry testimony), 6–10 April 1919: ibid., box 1, folder 8, p. 757; K. M. Bitner (inquiry testimony), July 1919: ibid., box 1, folder 8, p. 1018.
34. Ye. S. Kobylinskii (inquiry testimony), 6–10 April 1919: ibid., box 1, folder 8, p. 757.
35. Ibid.

7: THE PROVISIONAL GOVERNMENT

1. Interview of A. F. Kerenskii, 14–20 August 1920: DAVP, HIA, box 22, p. 111a.
2. Ibid., pp. 107b–108a; Ye. S. Kobylinskii (inquiry testimony), 6–10 April 1919: AMDP, HIA, box 1, folder 8, pp. 713–14.
3. Ibid.
4. Interview of A. F. Kerenskii, 14–20 August 1920: DAVP, HIA, box 22, pp. 107b–108a; Ye. S. Kobylinskii (inquiry testimony), 6–10 April 1919: AMDP, HIA, box 1, folder 8, pp. 713–14; S. Mstislavskii, *Pyat' dnei: nachalo i konets fevral'skoi revolyutsii* (Moscow: Z. I. Grzhebin, 1922), pp. 55–9.
5. N. de Basily, notes on departure of Nicholas II and his family: NABP, HIA, box 27, folder 11, p. 13.
6. A. A. Volkov, *Okolo tsarskoi sem'i* (Paris: Moscow, 1928), pp. 52–3.
7. A. A. Volkov (inquiry testimony), 20–23 August 1919: AMDP, HIA, box 1, folder 9, p. 1102.
8. Volkov, *Okolo tsarskoi sem'i*, p. 53.
9. Interview of A. F. Kerenskii, 14–20 August 1920: DAVP, HIA, box 22, pp. 106a–b.
10. Ibid., p. 107b.
11. Ibid., p. 109a; Ye. S. Kobylinskii (inquiry testimony), 6–10 April 1919: AMDP, HIA, box 1, folder 8, p. 715.
12. Interview of A. F. Kerensky, August 1920: DAVP, HIA, box 22, p. 106b.
13. Ye. S. Kobylinskii (inquiry testimony), 6–10 April 1919: AMDP, HIA, box 1, folder 8, p. 715.

14. A. A. Volkov (inquiry testimony), 20–23 August 1919: AMDP, HIA, box 1, folder 9, p. 1099.
15. Interview of A. F. Kerenskii, August 1920: DAVP, HIA, box 22, pp. 107b and 111a–112b.
16. A. A. Volkov (inquiry testimony), 20–23 August 1919: AMDP, HIA, box 1, folder 9, p. 1102.
17. Ibid.
18. Ibid., pp. 1102–3.
19. Pankratov, *So tsarëm v Tobol'ske: iz vospominanii* (Leningrad: Kooperativnoe izdatel'skoe t-vo 'Byloe', 1925), p. 63.
20. S. K. Buksgevden (sic), 'Gosudar' Imperator Nikolai II: iz vospominanii', part 1: NABP, HIA, box 23, folder 1, p. 24.
21. A. A. Volkov (inquiry testimony), 20–23 August 1919: AMDP, HIA, box 1, folder 9, p. 1102.
22. S. K. Buksgevden (sic), 'Gosudar' Imperator Nikolai II: iz vospominanii', part 1: NABP, HIA, box 23, folder 1, p. 23.
23. Ibid., p. 24.
24. P. Gilliard to N. de Basily, 29 April 1934 (notes): NABP, HIA, box 2, folder 62, pp. 2–3.
25. Ibid., p. 3.
26. S. K. Buksgevden (sic), 'Gosudar' Imperator Nikolai II: iz vospominanii', part 1: NABP, HIA, box 23, folder 1, pp. 23–4.

8: THE BRITISH OFFER

1. Cabinet discussion, 15 March 1917: *SPR*, p. 39.
2. *Krasnyi arkhiv*, vol. 23, p. 53, quoted N. de Basily, notes on departure of Nicholas II and his family: NABP, HIA, box 27, folder 11, p. 1.
3. N. de Basily, notes on departure of Nicholas II and his family: NABP, HIA, box 27, folder 11, pp. 2–3; conversation between N. de Basily and A. S. Lukomskii, 24 February 1933: ibid., box 22, p. 2.
4. N. de Basily, notes on departure of Nicholas II and his family: ibid., box 27, folder 11, pp. 4–5.
5. Ibid., p. 6.
6. Ibid.
7. Executive Committee meeting, 22 March 1917: *SPR*, pp. 63–4.
8. N. de Basily, notes on departure of Nicholas II and his family: NABP, HIA, box 27, folder 11, pp. 12–13.
9. M. Paléologue, *La Russie des tsars pendant la Grande Guerre*, vol. 3 (Paris: Plon, 1922), p. 264, cited ibid., p. 7.
10. Conversation between N. de Basily and A. S. Lukomskii, 24 February 1933: NABP, HIA, box 22, pp. 2–3.
11. N. de Basily, notes on departure of Nicholas II and his family: ibid., box 27, folder 11, pp. 7–8.

12. G. Buchanan, *My Mission to Russia and Other Diplomatic Memories*, vol. 2 (London: Cassell and Co., 1923), p. 105.

13. N. de Basily, notes on departure of Nicholas II and his family: NABP, HIA, box 27, folder 11, p. 10.

14. Ibid., p. 11.

15. *Petrogradskii Sovet rabochikh i soldatskikh deputatov v 1917 godu*, pp. 587–9.

16. P. Gilliard to N. de Basily, 29 April 1934 (letter): NABP, HIA, box 2, folder 62.

17. S. Gibbes to his Aunt Hattie, 21 April 1917: SGC, SCBLOU, box 2.

9: RULES AND ROUTINES

1. Instruction to the Tsarskoe Selo garrison commander, 30 March 1917: *SPR*, p. 68.

2. S. Gibbes to Grand Duke Alexander Nikolaevich, untitled memoir, 1 December 1928: SGC, SCBLOU, box 1, p. 4.

3. Markov, *Pokinutaya tsarskaya sem'ya*, p. 154.

4. Ye. S. Kobylinskii (inquiry testimony), 6–10 April 1919: AMDP, HIA, box 1, folder 8, pp. 712 and 718.

5. Executive Committee meeting, 22 March 1917: *Petrogradskii Sovet rabochikh i soldatskikh deputatov*, vol. 1, pp. 29–33.

6. N. A. Romanov to X. A. Romanova, 18 November 1917 (OS): *SPR*, pp. 115–16.

7. Ye. S. Kobylinskii (inquiry testimony), 6–10 April 1919: AMDP, HIA, box 1, folder 8, p. 756.

8. Ibid., p. 712.

9. P. A. (sic) Gilliard (inquiry testimony), 5–6 March 1919 (OS): ibid., box 1, folder 7, p. 457.

10. N. A. Mundel (inquiry testimony), 6 August 1919: ibid., box 1, folder 8, p. 1045; L. S. Tugan-Baranovskii (oral testimony from the Polievktov Collection): Lyandres (ed.), *The Fall of Tsarism*, p. 131.

11. A. A. Volkov (inquiry testimony), 20–23 August 1919: AMDP, HIA, box 1, folder 9, p. 1102.

12. Ibid., pp. 1100–1.

13. Ye. S. Kobylinskii (inquiry testimony), 6–10 April 1919: ibid., box 1, folder 8, p. 717.

14. A. A. Volkov (inquiry testimony), 20–23 August 1919: ibid., box 1, folder 9, p. 1101.

15. Ye. S. Kobylinskii (inquiry testimony), 6–10 April 1919: ibid., box 1, folder 8, p. 716.

16. P. Gilliard, *Le tragique destin de Nicolas II et de sa famille* (Paris: Payot, 1921), p. 193; Ye. S. Kobylinskii (inquiry testimony), 6–10 April 1919: AMDP, HIA, box 1, folder 8, p. 717.

17. N. A. Romanov to M. F. Romanova, letters of summer 1917: Kseniia

Aleksandrovna, Grand Duchess of Russia Papers (hereafter KAGDRP), HIA, box 8, file 38. Nicholas did not always date these letters.

18. *Skorbnaya pamyatka*, ed. A. V. Syroboyarskii (New York: Kassa Pomoshchi Blizhnim v Pamyat' v Tsarskoi Sem'e, 1928), p. 48: A. F. Romanova to A. V. Syroboyarski, 29 May 1917 (OS); Fuhrman (ed.), *Complete Wartime Correspondence*, p. 529.

19. *Skorbnaya pamyatka*, pp. 48–9.

18: ON THE LIVES OF RULERS

1. N. A. Romanov (diary), 24 March 1917 (OS): *DINII*, vol. 2, part 2, p. 300.
2. N. A. Romanov (diary), 29 April 1917 (OS), ibid., pp. 304 and 307.
3. N. A. Romanov (diary), 4 May 1917 (OS), ibid., p. 308.
4. N. A. Romanov (diary), 2 May 1917 (OS), ibid., p. 308.
5. L. A. Kasso, *Rossiya na Dunae i obrazovanie Bessarabskoi oblasti* (Moscow: A. Snegirëva, 1913), pp. 229–30.
6. A. N. Kuropatkin, *Zadachi russkoi armii* (St Petersburg: V. A. Berezovskii, 1910), vol. 3, pp. 13–14, 61, 66–7 and 339–43.
7. F. I. Uspenskii, *Istoriya vizantiiskoi imperii* (St Petersburg: Brokgauz-Efron, 1913), vol. 1, pp. 99–135.
8. Ibid., pp. 126–31.
9. Ibid., vol. 2, pp. 813–72.
10. N. A. Romanov (diary), 3 April 1917 (OS): *DINII*, vol. 2, part 2, p. 303.
11. N. A. Romanov (diary), 21 June 1917 (OS), ibid., p. 317.
12. N. A. Romanov (diary), 22 June 1917 (OS), ibid., p. 317.
13. D. S. Merezhkovskii, *Khristos i Antikhrist* (St Petersburg: M. V. Pirozhkov, 1907), vol. 2, *Voskresshie bogi. Leonardo da-Vinchi*, p. 816.
14. N. A. Romanov (diary), 4 July 1917 (OS): *DINII*, vol. 2, part 2, p. 319.
15. Merezhkovskii, *Khristos i Antikhrist*, vol. 3: *Antikhrist: Pëtr i Aleksei*, p. 550.
16. N. A. Romanov (diary), 11 July 1918 (OS): *DINII*, vol. 2, part 2, p. 320.
17. D. S. Merezhkovskii, *Aleksandr I*, vol. 6, in *Polnoe sobranie sochinenii*, 24 vols (Moscow: I. D. Sytin, 1914), pp. 189–90.
18. Ibid., pp. 237 and 239.
19. D. S. Mérejkowsky, 'Préface', in D. Mérejkowsky, Z. Hippius and Dm. Philosophoff, *Le Tsar et la Révolution* (Paris: Société du Mercure de France, 1907), p. 14.
20. D. S. Mérejkowsky, 'Religion et Révolution', ibid., pp. 147–8.
21. N. A. Romanov (diary), 3 June 1918 (OS): *DINII*, vol. 2, part 2, p. 430.
22. N. K. Shil'der, *Imperator Pavel Pervyi. Istoriko-biograficheskii ocherk* (St Petersburg: A. S. Suvorin, 1901), p. 503.
23. Ibid., pp. 26 and 477–504.
24. N. A. Romanov (diary), 3 June 1918 (OS): *DINII*, vol. 2, part 2, p. 430.
25. N. A. Romanov (diary), 9 November 1917 (OS), ibid., p. 339.
26. V. Hugo, *Quatre-vingt-treize*, p. 180.

27. Ibid., pp. 494–7.

11: KERENSKY'S DILEMMA

1. *Nikolai II-oi Romanov: ego zhizn' i deyatel'nost, 1894–1917 g.g., po inostrannym i russkim istochnikam* (Petrograd: Gosudarstvennaya tipografiya, 1917), pp. 1, 59, 69 and 72–3.
2. See B. I. Kolonitski, *Simvoly vlasti i bor'ba za vlast': k izucheniyu politicheskoi kul'tury Rossiiskoi revolyutsii 1917 goda* (St Petersburg: Dmitrii Bulanin, 2001), pp. 132–40.
3. See B. I. Kolonitskii, *'Tragicheskaya erotika': obrazy imperatorskoi sem'i v gody pervoi mirovoi voiny* (St Petersburg: Novoe Literaturnoe Obozrenie, 2010), pp. 236–40.
4. Interview of A. F. Kerenskii, 14–20 August 1920: DAVP, HIA, box 22, pp. 107b–108a.
5. N. de Basily, notes on conversation with M. Tereshchenko, 23 April 1934: NABP, HIA, box 27, folder 11, p. 1.
6. Ibid., p. 2.
7. Ibid., p. 4.
8. Interview of A. F. Kerenskii, August 1920: DAVP, HIA, box 22, p. 108b.
9. N. A. Romanov (diary), 5 July 1917 (OS): *DINII*, vol. 2, part 2, p. 319.
10. L. Sukacev, 'Soldier Under Three Flags: The Personal Memoirs of Lev Pavlovich Sukacev' (Washington, DC: typescript, 1974): Lev Sukacev Papers, HIA, p. 100.
11. M. A. Romanov to M. F. Romanova, 27 March 1917: KAGDRP, HIA, box 8, folder 37.
12. See Ioffe, *Revolyutsiya i sem'ya Romanovykh*, p. 194.

12: DISTANT TRANSFER

1. See Ioffe, *Revolyutsiya i sem'ya Romanovykh*, pp. 194–5.
2. Interview of A. F. Kerenskii, 14–20 August 1920: DAVP, HIA, box 22, p. 108b.
3. Ye. S. Kobylinskii (inquiry testimony), 6–10 April 1919: AMDP, HIA, box 1, folder 8, pp. 717–18.
4. Ibid., pp. 719–20.
5. Ibid., p. 720.
6. Ibid., pp. 720–1.
7. T. E. Mel'nik-Botkina, *Vospominaniya o tsarskoi sem'e i eë zhizni do i posle revolyutsii* (Belgrade: M. I. Stefanovich, 1921; repr. Moscow: Ankor, 1993), p. 64.
8. Ibid., pp. 63–4.
9. Ye. S. Kobylinskii (inquiry testimony), 6–10 April 1919: AMDP, HIA, box 1, folder 8, pp. 721–2.

10. S. K. Buksgevden (sic), 'Gosudar' Imperator Nikolai II: iz vospominanii', part 1: NABP, HIA, box 23, folder 1, p. 24.
11. Ibid.
12. Interview of A. F. Kerenskii, 14–20 August 1920: DAVP, HIA, box 22, p. 108b.
13. Benkendorf, *Last Days at Tsarskoe Selo*, p. 107.
14. Interview of A. F. Kerenskii, 14–20 August 1920: DAVP, HIA, box 22, p. 109a.
15. Ye. S. Kobylinskii (inquiry testimony), 6–10 April 1919: AMDP, HIA, box 1, folder 8, p. 722.
16. A. A. Volkov (inquiry testimony), 20–23 August 1919: ibid., box 1, folder 9, p. 1105.
17. Ye. S. Kobylinskii (inquiry testimony), 6–10 April 1919: ibid., box 1, folder 8, pp. 722–3.
18. M. A. Romanov to M. F. Romanova, 8 August 1917 (OS): KAGDRP, HIA, box 8, file 37.
19. A. A. Volkov (inquiry testimony), 20–23 August 1919: AMDP, HIA, box 1, folder 9, p. 1104.
20. E. A. Naryshkina (diary), 1 August 1917 (OS): *SPR*, p. 89.
21. Ye. S. Kobylinskii (inquiry testimony), 6–10 April 1919: AMDP, HIA, box 1, folder 8, p. 722.
22. M. A. Romanov to M. F. Romanova, 8 August 1917 (OS): KAGDRP, HIA, box 8, file 37.
23. S. K. Buksgevden (sic), 'Gosudar' Imperator Nikolai II: iz vospominanii', part 1: NABP, HIA, box 23, folder 1, p. 25.
24. M. A. Romanov to M. F. Romanova, 8 August 1917 (OS): KAGDRP, HIA, box 8, file 37; E. A. Naryshkina (diary), 1 August 1917 (OS): *SPR*, p. 89.
25. Mel'nik-Botkina, *Vospominaniya o tsarskoi sem'e*, pp. 62–3.
26. E. A. Naryshkina (diary), 1 August 1917 (OS): *SPR*, p. 89.
27. Mel'nik-Botkina, *Vospominaniya o tsarskoi sem'e*, p. 63.
28. Ibid., p. 86.
29. A. A. Volkov (inquiry testimony), 20–23 August 1919: AMDP, HIA, box 1, folder 9, p. 1104.
30. Ye. S. Kobylinskii (inquiry testimony), 6–10 April 1919: ibid., box 1, folder 8, p. 723.
31. Ibid., p. 724.
32. Ibid.
33. Ibid., pp. 724–5.
34. Ibid., p. 724.
35. A. N. Romanova, exercise book (n.d.): SGC, SCBLOU, box 1.
36. N. A. Romanov (diary), 4 August 1917 (OS): *DNIIAF*, p. 17.
37. A. A. Volkov (inquiry testimony), 20–23 August 1919: AMDP, HIA, box 1, folder 9, p. 1120.
38. Interview of A. F. Kerenskii, 14–20 August 1920: DAVP, HIA, box 22, p. 108b; see also Ioffe, *Revolyutsiya i sem'ya Romanovykh*, p. 198.
39. F. N. Gorshkov (inquiry testimony), 31 July 1918: AMDP, HIA, box 1, folder 6, p. 7; Ye. S. Kobylinskii (inquiry testimony), 6–10 April 1919: ibid., folder

8, p. 725; Volkov, *Okolo tsarskoi sem'i*, p. 57; A. F. Romanova (diary), 6 and 13 August 1917 (OS): *DNIIAF*, pp. 21 and 29.

40. Ye. S. Kobylinskii (inquiry testimony), 6–10 April 1919: AMDP, HIA, box 1, folder 8, p. 728.
41. A. F. Kerenskii to the Tobolsk Procurator (n.d.): ibid., box 1, folder 9, pp. 1401–2.
42. Interview of A. F. Kerenskii, 14–20 August 1920: DAVP, HIA, box 22, p. 109a.
43. Ye. S. Kobylinskii (inquiry testimony), 6–10 April 1919: AMDP, HIA, box 1, folder 8, p. 725.
44. A. F. Romanova (diary), 13 August 1917 (OS): *DNIIAF*, p. 29.

13: DESTINATION TOBOLSK

1. N. A. Romanov to M. F. Romanova, 27 October 1917: KAGDRP, HIA, box 8, folder 38.
2. *Baedeker's Russia*, p. 527.
3. Ibid., p. 527; R. S. Latimer, *Dr. Baedeker and his Apostolic Work in Russia* (London: Morgan and Scott, 1907), p. 121.
4. *Neobkhodimost' otkrytiya porto-franko v ust'yakh rek Obi i Yeniseya* (Tobolsk: Gubernskaya Tipografia, 1907), p. 24. See also D. W. Treadgold, *The Great Siberian Migration: Government and Peasant in Resettlement from Emancipation to the First World War* (Princeton, NJ: Princeton University Press, 1957), p. 100.
5. J. Snodgrass, *Bureau of Foreign and Domestic Commerce: Russia: A Handbook on Commercial and Industrial Conditions* (Washington, DC: Government Printing Office, 1913), pp. 217–18.
6. *Neobkhodimost' otkrytiya porto-franko v ust'yakh rek Obi i Yeniseya*, p. 7.
7. Ibid., pp. 15–18 and 22.
8. Mel'nik-Botkina, *Vospominaniya o tsarskoi sem'e*, p. 78.
9. D. Beer, 'Vae Victis: Siberian Exile as a Revolutionary Battleground, 1900–1914': St Antony's College (Oxford) history seminar series, 2 March 2015. See also D. Beer, *The House of the Dead: Siberian Exile under the Tsars* (London: Allen Lane, 2016), pp. 373–81.
10. S. Kallistov, *Tobol'skii Tsentral* (Moscow: Vsesoyuznoe obshchestvo politkatorzhan i ss-poselentsev, 1925), p. 4.
11. 'Golos s katorgi' (complaint-report on the troubles of 1906–1908), pp. 1–6 and 57–8: B. I. Nicolaevsky Collection, HIA, box 112, folder 6; Kallistov, *Tobol'skii Tsentral*, p. 11.
12. Beer, 'Vae Victis'.
13. Latimer, *Dr. Baedeker and his Apostolic Work in Russia*, p. 120.
14. Pankratov, *So tsarëm v Tobol'ske*, p. 30.
15. See Ioffe, *Revolyutsiya i sem'ya Romanovykh*, p. 197.

14: PLENIPOTENTIARY PANKRATOV

1. Interview of A. F. Kerenskii, 14–20 August 1920: DAVP, HIA, box 22, p. 109a; Pankratov, *So tsarëm v Tobol'ske*, pp. 14–15; Gilliard, *Le tragique destin de Nicolas II et de sa famille*, p. 201.

2. Pankratov, *So tsarëm v Tobol'ske*, pp. 14–15 and 24; Tobolsk Procurator Koryakin to A. F. Kerenskii, 4 September 1917: *SPR*, p. 107.

3. Ye. S. Kobylinskii (inquiry testimony), 6–10 April 1919: AMDP, HIA, box 1, folder 8, pp. 729–30.

4. 'Plebei' [V. S. Pankratov], 'Polozhenie uchenikov na zavodakh', *Literaturnye Otgoloski: Sbornik, Neperiodicheskii Izdanie*, no. 1 (7 February 1893 (OS)): Boris Nicolaevsky Collection, box 192, pp. 97–115.

5. Unsigned introduction to Pankratov, *So tsarëm v Tobol'ske*, pp. 7–11.

6. K. M. Bitner (inquiry testimony), July 1919: AMDP, HIA, box 1, folder 8, pp. 1012–13.

7. P. Gilliard to N. de Basily, 29 April 1934 (notes): NABP, HIA, box 2, folder 62, p. 3.

8. N. A. Romanov (diary), 1 September 1917 (OS): *DINII*, vol. 2, part 2, p. 330.

9. Volkov, *Okolo tsarskoi sem'i*, p. 57.

10. Ye. S. Kobylinskii (inquiry testimony), 6–10 April 1919: AMDP, HIA, box 1, folder 8, pp. 729–30.

11. Gilliard, *Le tragique destin de Nicolas II et de sa famille*, p. 201.

12. Ye. S. Kobylinskii (inquiry testimony), 6–10 April 1919: AMDP, HIA, box 1, folder 8, pp. 729–30.

13. Mel'nik-Botkina, *Vospominaniya o tsarskoi sem'e*, p. 85.

14. Pankratov, *So tsarëm v Tobol'ske*, p. 24.

15. Ibid., pp. 25 and 67.

16. Ibid., p. 67.

17. Ibid., p. 60; N. A. Romanov (diary), 22 September 1917 (OS): *DINII*, vol. 2, part 2, p. 333.

18. T. N. Romanova to M. S. Khitrovo, 17 October 1917 (OS): Alexandre Tarsaidze Papers, Subject File, Letters, HIA.

19. Pankratov, *So tsarëm v Tobol'ske*, p. 60; N. A. Romanov (diary), 22 September 1917 (OS): *DINII*, vol. 2, part 2, p. 333.

20. V. S. Pankratov to A. F. Kerenskii, 13 October 1917: *SPR*, p. 110.

21. Pankratov, *So tsarëm v Tobol'ske*, pp. 60–2.

22. Ibid., p. 62.

23. Ibid., p. 63.

24. K. M. Bitner (inquiry testimony), July 1919: AMDP, HIA, box 1, folder 8, p. 1021.

25. Tobolsk Procurator Koryakin to A. F. Kerenskii, 4 September 1917: *SPR*, pp. 105–7; Ye. S. Kobylinskii (inquiry testimony), 6–10 April 1919: AMDP, HIA, box 1, folder 8, p. 721.

26. Interview of A. F. Kerenskii, 14–20 August 1920: DAVP, HIA, box 22, p. 109a.

27. Office chief-of-staff of A. F. Kerenskii to E. S. Botkin, 28 September 1917: *SPR*, p. 110.
28. Pankratov, *So tsarëm v Tobol'ske*, pp. 56–7 and 71.
29. Ibid., p. 57.
30. N. A. Romanov (diary), 29 September 1917 (OS): *DINII*, vol. 2, part 2, p. 334. For Pankratov's letter of 30 September 1917 (OS), see ibid., p. 396, fn. 106.
31. Volkov, *Okolo tsarskoi sem'i*, p. 58.
32. A. F. Romanova (diary), 1 October 1917 (OS): DNIIAF, p. 105.
33. Pankratov, *So tsarëm v Tobol'ske*, pp. 52–4.
34. N. A. Romanov to X. A. Romanova, 18 November 1917 (OS): *SPR*, p. 115.
35. Ye. S. Kobylinskii (inquiry testimony), 6–10 April 1919: AMDP, HIA, box 1, folder 8, p. 732.
36. Pankratov, *So tsarëm v Tobol'ske*, pp. 52–3.

15: THE OCTOBER REVOLUTION

1. Markov, *Pokinutaya tsarskaya sem'ya*, p. 174.
2. Ibid.
3. Gilliard, *Le tragique destin de Nicolas II et de sa famille*, p. 204.
4. L. G. Kornilov, testimony to the Extraordinary Commission of Investigation, 2–5 September 1917 (OS): G. N. Sevastyanov et al. (eds), *Delo generala Kornilova: materialy Chrezvychainoi komissii po rassledovaniyu dela o byvshem Verkhovnom glavno komanduyushchem generale L. G. Kornilove i ego souchastnikakh, avgust 1917 g. – iyun' 1918 g.*, 2 vols (Moscow: Materik, 2003), vol. 2, p. 202.
5. L. G. Kornilov, 'Appeal to the People', 28 August 1917 (OS): ibid., p. 493.
6. N. A. Romanov (diary), 29 August 1917 (OS): *DINII*, vol. 2, part 2, p. 330.
7. N. A. Romanov (diary), 5 September 1917 (OS): ibid., p. 331.
8. See D. Koenker, *Moscow Workers and the 1917 Revolution* (Princeton, NJ: Princeton University Press, 1981), p. 132.
9. N. A. Romanov (diary), 25 October 1917 (OS): *DINII*, vol. 2, part 2, p. 337; A. F. Romanova (diary), 25 October 1917 (OS): *DNIIAF*, pp. 135–6.
10. Pankratov, *So tsarëm v Tobol'ske*, p. 81.
11. N. A. Romanov (diary), 11 November 1917 (OS): *DINII*, vol. 2, part 2, p. 339.
12. Father Nicholas (S. Gibbes), 'Ten Years with the Russian Imperial Family' (typescript): SGC, SCBLOU, box 1, p. 3.
13. N. A. Romanov (diary), 18 November 1917 (OS): *DINII*, vol. 2, part 2, p. 340.

16: THE ROMANOV DISPERSAL

1. G. M. Romanov to X. G. Romanova, 1 and 29 June 1917 (OS): Georgi Mikhailovich, Grand Duke of Russia Papers, HIA, box 2.
2. G. M. Romanov to X. G. Romanova, 29 June 1917 (OS): ibid.

3. N. M. Romanov to M. F. Romanova, 27 April 1917: KAGDRP, HIA, box 8, folder 39.

4. G. M. Romanov to X. G. Romanova, 29 September 1917 (OS): Georgi Mikhailovich, Grand Duke of Russia Papers, HIA, box 2.

5. G. M. Romanov to M. F. Romanova, 28 October 1917 (OS): KAGDRP, HIA, box 8, file 25.

6. N. A. Romanov to M. F. Romanova, 19 September 1917 (OS): ibid., box 8, file 38.

7. X. A. Romanova to N. A. Romanov, 6 December 1917 (OS): *DINII*, vol. 2, part 2, pp. 433–4.

8. N. A. Romanov to X. A. Romanova, 6 December 1917 (OS): *Pis'ma svyatykh tsarstvennykh muchennikov iz zatocheniya*, ed. E. E. Alfer'evym, D. S. Tatishchev and S. P. Andolenko (St Petersburg: Spaso-Preobrazhenskii Valaamskii monastyr', 1996), pp. 181–2, cited ibid., p. 435.

9. X. A. Romanova to N. A. Romanov, 6 December 1917 (OS): *DINII*, vol. 2, part 2, p. 434. On Mikhail's conditions of custody in Petrograd, see R. Crawford and D. Crawford, *Michael and Natasha: The Life and Love of the Last Tsar of Russia* (Weidenfeld and Nicolson: London, 1997), pp. 336–7.

10. O. A. Romanova to N. A. Romanov, 27 January 1918 (OS): ibid., p. 438.

11. X. A. Romanova to N. A. Romanov, 1/14 February 1918: ibid.

12. M. A. Romanov to M. F. Romanova, 11 October 1917 (OS): KAGDRP, HIA, box 8, file 37.

13. M. A. Romanov to M. F. Romanova, 25 October 1917 (OS): ibid.

14. M. A. Romanov to M. F. Romanova, 5 November 1917 (OS): ibid.

17: FREEDOM HOUSE

1. A. A. Volkov (inquiry testimony), 20–23 August 1919: AMDP, HIA, box 1, folder 9, p. 1106.

2. S. Gibbes, untitled memoir, 1 December 1928: SGC, SCBLOU, box 1, p. 5.

3. Mel'nik-Botkina, *Vospominaniya o tsarskoi sem'e*, p. 81.

4. Father Nicholas (S. Gibbes), 'Ten Years with the Russian Imperial Family' (typescript): SGC, SCBLOU, box 1, p. 8.

5. N. A. Romanov (diary), 18 January 1918 (OS): *DINII*, vol. 2, part 2, p. 407.

6. Photographs were itemized by N. A. Sokolov in a list of discovered belongings, 27 October 1919: AMDP, HIA, box 1, folder 9, p. 1333.

7. 'Bezique as always': N. A. Romanov (diary), 21 January 1918 (OS): *DINII*, vol. 2, part 2, p. 408.

8. M. N. Romanova to M. F. Romanova, 23 September 1917 (OS): KAGDRP, HIA, box 8, file 35.

9. A. N. Romanova to Ye. E. Zborovskaya, 20 September 1917 (OS): Ekaterina Zborovskaia Papers, HIA, box 2.

10. A. N. Romanova to Ye. E. Zborovskaya, 10 December 1917 (OS): ibid.

11. A. N. Romanov to M. F. Romanova, 5 November 1917: ibid., box 8, folder 10.

12. Ye. S. Kobylinskii (inquiry testimony), 6–10 April 1919: AMDP, HIA, box 1, folder 8, p. 728.
13. A. N. Romanova to Ye. E. Zborovskaya, 19 January 1918 (OS): Ekaterina Zborovskaia Papers, box 2.
14. Photographs were itemized by N. A. Sokolov in a list of discovered belongings, 27 October 1919: AMDP, HIA, box 1, folder 9, p. 1333.
15. T. N. Romanova to M. S. Khitrovo, 23 January 1918 (OS): Alexandre Tarsaidze Papers, HIA, Subject File, Letters.
16. Mel'nik-Botkina, *Vospominaniya o tsarskoi sem'e*, pp. 86–7.
17. Pankratov, *So tsarëm v Tobol'ske*, pp. 46–7.
18. Ye. S. Kobylinskii (inquiry testimony), 6–10 April 1919: AMDP, HIA, box 1, folder 8, p. 735; Mel'nik-Botkina, *Vospominaniya o tsarskoi sem'e*, p. 87.
19. Ye. S. Kobylinskii (inquiry testimony), 6–10 April 1919: AMDP, HIA, box 1, folder 8, p. 728.
20. Gilliard, *Le tragique destin de Nicolas II et de sa famille*, p. 207.
21. Pankratov, *So tsarëm v Tobol'ske*, p. 83; Ye. S. Kobylinskii (inquiry testimony), 6–10 April 1919: AMDP, HIA, box 1, folder 8, pp. 732–3.
22. *Tobol'skie eparkhal'nye vedomosti*, nos 29–31, 10/23 December – 1/14 December 1918, p. 285.
23. Ye. S. Kobylinskii (inquiry testimony), 6–10 April 1919: AMDP, HIA, box 1, folder 8, p. 732.
24. 'Beseda s episkopom Germogenom', *Svet* (St Petersburg), January 1912.
25. Ye. S. Kobylinskii (inquiry testimony), 6–10 April 1919: AMDP, HIA, box 1, folder 8, p. 733.
26. Ibid., pp. 733–4.

18: LEARNING FROM OTHERS

1. Pankratov, *So tsarëm v Tobol'ske*, pp. 68–9.
2. Ibid., pp. 65–7.
3. P. Gilliard to N. de Basily, 29 April 1934 (notes): NABP, HIA, box 2, folder 62, p. 4.
4. Pankratov, *So tsarëm v Tobol'ske*, p. 58.
5. Ibid., pp. 73–4.
6. Ibid., pp. 68–9.
7. N. A. Romanov (diary), 18 January 1918 (OS): *DINII*, vol. 2, part 2, p. 407; S. Nilus, *Velikoe v malom*, a book itemized by N. A. Sokolov in a list of discovered belongings, 6 September 1919: AMDP, HIA, box 1, folder 9, p. 1237. Sokolov recorded it as having belonged to Alexandra.
8. N. A Romanov to M. F. Romanova, 27 October 1917: KAGDRP, HIA, box 8, folder 38.
9. Pankratov, *So tsarëm v Tobol'ske*, p. 42.
10. Ibid., pp. 42–3; Markov, *Pokinutaya tsarskaya sem'ya*, p. 47.

11. K. M. Bitner (inquiry testimony), July 1919: AMDP, HIA, box 1, folder 8, pp. 1012–13.
12. Ibid., p. 1015.
13. Ibid., p. 1013.
14. Pankratov, *So tsarëm v Tobol'ske*, pp. 42–3.
15. Ibid., p. 43.
16. K. M. Bitner (inquiry testimony), July 1919: AMDP, HIA, box 1, folder 8, p. 1020.
17. Ibid., p. 1019.
18. Ibid., p. 1020.
19. Ibid., p. 1019.
20. Pankratov, *So tsarëm v Tobol'ske*, pp. 44–5.

19: TIME ON THEIR HANDS

1. *The Last Diary of Tsaritsa Alexandra*, ed. V. A. Kozlov and V. M. Khrustalëv (New Haven, CT: Yale University Press, 1997), 11 February 1918, p. 35.
2. Ibid., 11 January 1918 (OS), p. 17, and 11 February 1918, p. 35.
3. N. A. Romanov (diary), 9 January 1918 (OS): *DINII*, vol. 2, part 2, p. 406.
4. N. A. Romanov (diary), 7 January 1918 (OS): ibid.
5. Father Nicholas (S. Gibbes), 'My Tobolsk Books, Etc., Etc.' (typescript): SGC, SCBLOU, box 1, pp. 2–3, 8; N. A. Romanov (diary), 13 March 1918 (OS): *DINII*, vol. 2, part 2, pp. 414 and 416.
6. N. A. Romanov (diary), 26 and 29 September, 2, 9 and 17, 23 and 29 October 1917 (OS): *DINII*, vol. 2, part 2, pp. 332–4 and 336–7.
7. N. A. Romanov (diary), 16 October 1917 (OS): ibid., p. 335.
8. N. A. Romanov (diary), 3 October 1917 (OS): ibid.
9. N. A. Romanov (diary), 19 October 1917 (OS): ibid., p. 336.
10. N. A. Romanov (diary), 1 and 4 March 1918 (OS): ibid., p. 411.
11. N. A. Romanov (diary), 13 March 1918 (OS): ibid., p. 412.
12. N. A. Romanov (diary), 6 April 1918 (OS): ibid., p. 418.
13. N. A. Romanov (diary), 10 November; 3 and 13 December 1917; 26 March 1918 (OS): ibid., pp. 339, 342–3 and 414.
14. N. A. Romanov (diary), 19 August 1917 (OS): ibid., p. 329.
15. Baroness Orczy, *The Scarlet Pimpernel* (London: Hodder and Stoughton, 1960), p. 9.
16. N. A. Romanov (diary), 1 and 3 November 1917 (OS): *DINII*, vol. 2, part 2, p. 338 (with reference to: *I Will Repay*; *The Elusive Pimpernel*; *Fire in Stubble*).
17. Baroness Orczy, *The Scarlet Pimpernel*, chap. 28.
18. Ye. S. Kobylinskii (inquiry testimony), 6–10 April 1919: AMDP, HIA, box 1, folder 8, p. 754.
19. N. A. Romanov to M. F. Romanova, 5 March 1918: KAGDRP, HIA, box 8, folder 38.
20. N. A. Romanov to X. A. Romanova, 18 November 1917 (OS): *SPR*, p. 116.

21. N. A. Romanov (diary), 25 and 26 March 1918 (OS): *DINII*, vol. 2, part 2, p. 414.

22. N. A. Romanov (diary), 27 March 1918 (OS): ibid., p. 416.

23. N. Cohn, *Warrant for Genocide: The Myth of the Jewish World-Conspiracy and the Protocols of the Elders of Zion* (London: Eyre and Spottiswood, 1967), p. 115.

24. *The Last Diary of Tsaritsa Alexandra*, 22, 24, 25 and 29 April 1918 (OS), pp. 126–33; N. A. Romanov (diary), 27 March 1918 (OS): *DINII*, vol. 2, part 2, p. 416.

25. N. A. Romanov (diary), 27 March 1918 (OS): ibid., p. 416.

26. K. M. Bitner (inquiry testimony), July 1919: AMDP, HIA, box 1, folder 8, p. 1014.

28: 'OCTOBER' IN JANUARY

1. Father Nicholas (S. Gibbes), 'My Tobolsk Books, Etc., Etc.' (typescript): ibid., pp. 2–3.

2. N. A. Romanov (diary), 18 November 1917 (OS): *DINII*, vol. 2, part 2, p. 340.

3. Ye. S. Kobylinskii (inquiry testimony), 6–10 April 1919: AMDP, HIA, box 1, folder 8, p. 734.

4. Ibid., pp. 734 and 736.

5. Ibid., p. 755.

6. N. A. Romanov (diary), 14 March 1918 (OS): *DINII*, vol. 2, part 2, p. 414.

7. Pankratov, *So tsarëm v Tobol'ske*, pp. 58–60.

8. Markov, *Pokinutaya tsarskaya sem'ya*, photo opposite p. 240.

9. Ye. S. Kobylinskii (inquiry testimony), 6–10 April 1919: AMDP, HIA, box 1, folder 8, p. 729.

10. Father Nicholas (S. Gibbes), 'Ten Years with the Russian Imperial Family' (typescript): SGC, SCBLOU, box 1, p. 7.

11. Pankratov, *So tsarëm v Tobol'ske*, p. 81.

12. *The Last Diary of Tsaritsa Alexandra*, 29 January 1918, p. 22.

13. Ibid., 30 January 1918, p. 23.

14. A. N. Romanova to Ye. E. Zborovskaya, 19 January 1918 (OS): Ekaterina Zborovskaia Papers, box 2.

15. A. N. Romanova to Ye. E. Zborovskaya, 15 October 1917 (OS): ibid.

16. Ye. S. Kobylinskii (inquiry testimony), 6–10 April 1919: AMDP, HIA, box 1, folder 8, pp. 730–1.

17. N. A. Mundel (inquiry testimony), 6 August 1919: ibid., box 1, folder 8, p. 1047.

18. Pankratov, *So tsarëm v Tobol'ske*, pp. 78–9; Ye. S. Kobylinskii (inquiry testimony), 6–10 April 1919: AMDP, HIA, box 1, folder 8, p. 730.

19. Ibid., p. 734.

20. N. A. Romanov (diary), 1–5 January 1918 (OS): *DINII*, vol. 2, part 2, p. 405. Anastasia went down with the illness on 28 January 1918: ibid., p. 407; S. Buxhoeveden (diary), 1 January 1918 (OS): AMDP, HIA, box 1, folder 7,

p. 440. I have identified Buxhoeveden from the internal evidence of the diary, notably from the date of her expulsion from the Kornilov house.

21. S. Buxhoeveden (diary), 18 January 1918 (OS): AMDP, HIA, box 1, folder 7, p. 440.
22. Pankratov, *So tsarëm v Tobol'ske*, p. 86.
23. Ibid.
24. Ibid., p. 87.
25. Ibid., p. 89.
26. N. A. Romanov to M. F. Romanova, 5 March 1918 (OS): KAGDRP, HIA, box 8, folder 38.
27. *The Last Diary of Tsaritsa Alexandra*, 24 January 1918, p. 17.
28. Mel'nik-Botkina, *Vospominaniya o tsarskoi sem'e*, p. 80; S. Buxhoeveden, *The Life and Tragedy of Alexandra Feodorovna, Empress of Russia: A Biography* (London: Longman, Green and Co., 1929), pp. 314–15.
29. *The Last Diary of Tsaritsa Alexandra*, 24 January 1918, p. 17.
30. S. Buxhoeveden (diary), 27 January 1918 (OS): AMDP, HIA, box 1, folder 7, p. 441.
31. Mel'nik-Botkina, *Vospominaniya o tsarskoi sem'e*, p. 86.
32. Pankratov, *So tsarëm v Tobol'ske*, p. 88.
33. O. N. Romanova to M. S. Khitrovo, 19 February 1918 (OS): Alexandre Tarsaidze Papers, Subject File, Letters, HIA, box 16, folder 4.
34. Mel'nik-Botkina, *Vospominaniya o tsarskoi sem'e*, p. 86.
35. Ibid.
36. Ye. S. Kobylinskii (inquiry testimony), 6–10 April 1919: AMDP, HIA, box 1, folder 8, p. 734.
37. O. N. Romanova to M. S. Khitrovo, 19 February 1918: Alexandre Tarsaidze Papers, Subject File, Letters, HIA, box 16, folder 4.
38. T. N. Romanova to M. S. Khitrovo, 19 February 1918: ibid.

21: THE MOSCOW DISCUSSIONS

1. Sovnarkom minutes, 29 January 1918: Gosudarstvennyi Arkhiv Rossiiskoi Federatsii (hereafter GARF), f. 130, op. 23, d. 7, p. 170.
2. L. Bryant, *Six Red Months in Russia: An Observer's Account of Russia before and during the Proletarian Dictatorship* (New York: George H. Doran, 1918), chap. 24.
3. Sovnarkom minutes, 29 January 1918: GARF, f. 130, op. 23, d. 7, p. 170; M. P. Iroshnikov, *Sozdanie sovetskogo tsentral'nogo apparata: Sovet narodnykh komissarov i narodnye komissariaty, oktyabr' 1917 g. – yanvar' 1918 g.* (Moscow/Leningrad: Nauka, 1966), p. 265.
4. Sovnarkom minutes, 20 February 1918: GARF, f. 130, op. 23, d. 8, p. 204.
5. Gilliard, *Le tragique destin de Nicolas II et de sa famille*, p. 213; Ye. S. Kobylinskii (inquiry testimony), 6–10 April 1919: AMDP, HIA, box 1, folder 8,

p. 736; S. Buxhoeveden (diary), 10 March 1918 (OS): ibid., box 1, folder 7, p. 442.

6. N. A. Romanov (diary), 14 February 1918 (OS): *DINII*, vol. 2, part 2, p. 410.

7. P. Gilliard (inquiry testimony), 5–6 March 1919: AMDP, HIA, box 1, folder 7, p. 461.

8. F. N. Gorshkov (inquiry testimony), 31 July 1918: ibid., folder 8, p. 7; S. Buxhoeveden (diary), 10 March 1918 (OS): ibid., box 1, folder 7, p. 442. In the latter source the number of fired staff is put at eleven.

9. Mel'nik-Botkina, *Vospominaniya o tsarskoi sem'e*, p. 87.

10. Ibid.

11. *The Last Diary of Tsaritsa Alexandra*, 4 and 17 March and 2 April 1918, pp. 56, 69 and 85.

12. Mel'nik-Botkina, *Vospominaniya o tsarskoi sem'e*, p. 87.

13. Ibid.

M. A. Medvedev, 'Predystoriya rasstrela tsarskoi sem'i Romanovykh v 1918 godu': Rossiiskii Gosudarstvennyi Arkhiv Sotsial'no-Politicheskoi Istorii (hereafter RGASPI), f. 558, op. 3s, d. 12, in DAVP, HIA, box 15, p. 20.

14. N. A. Romanov (diary), 13 March 1918 (OS): *DINII*, vol. 2, part 2, p. 414.

15. Central Committee meeting, 23 February 1918: *Protokoly Tsentral'nogo Komiteta RSDRP(b), avgust 1917 – fevral' 1918* (Moscow: Gosudarstvennoe izdatel'stvo politicheskoi literatury, 1958), p. 215.

16. *Skorbnaya pamyatka*, p. 64.

17. P. Gilliard, notes appended to letter (29 April 1934?) to N. de Basily, p. 2.

18. *Skorbnaya pamyatka*, p. 68.

22: RESCUE PLANS

1. Diterikhs, *Ubiistvo tsarskoi sem'i i chlenov doma Romanovykh na Urale*, part 1, p. 81; see also P. M. Bykov, *Poslednie dni Romanovykh* (Sverdlovsk: Izdatel'stvo 'Ural'skiï rabochiï', 1990), p. 81; P. P. Bulygin, *The Murder of the Romanovs: the Authentic Account* (London: Hutchinson, 1935), p. 216.

2. B. N. Solo'ëv, 29 December 1919 (inquiry testimony): N. Ross, *Gibel' tsarskoi sem'i: materialy sledstviya* (Frankfurt am Main: Posev, 1986) (hereafter *GTSMS*), p. 497.

3. Interview of A. F. Kerenskii, 14–20 August 1920: DAVP, HIA, box 22, pp. 109b and 117.

4. N. Sokolov, *Ubiistvo tsarskoi sem'i* (Berlin: Slovo, 1925), pp. 95–6.

5. B. N. Solo'ëv, 29 December 1919 (inquiry testimony): *GTSMS*, p. 496.

6. Ibid., p. 497.

7. Ibid.

8. Sokolov, *Ubiistvo tsarskoi sem'i*, pp. 89–90.

9. B. N. Solo'ëv, 29 December 1919 (inquiry testimony): *GTSMS*, p. 498.

10. *The Last Diary of Tsaritsa Alexandra*, 4 February 1918, p. 28.

11. B. N. Solo'ëv, 29 December 1919 (inquiry testimony): *GTSMS*, p. 498.

12. *The Last Diary of Tsaritsa Alexandra*, 6 February 1918, p. 30; Markov, *Pokinutaya tsarskaya sem'ya*, p. 256.
13. Ibid., p. 259.
14. Ibid., p. 262.
15. Sokolov, *Ubiistvo tsarskoi sem'i*, pp. 89–90 and 94.
16. Ibid., p. 103.
17. Ibid.
18. Ibid., pp. 94–5.
19. Mel'nik-Botkina, *Vospominaniya o tsarskoi sem'e*, p. 75.
20. K. S. Melnik, 2 November 1919 (inquiry testimony): *GTSMS*, p. 491; Sokolov, *Ubiistvo tsarskoi sem'i*, pp. 94–5.
21. Mel'nik-Botkina, *Vospominaniya o tsarskoi sem'e*, p. 76.
22. Ibid., p. 75.
23. Ibid., pp. 76–7.
24. Ibid., pp. 89–90 and 94; Bulygin, *The Murder of the Romanovs: the Authentic Account*, p. 217.
25. K. S. Mel'nik, 2 November 1919 (inquiry testimony): *GTSMS*, p. 491.
26. Markov, *Pokinutaya tsarskaya sem'ya*, pp. 83–4.
27. Ibid., p. 47.
28. Ibid., p. 188.
29. Ibid., pp. 194–5, 197 and 216.
30. Ibid., p. 248.
31. Ibid., p. 249.
32. Ibid., pp. 256 and 261.
33. Mel'nik-Botkina, *Vospominaniya o tsarskoi sem'e*, pp. 78–9.
34. Markov, *Pokinutaya tsarskaya sem'ya*, p. 220.
35. Ibid., p. 221.
36. *The Last Diary of Tsaritsa Alexandra*, 25 March 1918, p. 77.
37. Markov, *Pokinutaya tsarskaya sem'ya*, p. 260.
38. Ibid., p. 233.
39. Mel'nik-Botkina, *Vospominaniya o tsarskoi sem'e*, pp. 77–8.
40. Ibid., p. 78.
41. Ibid.
42. Ibid., pp. 77–8.
43. Ibid., p. 77.

23: THE RUSSIAN FUTURE

1. P. Gilliard to N. de Basily, 29 April 1934 (notes): NABP, HIA, box 2, folder 62, p. 1.
2. N. A. Romanov (diary), 1 February 1918 (OS): *DINII*, vol. 2, part 2, p. 409.
3. N. A. Romanov (diary), 7 February 1918 (OS): ibid., p. 410.
4. N. A. Romanov (diary), 12 February 1918 (OS): ibid.

5. P. A. (sic) Gilliard (inquiry testimony), 5–6 March 1919 (OS): AMDP, HIA, box 1, folder 7, p. 462.

6. Ibid.; Gilliard, *Le tragique destin de Nicolas II et de sa famille*, p. 215.

7. P. A. (sic) Gilliard (inquiry testimony), 27 August 1919: AMDP, HIA, box 1, folder 9, p. 1129.

8. Ye. S. Kobylinskii (inquiry testimony), 6–10 April 1919: ibid., box 1, folder 8, p. 758; K. M. Bitner (inquiry testimony), July 1919: ibid., box 1, folder 8, p. 1016; *Skorbnaya pamyatka*, p. 64.

9. Gilliard, *Le tragique destin de Nicolas II et de sa famille*, p. 215.

10. Ye. S. Kobylinskii (inquiry testimony), 6–10 April 1919: AMDP, HIA, box 1, folder 8, p. 759.

11. A. F. Romanova to A. A. Vyrubova, 22 January 1918: *SPR*, p. 129.

12. Mel'nik-Botkina, *Vospominaniya o tsarskoi sem'e*, p. 84.

13. K. M. Bitner (inquiry testimony), July 1919: AMDP, HIA, box 1, folder 8, p. 1014.

14. Ibid., pp. 1014–15.

15. Ibid., p. 1021.

16. Ibid., pp. 1014–15.

17. S. Gibbes, untitled memoir (typescript): SGC, SCBLOU, box 1, pp. 21–2.

18. K. M. Bitner (inquiry testimony), July 1919: AMDP, HIA, box 1, folder 8, pp. 1016–17.

19. Ibid., p. 1014.

20. Ye. S. Kobylinskii (inquiry testimony), 6–10 April 1919: ibid., box 1, folder 8, p. 755.

21. P. Gilliard to N. de Basily, 29 April 1934 (letter): NABP, HIA, box 2, folder 62.

22. Ibid.

23. K. M. Bitner (inquiry testimony), July 1919: AMDP, HIA, box 1, folder 8, p. 1019.

24. Ibid., p. 1020.

CHAPTER 24: COMRADES ON THE MARCH

1. Testimony of guard official Zentsov, *Poslednie dni poslednego tsarya: inochtozhenie dinastii Romanovykh* (Tver: Tverskoe izdatel'stvo, 1922), p. 11.

2. Gilliard, *Le tragique destin de Nicolas II et de sa famille*, p. 216: 26 March 1918 (diary).

3. Sokolov, *Ubiistvo tsarskoi sem'i*, p. 88.

4. Ye. S. Kobylinskii (inquiry testimony), 6–10 April 1919: AMDP, HIA, box 1, folder 8, p. 738.

5. Ya. M. Yurovskii, 'Poslednii tsar' nashël svoë mesto': RGASPI, f. 3, op. 58, d. 280, in DAVP, HIA, box 15, p. 5.

6. Ibid.

7. Testimony of guard official Zentsov, *Poslednie dni poslednego tsarya: inochtozhenie dinastii Romanovykh*, p. 11.

8. S. Buxhoeveden (diary), 11 and 13 March 1918 (OS): AMDP, HIA, box 1, folder 7, p. 443.

9. Mel'nik-Botkina, *Vospominaniya o tsarskoi sem'e*, p. 86.

10. Ibid.

11. Ibid., p. 84.

12. Gilliard, *Le tragique destin de Nicolas II et de sa famille*, p. 216; N. A. Romanov (diary), 29 March 1918 (OS): *DINII*, vol. 2, part 2, p. 416.

13. N. A. Mundel (inquiry testimony), 6 August 1919: AMDP, HIA, box 1, folder 8, p. 1047.

14. Ye. S. Kobylinskii (inquiry testimony), 6–10 April 1919: ibid., box 1, folder 8, p. 738.

15. V. M. Kosarev to V. I. Lenin and L. D. Trotskii, 28 March 1918: *SPR*, p. 137.

16. N. A. Romanov (diary), 22 March 1918 (OS): *DINII*, vol. 2, part 2, p. 415.

17. N. A. Romanov (diary), 28 March 1918 (OS): ibid., p. 416.

18. N. A. Romanov (diary), 23 March 1918 (OS): ibid.; A. V. Gendrikova (diary), 1 April 1918: ibid., p. 443.

19. Mel'nik-Botkina, *Vospominaniya o tsarskoi sem'e*, p. 84.

20. N. A. Romanov (diary), 22 March 1918 (OS): *DINII*, vol. 2, part 2, p. 415.

21. A. G. Beloborodov, 'Iz vospominanii', dated February 1922: A. N. Avdonin, *V zhernovakh revolyutsii: dokumental'nyi ocherk o komissare V. V. Yakovleve* (Ekaterinburg: Bank kul'turnoi informatsii, 1995) (hereafter *VZR*), p. 203.

22. Ibid.

23. P. M. Bykov, 'Poslednie dni poslednego tsarya', in N. I. Nikolaev (ed.), *Rabochaya revolyutsiya na Urale: epizody i fakty* (Ekaterinburg: Gosizdat, Ural'skoe Oblastnoe Upravlenie, 1921), pp. 6–7.

24. Testimony of guard official Zentsov, *Poslednie dni poslednego tsarya: inochtozhenie dinastii Romanovykh*, p. 11.

25. Bykov, *Poslednie dni Romanovykh*, p. 88.

26. Ya. M. Yurovskii, 'Poslednii tsar' nashël svoë mesto': RGASPI, f. 3, op. 58, d. 280, in DAVP, HIA, box 15, p. 5; Ye. S. Kobylinskii (inquiry testimony), 6–10 April 1919: AMDP, HIA, box 1, folder 8, p. 751.

27. F. N. Gorshkov (inquiry testimony), 31 July 1918: ibid., box 1, folder 6, p. 9.

28. A. G. Beloborodov, 'Iz vospominanii', dated February 1922: *VZR*, p. 204.

29. Bykov, *Poslednie dni Romanovykh*, p. 88.

30. Ya. M. Yurovskii, 'Poslednii tsar' nashël svoë mesto': RGASPI, f. 3, op. 58, d. 280, in DAVP, HIA, box 15, p. 5.

31. A. G. Beloborodov, 'Iz vospominanii', dated February 1922: *VZR*, p. 204.

32. Bykov, 'Poslednie dni poslednego tsarya', pp. 6–7.

33. Ibid.

34. See Bykov, *Poslednie dni Romanovykh*, p. 88.

35. Ye. S. Kobylinskii (inquiry testimony), 6–10 April 1919: AMDP, HIA, box 1, folder 8, p. 766.

36. S. Buxhoeveden (diary), 11 and 13 March 1918 (OS): ibid., box 1, folder 7, pp. 443–4.
37. Bykov, 'Poslednie dni poslednego tsarya', p. 9.
38. Ye. S. Kobylinskii (inquiry testimony), 6–10 April 1919: AMDP, HIA, box 1, folder 8, pp. 738–9.
39. Imperial family breakfast and lunch menus, 22–29 April 1918 (OS?): SGC, SCBLOU, box 2.
40. K. M. Bitner (inquiry testimony), July 1919: AMDP, HIA, box 1, folder 8, p. 1022.
41. N. A. Romanov (diary), 11 April 1918 (OS): DINII, vol. 2, part 2, p. 419.
42. N. A. Romanov (diary), 19 March 1918 (OS): DINII, vol. 2, part 2, p. 415.

25: TOBOLSK AND MOSCOW

1. S. Buxhoeveden (diary), 7 March 1918 (OS): ibid., box 1, folder 7, p. 442.
2. Tobol'skii rabochii, 31 March 1918.
3. Ibid., 16 April 1918.
4. S. Buxhoeveden (diary), 3 March 1918 (OS): AMDP, HIA, box 1, folder 7, p. 443.
5. Ye. S. Kobylinskii (inquiry testimony), 6–10 April 1919: ibid., box 1, folder 8, p. 732.
6. V. D. Bonch-Bruevich to V. A. Avanesov, 1 April 1918: DINII, vol. 2, part 2, pp. 442–3.
7. Minutes of VTsIK Presidium, 1 April 1918: V. V. Alexeev, Gibel' tsarskoi sem'i: mify i real'nost': novye dokumenty o tragedii na Urale (Ekaterinburg: Bank kul'turnoi informatsii, 1993), p. 52.
8. F. N. Gorshkov (inquiry testimony), 31 July 1918: AMDP, HIA, box 1, folder 6, p. 7.
9. Minutes of VTsIK Presidium, 6 April 1918: SPR, p. 53.
10. Ya. M. Sverdlov to Urals Regional Soviet, 9 April 1918: ibid., pp. 53–4.
11. See I. F. Plotnikov, Pravda Istorii: gibel' tsarskoi sem'i (Ekaterinburg: Sverdlovskaya regional'naya obshchestvennaya organizatsiya, 2002) (hereafter PIGTS), p. 156.
12. F. P. Proskuryakov (inquiry testimony), 1–3 April 1919: AMDP, HIA, box 1, folder 7, p. 644.
13. S. G. Loginov, 4 April 1919 (inquiry testimony): GTSMS, p. 289.
14. Ibid.
15. V. V. Yakovlev's notes (from the personal archives of L. K. Karpovaya), reproduced in VZR, p. 18.
16. Aksyuta (speech), minutes of general meeting of guard detachment, 22 April 1918: SPR, p. 142.
17. Ye. S. Kobylinskii (inquiry testimony), 6–10 April 1919: AMDP, HIA, box 1, folder 8, p. 732.

18. Ibid., p. 737; Father Nicholas (S. Gibbes), 'Ten Years with the Russian Imperial Family' (typescript): SGC, SCBLOU, box 1, p. 8.
19. K. A. Stoyanovich (V. V. Yakovlev), draft notes for projected book, June–July 1928, reproduced in *VZR*, p. 162.
20. N. A. Romanov (diary), 30 March 1918 (OS): *DINII*, vol. 2, part 2, p. 417.
21. N. A. Romanov (diary), 31 March 1918 (OS): ibid.
22. N. A. Romanov (diary), 1 April 1918 (OS): ibid.
23. B. V. Didkovskii to V. I. Lenin and Ya. M. Sverdlov, 13 April 1918: *SPR*, p. 54.
24. N. A. Romanov (diary), 2 April 1918 (OS): *DINII*, vol. 2, part 2, p. 417; Ye. S. Kobylinskii (inquiry testimony), 6–10 April 1919: AMDP, HIA, box 1, folder 8, p. 734.
25. Ibid., p. 735.
26. Ibid., p. 736; N. A. Romanov (diary), 8 April 1918 (OS): *DINII*, vol. 2, part 2, p. 418.
27. F. I. Goloshchëkin to P. D. Khokhryakov, 21 April 1918: *SPR*, p. 140.

26: COMMISSAR YAKOVLEV

1. Ya. M. Sverdlov to Urals leaders (Ekaterinburg), 9 April 1918, reproduced in *PIGTS*, p. 38.
2. Ye. S. Kobylinskii (inquiry testimony), 6–10 April 1919: AMDP, HIA, box 1, folder 8, p. 739.
3. K. A. Stoyanovich (V. V. Yakovlev) to I. V. Stalin and V. R. Menzhinskii, 15 March 1928, reproduced in *VZR*, p. 152.
4. Ibid., p. 153.
5. Ibid., p. 154.
6. Minutes of guard detachment meeting, 22 April 1918: *SPR*, p. 141.
7. Ibid., pp. 141–2; N. A. Mundel (inquiry testimony), 6 August 1919: AMDP, HIA, box 1, folder 8, p. 1048.
8. Minutes of general meeting of guard detachment, 22 April 1918: *SPR*, pp. 141–2; K. A. Stoyanovich (V. V. Yakovlev), draft notes for projected book, June–July 1928, reproduced in *VZR*, p. 162.
9. Minutes of guard detachment meeting, 22 April 1918: *SPR*, pp. 46 and 55–6; N. A. Mundel (inquiry testimony), 6 August 1919: AMDP, HIA, box 1, folder 8, p. 1048.
10. N. A. Romanov (diary), 9 April 1918 (OS): *DINII*, vol. 2, part 2, p. 418.
11. N. A. Romanov (diary), 10 April 1918 (OS): ibid., p. 419.
12. The inspection report of 23 April 1918 is reproduced in *PIGTS*, pp. 42–3; N. A. Romanov (diary), 10 April 1918 (OS): *DINII*, vol. 2, part 2, p. 419.
13. Inspection report of 23 April 1918: *PIGTS*, p. 43.
14. A. A. Volkov (inquiry testimony), 20–23 August 1919: AMDP, HIA, box 1, folder 9, p. 1107.
15. Father Nicholas (S. Gibbes), 'Ten Years with the Russian Imperial Family' (typescript): SGC, SCBLOU, box 1, p. 8.

16. N. A. Mundel (inquiry testimony), 6 August 1919: AMDP, HIA, box 1, folder 8, p. 1048; Ye. S. Kobylinskii (inquiry testimony), 6–10 April 1919: ibid., HIA, box 1, folder 8, p. 739.

17. Father Nicholas (S. Gibbes), untitled memoir (typescript): SGC, SCBLOU, box 1, p. 15.

18. V. V. Yakovlev: minutes of Ufa meeting of 1st and 2nd Red Army *druzhiny*, 3 May 1918, reproduced in *VZR*, p. 147; A G. Beloborodov, 'Iz vospominanii', dated February 1922: *VZR*, p. 205.

19. Ibid., p. 204.

20. Ibid., p. 205.

21. V. V. Yakovlev: minutes of Ufa meeting of 1st and 2nd Red Army *druzhiny*, 3 May 1918, reproduced in *VZR*, p. 147.

22. Ya. M. Yurovskii, 'Poslednii tsar' nashël svoë mesto': RGASPI, f. 3, op. 58, d. 280, in DAVP, HIA, box 15, pp. 5–6.

27: THE ORDER TO MOVE

1. Ye. S. Kobylinskii (inquiry testimony), 6–10 April 1919: AMDP, HIA, box 1, folder 8, pp. 742–3.

2. Ibid., p. 743.

3. Ibid.

4. P. A. (sic) Gilliard (inquiry testimony), 27 August 1919: ibid., box 1, folder 9, pp. 1125–7.

5. Ibid., p. 1127.

6. Ye. S. Kobylinskii (inquiry testimony), 6–10 April 1919: ibid., box 1, folder 8, p. 744; S. Buxhoeveden (diary), 7 March 1918 (OS): ibid., box 1, folder 7, p. 445.

7. A. A. Volkov (inquiry testimony), 20–23 August 1919: ibid., box 1, folder 9, p. 1109.

8. Ibid.

9. P. A. (sic) Gilliard (inquiry testimony), 27 August 1919: ibid., box 1, folder 9, p. 1126.

10. M. G. Tutelberg (inquiry testimony), 1919: ibid., box 1, folder 8, p. 978.

11. Interview with V. V. Yakovlev: *Izvestiya*, 16 May 1918.

12. Ye. S. Kobylinskii (inquiry testimony), 6–10 April 1919: AMDP, HIA, box 1, folder 8, p. 744.

13. Ibid.

14. I. A. Teodorovich and V. V. Yakovlev (Hughes telegraph conversation), n.d.: *SPR*, pp. 143–4.

15. N. A. Mundel (inquiry testimony), 6 August 1919: AMDP, HIA, box 1, folder 8, p. 1049.

16. Ye. S. Kobylinskii (inquiry testimony), 6–10 April 1919: ibid., box 1, folder 8, pp. 745–6.

17. V. V. Yakovlev: minutes of Ufa meeting of 1st and 2nd Red Army *druzhiny*, 3 May 1918, reproduced in *VZR*, p. 147.
18. D. M. Chudinov, 'Kak my pervozili byvshuyu tsarskuyu sem'yu': *VZR*, p. 210.
19. Ibid.
20. F. N. Gorshkov (inquiry testimony), 31 July 1918: AMDP, HIA, box 1, folder 6, p. 8.
21. M. G. Tutelberg (inquiry testimony), 23–27 July 1919: ibid., box 1, folder 8, p. 979.
22. Father Nicholas (S. Gibbes), 'Ten Years with the Russian Imperial Family' (typescript): SGC, SCBLOU, box 1, p. 9.
23. Ibid., pp. 9–10.
24. Ye. S. Kobylinskii (inquiry testimony), 6–10 April 1919: AMDP, HIA, box 1, folder 8, p. 746.
25. S. I. Ivanov (inquiry testimony), 19 July 1919: ibid., box 1, folder 8, p. 950; A. A. Volkov (inquiry testimony), 20–23 August 1919: ibid., box 1, folder 9, p. 1110.

28: SOUTH TO TYUMEN

1. D. M. Chudinov, 'Kak my pervozili byvshuyu tsarskuyu sem'yu': *VZR*, pp. 210–11.
2. Father Nicholas (S. Gibbes), 'Ten Years with the Russian Imperial Family' (typescript): SGC, SCBLOU, box 1, pp. 9–10.
3. D. M. Chudinov, 'Kak my pervozili byvshuyu tsarskuyu sem'yu': *VZR*, p. 211.
4. N. A. Mundel (inquiry testimony), reporting on what he heard from the returning escort, 6 August 1919: AMDP, HIA, box 1, folder 8, p. 1050.
5. N. A. Romanov (diary), 13 April 1918 (OS): *DINII*, vol. 2, part 2, p. 419; *The Last Diary of Tsaritsa Alexandra*, 26 April 1918, p. 109.
6. Ye. S. Kobylinskii (inquiry testimony), 6–10 April 1919: AMDP, HIA, box 1, folder 8, p. 749.
7. See Bykov, *Poslednie dni Romanovykh*, p. 96.
8. V. V. Yakovlev to F. I. Goloshchëkin, 27 April 1918: *SPR*, pp. 144–6.
9. N. A. Romanov (diary), 14 April 1918 (OS): *DINII*, vol. 2, part 2, pp. 419–20.
10. V. V. Yakovlev to Ya. M. Sverdlov, 27 April 1918, reproduced in *SPR*, p. 58; V. V. Yakovlev to F. I. Goloshchëkin, 27 April 1918, reproduced ibid., p. 60.
11. N. A. Romanov (diary), 14 April 1918 (OS): *DINII*, vol. 2, part 2, pp. 419–20.
12. Interview with V. V. Yakovlev: *Izvestiya*, 16 May 1918.
13. D. M. Chudinov, 'Kak my perevozili byvshuyu tsarskuyu sem'yu': *VZR*, p. 212.
14. Ibid., p. 211.
15. Ibid., p. 212.
16. N. A. Romanov (diary), 14 April 1918 (OS): *DINII*, vol. 2, part 2, p. 420; Ye. S. Kobylinskii (inquiry testimony), 6–10 April 1919: AMDP, HIA, box 1,

folder 8, p. 747; D. M. Chudinov, 'Kak my pervozili byvshuyu tsarskuyu sem'yu': *VZR*, p. 212.

17. V. V. Yakovlev: minutes of Ufa meeting of 1st and 2nd Red Army *druzhiny*, 3 May 1918, reproduced in *VZR*, pp. 147–8; A. I. Nevolin (written testimony), 3 May 1918: *SPR*, pp. 156–7.

18. V. V. Yakovlev: minutes of Ufa meeting of 1st and 2nd Red Army *druzhiny*, 3 May 1918, reproduced in *VZR*, pp. 147–8; A. I. Nevolin (written testimony), 3 May 1918: *SPR*, pp. 156–7.

19. N. A. Romanov (diary), 14 April 1918 (OS): *DINII*, vol. 2, part 2, p. 420; Ye. S. Kobylinskii (inquiry testimony), 6–10 April 1919: AMDP, HIA, box 1, folder 8, p. 747.

20. M. G. Tutelberg (inquiry testimony), 1919: ibid., box 1, folder 8, p. 978.

21. N. A. Romanov (diary), 14 April 1918 (OS): *DINII*, vol. 2, part 2, p. 420; interview with V. V. Yakovlev: *Izvestiya*, 16 May 1918.

22. Markov, *Pokinutaya tsarskaya sem'ya*, p. 295.

23. Ibid.

24. Ibid.

25. N. A. Romanov (diary), 14 April 1918 (OS): *DINII*, vol. 2, part 2, p. 420; *The Last Diary of Tsaritsa Alexandra*, 14 April 1918 (OS), p. 112.

26. Markov, *Pokinutaya tsarskaya sem'ya*, pp. 273, 280 and 297.

27. Ibid., p. 295.

28. N. A. Romanov (diary), 14 April 1918 (OS): *DINII*, vol. 2, part 2, p. 420.

29. See Bykov, *Poslednie dni Romanovykh*, p. 97.

30. Ibid.

31. Ya. M. Yurovskii, 'Poslednii tsar' nashël svoë mesto': RGASPI, f. 3, op. 58, d. 280, in DAVP, HIA, box 15, p. 6.

32. V. V. Yakovlev to Ya. M. Sverdlov, 27 April 1918, reproduced in *SPR*, pp. 58–9.

33. V. V. Yakovlev to Ya. M. Sverdlov (Hughes apparatus exchange), 27 April 1918, reproduced ibid., p. 59.

34. V. V. Yakovlev to F. I. Goloshchëkin, 27 April 1918, reproduced ibid., p. 60.

35. Ya. M. Yurovskii, 'Poslednii tsar' nashël svoë mesto': RGASPI, f. 3, op. 58, d. 280, in DAVP, HIA, box 15, p. 6.

29: DESTINATION TO BE CONFIRMED

1. Bykov, *Poslednie dni Romanovykh*, p. 97.

2. Snodgrass, *Bureau of Foreign and Domestic Commerce*, p. 43.

3. V. V. Yakovlev: minutes of Ufa meeting of 1st and 2nd Red Army *druzhiny*, 3 May 1918, reproduced in *VZR*, p. 148; A. G. Beloborodov, 'Iz vospominanii', dated February 1922: *VZR*, p. 206.

4. Ya. M. Yurovskii, 'Poslednii tsar' nashël svoë mesto': RGASPI, f. 3, op. 58, d. 280, in DAVP, HIA, box 15, p. 6.

5. Ibid., pp. 6–7.

6. Ibid., p. 7.

7. A. G. Beloborodov and G. I. Safarov to V. I. Lenin and Ya. M. Sverdlov, 28 April 1918: *SPR*, pp. 147–8.

8. A. G. Beloborodov, telegram to Omsk and elsewhere, 28 April 1918, reproduced in *SPR*, pp. 148–8; A. G. Beloborodov, 'Iz vospominanii', dated February 1922: *VZR*, p. 206.

9. Bykov, 'Poslednie dni poslednego tsarya', p. 11.

10. Ibid.

11. Ye. S. Kobylinskii (inquiry testimony), 6–10 April 1919: AMDP, HIA, box 1, folder 8, p. 747.

12. Interview with V. V. Yakovlev: *Izvestiya*, 16 May 1918.

13. N. A. Romanov (diary), 14–15 April 1918 (OS): *DINII*, vol. 2, part 2, p. 420.

14. Bykov, *Poslednie dni Romanovykh*, pp. 98–9; S. Gibbes to Sir Charles Elliot (note), n.d., but possibly an attachment to letter of 15 April 1919: SGC, SCBLOU, box 2.

15. A. G. Beloborodov, 'Iz vospominanii', dated February 1922: *VZR*, p. 206; G. I. Safarov and V. M. Kosarev (Hughes apparatus), 29 April 1918, reproduced in *SPR*, pp. 64–5.

16. V. V. Yakovlev: minutes of Ufa meeting of 1st and 2nd Red Army *druzhiny*, 3 May 1918, reproduced in *VZR*, p. 148; Bykov, *Poslednie dni Romanovykh*, pp. 98–9; Ya. M. Yurovskii, 'Poslednii tsar' nashël svoë mesto': RGASPI, f. 3, op. 58, d. 280, in DAVP, HIA, box 15, p. 7.

17. Ya. M. Sverdlov to V. V. Yakovlev, 28 April 1918: *SPR*, p. 149.

18. V. V. Yakovlev: minutes of Ufa meeting of 1st and 2nd Red Army *druzhiny*, 3 May 1918, reproduced in *VZR*, p. 148.

19. Ya. M. Sverdlov to Urals Regional Soviet leadership, 29 April 1918, reproduced in *SPR*, p. 63.

20. Urals Regional Soviet to Ya. M. Sverdlov (telegram), 29 April 1918, reproduced in *VZR*, p. 139.

21. L. A. Lykova (ed.), *Sledstvie po delu ob ubiistve Rossiiskoi imperatorskoi sem'i* (Moscow: Rosspen, 2007), pp. 269–70.

22. A. G. Beloborodov to V. M. Kosarev, 29 April, reproduced in *SPR*, p. 65.

23. A. G. Beloborodov to S. S. Zaslavski, 29 April, reproduced ibid., pp. 67–8.

24. Ya. M. Sverdlov to V. V. Yakovlev, 28 April 1918, reproduced ibid., p. 64.

25. Ibid.

26. Ibid.

27. G. I. Safarov and V. M. Kosarev (Hughes apparatus exchange), 29 April 1918, reproduced ibid., pp. 64–5.

28. V. M. Kosarev (telegram order), 29 April 1918, reproduced in *VZR*, p. 148.

29. V. V. Yakovlev to Ya. M. Sverdlov, 29 April 1918: *SPR*, p. 152.

30. See Bykov, *Poslednie dni Romanovykh*, p. 100.

31. Ibid., pp. 100–1.

32. N. A. Romanov (diary), 16 April 1918 (OS): *DINII*, vol. 2, part 2, p. 420.

33. N. A. Romanov (diary), 17 April 1918 (OS): ibid.

34. Interview with V. V. Yakovlev: *Izvestiya*, 16 May 1918.

38: TO THE IPATEV HOUSE

1. A. G. Beloborodov, 'Iz vospominanii', dated February 1922: *VZR*, p. 206; see also *PIGTS*, p. 71.
2. Site report of N. A. Sokolov, 15–25 April 1919: AMDP, HIA, box 1, folder 9, p. 1381.
3. Preston, *Before the Curtain*, p. 99.
4. Bykov, 'Poslednie dni poslednego tsarya', p. 14.
5. N. N. Ipatev (interview by I. A. Sergeev), 30 November 1918: Lykova (ed.), *Sledstvie po delu ob ubiistve Rossiiskoi imperatorskoi sem'i*, pp. 145–6.
6. A. G. Beloborodov, manuscript memoirs, reproduced in *DINII*, vol. 2, part 2, pp. 450–1; N. N. Ipatev (interview by I. A. Sergeev), 30 November 1918: Lykova (ed.), *Sledstvie po delu ob ubiistve Rossiiskoi imperatorskoi sem'i*, p. 146. See also *PIGTS*, p. 71.
7. Bykov, 'Poslednie dni poslednego tsarya'; Bykov, *Poslednie dni Romanovykh*, p. 102.
8. A. G. Beloborodov, manuscript memoirs, reproduced in *DINII*, vol. 2, part 2, pp. 450–1; see also *PIGTS*, p. 71.
9. R. L. Jefferson, *Roughing It In Siberia, With Some Account of the Trans-Siberian Railway, and the Gold-Mining Industry of Asiatic Russia* (London: Sampson, Low, Marston and Co., 1897), p. 5.
10. N. A. Romanov (diary), 17 April 1918 (OS): *DINII*, vol. 2, part 2, p. 420; Bykov, 'Poslednie dni poslednego tsarya', p. 12; Bykov, *Poslednie dni Romanovykh*, p. 101.
11. V. Yakovlev, 'Poslednii reis Romanovykh', *Ural*, no. 8 (1988): *DINII*, vol. 2, part 2, pp. 446–7.
12. N. A. Romanov (diary), 17 April 1918 (OS): ibid., p. 420; Bykov, 'Poslednie dni poslednego tsarya', p. 12; Bykov, *Poslednie dni Romanovykh*, p. 101; V. Yakovlev, 'Poslednii reis Romanovykh', *Ural*, no. 8 (1988): *DINII*, vol. 2, part 2, p. 447; A. G. Beloborodov, 'Iz vospominanii', dated February 1922: *VZR*, p. 207.
13. N. A. Romanov (diary), 17 April 1918 (OS): *DINII*, vol. 2, part 2, p. 420; Bykov, 'Poslednie dni poslednego tsarya', p. 12; Bykov, *Poslednie dni Romanovykh*, p. 101; V. Yakovlev, 'Poslednii reis Romanovykh', *Ural*, no. 8 (1988): *DINII*, vol. 2, part 2, p. 447.
14. N. A. Romanov (diary), 17 April 1918 (OS): *DINII*, vol. 2, part 2, p. 420; Bykov, 'Poslednie dni poslednego tsarya', p. 12; Bykov, *Poslednie dni Romanovykh*, p. 101; V. Yakovlev, 'Poslednii reis Romanovykh', *Ural*, no. 8 (1988): *DINII*, vol. 2, part 2, p. 447.
15. A. G. Beloborodov, manuscript memoirs, reproduced in *DINII*, vol. 2, part 2, p. 447.
16. A. G. Beloborodov and B. Z. Didkovski, 30 April 1918: AMDP, HIA, box 1, folder 9, pp. 1397–8. See the photo in N. Sokoloff, *Enquête judiciaire sur*

l'assassinat de la famille impériale russe, avec les preuves, les interrogatoires et les dépositions des témoins et des accusés (Paris: Payot, 1924), p. 16.

17. A. G. Beloborodov, 'Iz vospominanii', dated February 1922: *VZR*, p. 207; Bykov, 'Poslednie dni poslednego tsarya', p. 12.

18. P. T. Samokhvalov, 20–21 November 1919 (inquiry testimony): *GTSMS*, p. 494.

19. P. A. (sic) Gilliard (inquiry testimony) (who reported on what Nabokov and Matveev told him), 5–6 March 1919 (OS): AMDP, HIA, box 1, folder 7, p. 465. According to his book, the soldiers were arrested for only two days: Gilliard, *Le tragique destin de Nicolas II et de sa famille*, p. 223.

20. Ye. S. Kobylinskii (inquiry testimony), 6–10 April 1919: ibid., box 1, folder 8, p. 748.

21. N. A. Mundel (inquiry testimony), 6 August 1919: ibid., box 1, folder 8, p. 1050; Ye. S. Kobylinskii (inquiry testimony), 6–10 April 1919: ibid., box 1, folder 8, p. 748.

22. Bykov, 'Poslednie dni poslednego tsarya', p. 13; Bykov, *Poslednie dni Romanovykh*, p. 103.

23. Urals Regional Soviet Presidium decree, 30 April 1918, reproduced in *SPR*, p. 69.

24. A. G. Beloborodov to V. I. Lenin and Ya. M. Sverdlov, 30 April 1918, reproduced ibid., pp. 70–1.

25. V. V. Yakovlev's notes, quoted in *VZR*, p. 25.

26. Bykov, *Poslednie dni Romanovykh*, p. 104; Bykov, 'Poslednie dni poslednego tsarya', p. 13.

27. V. V. Yakovlev: minutes of Ufa meeting of 1st and 2nd Red Army *druzhiny*, 3 May 1918, reproduced in *VZR*, pp. 147–9.

28. N. A. Mundel (inquiry testimony), 6 August 1919: AMDP, HIA, box 1, folder 8, p. 1050; Ye. S. Kobylinskii (inquiry testimony), 6–10 April 1919: ibid., box 1, folder 8, p. 748.

31: THE URALS AND ITS BOLSHEVIKS

1. Bykov, 'Poslednie dni poslednego tsarya', p. 96.

2. G. Kennan, *Siberia and the Exile System*, vol. 2 (New York: The Century Co., 1891), p. 420.

3. Snodgrass, *Bureau of Foreign and Domestic Commerce*, pp. 123–4 and 139.

4. P. M. Bykov, 'Yekaterinburgskii Sovet', in N. I. Nikolaev (ed.), *Rabochaya revolyutsiya na Urale: epizody i fakty* (Ekaterinburg: Gosizdat, Ural'skoe Oblastnoe Upravlenie, 1921), p. 93.

5. Ibid., pp. 94–5.

6. Ibid.

7. Ibid., p. 98.

8. Ibid.

9. Ibid., pp. 97–9.

10. I. I. Radzinskii, taped memoirs (1963): RGASPI, f. 588, op. 3, d. 14, in DAVP, box 15, pp. 10–11.
11. L. A. Krol, 'Polozhenie na gornozavodskom Urale v kontsa 1917 – pervoi polovine 1918', reproduced in M. Bernshtam (ed.), *Ural i Prikam'e, noyabr' 1918 – yanvar' 1919: dokumenty i materialy* (Paris: YMCA-Press, 1982), p. 50.
12. J. Harris, *The Great Urals: Regionalism and the Evolution of the Soviet System* (Ithaca, NY: Cornell University Press, 1999), p. 22.
13. 'Dioneo' (V. I. Shklovsky), *Russia under the Bolsheviks* (London: Russian Liberation Committee, 1919), pp. 8–12.
14. See V. V. Dublënnykh, *Belaya armiya na Urale: istoricheskie spravki chastei i soedinenii* (Ekaterinburg: Izd. Ural'skogo Universiteta, 2008), p. 313; Yu. Zhuk, *Voprositel'nye znaki v 'tsarskom dele'* (St Petersburg: BkhV-Peterburg, 2013), p. 133.
15. I. I. Serebrennikov, 'Moi vstrechi s atamanom A. I. Dutov': Ivan I. Serebrennikov Papers, HIA, box 11, folder 1, p. 1.
16. Bykov, 'Yekaterinburgskii Sovet', p. 100.
17. Harris, *The Great Urals*, p. 22.
18. Ibid.
19. Ibid.
20. Bykov, 'Yekaterinburgskii Sovet', p. 97.
21. F. I. Goloshchëkin, report to the Regional Party Conference, *Ural'skii rabochii*, 5 January 1918.
22. *Ural'skii rabochii*, 26 January 1918.
23. Ibid., 11 April 1918.
24. M. A. Medvedev, 'Predystoriya rasstrela tsarskoi sem'i Romanovykh v 1918 godu': RGASPI, f. 558, op. 3s, d. 12, in DAVP, box 15, p. 2.
25. N. A. Sakovich (inquiry testimony), 24 August 1918: AMDP, HIA, box 1, folder 6, pp. 19–20.
26. Ibid., p. 20.
27. A. S. Kotousova (inquiry testimony), 18 November 1918: ibid., box 1, folder 6, p. 99.
28. Ye. T. Lobanova (inquiry testimony), 1 August 1918: ibid., box 1, folder 6, p. 12.

32: MEANWHILE, IN TOBOLSK

1. Bykov, 'Poslednie dni poslednego tsarya', p. 13.
2. F. N. Gorshkov (inquiry testimony), 31 July 1918: AMDP, HIA, box 1, folder 6, p. 10.
3. P. A. (sic) Gilliard (inquiry testimony), 5–6 March 1919 (OS): ibid., box 1, folder 7, p. 464; Ye. S. Kobylinskii (inquiry testimony), 6–10 April 1919: ibid., box 1, folder 8, p. 747.
4. Ibid., p. 749; S. Buxhoeveden (diary), 3–4 May 1918 (OS): ibid., box 1, folder 7, p. 446.

5. S. Buxhoeveden (diary), 15 April 1918 (OS): ibid., p. 445.

6. Ye. S. Kobylinskii (inquiry testimony), 6–10 April 1919: AMDP, HIA, box 1, folder 8, p. 749; A. A. Volkov (inquiry testimony), 20–23 August 1919: ibid., box 1, folder 9, p. 1111; A. G. Beloborodov to P. D. Khokhryakov, 6 May 1918: SPR, p. 202.

7. S. Buxhoeveden (diary), 3–4 May 1918 (OS): AMDP, HIA, box 1, folder 7, p. 446.

8. Ye. S. Kobylinskii (inquiry testimony), 6–10 April 1919: ibid., box 1, folder 8, p. 749; A. A. Volkov (inquiry testimony), 20–23 August 1919: ibid., box 1, folder 9, p. 1111; A. G. Beloborodov to P. D. Khokhryakov, 6 May 1918: SPR, p. 202.

9. Markov, Pokinutaya tsarskaya sem'ya, p. 298.

10. A. G. Beloborodov to P. D. Khokhryakov, 6 May 1918: SPR, p. 202.

11. P. A. (sic) Gilliard (inquiry testimony), 5–6 March 1919 (OS): AMDP, HIA, box 1, folder 7, p. 465; Gilliard, Le tragique destin de Nicolas II et de sa famille, p. 223.

12. P. A. (sic) Gilliard (inquiry testimony), 27 August 1919: AMDP, HIA, box 1, folder 9, pp. 1127–8.

13. Gilliard, Le tragique destin de Nicolas II et de sa famille, p. 223; Ye. S. Kobylinskii (inquiry testimony), 6–10 April 1919: AMDP, HIA, box 1, folder 8, pp. 750–1 and 762.

14. Gilliard, Le tragique destin de Nicolas II et de sa famille, p. 223.

15. Volkov, Okolo tsarskoi sem'i, p. 62.

16. Ye. S. Kobylinskii (inquiry testimony), 6–10 April 1919: AMDP, HIA, box 1, folder 8, p. 750.

17. P. A. (sic) Gilliard (inquiry testimony), 5–6 March 1919 (OS): ibid., box 1, folder 7, pp. 464–5.

18. Menu of 29 April 1918: SGC, SCBLOU, box 1.

19. S. Buxhoeveden (diary), 3–4 May 1918 (OS): AMDP, HIA, box 1, folder 7, p. 446.

20. Gilliard, Le tragique destin de Nicolas II et de sa famille, p. 224.

21. P. A. (sic) Gilliard (inquiry testimony), 5–6 March 1919 (OS): AMDP, HIA, box 1, folder 7, p. 466.

22. Ye. S. Kobylinskii (inquiry testimony), 6–10 April 1919: ibid., box 1, folder 8, p. 750.

23. P. A. (sic) Gilliard (inquiry testimony), 5–6 March 1919 (OS): ibid., box 1, folder 7, p. 466.

24. M. G. Solovëva (Rasputina) (diary), 22 May 1918: SPR, p. 206.

25. M. G. Tutelberg (inquiry testimony), 1919: AMDP, HIA, box 1, folder 8, p. 979.

26. P. A. (sic) Gilliard (inquiry testimony), 5–6 March 1919 (OS): ibid., box 1, folder 7, p. 466. According to F. N. Gorshkov, the train arrived in Ekaterinburg on 22 May 1918: F. N. Gorshkov (inquiry testimony), 31 July 1918: ibid., box 1, folder 6, p. 10.

27. P. A. (sic) Gilliard (inquiry testimony), 5–6 March 1919 (OS): ibid., box 1, folder 7, p. 466.
28. Ibid., pp. 466–7.
29. Ipatev house guard duty book, 22 May 1918, reproduced in *SPR*, p. 88.

33: ENDURING EKATERINBURG

1. M. N. Romanova to Tobolsk, 1 May 1918: *SPR*, p. 199.
2. Bykov, 'Poslednie dni poslednego tsarya', p. 17.
3. Bykov, 'Yekaterinburgskii Sovet', p. 101.
4. F. N. Gorshkov (inquiry testimony), 31 July 1918: AMDP, HIA, box 1, folder 6, p. 8; Bykov, 'Poslednie dni poslednego tsarya', p. 14.
5. F. N. Gorshkov (inquiry testimony), 31 July 1918: AMDP, HIA, box 1, folder 6, p. 10.
6. Ya. M. Sverdlov to A. G. Beloborodov, 3 May 1918, *SPR*, p. 201.
7. A. G. Beloborodov to Ya. M. Sverdlov, 3 May 1918: ibid., pp. 201–2.
8. F. P. Proskuryakov (inquiry testimony), 1–3 April 1919: AMDP, HIA, box 1, folder 7, p. 644.
9. This evidently somewhat shocked even the Bolsheviks in Ekaterinburg.
10. I. D. Sednëv and K. G. Nagorny to A. G. Beloborodov, 28 May 1918: AMDP, HIA, box 1, folder 9, pp. 1337–8.
11. P. A. (sic) Gilliard (inquiry testimony), 5–6 March 1919 (OS): ibid., box 1, folder 7, p. 467.
12. G. N. Kotechev (inquiry testimony): ibid., box 1, folder 6, p. 51.
13. M. D. Medvedeva (inquiry testimony), 9–10 November 1918: ibid., box 1, folder 6, p. 57; A. A. Yakimov (inquiry testimony), 2 April 1919: ibid., box 1, folder 8, pp. 803–4; A. G. Beloborodov, 'Iz vospominanii', dated February 1922: *VZR*, p. 208.
14. G. M. Suetin (inquiry testimony, n.d.): AMDP, HIA, box 1, folder 6, p. 52.
15. F. P. Proskuryakov (inquiry testimony), 1–3 April 1919: ibid., box 1, folder 7, p. 640.
16. M. I. Letemin (inquiry testimony), 7 August 1918: ibid., box 1, folder 6, p. 28.
17. F. P. Proskuryakov (inquiry testimony), 1–3 April 1919: ibid., box 1, folder 7, p. 639.
18. Ibid., p. 641.
19. I. V. Storozhev (inquiry testimony), 8–10 October 1918: AMDP, HIA, box 1, folder 6, pp. 71–2.
20. Ibid., pp. 72–4.
21. Ibid., pp. 74–7.
22. F. P. Proskuryakov (inquiry testimony), 1–3 April 1919: AMDP, HIA, box 1, folder 7, p. 643.
23. M. L. Krokhaleva (inquiry testimony), 9 July 1919: ibid., box 1, folder 8, p. 909; P. Ya. Shamarin (procurator) reporting on the testimony of P. Medvedev, 3–5 October 1919: ibid., box 1, folder 9, p. 1353.

24. Ya. M. Yurovskii, 'Poslednii tsar' nashël svoë mesto': RGASPI, f. 3, op. 58, d. 280, in DAVP, HIA, box 15, p. 9.

25. F. N. Gorshkov (inquiry testimony), 31 July 1918: AMDP, HIA, box 1, folder 6, p. 8.

26. P. A. (sic) Gilliard (inquiry testimony), 5–6 March 1919 (OS): ibid., box 1, folder 7, p. 468.

27. F. P. Proskuryakov (inquiry testimony), 1–3 April 1919: ibid., box 1, folder 7, p. 644.

28. N. A. Romanov (diary), 1 May 1918 (OS): *DINII*, vol. 2, part 2, p. 424.

29. *The Last Diary of Tsaritsa Alexandra*, 31 May and 3 June 1918, pp. 152 and 155.

30. Ibid., 21 June 1918, p. 173.

31. P. Ya. Shamarin (procurator) reporting on testimony of P. Medvedev, 3–5 October 1919: AMDP, HIA, box 1, folder 9, p. 1354.

32. G. M. Suetin (inquiry testimony, n.d.): ibid., box 1, folder 6, p. 52.

33. P. Ya. Shamarin (procurator) reporting on testimony of P. S. Medvedev, 3–5 October 1919: ibid., box 1, folder 9, p. 1364.

34. Ya. M. Yurovskii, 'Poslednii tsar' nashël svoë mesto': RGASPI, f. 3, op. 58, d. 280, in DAVP, HIA, box 15, p. 11.

35. F. P. Proskuryakov (inquiry testimony), 1–3 April 1919: AMDP, HIA, box 1, folder 7, p. 643.

36. N. A. Romanov (diary), 24 and 25 May 1918 (OS): *DINII*, vol. 2, part 2, p. 429.

37. Testimony of K. L. Sobolev, 30 August 1919 (OS): AMDP, HIA, box 1, folder 9, p. 1131.

38. I. I. Radzinskii, taped memoirs (1963): RGASPI, f. 588, op. 3, d. 14, in DAVP, box 15, p. 10.

39. Preston, *Before the Curtain*, p. 98.

40. *Poslednie dni poslednego tsarya: inochtozhenie dinastii Romanovykh*, p. 9; M. A. Medvedev, 'Predystoriya rasstrela tsarskoi sem'i Romanovykh v 1918 godu': RGASPI, f. 558, op. 3s, d. 12, in DAVP, box 15, p. 7.

41. Bykov, 'Poslednie dni poslednego tsarya', pp. 16–17.

42. I. I. Radzinskii, taped memoirs (1963): RGASPI, f. 588, op. 3, d. 14, in DAVP, box 15, p. 28.

43. A. D. Avdeev, 'Nikolai Romanov v Tobol'ske I Yekaterinburge. Iz vospomina-nii komendanta', *Krasnaya nov'*, no. 5 (1928), pp. 185–209.

44. I. I. Radzinskii, taped memoirs (1963): RGASPI, f. 588, op. 3, d. 14, in DAVP, box 15, pp. 23–5.

45. First letter of an 'officer' to the Romanov family, no later than 20 June 1918: *SPR*, p. 210.

46. Letters between an 'officer' and the Romanov family, ending no later than 4 July 1918: ibid., pp. 212–14.

47. N. A. Romanov (diary), 19 April 1918 (OS): *DINII*, vol. 2, part 2, p. 421; Ipatev house guard duty book, 7 June 1918, reproduced in *SPR*, p. 89.

48. N. A. Romanov (diary), 28 May 1918 (OS): *DINII*, vol. 2, part 2, p. 429.

49. Ipatev house guard duty book, 9 July 1918, reproduced in *SPR*, p. 91.

34: A SENSE OF THE WORLD

1. N. A. Romanov (diary), 28 May 1918 (OS): *DINII*, vol. 2, part 2, p. 429.
2. *The Last Diary of Tsaritsa Alexandra*, 24 April 1918 (OS), p. 128.
3. M. Maeterlinck, *Wisdom and Destiny* (George Allen: London, 1898), p. 53.
4. Ibid., p. 55.
5. Ibid., p. 58.
6. Ibid., p. 63.
7. Ibid., p. 64.
8. Ibid., p. 71.
9. N. A. Romanov (diary), 30 April 1918 (OS): *DINII*, vol. 2, part 2, p. 424.
10. On Nicholas's disdain for merchants, see Wortman, *Scenarios of Power*, pp. 387–8.
11. See L. McReynolds, *The News Under Russia's Old Regime: The Development of a Mass-Circulation Press* (Princeton, NJ: Princeton University Press, 1991), pp. 68–70.
12. Ibid., p. 195.
13. N. A. Romanov (diary), 13 and 18 May 1918 (OS): *DINII*, vol. 2, part 2, pp. 427–8.
14. Ibid., 8 May 1918 (OS): p. 426.

35: CIVIL WAR

1. *Tobol'skie eparkhal'nye vedomosti*, nos 29–31, 10/23 December – 1/14 December 1918, p. 261.
2. 'Ocherednye zadachi sovetskoi vlasti', *Pravda*, 28 April 1918.
3. Calculation by M. Bernshtam in his *Ural i Prikam'e, noyabr' 1918 – yanvar' 1919*, p. 55.
4. M. A. Medvedev, 'Predystoriya rasstrela tsarskoi sem'i Romanovykh v 1918 godu': RGASPI, f. 558, op. 3s, d. 12, in DAVP, box 15, p. 2.
5. Bykov, 'Yekaterinburgskii Sovet', pp. 106–7.
6. P. V. Kukhtenkov (inquiry testimony), 13 November 1918: AMDP, HIA, box 1, folder 6, p. 60.
7. *Ural'skii rabochii*, 28 April 1918.
8. M. Golubykh, *Ural'skie partizany: pokhod otryadov Blyukhera-Kashirina v 1918 godu* (Ekaterinburg: Uralkniga, 1924), pp. 8–9.
9. B. Mueggenberg, *The Czecho-Slovak Struggle for Independence, 1914–1920* (Jefferson, NC: McFarland and Co., 2014), p. 174.
10. See Zhuk, *Vpositel'nye znaki v 'tsarskom dele'*, p. 135.
11. Bykov, 'Yekaterinburgskii Sovet', p. 101.
12. G. Strumillo, 'Iz zapisok rabochego', *Zarya* (Berlin), nos 4 and 6 (1922),

reproduced in Bernshtam (ed.), *Ural i Prikam'e, noyabr' 1918 – yanvar' 1919*, p. 45.

13. M. A. Medvedev, 'Predystoriya rasstrela tsarskoi sem'i Romanovykh v 1918 godu': RGASPI, f. 558, op. 3s, d. 12, in DAVP, box 15, p. 7.

14. Markov, *Pokinutaya tsarskaya sem'ya*, pp. 323–4.

15. See Bernshtam (ed.), *Ural i Prikam'e, noyabr' 1918 – yanvar' 1919*, pp. 70–2.

16. G. Strumillo, 'Iz zapisok rabochego', *Zarya* (Berlin), nos 4 and 6 (1922), reproduced in Bernshtam (ed.), *Ural i Prikam'e, noyabr' 1918 – yanvar' 1919*, p. 32.

17. See Zhuk, *Voprositel'nye znaki v 'tsarskom dele'*, p. 134.

36: GERMAN MANOEUVRES

1. J. Sadoul, *Notes sur la révolution bolchévique, octobre 1917 – janvier 1919* (Paris: Sirène, 1920), p. 319: letter to A. Thomas, 26 April 1918.

2. Ibid., p. 322: letter to A. Thomas, 27 April 1918.

3. Ibid., p. 365: letter to A. Thomas, 27 May 1918; Sovnarkom meeting, 25 June 1918: GARF, f. R-130, op. 2, d. 2.

4. D. B. Neidgart (inquiry testimony), 27 and 29 January 1921, in Sokolov, *Ubiistvo tsarskoi sem'i*, p. 106.

5. Ibid.

6. A. F. Trepov (inquiry testimony), 16 February 1921, in Sokolov, *Ubiistvo tsarskoi sem'i*, pp. 106–7.

7. Ibid., p. 108.

8. See A. Olano-Eren'ya, 'Ispanskii korol' i politika spaseniya sem'i Nikolaya II', *Novaya i noveishaya istoriya*, no. 5 (1993), pp. 152–65.

9. K. von Bothmer, *Mit Graf Mirbach in Moskau: Tagebuch-Aufzeichnungen und Aktenstücke vom 19. April bis 24. August 1918* (Tübingen: Osiander'sche Buchhandlung, 1922), p. 103 (22 July 1918).

10. P. A. (sic) Gilliard (inquiry testimony), 27 August 1919: AMDP, HIA, box 1, folder 9, p. 1128.

11. Markov, *Pokinutaya tsarskaya sem'ya*, pp. 305 and 318.

12. Ibid., pp. 304 and 319–20.

13. V. A. Kislitsyn (inquiry testimony), 27 August 1919: AMDP, HIA, box 1, folder 9, pp. 1153–4.

14. Ibid., p. 1154.

15. V. V. Golitsyn (inquiry testimony), 2 October 1919: ibid., box 1, folder 9, pp. 1145–6.

16. E. Pantazzi, *Roumania in Light and Shadow* (London: T. F. Unwin, 1921), pp. 243–6.

17. A. I. Mosolov, *Pri dvore imperatora*, pp. 220–2, cited in Ioffe, *Revolyutsiya i sem'ya Romanovykh*, p. 300.

18. N. I. Kanishcheva et al. (eds), *Dnevnik P. N. Milyukova, 1918–1921* (Moscow: Rosspen, 2015), p. 34 (21 June 1918).

19. Ibid., p. 20 (12 June 1918).

20. Ibid., pp. 33, 35 and 38–9 (21 June 1918).
21. Ibid., p. 66 (4 July 1918).
22. Ibid., pp. 82–3 (10 July 1918).
23. See Ioffe, *Revolyutsiya i sem'ya Romanovykh*, pp. 293–4.

37: LAST DAYS IN THE HOUSE

1. F. P. Proskuryakov (inquiry testimony), 1–3 April 1919: AMDP, HIA, box 1, folder 7, p. 641.
2. Serebryakova, 'Moei docheri Zore, ob eë ottse': Serebryakova Papers, HIA, p. 3.
3. A. I. Belogradskii (inquiry testimony), 22 July 1919: AMDP, HIA, box 1, folder 8, p. 964.
4. Ya. M. Yurovskii, 'Poslednii tsar' nashël svoë mesto': RGASPI, f. 3, op. 58, d. 280, in DAVP, HIA, box 15, p. 8.
5. Ibid., pp. 8–9.
6. P. Ya. Shamarin (procurator) reporting on testimony of P. S. Medvedev, 3–5 October 1919: AMDP, HIA, box 1, folder 9, pp. 1352–3.
7. F. P. Proskuryakov (inquiry testimony), 1–3 April 1919: ibid., box 1, folder 7, p. 642.
8. N. A. Romanov (diary), 21 June 1918 (OS): *DINII*, vol. 2, part 2, p. 431; F. P. Proskuryakov (inquiry testimony), 1–3 April 1919: AMDP, HIA, box 1, folder 7, p. 644; Ya. M. Yurovskii, 'Poslednii tsar' nashël svoë mesto': RGASPI, f. 3, op. 58, d. 280, in DAVP, HIA, box 15, pp. 8–9.
9. Ya. M. Yurovskii, 'Poslednii tsar' nashël svoë mesto': RGASPI, f. 3, op. 58, d. 280, in DAVP, HIA, box 15, p. 9.
10. N. A. Romanov (diary), 23 June 1918 (OS): *DINII*, vol. 2, part 2, p. 432.
11. Ya. M. Yurovskii, 'Poslednii tsar' nashël svoë mesto': RGASPI, f. 3, op. 58, d. 280, in DAVP, HIA, box 15, pp. 8–9.
12. F. P. Proskuryakov (inquiry testimony), 1–3 April 1919: AMDP, HIA, box 1, folder 7, pp. 643–4.
13. Ya. M. Yurovskii, 'Poslednii tsar' nashël svoë mesto': RGASPI, f. 3, op. 58, d. 280, in DAVP, HIA, box 15, pp. 9 and 21.
14. M. L. Krokhaleva (inquiry testimony), 9 July 1919: AMDP, HIA, box 1, folder 8, pp. 909–10.
15. F. P. Proskuryakov (inquiry testimony), 1–3 April 1919: ibid., box 1, folder 7, pp. 645–6.
16. Inquiry materials file, 5 September 1918: A. G. Beloborodov to Ya. M. Sverdlov (telegram received on 4 July 1918): ibid., box 1, folder 6, p. 22.
17. Inquiry materials file, 23 February 1919: French vice-consul, telegram from Ekaterinburg to Moscow, 9 July 1918: ibid., box 1, folder 7, p. 407.
18. I. V. Storozhev (inquiry testimony), 8–10 October 1918: ibid., box 1, folder 6, p. 81.
19. Ibid., p. 82.
20. *The Last Diary of Tsaritsa Alexandra*, 12 July 1918, p. 194.

38: THE EKATERINBURG TRAP

1. See R. Service, *Lenin: A Biography* (London: Macmillan, 1998), p. 317.
2. V. I. Lenin, *Biograficheskaya khronika*, vol. 5 (Moscow: Gosudarstvennoe izdatel'stvo, 1974), p. 413.
3. Sovnarkom minutes, 2 May: *SPR*, p. 52. Citing GARF, f. 130, op. 23, d. 13, pp. 58–9.
4. Interview with V. V. Yakovlev: *Izvestiya*, 16 May 1918.
5. Bolshevik Central Committee, 19 May 1918: RGASPI, f. 3, op. 58, d. 280, in DAVP, HIA, box 15.
6. See Zhuk, *Voprositel'nye znaki v 'tsarskom dele'*, p. 141, and Yu. A. Buranov and V. M. Khrustalëv, *Gibel' imperatorskogo doma* (Moscow: Progress, 1992), p. 251.
7. Inquiry materials file, 24 March 1919: R. Bērziņš, commander-in-chief of the North Urals and Siberian Front, to Sovnarkom and VTsIK, 24 June 1918: AMDP, HIA, box 1, folder 7, p. 574.
8. Inquiry materials file, 12 March 1919: V. D. Bonch-Bruevich to A. G. Beloborodov, 20 and 21 June 1918: ibid., box 1, folder 7, p. 494.
9. Inquiry materials file, 24 March 1919: R. Bērziņš, commander-in-chief of the North Urals and Siberian Front, to Sovnarkom and VTsIK, 24 June 1918: ibid., box 1, folder 7, p. 574.
10. M. A. Medvedev, 'Predystoriya rasstrela tsarskoi sem'i Romanovykh v 1918 godu': RGASPI, f. 558, op. 3s, d. 12, in DAVP, box 15, p. 3.
11. Ibid., p. 6.
12. I. I. Radzinskii, taped memoirs (1963): RGASPI, f. 588, op. 3, d. 14, in DAVP, box 15, pp. 9 and 13.
13. M. A. Medvedev, 'Predystoriya rasstrela tsarskoi sem'i Romanovykh v 1918 godu': ibid., pp. 6–7.
14. Bykov, 'Yekaterinburgskii Sovet', p. 101.
15. Preston, *Before the Curtain*, p. 91.
16. N. A. Sakovich (inquiry testimony), 24 August 1918: AMDP, HIA, box 1, folder 6, p. 21.
17. See Zhuk, *Voprositel'nye znaki v 'tsarskom dele'*, p. 148, quoting A. G. Beloborodov's memoir.
18. L. A. Krol, 'Polozhenie na gornozavodskom Urale v kontsa 1917 – pervoi polovine 1918', reproduced in Bernshtam (ed.), *Ural i Prikam'e, noyabr' 1918 – yanvar' 1919*, p. 49.
19. Bykov, 'Poslednie dni poslednego tsarya', p. 17.
20. I. I. Radzinskii, taped memoirs (1963): RGASPI, f. 588, op. 3, d. 14, in DAVP, box 15, p. 21.

39: THE MOSCOW FULCRUM

1. Von Bothmer, *Mit Graf Mirbach in Moskau*, pp. 97–8 (diary entry for 19 July 1918).
2. N. S. Angarskii in interview with Boris Nicolaevsky, 29 April 1928 (Werder, Germany): Boris I. Nicolaevsky Collection, HIA, box 525, folder 8.
3. I. I. Radzinskii, taped memoirs (1963): RGASPI, f. 588, op. 3, d. 14, in DAVP, box 15, p. 14.
4. G. A. Hill, *Go Spy the Land* (London: Cassell, 1932), p. 207.
5. F. Grenard, *La révolution russe* (Paris: Armand Colin, 1933), p. 321.
6. Sadoul, *Notes sur la révolution bolchévique*, p. 405: letter to A. Thomas, 10 July 1918.
7. Sovnarkom, 15 July 1918: GARF, f. R-130, op. 2, d. 2.
8. Hill, *Go Spy the Land*, pp. 210–11.
9. Sadoul, *Notes sur la révolution bolchévique*, p. 405: letter to A. Thomas, 10 July 1918.
10. Savinkov's testimony in 'Sudebnoe razbiratel'stvo', *Pravda*, 30 August 1924, pp. 4–5.
11. Lockhart's telegram, 26 May 1918: FO 371/3332/9748 (NA).
12. Savinkov's testimony in 'Sudebnoe razbiratel'stvo', *Pravda*, 30 August 1924, pp. 4–5.
13. Grenard, *La révolution russe*, p. 322.
14. Savinkov's testimony in 'Sudebnoe razbiratel'stvo', *Pravda*, 30 August 1924, pp. 4–5.
15. Urals Regional Soviet to Press Bureau, Central Executive Committee of Congress of Soviets, 13 July 1918: inquiry materials file, 24 March 1919: AMDP, HIA, box 1, folder 7, p. 578.
16. G. I. Safarov to V. I. Lenin, 13 July 1918: ibid., box 1, folder 7, p. 577; see also Lykova (ed.), *Sledstvie po delu ob ubiistve Rossiiskoi imperatorskoi sem'i*, p. 72.
17. V. Gorin to V. I. Lenin, 17 July 1918: AMDP, HIA, box 1, folder 7, p. 574; see also Lykova (ed.), *Sledstvie po delu ob ubiistve Rossiiskoi imperatorskoi sem'i*, p. 72.
18. Inquiry materials file, 12 March 1919: V. D. Bonch-Bruevich to A. G. Beloborodov, 20 and 21 June 1918: AMDP, HIA, box 1, folder 7, p. 494.
19. Lenin, *Biograficheskaya khronika*, vol. 5, p. 616.

40: THE MAN WHO WOULD NOT BE TSAR

1. G. M. Romanov to X. G. Romanova, 5 April, 21 July and 23 August 1918: Georgi Mikhailovich, Grand Duke of Russia Papers, HIA, box 2.
2. *Poslednie dni poslednego tsarya: inochtozhenie dinastii Romanovykh*, pp. 8–9. See also V. M. Khrustalëv, *Alapaevsk: zhertvy i palachi* (Moscow: Dostoinstvo, 2010), pp. 12–13.

3. M. A. Medvedev, 'Predystoriya rasstrela tsarskoi sem'i Romanovykh v 1918 godu': RGASPI, f. 558, op. 3s, d. 12, in DAVP, box 15, p. 8.
4. Ibid.
5. Ibid., pp. 3–4.
6. I. I. Radzinskii, taped memoirs (1963): RGASPI, f. 588, op. 3, d. 14, in DAVP, box 15, p. 36.
7. Ibid., pp. 38–9.
8. See *PIGTS*, pp. 258–9. I. F. Plotnikov quotes A. V. Markov as reproduced in *Literaturnaya Rossiya*, no. 38 (1990), p. 19.
9. V. I. Lenin to A. G. Beloborodov, 10 June 1919: Trotsky Collection, HIA, box 6, folder 6.
10. M. V. Alexeev (military report), probably June 1918: Mikhail V. Alekseev Papers, HIA, box 1, folder 22, p. 3.
11. Ibid.

41: NARROWED OPTIONS

1. The decree is given in *DINII*, vol. 2, part 2, p. 474.
2. See Zhuk, *Voprositel'nye znaki v 'tsarskom dele'*, pp. 145–7, citing G. Z. Besedovskii, *Na putyakh k termidoru* (Moscow: Sovremennik, 1997), pp. 111–13.
3. This was the conclusion reached by N. A. Sokolov who led the anti-Bolshevik inquiry in 1919: Sokoloff, *Enquête judiciaire sur l'assassinat de la famille impériale russe*, pp. 287–9.
4. See Bykov, *Poslednie dni Romanovykh*, p. 114.
5. Mueggenberg, *The Czecho-Slovak Struggle for Independence*, pp. 141 and 175.
6. See Bykov, *Poslednie dni Romanovykh*, p. 114.
7. Ipatev house guard duty book, 9 July 1918, reproduced in *SPR*, p. 91.
8. Preston, *Before the Curtain*, p. 102.
9. This comes from an anti-Bolshevik secret agent's report delivered to sub-inspector M. Talashmanov, which he passed to the Ekaterinburg Criminal Inquiry Department on 22 August 1918: *GTSMS*, pp. 66–7. The date in the source is given as a Sunday 'around 15 July'. 14 July is the only possible Sunday. On Anuchin, the information comes in V. Gorin to V. I. Lenin, 17 July 1918: AMDP, HIA, box 1, folder 7, p. 574.
10. F. P. Proskuryakov (inquiry testimony), 1–3 April 1919: ibid., box 1, folder 7, pp. 649–50.
11. A. N. Shveikina (inquiry testimony), 26 February 1919: ibid., box 1, folder 6, p. 230.
12. M. A. Medvedev, 'Rasstrel tsarskoi sem'i Romanovykh v gorode Yekaterinburge v noch' na 17 iyulya 1918 goda: vospominaniya uchastnika rasstrela': RGASPI, f. 588, op. 3, d. 12, in DAVP, box 15, pp. 1–2.
13. Besedovskii, *Na putyakh k termidoru*, p. 113.
14. Ibid.

15. F. P. Proskuryakov (inquiry testimony), 1–3 April 1919: AMDP, HIA, box 1, folder 7, pp. 649–50.
16. P. Ya. Shamarin (procurator) reporting on testimony of P. Medvedev, 3–5 October 1919: ibid., box 1, folder 9, p. 1354.
17. The telegram from G. E. Zinoviev to Ya. M. Sverdlov and V. I. Lenin (16 July 1918) is reproduced in *PIGTS*, p. 207.
18. Ibid.
19. See *PIGTS*, p. 208.
20. Ibid., pp. 208 and 258. Plotnikov quotes A. I. Akimov's memoir as reproduced in *Ogonëk*, no. 38 (1990), p. 29 and *Argumenty i fakty*, no. 46 (1990).
21. See G. Z. Ioffe, *Revolyutsiya i sud'ba Romanovykh* (Moscow: Respublika, 1992), pp. 308–12; Buranov and Khrustalëv, *Gibel' imperatorskogo doma*, pp. 257–9; E. Radzinskii, *Gospodi – spasi i usmiri Rossiyu': Nikolai II, zhizn' i smert'* (Moscow: Vagrius, 1993), pp. 401–4.

42: DEATH IN THE CELLAR

1. Ya. M. Yurovskii, 'Poslednii tsar' nashël svoë mesto': RGASPI, f. 3, op. 58, d. 280, in DAVP, HIA, box 15, p. 12.
2. Ibid.
3. Preston, *Before the Curtain*, p. 102.
4. Ibid.
5. Ya. M. Yurovskii, 'Poslednii tsar' nashël svoë mesto': RGASPI, f. 3, op. 58, d. 280, in DAVP, HIA, box 15, p. 12.
6. Ibid.; F. P. Proskuryakov (inquiry testimony), 1–3 April 1919: AMDP, HIA, box 1, folder 7, p. 650; testimony of P. Ya. Shamarin (procurator) reporting on testimony of P. Medvedev, 3–5 October 1919: ibid., box 1, folder 9, p. 1355.
7. Ibid.
8. Ibid., p. 1356.
9. Ya. M. Yurovskii, 'Poslednii tsar' nashël svoë mesto': RGASPI, f. 3, op. 58, d. 280, in DAVP, HIA, box 15, pp. 12–13; F. P. Proskuryakov (inquiry testimony), 1–3 April 1919: AMDP, HIA, box 1, folder 7, p. 650; testimony of P. Ya. Shamarin (procurator) reporting on testimony of P. Medvedev, 3–5 October 1919: ibid., box 1, folder 9, p. 1355.
10. I. I. Radzinskii, taped memoirs (1963): RGASPI, f. 588, op. 3, d. 14, in DAVP, box 15, p. 29.
11. Ya. M. Yurovskii, 'Poslednii tsar' nashël svoë mesto': RGASPI, f. 3, op. 58, d. 280, in DAVP, HIA, box 15, pp. 12–13; F. P. Proskuryakov (inquiry testimony), 1–3 April 1919: AMDP, HIA, box 1, folder 7, p. 650; testimony of P. Ya. Shamarin (procurator) reporting on testimony of P. Medvedev, 3–5 October 1919: ibid., box 1, folder 9, p. 1355.
12. Testimony of P. Ya. Shamarin (procurator) reporting on testimony of P. Medvedev, 3–5 October 1919: AMDP, HIA, box 1, folder 9, p. 1356.

13. F. P. Proskuryakov (inquiry testimony), 1–3 April 1919: ibid., box 1, folder 7, p. 649.

14. Ibid., pp. 652–3.

43: RED EVACUATION

1. A. G. Beloborodov to V. D. Gorbunov, 17 July 1918: Nikolai Alekseevich Sokolov Papers, HIA, folder XX197–13.04. The telegram was first reproduced in Sokoloff, *Enquête judiciaire sur l'assassinat de la famille impériale russe*, p. 240.

2. I. I. Radzinskii, taped memoirs (1963): RGASPI, f. 588, op. 3, d. 14, in DAVP, box 15, p. 42.

3. Central Executive Committee minutes, 18 July 1918, reproduced in *SPR*, p. 105.

4. Sovnarkom minutes, 18 July 1918, reproduced ibid., pp. 105–6.

5. Ya. M. Sverdlov and probably A. G. Beloborodov, conversation, n.d. but likely 18 July 1918: AMDP, HIA, box 1, folder 9, p. 1340; see also Lykova (ed.), *Sledstvie po delu ob ubiistve Rossiiskoi imperatorskoi sem'i*, p. 76.

6. Ya. M. Sverdlov and probably A. G. Beloborodov, conversation, n.d. but likely 18 July 1918: AMDP, HIA, box 1, folder 9, p. 1338.

7. Ibid., p. 1339.

8. M. I. Letemin (inquiry testimony), 18–19 October 1918: ibid., box 1, folder 6, p. 88.

9. Agent Alexeev, report to inquiry, 26 February 1919: ibid., box 1, folder 6, p. 225.

10. F. P. Proskuryakov (inquiry testimony), 1–3 April 1919: ibid., box 1, folder 7, pp. 652–3.

11. Inquiry materials file, 5 September 1918: Ya. M. Yurovski to A. G. Beloborodov, 20 July 1918: ibid., box 1, folder 6, p. 22.

12. See H. Rappaport, *Ekaterinburg: The Last Days of the Romanovs* (London: Windmill Books, 2009), p. 206.

13. Preston, *Before the Curtain*, p. 105.

14. A. P. Belozerova (inquiry testimony), 28 September 1918: AMDP, HIA, box 1, folder 6, p. 48.

15. N. A. Sakovich (inquiry testimony), 24 August 1918: ibid., box 1, folder 6, p. 21.

16. I. A. Sergeev, report to inquiry, 20 February 1919: ibid., box 1, folder 6, p. 196.

17. P. Ya. Shamarin (procurator) reporting on testimony of P. Medvedev, 3–5 October 1919: ibid., box 1, folder 9, p. 1367.

18. M. L. Krokhaleva (inquiry testimony), 9 July 1919: ibid., box 1, folder 8, p. 910.

19. Quoted in Lykova (ed.), *Sledstvie po delu ob ubiistve Rossiiskoi imperatorskoi sem'i*, p. 147.

20. A. A. Volkov (inquiry testimony), 22 October 1918: AMDP, HIA, box 1, folder 6, p. 93; Volkov, *Okolo tsarskoi sem'i*, p. 67.
21. *Ural'skii rabochii*, 23 July 1918, quoted in AMDP, HIA, box 1, folder 6, pp. 145–8.
22. Third Army report to I. I. Vatsetis, 23 July 1918, in Bernshtam (ed.), *Ural i Prikam'e, noyabr' 1918 – yanvar' 1919*, p. 98.

44: MURDERS, COVER-UPS, PRETENDERS

1. I. S. Smolin, 'The Alapaevsk Tragedy' (typescript, translated): HIA, pp. 7–8.
2. Ibid., p. 8.
3. Ibid., pp. 8–9.
4. *Ural'skii rabochii*, 20 July 1918, in I. S. Smolin, 'The Alapaevsk Tragedy' (typescript, translated): HIA, p. 12.
5. *Izvestiya*, 19 July 1918.
6. M. N. Pokrovskii to L. N. Pokrovskaya, 26 July 1918, quoted in Lykova (ed.), *Sledstvie po delu ob ubiistve Rossiiskoi imperatorskoi sem'i*, p. 89.
7. A. A. Ioffe to V. I. Lenin, 24 June 1918, reproduced in *SPR*, p. 106.
8. A. A. Ioffe to G. V. Chicherin, 21 July 1918, reproduced ibid., p. 107.
9. A. A. Ioffe, 'N. Ioffe i nasha vneshnyaya politika' (dated 20 October 1927): Arkhiv Prezidenta Rossiiskoi Federatsii, f. 31, op. 1, d. 4, p. 216.
10. Ibid.
11. V. N. Karnaukhova (inquiry testimony), 2 July 1919: *GTSMS*, pp. 386–7.
12. A. Ya. Valek (inquiry testimony, n.d.): AMDP, HIA, box 1, folder 8, p. 702.
13. Ibid., pp. 701–2.
14. Ibid., p. 702.
15. P. A. (sic) Gilliard (inquiry testimony), 5–6 March 1919 (OS): AMDP, HIA, box 1, folder 7, p. 467.
16. Markov, *Pokinutaya tsarskaya sem'ya*, pp. 331, 335 and 336.
17. Ibid., p. 349.

45: THE CZECHOSLOVAK OCCUPATION

1. Diterikhs, *Ubiistvo tsarskoi sem'i i chlenov doma Romanovykh na Urale*, part 1, p. 23; Preston, *Before the Curtain*, p. 112.
2. F. N. Gorshkov (inquiry testimony), 31 July 1918: AMDP, HIA, box 1, folder 6, p. 1.
3. K. A. Agafonova, 13 November 1918: ibid., box 1, folder 6, p. 64. Agafonova had a Bolshevik brother who served as district commissar of justice.
4. V. Ya. Buyvid (inquiry testimony), 10 August 1918: ibid., box 1, folder 6, p. 33.
5. F. I. Ivanov (inquiry testimony), 13 September 1918: ibid., box 1, folder 6, p. 41.

6. A. G. Eliseeva (inquiry testimony), probably 13 September 1918: ibid., box 1, folder 6, p. 42.
7. F. N. Gorshkov (inquiry testimony), 31 July 1918: ibid., box 1, folder 6, p. 10.
8. Preston, *Before the Curtain*, pp. 113–14.
9. See Service, *Lenin: A Biography*, pp. 359–66.
10. *Komsomol'skaya pravda*, 12 February 1992.
11. Sokoloff, *Enquête judiciaire sur l'assassinat de la famille impériale russe*, pp. 9–10.
12. *Prikaz komendanta goroda Ekaterinburga*, no. 37, 8 September 1918: Vera Cattell Papers, HIA, box 4, Iskander Riza Kuli Mirza folder.
13. Report of N. Mirolyubov, Procurator of Kazan Palace of Justice, to Minister of Justice, 12 December 1918 (English translation), pp. 1–13: SGC, SCBLOU, box 2.

46: ROMANOV SURVIVORS

1. A. A. Volkov (inquiry testimony), 22 October 1918: AMDP, HIA, box 1, folder 6, p. 93; Volkov, *Okolo tsarskoi sem'i*, pp. 71–2.
2. L. Sukacev, 'Soldier under Three Flags: The Personal Memoirs of Lev Pavlovich Sukacev' (Washington, DC: typescript, 1974): Lev Sukacev Papers, HIA, pp. 100–1.
3. Princess Marie of Romania to M. F. Romanova, 1 September 1918: KAGDRP, HIA, box 8, folder 33.
4. Queen Marie of Romania to M. F. Romanova, 20 October 1918: ibid.
5. Hill, *Go Spy the Land*, pp. 115–48.
6. Pantazzi, *Roumania in Light and Shadow*, pp. 267–8.
7. Ibid., pp. 269–70.
8. Ibid., p. 270.
9. Ibid.
10. A. Calthorpe to M. F. Romanova, 19 November 1918: Kseniia Aleksandrovna Grand Duchess of Russia Papers, HIA, box 8, folder 16.
11. Queen Alexandra to M. F. Romanova, 21 December 1918: ibid., box 8, folder 11.
12. Bulygin, *The Murder of the Romanovs: the Authentic Account*, p. 187.
13. Quoted by V. M. Khrustalëv, *Petrograd: rasstrel Velikikh knyazei* (Moscow: Dostoinstvo, 2011), pp. 62 and 68–70.
14. *Evening News*, 4 November 1919. I am grateful to Nick Walshaw for this reference.
15. George V to M. F. Romanova, 19 April 1919: HIA, box 8, folder 24.
16. Queen Alexandra to M. F. Romanova, 16 April 1919: ibid., box 8, folder 11.
17. Queen Alexandra to M. F. Romanova, 22 April 1919: ibid.
18. George V to M. F. Romanova, 21 April 1919: ibid., box 8, folder 24.

47: THE ANTI-BOLSHEVIK INQUIRY

1. D. M. Fedichkin, 'Izhevskoe vosstanie v period s 8-go avgusta po 15-go okt-yabrya 1918 goda' (San Francisco: manuscript, 1931): Dmitri I. Fedichkin Papers, HIA.

2. M. A. Medvedev, 'Predystoriya rasstrela tsarskoi sem'i Romanovykh v 1918 godu': RGASPI, f. 558, op. 3s, d. 12, in DAVP, box 15, p. 38.

3. M. I. Letemin (inquiry testimony), 18–19 October 1918: AMDP, HIA, box 1, folder 6, pp. 87–8.

4. Sokoloff, *Enquête judiciaire sur l'assassinat de la famille impériale russe*, pp. 10–12; Diterikhs, *Ubiistvo tsarskoi sem'i i chlenov doma Romanovykh na Urale*, part 1, p. 14.

5. Ibid.

6. Diterikhs, *Ubiistvo tsarskoi sem'i i chlenov doma Romanovykh na Urale*, part 1, p. 17.

7. Ibid., p. 21.

8. I. A. Sergeev, report to inquiry, 20 February 1919: AMDP, HIA, box 1, folder 6, p. 198.

9. Inquiry testimonies, *GTSMS*, pp. 176 (A. Ya. Neustroev), 180 (S. F. Podor-ova), 181 (T. L. Sitnikova), 182 (F. F. Onyanov) and 186 (M. I. Solo'ëv).

10. F. V. Sitnikov (inquiry testimony), 28 March 1919: ibid., pp. 185–6.

11. N. V. Mutnykh (inquiry testimony), 8 March 1919: ibid., pp. 179 and 188.

12. P. Ya. Shamarin (procurator) reporting on testimony of P. Medvedev, 3–5 October 1919: AMDP, HIA, box 1, folder 9, pp. 1372–3.

13. V. Iordanskii to N. I. Mirolyubov (Procurator of the Kazan Palace of Justice), 19 February 1919: Nikander I. Miroliubov Papers, HIA, box 1, folder V. Iordanskii (1919).

14. V. Iordanskii to N. I. Mirolyubov, 23 February 1919: ibid.

15. P. Ya. Shamarin (inquiry testimony), 3–5 October 1919: AMDP, HIA, box 1, vol. 9, pp. 1373–7. When testifying in autumn 1919, Shamarin was describing his experiences of the winter of 1918–1919.

16. S. Gibbes to Grand Duke Alexander Nikolaevich, untitled memoir, 1 December 1928: SGC, SCBLOU, box 1, p. 7.

17. P. I. Utkin (inquiry testimony), 28 March 1919: *GTSMS*, pp. 355–60.

18. N. A. Sokolov, preliminary report to inquiry, 1 April 1918: AMDP, HIA, box 1, folder 7, pp. 633–6.

19. N. A. Sokolov to N. I. Mirolyubov, 9 October 1919: Nikander I. Miroliubov Papers, HIA, box 1, folder N. A. Sokolov; Bulygin, *The Murder of the Romanovs: the Authentic Account*, p. 265.

20. N. A. Sokolov to N. I. Mirolyubov, 20 December 1919: ibid.; Bulygin, *The Murder of the Romanovs: the Authentic Account*, pp. 265–6.

21. Ibid., pp. 268–9.

48: DISPUTE WITHOUT BONES

1. Individual questions for Lenin at the eighth party congress, March 1919: RGASPI, f. 5, op. 2, d. 2, p. 5.
2. *Poslednie dni poslednego tsarya: inochtozhenie dinastii Romanovykh*, pp. 4–5 and 14–16.
3. *Ubiistvo tsarskoi sem'i i eë svity: offitsial'nye dokumenty* (Constantinople: Russkaya Mysl', 1920), pp. 1–5 and 14–15.
4. R. Wilton, *The Last Days of the Romanovs, from 15th March 1917* (London: Thornton Butterworth, 1920).
5. Receipt signed by F. Finlayson, 18 March 1919: AMDP, HIA, box 1.
6. Quoted by Bykov, *Poslednie dni Romanovykh*; Bykov, 'Poslednie dni poslednego tsarya', p. 24.
7. Receipt signed by F. Finlayson, 18 March 1919: AMDP, HIA, box 1.
8. Bykov, 'Poslednie dni poslednego tsarya', pp. 20–1.
9. Ibid.
10. Ibid., p. 21.
11. *Poslednie dni poslednego tsarya: inochtozhenie dinastii Romanovykh*, pp. 14–16.
12. Ibid., pp. 4–5 and 14–16.
13. Diterikhs, *Ubiistvo tsarskoi sem'i i chlenov doma Romanovykh na Urale*, part 1 (Vladivostok: Voennaya Akademiya, 1922).
14. N. A. Sokolov to S. Gibbes, 19 February 1920: SGC, SCBLOU, box 2.
15. Bulygin, *The Murder of the Romanovs: the Authentic Account*, p. 269.
16. N. A. Sokolov to M. K. Nikiforov, 22 April 1922: AMDP, HIA, box 1, folder 2; Bulygin, *The Murder of the Romanovs: the Authentic Account*, pp. 270–1.
17. N. A. Sokolov to M. K. Nikiforov, 22 April 1922; Bulygin, *The Murder of the Romanovs: the Authentic Account*, p. 155.
18. N. A. Sokolov to M. K. Nikiforov, 22 April 1922.
19. Sokoloff, *Enquête judiciaire sur l'assassinat de la famille impériale russe*.
20. Sokolov, *Ubiistvo tsarskoi sem'i*.
21. Gilliard, *Le tragique destin de Nicolas II et de sa famille*.
22. Mel'nik-Botkina, *Vospominaniya o tsarskoi sem'e*; Buxhoeveden, *The Life and Tragedy of Alexandra Feodorovna*; *Skorbnaya pamyatka*; Markov, *Pokinutaya tsarskaya sem'ya*.
23. J. Klier and H. Mingay, *The Quest for Anastasia: Solving the Mystery of the Lost Romanovs* (Edgware: Smith Gryphon, 1997).
24. *PTR*, vols. 1–7.

49: AFTERWORD

1. R. and S. Massie, *Nicholas and Alexandra* (New York: Atheneum, 1967).
2. *Rasputin the Mad Monk* (Hammer Films UK; dir. D. Sharp, 1966).

3. A. Summers and T. Mangold, *File on the Tsar* (London: Gollancz, 1976).
4. Wortman, *Scenarios of Power*; D. Lieven, *Nicholas II: Emperor of all the Russias* (London: John Murray, 1993).
5. G. Hosking, *The Russian Constitutional Experiment: Government and Duma, 1907–1914* (Cambridge: Cambridge University Press, 1973).
6. Löwe, *The Tsars and the Jews*.
7. Montefiore, *The Romanovs*.
8. Rappaport, *Ekaterinburg*.
9. Ioffe, *Revolyutsiya i sud'ba Romanovykh*.
10. Radzinskii, *'Gospodi – spasi i usmiri Rossiyu'*.
11. *SPR*; Lykova (ed.), *Sledstvie po delu ob ubiistve Rossiiskoi imperatorskoi sem'i*; *PIGTS*; Zhuk, *Voprositel'nye znaki v 'tsarskom dele'*.

INDEX

Prayer at end of growth in grace teaching

Dear Father, we're asking to remember what Jesus has done for us. Help us by your Holy Spirit to see what He did for us. How will we love other people – not selfishly, but just for who they are, unless we sense the reality of who we are by Jesus Christ dying for us -- just for who we are, just because he loves us? How will we get joy, unless we see the beauty of what He's done? How will we get peace unless we realize that if we can't trust Him, who in the world can we trust? How can we get patience unless we see Him up there on the cross saying, "Father, forgive them"? How can we get kindness unless we see Him pour Himself out for us? How will we get integrity until we see we don't need anybody else's approval but His? How will we get faithfulness until we see He has never let us down? How can we get humbleness and gentleness unless we see we can say, 'Oh my Lord, you who are meek and lowly of heart, who am I?? How will we get self-control unless we see we've already got the thing that will ravish our hearts the most? Father, help us!

In Jesus' name we pray, Amen.